CURIOUS GOODS

CURIOUS GOODS

Behind the Scenes of

FRIDAY
the 13th
The Series

by Alyse Wax

BearManor Media

2015

Curious Goods: Behind the Scenes of Friday the 13th: The Series

© 2015 Alyse Wax

For information, address:

BearManor Media
P. O. Box 71426
Albany, GA 31708

bearmanormedia.com

Typesetting and layout by John Teehan

Published in the USA by BearManor Media

ISBN—1-59393-894-2
978-1-59393-894-9

Table of Contents

Acknowledgements

IF YOU WOULD HAVE TOLD ME twenty years ago that I would make *Friday the 13th: The Series* a huge part of my career, I wouldn't have believed you. The series always seemed so far removed from regular life. As a teen, my fandom into the series felt like fantasy role-play. It didn't feel real. Ironically, it was Marc Scott Zicree's *The Twilight Zone Companion* that made me realize that a book about an old television show could find an audience. Now, here I am, with an actual book in my hands, one that other people will read. It is an ode to my obsession. I guess obsessions can, in fact, be productive.

I want to thank everyone who I interviewed for this book. I asked people to dig through memories from twenty years ago, and was duly impressed with the results. I also want to thank all the agents and managers who helped facilitate the interviews.

Many thanks go to Rebekah McKendry for becoming my unwitting "mentor" through this whole book process; and to Patrick Doody for getting me that one, elusive interview.

Finally, to my husband, Tim. He put up with my mania and my obsession; he is my calming force, my biggest cheerleader, my best friend. I quite literally could not have written this book if you weren't in my corner.

Introduction

I **FIRST SAW** *Friday the 13th: The Series* when I was about nine years old. It was Saturday morning, the eleven o'clock hour—the awkward television time when morning cartoons were over but old sitcoms like *The Munsters* and *I Love Lucy* were still a couple hours away. I was flipping channels, and landed on KCOP 13, a local Los Angeles station. There was something incredibly gory on the TV, a man with throbbing, oozing pustules all over his head. I was fascinated. Entranced.

That show was *Friday the 13th: The Series*. The episode? "Stick It in Your Ear," with the cursed hearing aid. The obsession had begun.

Around that same time, I was just getting into horror movies. My first one was *Nightmare on Elm Street: The Dream Child*, shown to me by a school friend, who promised it wasn't actually scary. After watching that movie, I realized I was scared of the idea of horror movies; the movies themselves were not scary. In fact, I found a lot of humor in it. It was a few more years before my parents gave in to my horror obsession by renting me videos and getting me a subscription to *Fangoria*, but somehow, if it was on television—Saturday mornings, no less—it was "safe" to watch.

I recorded each episode on VHS, then would watch them after school, when I was done with my homework. This was 1989. The Internet was scarcely more advanced than CompuServe and BBS. I knew nothing about this wonderful mystery show; I just enjoyed it.

My obsession was deeply rooted in two aspects of the show: the gore and the lead. Micki Foster. Micki was the most beautiful woman I had ever seen (still is) and as a ginger kid, she was my first exposure to a beautiful redhead on television. I don't remember ever being teased for having red hair, but it was somehow validating to see a redhead on TV.

Micki was my idol. She was smart, she was capable, and she always took care of herself. More often than not, she got herself out of dangerous situations ("And Now the News" and "Bedazzled" come to mind immediately) without needing to be rescued by the boys. The "final girls" of

1

horror movies of that era were generally all either bubble-headed idiots or fleshpots there to add a little T&A before getting ripped to shreds. Micki was neither of those things. I loved that she wasn't afraid to use her sexuality, but there was always intention behind it. Plus she had a fantastic wardrobe.

It was frustrating, because all I ever wanted to talk about was *F13*, but I couldn't find anyone who had seen an episode. For a while, I started to wonder if I had made up the show all together. One morning, I woke up fifteen minutes into the episode; from that day on, I set my alarm to make sure that never happened again. Sometimes I would wake up 3:33 a.m. and I would lie still, waiting to see if anything weird happened (nothing ever did). I can trace my intense phobia of snakes back to "And Now the News."

The local station took *F13* off the air at some point. I don't remember how long it was before it disappeared, but I was devastated. Another show, *She-Wolf of London*, appeared in the same time slot, and that held me over for a few months, but with a mere twenty episodes, it didn't last long.

I remember going to Florida with my mom in 1992, a short trip to see an old friend of hers. There wasn't a lot to do, so I studied the TV Guide—and found an episode of *F13* playing at 1:00 a.m. "The Butcher," I believe. I was ecstatic; it was the highlight of the trip for me. I remember sneaking out to the living room late at night, waiting for the show to come on… and I couldn't quite make it. I fell asleep about a half-hour before it aired and didn't realize until my mom found me passed out on the couch in the morning. I was heartbroken.

Friday the 13th: The Series returned to television when I was thirteen. Flipping channels on a Saturday evening, I passed something with Chris Wiggins in it. Doubling back, I discovered my beloved series was back! The newly launched Sci-Fi channel (before it became Syfy) was running the series, allowing me to record the remaining episodes I didn't already have on VHS. Sci-Fi Channel ran the series regularly for a number of years. Every Friday the thirteenth, they would run a marathon of the series, hosted by Ron Perlman, which even included a few exclusive interview clips with Louise Robey.

Sometime around 1994, the Internet was really becoming consumer-friendly, thanks to America Online and "blazing fast" 14.4k modems. I soon discovered that, on the Internet, you could *always* find someone who was into the same weird stuff as you. I quickly found other fans and started what was the first *Friday the 13th: The Series* Internet fan club. I wrote my first-ever episode guide, an embarrassingly bad piece of fan fiction. I had over a hundred people with which to discuss my favorite topic (a few of which even thought I was Micki—I didn't dissuade them). I even had a terrible, bare-bones web page devoted to the show. To this day, my techy husband is still a little bitter that, even though he built his first computer at age eight, I had a website long before he did.

In 1996, my obsession showed no signs of abating, and I devoted months to creating my first (and only) *Friday the 13th: The Series* fanzine. Filled with my afore-mentioned atrocious episode guide and worse fan fiction, some short stories and poems from other fans, generic clip art, and some pretty good original drawings, I sold over sixty copies and didn't make a penny profit. (I sold them at cost, which was still nearly $20.)

By the time I went to college, I had my obsession (mostly) under control. I had a boyfriend, a social life, and classes that were interesting. I didn't watch the series on a daily basis, but every once in a while I would find an episode on cable late at night, and my heart would skip a beat.

It wasn't until writing this book that I found out that "The Inheritance" wasn't the first episode shot, like a traditional pilot. That was probably one of the reasons it didn't feel like a pilot episode to me, but it was also the skilled script by Bill Taub. The episode was laid out in a 50/50 split, divided between meeting our heroes and exploring what the show will be. It wasn't crowded with a lot of extra back story or mythology. So many traditional pilots jam all that in to appease network executives. No network, no need to appease them. "The Inheritance" is one of the few "pilots" that just works.

I am tempted to say that Season 2 was the least memorable season of *Friday the 13th: The Series*, but then I look at the list of episodes, and there are so many good ones. The violence of "Better Off Dead;" the two-for-one of "A Friend to the End;" the real-life terror of "And Now the News;" the creepy carnival setting of "Wax Magic." Over the course of Season 2, Micki dies, comes back to life, discovers she has occult powers, and puts Johnny in his place. Ryan falls for no fewer than three girls who all fall victims to cursed objects. And Jack fights Nazis!

The big change in Season 3 was, of course, John LeMay's exit. Everyone was surprised that the young actor would want to leave a hit television series, especially after only two seasons.

Brought in to replace LeMay was Steve Monarque, who had been introduced as a minor recurring character in Season 2. From the start, it was clear that Johnny would be a very different character than Ryan. That was fine when he was a recurring character, but as a series regular, he really threw off the balance of the show. Whereas Ryan was intelligent, sensitive, and thoughtful, Johnny was brutish, self-serving, and just plain dumb. It was a good decision not to simply recast Ryan, but a new character could not match the magic that we had in the first two seasons. I never liked Johnny. Not because he wasn't Ryan, but because he was Johnny. *Friday the 13th: The Series* was always a show that aimed to elevate the genre. Johnny brought the show down. Decades later, and he still gets me riled up.

Despite the casting change-up, Season 3 had some of the strongest episodes of the series. "The Charnel Pit" was a sumptuous swan song that didn't hold back—why would it? "The Long Road Home" was a genuinely well-paced and scary episode that borrows from films like *Texas Chainsaw Massacre* without copying them. "Repetition" used a different story format that proved delightfully ironic. "Hate on Your Dial" tackled racism in a direct, yet non-preachy way. "Mightier Than the Sword" was one of the earliest film depictions of a sociopathic female serial killer.

Frank Mancuso, Jr. is unequivocal about the reason *Friday the 13th: The Series* was canceled: conservative groups started to boycott the show's sponsors, who eventually pulled out. No sponsors, no money, and since this was a syndicated show, there was no network to back them up.

Interestingly, in an article from the *Los Angeles Times*[1], Paramount denied reports that *Friday the 13th: The Series* was canceled due to "advertiser resistance." Instead, they claimed that *Friday the 13th: The Series* and *War of the Worlds* had been pulled "because of lackluster ratings and because sufficient *Friday the 13th* episodes had been produced to ensure its future in syndication." Later in that same article, spokespeople from the U.S. Department of Defense (who ran recruitment ads) and SmithKline Beecham Consumer Brands (who sold products like Oxy-10 zit cream) admitted they pulled their advertising because of viewer complaints. However, the complaints seem tiny. The Department of Defense guessed they averaged "maybe one letter every couple of weeks;" while SmithKline admitted less than a hundred complaints prompted their decision. David Boyd of the National Coalition on Television Violence claimed responsibility for a letter-writing campaign. Most of the crew involved with *Friday the 13th: The Series* blamed Donald Wildmon of the American Family Association for the letter-writing campaign, and

---

1. Mahler, R. (1990, May 6). The New Power of TV Advertisers. *Los Angeles Times*.

while that may be true, I could not find any news articles or press releases in which Wildmon or his organization specifically name *Friday the 13th: The Series.*

Clearly, *Friday the 13th: The Series* is a topic that is near and dear to my heart. I never wanted to be a writer—my mother is a journalist so that was my "rebellion"—but as it turns out, I have a knack for it. I fell into horror journalism many years ago, without even realizing that was a "thing," but once I was there, I knew I found a home. I have always been a rabid television viewer—if my husband doesn't hear it on while I am home, he worries that I might be dead. Ironically, it was a copy of *The Twilight Zone Companion,* written by Marc Scott Zicree that showed me there was a market for writing about television. This book feels like a culmination of all these factors. Plus, I like being able to point out to my parents that my obsession led to something.

Season 1

FRANK MANCUSO JR. (creator, executive producer) – Mel Harris, who used to be the head of television at Paramount, came to me and said that he wanted to create a *Friday the 13th* television series. They had a great deal of success in syndication with *Star Trek*, so they were looking through their sci-fi/horror catalogue, saying, "What titles do we believe we could get traction on, that have enough name value that it wouldn't require sizable casting or a lot of advertising dollars spent on making people aware of what the show is?" At the time, I felt as though I'd kind of done *Friday the 13th* and I wasn't really interested in revisiting it. I felt like it ultimately was limiting how people perceived what I was capable of doing. So, I said, "Yeah, I really don't want to do this. I don't watch television, so I don't think I'd be very good at making it. I've made these other films and people are finally starting to put that *Friday the 13th* thing behind me." Now, all of a sudden, I would be jumping right back in the middle of it. Then, there was the obvious part of it: the certain limitations of what you could put on television. *Friday the 13th* movies are known for certain scenes of real aggression, and that would be a real limitation if you brought it to television. He basically said, "Look, we really want to do this, and you are really the only one who can do it. I don't care *what* the show is; just call it *Friday the 13th*. You make it anything you want for an hour, and we will put it on the air." I told them I get it, but I just don't want to do it.

My dad, who was the chairman of Paramount at that time, said, "Look, this is a real opportunity to do something you've never done before. Theoretically, they can sell this thing."

So, I said, "It can be *anything* we want?"

He said, "Absolutely. Because it is syndication, you aren't going to get a lot of notes, you aren't going to get a lot of structure from us. You are just going to get a budget from us, then you can go do whatever the hell you want."

That, ultimately, made me curious enough to start thinking about, *Well, if I was going to do this, what would the show be?* I started meeting with people about various scenarios in which this might be fun. I was certainly drawn towards a sort of anthological premise because I felt like that most naturally suited the way my head worked. They kept wanting some common openings and closings, so it will feel more like a TV series and less like a movie. So, we started thinking about *The Twilight Zone* and how that had common elements and they were bound thematically but they weren't necessarily a traditional series. We started riffing off that, and that's sort of how it all got going.

TOM MCLOUGHLIN (director, story editor) – Right after I finished *Jason Lives: Friday the 13th Part VI*, Frank Mancuso said, "You know, there's this guy who came in, who is talking to me about doing this as a series."

I said, "A weekly thing with Jason?"

He said, "No, no, it's like with cursed objects and stuff. I don't know if it is going to work."

I said, "Why the title?"

He said, "Meh, we own the title."

It was my second feature film, and as far as I was concerned, my career was doing features. I wasn't interested in signing up for a series. That was kind of the end of it. Then, the conversation swung over to *Jason vs. Freddy*. We started talking about that back then—it was 1986. That went nowhere because New Line wasn't about to give up Freddy.

WILLIAM TAUB (executive story editor) – My agents set me up with a meeting with Paramount for this project called *Friday the 13th*. That is not my genre, I've never done anything like that, and I couldn't be less interested in that. I went through interview after interview after interview. This was the first show that Paramount, through a subsidiary, was going to shoot in Toronto. The way it was explained to me was that I would be responsible for thirteen episodes in Los Angeles, and they would hire the equivalent to me in Toronto to be responsible for the Toronto thirteen. I would only have to worry about the U.S. half. But that never happened. They never found anybody in Toronto. It was hard. I had to do the whole twenty-six. So, it was very different from the way it was described.

The first thing I did when I got on *Friday the 13th* was hire someone—I had to. Someone brought to my attention *The Twilight Zone Companion*, so I said, "Get me the writer who did that."

MARC SCOTT ZICREE (story consultant) – My agent told me that *Friday the 13th* was going to be a series. I knew about the movies but I had never seen them. If the series had been like the movies, just a serial killer sadistically murdering, I would not have done the show. I didn't want to do anything that I thought might cause harm in the world. I found out it wasn't going to be anything like the movies, they were just using that as branding to get the show greenlit.

ROB HEDDEN (writer, director) – I was hired as story consultant one month before Season 1 was scheduled to go into production in Toronto. While there were a half dozen or so scripts already written, they needed various degrees of polish to make them as great as possible and set a consistent tone for the series. I ended up revising the first four episodes and tossing in my two cents on several others, though the writing credit deservedly went to the original writers. In exchange for being story consultant on the initial episodes, I was able to write several episodes of my own and direct one of them. I ended up writing four and directing two before shifting into writing and directing *Friday the 13th VIII: Jason Takes Manhattan.*

J. MILES DALE (line producer) – I started in this job that wasn't really a job. I was just like the "production observer" for Paramount, and I really had no idea what I was doing. Then the line producer on episode four quit, and they offered me the job. I was not the least bit qualified to do it. They told me it would be another $600 or $700 a week, and I took it immediately. I said, "I'll learn on the job, I don't give a shit." It was literally the longest year of my life. It probably took years off my life.

FRED MOLLIN (composer) – I was still pretty new to the game. I had just gotten the Kurzweil 250, which was a really wonderful instrument which was miraculous for 1987. It gave me a keyboard with a built-in digital digital recorder and sequencer, great sound, samples of real strings. I had to do a demo of music "inspired by" the script that I saw. It was probably about seven minutes long, an idea for a theme song. I did it on the Kurzweil and made a cassette of it and listened to that and other pieces. I was driving in my neighborhood in Toronto, and a church bell chimed. I was listening to my cassette of the theme, which was pretty close to what the final theme was, but then the church bell hit at the right time, and it was sort of eerie. It worked like a charm. It was in the right key, and I went home and added a tolling bell at the end. It was very fortuitous because I think it really caps that theme.

LOUISE ROBEY (Micki Foster) – The callbacks were on Pico Boulevard, not anywhere near the Paramount Studios. I showed up very late. I was the only one there, and I went in and I did my bit. Next thing I knew, my next call-back *was* on the Paramount lot. That was interesting because I had never been to the Paramount lot. They told me to park under the big blue sky and I thought they were making fun of me. But it turned out there was a big blue sky painted on the side of a building! I finally find this one bloody office, and there was Frank Mancuso Jr., and his father, Senior, who was the head of Paramount. It meant very little to me. It was lucky I was so naive. I did my readings, and oddly enough I did them with John LeMay. He hadn't been cast yet, but they were looking for people [to pair up]. So, we went behind a dumpster and rehearsed our lines! Then we went in and did them. That led to another callback. It was still us two, which I found to be unusual.

After I had done the audition, I got a great big wink from the casting people. It was a couple of days and I heard I got the job. The news went around Hollywood because, as it turned out, it was a huge job to get.

JOHN LEMAY (Ryan Dallion) – I remember going behind the dumpster and rehearsing with Louise before our callback. It was just a dumpster sitting in the corner of the lot. Two or three callbacks and I worked my tail off rehearsing the scenes. Then I think they actually offered it to someone else, a guy who had just done a series of 7-Up commercials. He turned it down. Lo and behold, I get a call at my apartment that I was to fly to Toronto the next day. I hadn't heard it from anyone but this wardrobe person who called me. She wanted me to come in for my fitting. I go, "What? Um, okay." So, I called my agent and yes, indeed, I got the part. They offered me the role, and the details had to be worked out, but that was the plan. Then it all happened really quickly. The next week I was in Toronto.

FRANK MANCUSO JR. – Chris Wiggins was like the emotional and spiritual anchor of things. The kids, Robey and John LeMay, were more involved in doing the heavy lifting. But the truth of it is, after Chris [was cast], it was easier. We always knew that he would sort of ground the show in a way that I thought was important. The guest stars were more the "sexier" parts, for lack of a better word. They were the ones that had the most fun associated with them because the Robey-LeMay parts were more of the "procedural" aspect of trying to get the thing back. So, Chris kind of grounded it, then they were our protagonists that were out there trying to save the world from whatever it was that was being unleashed. Then you've got the guys who are making the deals with the devil, who were the more fun people to watch. They are the ones benefiting in some real way from the implementation of the device.

JIM HENSHAW (executive story consultant) – Chris was a really great guy to work with and write for. A really bright, old-school English-trained actor. He had a classical theater background. You could give him anything and it was a lot of fun to see what he would do with it. I remember having many discussions with him where he would ask if he could try it this way or that.

John was kind of a Method actor, he came from theater, that sort of thing. Real quick study, whatever you gave him.

Robey wasn't really an actress; she was really more a singer, and had done a lot of modeling before. She was very instinctive about everything she did. Whenever you talked to her about scripts and things, she always came at it from a very emotional, instinctive way.

TOM MCLOUGHLIN – Chris was one of those actors who could make the worst dialogue sound good. He would take the proper amount of beats between lines. You could see him processing certain things without it looking like acting. He could just do nothing and be interesting.

TIM BOND (director) – Robey was inexperienced and a little frustrating at times because she was kind of a live wire. I was fond of her, but it took a lot of effort to "trick" something good out of her. I guess that's one way of putting it. She was a strong personality but she was inexperienced, and she thought she was right because she had the lead in a series. She was a little tricky at times, but dependable. A professional.

RODNEY CHARTERS (cinematographer, director) – We were very close as a team. Chris Wiggins set the tone for the actors, and he was like a schoolteacher occasionally. He would demand we focus a little better because we would get a little ragged, having too much fun. I have fond, fond memories of him. He really set the tone for those moments when we had to focus in on the horror aspect of the storytelling. He was a great storyteller and wonderful on camera.

Robey and John fit in well with that. That was the contrast. They were young and vibrant and somehow got saddled with this impossible task.

LOUISE ROBEY – I used to skip school when I was younger, to watch *Paul Bernard, Psychiatrist*. And that was Chris! Years later, there I was, working with the man. He's a lovely man, a true pro. He told me never, ever argue on set. He said to take it off-set. If you have a problem, take it off-set. Don't upset everyone else.

JOHN LEMAY – Chris was the seasoned professional. He was an incredible mentor to me throughout the production. Robey really understood the publicity and "selling yourself" aspect of the whole thing. They both had a lot to teach. I think I had more training than Robey did. I wanted to be the consummate actor. She had a lot of expertise on selling herself, preparing for interviews, she seemed to be really good at that. There aren't many people who go by one name! There's Cher, there's Madonna… there's Robey. There are iconic aspirations there, right?

LOUISE ROBEY – I had a manager who thought I should just use my last name. He's a really silly person, and he is no longer my manager. He decided, if Madonna can do it, I can do it. I said, "But that's her real first name! Mine's Louise!" They did ask me at Paramount if I would [go by] Louise Robey, but nope, stuck with Robey. It seems to be what I have to live with. A lot of people never realized that that wasn't my first name.

J. MILES DALE – Robey was a character for sure. She told me they would rename Hollywood "Robeywood."

ROB HEDDEN – We had tremendous freedom to brainstorm all sorts of cursed objects. Generally an evil artifact was the springboard for each storyline, but character relationships were always crucial. If you didn't care about Ryan, Micki and Jack, the jeopardy would be pointless. Having memorable antagonists was essential too. The beauty of the series was that not everyone who acquired a cursed artifact was pure evil; quite often there was a moral dilemma. While this conflict gave the show more depth, there's no denying that the de-facto hook was the antique itself. Our mission was to be as creative as possible in their selection, as well as utilization.

WILLIAM TAUB – I had a list of objects. We wanted the most obscure, interesting, out-of-the-mainstream ways for people to die. So, we had a list of objects. Like, we had a lantern, or Doctor Jack's scalpel… can you come up with a storyline? Or else they would come to us. Often they wouldn't have an object as good as ours, but they would have a story, and we'd say that would work well with such-and-such an object.

There is only one [antique] that never got an episode. It was Paramount who nixed it. We had one that had a gas oven from Nazi Germany. We had the story, we had an outline, everything. Paramount said no. No way can you do a gas oven. I said, "After the way we've killed two dozen people, you are saying no to a gas oven?" That became the leaf mulcher.

I'm Jewish, and the truth of the matter is, I never put it together. After they said it, I did. That's the only one.

MARC SCOTT ZICREE – I remember one time this woman came in [to pitch] and she said: "The Midas touch." I said, "Yes?" She said, "That's it." I said, "You don't understand how this works."

I know I was generating a ton of stories. Sometimes they would gel, sometimes they would not. I tried to do one about a motorcycle gang that turns into werewolves [that never worked out]. We were shooting in Toronto so I would get guide books to Toronto, and learning about the city, and the varied locations we could shoot at.

I liked the idea of Micki and Ryan and Jack doing good in the world. Their uncle had done evil, and they were going everywhere they could to find these things and lock them down. I said to Bill, "Our villains can be perverse, but we must not be. The spirit of the show must not be."

TIM BOND – Frank gave us strict orders at the beginning of the show. He said, "This is aimed at teenagers. It is going to appeal to boys more than girls. We are going to try to persuade the girlfriends to watch it with their boyfriends on Friday nights, make it a "date night" show. So, film it really, really dark so in order to see it on the TV they have to turn the lights off in the room. Then the boy can cop a feel." That was the philosophy of the show.

LOUISE ROBEY – At the beginning, the wardrobe mistress—who left after one week—put me in loose, drab brown and grey things. I don't know what they thought I was going to be. I said to them, "If you want the girl next door, you should have hired her." I had wonderful hair and makeup people who understood me. I would instruct wardrobe, and lent them a lot of my clothing. Micki became a much flashier, more colorful person. I think that helped the show in a way.

FRED MOLLIN - The Kurzweil I was using was very, very deep for that era, so I had lots of sounds and lots of extra libraries of sounds to use. I just learned as I went. If I was doing an episode that was very Gothic, like "The Poison Pen" or something like that, I knew I would have lots of bells tolling, lots of weird pipe organs. It was just my instincts. I am a musical person and my instincts were pretty good, so I knew where I wanted to feature certain instruments. I could be improvising as I watched the show. I would play along to the picture, record it, try a different sound on top of that, a lot of overdubbing. It was all me playing almost every single instrument for every show, except maybe two or three episodes. Then at night, I had two assistants come in. One would take what I had written and dump it out onto an actual analogue, multi-track tape. The other person would engineer that. Then we would take that tape to another studio and I would mix the cues. It was really like a factory going on for awhile. Every episode was different because every cursed object was different. So, I would have to come up with a new theme every week for the item, different sounds.

J. MILES DALE - It was a young group, but smart. We were all very young and nobody knew what they hell they were doing. We were sort of fighting our own inexperience in a way. Like, if we knew any better...

The show was, in the first season, $411,000 an episode—on 35mm. Doing visual effects before there were visual effects. It was kind of crazy. It was all nights for obvious reasons: scary stuff happens at night. There were some really good shows—then there were some shows that weren't as good...

"The Inheritance"

Written by: William Taub
Directed by: William Fruet
Original airdate: September 28, 1987
Cursed antique: Porcelain doll

It is a dark and stormy night when Mr. and Mrs. Simms (Michael Fletcher, Lynne Cormack) and their daughter Mary (Sarah Polley) seek refuge in Vendredi Antiques. Lewis (R.G. Armstrong) is quite annoyed; he is ready to close. Mrs. Simms chastises her stepdaughter for touching things, and Mr. Simms distracts his wife. Mary spies an old porcelain doll on the shelf and scoops her up. She sneaks into the back alley with the doll and finds a string in her back. The doll introduces herself as Veda and promises she can do a lot of things. A couple of guys approach and start giving her a hard time. Mary warns them away. Veda snaps into action. She snarls and slits one guy's throat. Mary and Veda run back into the store, where her parents are mad and worried. She tells them what happened, and Lewis is incensed. "Nothing is for sale!" he cries, grabbing Veda and pushing them out of the store. "No more, no more. I'm not going to do your bidding anymore," he shouts into the empty store. "I don't want to be responsible for the deaths of innocent people anymore." (Interestingly, this line is very hard to hear, as if attempting to hide a "softer" side of Lewis.)

Lewis rushes an armload of antiques down into the vault. The wind blows the front door open, as if the gates of hell were opening to let Satan in. Sure enough, flaming hoof prints come down the stairs, and a deep, evil laugh echoes through the store. Lewis tries to escape, but he is trapped. The antiques in the vault go crazy: Veda sits up, a piano plays, a thermometer boils, a radio lights up. The vault doors swing open and ghostly apparitions of the objects appear and swirl around Lewis. A cross floats before Lewis and turns solid. "Merciful god," he murmurs as he reaches for it—but it burns him. The gates to the never-used elevator (maybe it is more appropriately a dumbwaiter?) open for Lewis. He takes the opportunity to escape, but it soon proves his downfall. Demonic markings and flames engulf the car, and the floor opens up and swallows

Enjoying the Mercedes in "The Inheritance." Photo courtesy of John LeMay.

him into hell. It is an adorably 1980s graphic that really hasn't come very far since *Vertigo*.

And so ends Lewis Vendredi.

Six months later, we first see Micki Foster (Louise Robey) saying goodbye to her yuppy fiancé Lloyd (Barclay Hope). She has never met Lewis or this cousin Ryan (John D. LeMay) she is supposed to split her inheritance with. Lloyd wants to sue the cousin for a greater portion of the inheritance. Micki rolls her eyes and gets in the cab.

It is night when the cab drops Micki off at Vendredi Antiques. She has an awful lot of luggage for "a couple of days." The door to the antique shop is ajar. Inside, much is covered with drop cloths. She peeks under one and discovers a hideous mask. Suddenly someone in an equally strange mask jumps out from behind the counter. Micki smashes him with a vase. A dweeby, nerdy kid takes off his mask, rubbing his head. He is excited to see a beautiful young woman in front of him. "You must be Ryan Dallion," Micki says, pronouncing his last name with a French accent. "Ryan Da-Lion," he says. She introduces herself as Micki, and Ryan is wary. So, she tries again, with her full name:

"Michelle Foster?" Ryan laughs. He thought the cousin he was waiting for was named Michael. He was waiting for a guy.

"This sure does change things," he says.

Micki tightens her jacket across her chest. "Not really."

Ryan is excited about the shop, and predicts they will have a "blast" fixing it up. Micki wants to call Lloyd, but the phones and electricity are still off. They use flashlights to peek around at their inheritance. Ryan is impressed; Micki is disturbed. She reveals that the shop wasn't left to them specifically; it was in probate. They won by default.

They move into the garage and Ryan prays that this is the most amazing car he's ever seen. He removes the cover with much fanfare, and is in love with the Mercedes beneath. The place gives Micki the creeps, but she does admit the car is "not bad." She sits in the backseat and plays along. "Home, James. And don't spare the horses," she tells him. She is starting to get into it when a black cat jumps into the seat beside her, scaring her. Micki storms off.

Ryan follows her to the basement, and Micki is ready to get to business. The first thing they need to do is get an appraisal. Ryan sees the vault and looks for a way to open it. "Don't you want to know what you inherited? All the ins and outs, nooks and crannies? Good, bad, or indifferent, whatever is behind that door is ours! Listen to me, I'm beginning to sound like Monty Hall."

Ryan finally pries the doors open and finds a "veritable gold mine." He wedges the doors open with a poker and they enter. A noise draws Ryan out of the vault, and the poker folds, slamming the doors shut. Micki immediately starts screaming, then freezes when she sees Veda sit up and look at her. She is spooked and starts tripping over things, until Ryan triggers the door release and she runs out. She heads straight up the stairs but trips and grabs onto a railing for support. A trap door opens in the ceiling, and a heavy book drops down beside her. The manifest. There is a moment of pure stillness as the cousins stare at this new surprise. Micki doesn't care what is in the book; she just cares that she nearly suffocated in the vault. "Then there was this doll... never mind." She brushes off Veda after Ryan gives her a strange look.

The two return to the main floor. "You really are a tight ass, aren't you?" Ryan asks. Micki has had enough.

She throws a curio at him.

He ducks, but promises, "That is coming out of your half."

She moves to throw another, but he stops her. "This might come as a great shock to you, but I don't want the store," she tells him. "I came here to sell it off."

Ryan doesn't want to sell. "Over my dead body."

Cut to the next morning: Vendredi Antiques is having a going out of business sale. Mr. Simms comes in, looking for the doll Mary had been so taken with. Micki sees Ryan hand it over and steps in. She can't explain it, but she doesn't want to sell the doll. Ryan reminds her she said everything must go, and he sells it to Mr. Simms.

That night, the cousins are going through the vault. By tomorrow, they should have just about everything sold. On the main floor, a hooded figure sneaks into the store, stops by the cash register, then sneaks upstairs. Micki and Ryan hear this from the basement and creep up to the main floor. The hooded figure surprises them with a dagger. This is Jack Marshak (Chris Wiggins), and he supplies this store with antiques. He is looking for Lewis, who had a selective memory about paying him. They explain who they are, and Jack is suspicious. "You look too normal to relatives of Vendredi's." Micki informs him that Lewis is dead, and Jack is shocked. He drops the tough guy act and the three sit down for some tea.

Jack and Lewis were boyhood friends. Jack taught him his first magic trick, read him his first tarot, and opened his eyes to the world beyond our own, the world of spirits. Lewis was afraid of growing old and passionate about wealth. He started dabbling in things Jack wanted no part in: deucens. "Devil worship," Ryan translates, something he proudly learned from comic books. Jack returns to his story: Lewis said he was ready to make a pact with the devil, something to do with his antiques. He would gain immense wealth and immortality.

The cousins show Jack the manifest (decorated with black magic runes), and the secret compartment. "Lewis always did like secret compartments," he says, and locates another one in the wall, filled with news clippings about his antiques. Jack realizes that Lewis made the pact. But if he is dead, that means he tried to break the pact. He died, but the curse didn't die with him. "The doll," Micki exclaims, then explains the doll that she didn't want Ryan to sell "turned and stared at me like it was alive." Micki finds the sales receipt and she and Ryan intend to go over and collect the doll. Jack is going to stay at the shop, as "much in the manifest disturbs him." He gives the cousins a chance to go home and forget about all this. While Micki is not completely convinced of Jack's story, she is not going to take the chance of a little girl with a devil doll.

Mr. Simms gives the doll to Mary, who eagerly takes it upstairs to play with. When they are alone, Veda assures her she can still talk—and do a lot more. Downstairs, Mrs. Simms is furious with her husband for spoiling

The "happy family." Photo courtesy of Louise Robey.

Mary with that doll. Mary overhears this, and isn't happy. But she and Veda sit down for a tea party. Veda asks her about her "mommy," egging her on. Mrs. Simms comes in to talk with Mary, and decides that she needs to be punished. Mary offers to clean her room, but her stepmother informs her it is too late for that. She takes away Veda and tells her she can have her back in a week. Mary clutches Veda tight and runs from the room. Mrs. Simms follows and snatches the doll away. She sends Mary to her room, then puts Veda at the top of the linen closet. With her stepmother out of sight, Mary sneaks out to get Veda back, but Mrs. Simms catches her. "You're asking for it," she warns. Veda looks at Mary, who seems to give silent consent, and a roller skate quietly positions itself behind Mrs. Simms. Mary moves forward with Veda, who has begun to hiss. Mrs. Simms is startled and steps back onto the roller skate, and down the stairs she tumbles.

Ryan and Micki arrive at the Simms house after the ambulance. Mary is sitting on the curb, playing with Veda, and they go straight to her. "Don't be afraid, I'm your friend," Micki assures her in the least-convincing way possible. (Did they not have "stranger danger" in Canada in the 1980s?)

Mary sees right through this ruse and tells Micki to go away. Veda hisses, and Mary joins her dad in the ambulance.

Mrs. Simms is badly banged up, but alive. While her husband goes looking for the doctor, Veda encourages Mary to kill her, quick. Mary and Veda approach Mrs. Simms, who is scared and begging for her life. Veda locks eyes with Mrs. Simms, then "attacks." There isn't a lot of movement, but I think Veda is smothering her. By the time Mr. Simms returns, his wife has flatlined. Mary sits happily in the corner, playing with Veda, oblivious to her father's grief.

The next day, Mr. Simms leaves Mary with a kindly neighbor while he makes funeral arrangements. Mary introduces Veda to her other toys while the neighbor keeps watch from just outside her room. The little girl wants more cookies, and while her babysitter hesitates, she gives in. Even still, Mary is mad and screams that she wants the woman out of her house. "You know what to do, Mary," whispers Veda. Mary points Veda at a stack of records; they fly off the shelf and cut up the sitter. A look to the shelf, and the toys become a jungle's worth of animals. A jump rope slithers off the shelf and wraps itself around the babysitter's neck, then brings the bookcase down after it.

Micki and Ryan approach the house nervously, but the sitter's screams cause them to burst in. Ryan calls 911 and Micki sees Mary in her backyard playground, with Veda. She approaches gently and asks if she remembers her. "I don't want to take Veda; I have to," she insists. Mary isn't going to give in that easily. She and Veda make the swings fly up around Micki. It startles her, but just for a second. Mary climbs to the top of the slide and makes fire come from the mouth of a clown decoration, then makes a tether ball hit Micki.

Mary ends up on the merry-go-round, which seems to spin on its own. Micki jumps on and it spins faster and faster as the clouds grow dark and heavy, and the wind whips up. Ryan runs forward, seeing the scene, and, ever-so-helpful, tells Micki, "Don't let go!" Duh. But she is losing her grip, so Ryan jumps on and manages to wrest the doll away from Mary. The wind stops, the clouds fade, and the merry-go-round slows.

"It's all over now," Ryan assures Micki, still trying to catch her breath.

"Oh yeah? What about all the other antiques?"

Before Ryan can answer, Micki rushes to check on Mary, who was thrown clear of the merry-go-round and scraped her elbows.

Status: Veda is locked up in the vault, but is one of the few objects we see again, in the background, throughout the show. She will always be

Micki's "nemesis." Jack explains that cursed objects cannot be destroyed, so the vault is the safest option for them. Micki calls Lloyd and tells him they will have to postpone the wedding; "Lewis left his affairs in a terrible state." Lloyd is not happy. Ryan suggests they change the name of the store; it is Jack who suggests Curious Goods.

*   *   *

A porcelain doll is the perfect antique to feature in the pilot episode of a show about evil antiques. It's a very common antique—ease the viewer into the weirdness—and dolls are inherently scary: Talky Tina in *The Twilight Zone*. Chucky in *Child's Play*. Annabelle in *The Conjuring*. The dolls in *Dolls*.

Actor Channing Tatum admitted on *The Ellen Show* that he was terrified of porcelain dolls—and he has Veda from *Friday the 13th: The Series* to thank for that.[1] Veda became somewhat iconic to the show. Besides the items that got two full episodes (the coin and the compact), Veda was the only other antique that was "featured" in other episodes ("Root of All Evil," "Bottle of Dreams," and "Coven of Darkness" at minimum).

"The Inheritance" was the third or fourth episode filmed (memories vary), to give the crew a chance to gel and the actors a chance to settle in to their characters. "I think they were right to do it that way," says Louise Robey. "I think, because you have three main characters, you really have to get into a rhythm with each other. I couldn't say for certain if that happened, but I think it did."

"I'm not sure if that is typical, to be honest with you," says John LeMay, "but it makes sense to me: wait to shoot the initial episode until everyone is ready to put their best foot forward, let everything gel."

Composer Fred Mollin appreciated the out-of-order shooting, too. "By the time I got to 'The Inheritance,' I had two shows under my belt and I thought I was getting to a place where I was doing really good work and I understood what I wanted to do with the show. I think 'The Inheritance' really came off really well because of that."

Bill Taub remembers setting the pilot episode. "Some of the world was already set. The store was part of the premise. The one thing I wanted to do was to build [Micki and Ryan] out as real people. A lot of boy/girl shows were on at the time, like *Moonlighting*, stuff like that. That was what I wanted to stay away from. As soon as they get together [romantically],

---

1.   *The Ellen Show*, 9 September 2014. https://youtu.be/I6T7sh7T2lU

it's over. And if they're not going to get together, what are we doing here? They are each strong individual people and very strong characters." Making Micki and Ryan cousins was a simple, direct way to prevent them from hooking up.

"I made Ryan a little more innocent. And Micki… I called her Micki Foster because at the time I had a crush on an actress named Meg Foster," admits Taub. "I told this to Robey a few years ago, and she said, 'I wish I had known! I'm such good friends with her!' So, that is how she became Micki Foster.

"The philosophy of the show is very much Faust. We'll give you your wish, but you will pay a price; a pact with the devil. The store, Jack, Ryan, Micki, they all worked really well together."

The guest star of this episode was a then-unknown seven-year-old named Sarah Polley, who would go on to star in big-screen successes like *The Sweet Hereafter*, *Splice*, and the 2004 remake of *Dawn of the Dead*, as well as write and direct *Stories We Tell*. It is interesting that in the first episode of *Friday the 13th*, they chose to make the "villain" a child. This isn't the only time a child has gotten hold of cursed antiques ("The Playhouse," "Jack-in-the-Box," "A Friend to the End"), but it is surprising that the first (aired) episode made a child the villain. Children are normally very sheltered in television and film. Audiences don't like to see villainous children almost as much as they don't like to see children killed on-screen. People like to preserve the idea of the innocence of children.

Lynne Cormack played "evil stepmother" Mrs. Simms. "I think the first question you always ask with a role like that is, 'where is the love, and where is the lack of love?' Especially in 'The Inheritance,' all horrible behavior comes from wanting something you can't get. I don't think a person just wakes up and says, 'I'm going to be a horrible bitch today.' You always think you are justified in your behavior."

Cormack recalls bumping into Polley a few years ago and her shyly saying, "Hi mommy." "She told me for years she thought she *actually* killed me. I said, 'Well I hope your mom straightened that out!' She said, 'Yeah, eventually she did, but I was just sure I'd killed you.'"

"The Poison Pen"

Written by: Durnford King
Directed by: Timothy Bond
Original airdate: October 5, 1987
Cursed antique: Quilled pen

The Eternal Brotherhood is a cloistered religious sect located in the heart of the city. Amongst their numbers is Brother Currie (Larry Reynolds), the so-called "Oracle of Death," named so because he writes about the deaths of fellow brothers, and they all come true. Naturally a cursed object is behind this, and a photo in the newspaper of Brother Currie reveals which one: a quilled pen that Jack picked up in Tierra del Fuego, made from the tail feather of a giant Chilean condor. ("They're the worst kind.") The manifest lists the pen as being sold to a Rupert Seldon, who disappeared some years ago while a suspect in his business partner's murder. Because of the secretive nature of the Brotherhood, the only way to get close is to go undercover. For whatever reason, Micki will join Ryan instead of Jack, meaning Micki has to go undercover as a boy.

I never really understood this. I guess Jack wanted to stay behind and research, and it would be unwise to send Ryan in alone. But how on earth can anyone mistake Micki for a boy? Micki does take a vow of silence and she straps her breasts down, but her delicate features are far too feminine.

Anyway, Jack writes up a letter of introduction "that could fool the Pope," and Brothers Matthew and Simon from Yorkshire are born. Brother Drake (Alar Aedma) greets them at the gate and accepts them hesitantly, having not heard of any transfers and still reeling from the death of the abbot a couple days prior. Ryan is very excited to meet Brother Currie, but Brother Drake informs him he is in seclusion and cannot be disturbed.

Micki and Ryan are to share a room, which disgusts Micki, but not as much as when she discovers the shower and bathroom are communal. Ryan is still weirdly flirty with Micki at this point in the show, and Micki is still kind of stuck up and unhappy about her new life circumstances.

Brother Le Croix (Colin Fox) is cautious of the new recruits, but at first he thinks Matthew and Simon are, at worst, journalists. Le Croix clearly runs the joint, even though a new abbot has not been named, and he gives Drake the task of keeping an eye on them.

Ryan and Micki follow one brother as he delivers a tray of food to the cloistered Currie, but are scared away by Drake. They do find where they hide the guillotine. Foiled on their first attempt, they go do their chores (raking and lawn mowing) when Brother Arrupe (Gillie Fenwick) runs up, proclaiming that the Oracle of Death has made another prophecy: the abbot will choke tonight. Ryan reminds Arrupe that a new abbot has not been named, which calms him down.

As Arrupe goes to bed that night, he reads a letter. The home office has named him the new abbot. In his excitement he forgets about the prophecy, and goes to bed. He has barely gotten comfortable when the canopy starts to lower itself onto Arrupe. It doesn't crash down; it moves ominously and with purpose. Though Arrupe does manage to tear an air hole in the fabric, by the time others in the Brotherhood (including Micki and Ryan) answer his cries of distress, Arrupe is dead. The canopy is back where it should be, but there is a very noticeable hole in it. Jack decides the kids need help, so he arrives as another new transfer, this time from Ireland. During more chores, he shows Ryan and Micki the exact replica of the quilled pen he made to swap out with the cursed one. Their conversation (which they don't keep very secret) is overheard.

"Brother Currie" is actually a guy named Frank, and he runs to Le Croix in a panic, because the newbies know about the pen. Le Croix is really Rupert Seldon. He and Frank have been hiding out in the Brotherhood to avoid prison. Le Croix is not worried; he will just write up another epitaph for the transfers, but Frank wants out. Le Croix is now abbot, and he wants to sell the monastery to a developer for $10 million—something that previous abbots had all refused to do. Frank doesn't care about the money, and vows that the Oracle has made his last prediction. But the "Oracle" still has one more prediction: the "most gruesome death" of Brother Currie. It is meant as a suicide note, for when Micki and Ryan arrive, they find Currie laying beneath the guillotine, head already rolling around on the floor.

Le Croix writes up a new epitaph, this one for Brothers Simon and Matthew: death by spider bite. A huge, hairy tarantula creeps into Micki and Ryan's room, crawling up Micki's arm. She is terrified, and Ryan shoos it away, but they make a lot of noise, which brings Jack running. He assures them it is a harmless tarantula, and sends the arachnid on its way. In the morning, Le Croix tells Drake that Currie left behind a bunch of predictions, to cover his ass when more people start dying. He is shocked to see Micki and Ryan, alive and well, sitting down to their morning ration of brown rice. He greets them with fake charm and makes sure they haven't been bothered by any rodents, spiders, or other pests. Jack puts it together, and realizes Le Croix wrote an epitaph, but it was for Brother Matthew and Brother Simon, not Micki Foster and Ryan Dallion. It turns out that the real Brothers Matthew and Simon in Yorkshire were killed by a poisonous spider bite. I wonder, if those two people didn't exist, would the pen have killed Le Croix for not delivering what he promised?

Jack starts snooping around Le Croix's office. He doesn't find the pen, but he does find the prognostication book. He checks the handwriting against that of Rupert Seldon's signature on the original bill of sale, and finds they match: the same formal Gothic calligraphy. Even though the book has nothing to do with the curse, Jack takes it. While he does this, Ryan is standing guard outside the bathroom so Micki can shower, her first in something like three days. She enjoys herself immensely—and so does Drake—who is watching through a none-too-subtle peep hole. Considering this is men-only order, this glory hole takes on a whole new meaning.

Drake reports to Le Croix that the real Simon and Matthew never left Yorkshire and were killed. He also reveals, with a giggle, that the person they know as Brother Simon is a woman. Le Croix doesn't seem to care about this, and instructs Drake to remain quiet on the entire matter. Le Croix turns evening meditation over to Drake and rushes back to his office, where he finds Jack sneaking about. As soon as Le Croix produces a gun, Jack drops his accent, and sets up the best (and by best, I mean cheesiest) line in the whole series:

"I thought you were meditating."

"I was. Premeditating."

Le Croix ties Jack to the guillotine and admits to having the pen, but only Jack and his friends know about it. He doesn't need to write up an epitaph for Jack for whatever reason; he just leaves a lit candle burning beneath the rope that holds the blade up and leaves. He has a meeting with the developer and is ready to sign on the dotted line. Unfortunately, Drake is snooping about and overhears the deal. As possibly the only true believer left in the order, he is upset.

Micki and Ryan split up: she will find the pen and swap it with the fake, while Ryan goes hunting for Jack. Micki finds the quill hidden beneath Le Croix's desk chair, and swaps it out. She hides when Le Croix enters. He can't find his super-special prophecy book, so he settles for taking the pen and leaves. He does not know he has the fake.

Micki meets up with Ryan, who has just untied Jack from the guillotine. She proudly informs them of the switch, but Le Croix returns and thanks her for the warning. He demands the real antique at gunpoint, and Micki turns it over. Since he can't find his journal, he grabs a scrap of paper from Jack and begins writing out their epitaphs. Drake interrupts the festivities by rushing Le Croix with an axe. He sees Le Croix as a traitor, but he misses and ends up joining our crew as a hostage. Le Croix finishes writing and, like any good bad guy, says he "just has to fill in the names." Jack points out that he is writing on the back of the original bill of sale, with Rupert Seldon's name on it. The guillotine blade flies off the contraption and starts chasing him around the room. It gets stuck in the wall, and a smug Le Croix returns to his hostages.

Then the episode turns into a Bugs Bunny cartoon. The blade sneaks up behind Le Croix, and Micki weakly tries to point it out. "You really think I'm going to fall for an old trick like that?" The blade kindly waits until Le Croix is done mocking her before it implants itself into Le Croix's back. Strangely enough, the blade makes it all the way through his body, but stops short at ripping the front side of his tunic.

Status: Jack assures a worried Micki that the real pen is safely tucked away in the vault; the one on his desk is the copy. Ryan offers to find out the truth by using it to take the lunch order. He wants something "really sinful."

Mentioned but not explored: All these are seen as listings in the manifest. One ring of skeleton keys; two Venetian chairs, XIX (1 leg is missing); ring (silver) of MacCulloch family; 2x tapestry, Polish, XVII (animal motifs); doll house, 5'6" high, 1" scale, lights (could this have been the eponymous antique from "The Playhouse?"); Venus statue (planter) (marble); Queen Anne bed + canopy; magic lantern + 8 dispositives (I'm pretty sure this is the lantern from "Eye of Death").

*   *   *

John LeMay and Louise Robey were almost kicked off the set of *F13* during "The Poison Pen." Can you imagine a different Ryan and Micki? I can't.

Director Timothy Bond explains what happened: "On the first day of shooting 'The Poison Pen,' John LeMay and Robey still had not signed their contracts. They had agents who were grandstanding: 'You've already started shooting, what are you going to do now?'

"[Producer] Iain Paterson came to set just before the lunch break. He called them over and said 'We're taking a one-hour lunch break, and if you two haven't signed by the end of the hour, don't come back to set, because I will be replacing you.'

"So, they signed."

Ironic that it is during an episode about a pen that signs people's fates.

"I have a picture of mine," John LeMay admits. "I look so geeky in the picture. I'm in these shorts that the wardrobe person put me in. I have a huge grin on my face. The makeup person came over and took a picture of me while I was signing the contract."

As her first television role, Robey was more than a little green. "LeMay looked at me as if I were mad when I said, 'Where's the director?' after the first week.

"He said, 'They change directors, Louise, on television. Every week.'

"He was such a snotty kid to me! I didn't know!"

Snotty or not, Robey admits the two got along. "There was a chemistry."

"'The Poison Pen' was my first episode and there was lots of tension," director Tim Bond tells me. "When I got the script, I noticed that 75% took place outdoors at night. My shooting date was a couple of days before the longest day of the year (June 22). I had to do a little astronomy lesson for the producers, since I didn't think they would want their crew working six hours a day. As it turned out, the show soon fell into a regrettable pattern of shooting fifteen to eighteen hours a day."

Season 3 saw another cursed pen episode: "Mightier Than the Sword." Though both episodes are drastically different, the basic curse is the same: a pen that writes horrible things that come true. "Mightier" has the added bonus of controlling another human being. Seems like you get more curse for your buck with that pen. "I always confuse 'The Poison Pen' and 'Mightier than the Sword,'" admits line producer J. Miles Dale. "'The Poison Pen is Mightier than the Sword,' our joke used to be."

"Cupid's Quiver"

Written by: Stephen Katz
Directed by: Atom Egoyan
Original airdate: October 12, 1987
Cursed antique: Cupid statuette

An awkward, dorky man, Gerald Hastings, is hanging out at a dive bar when he takes an interest in a woman across the room. She turns down his request for a dance, perhaps because she is already talking with a man. Gerald retreats to the bar and unwraps an ugly cupid statue. He tries one more time with the woman, but she again rejects him—much more rudely. From across the room, the cupid shoots her with a little laser arrow, and her whole outlook changes. She eagerly accepts when he cuts in on her dance, and suggests they get a room. Gerald takes her to the honeymoon suite, a tacky room with a heart-shaped bed and pink light bulbs, and immediately has sex with her. The cupid statue actually turns its head to watch. As they lay in a post-coital haze, the woman tells Gerald she loves him. That is what Gerald was waiting to hear. He climbs on top of her and chokes her. A group of frat boys hears the commotion and breaks the door down, pulling Gerald off her. One of the frat boys, Bowser (Kevin Lund) is intrigued by the cupid statue and takes it with him.

Micki reads about the incident in the morning paper, and she remembers that there was a cupid statue in the manifest. Jack remembers picking it up in Cairo. It was commissioned by Salla Malek in Italy in 1493. It was said he was so ugly that no woman could look at him without turning away. He vowed vengeance on them and had the statue cast in his own image. Upon his arrest, Gerald claimed that he "had to kill for cupid's sake." Micki finds the statue in the manifest, item 00279, sold to a Frederick Mason four years prior. He was convicted of killing three women and sentenced to death.

After a chat with the motel manager, Micki and Ryan are directed to a local frat with a heart and arrow symbol. They stop a young couple, Eddie and Laurie (Denis Forest and Carolyn Dunn), to ask for directions. Except Eddie and Laurie aren't actually a couple. Laurie is a lovely, normal

Time to chill. Photo courtesy of John LeMay.

young co-ed, while Eddie is a creepy student who takes pictures of her from trees under the guise of bird watching. He has been obsessed with Laurie ever since she helped him with homework one day and mistook it for a date. Eddie is badgering her to go out with him, but she is creeped out. Micki and Ryan interrupt just as Laurie is threatening to report Eddie. Eddie knows the frat they are looking for, Delta Lambda Chi. He is wearing their t-shirt and lets Ryan think he is a member. He offers to give them a ride, but Laurie offers to walk them directly there. Micki picks up on the "girl signals" Laurie is sending and the two escort her to the frat. She is very grateful.

Eddie rushes back to the frat house in hopes of catching up with Laurie, but she doesn't come in. Eddie starts cleaning up, which is when we learn that he isn't actually part of the frat, he just cleans up in exchange for wearing one of their t-shirts. While cleaning, he finds the cupid in Bowser's room and is immediately drawn to it. Bowser warns him away from it, but Eddie clearly isn't going to stay away for long. Ryan's plan to go into the frat as cops backfires when frat president, Harold, won't let them look around without a warrant or badges.

Jack has a plan to get them into the frat. He will play bartender at the party tonight while Ryan and Micki snoop. Jack has dosed his special punch with sodium pentathol to help loosen lips. This may be the first time in history spiked punch at a frat party wasn't used to abuse women. After being plied with punch, Bowser says he has the cupid and takes Micki and Ryan to his room to show them. But it's gone, and he has one suspect: Eddie.

Eddie, after seeing Laurie smooch her boyfriend, gets kicked out of the party and takes the cupid to a bar (the same bar Gerald Hastings preyed at, it seems). The first girl who talks to him does so purely to insult the ugly statue. Eddie aims cupid at her, and her disdain turns to lust. They go take a ride up by Mason's Creek. In a secluded part of the woods, the couple fools around in the cab of Eddie's truck. The cupid watches them through the window. It is never mentioned as part of the curse, but it seems like part of the unspoken deal between the cupid and its master is that it gets to watch the naughty bits. After sex, the girl apologizes for being so mean and tells Eddie she loves him. He presents a bottle of honey to get her in the mood for round two, then excuses himself to pee while she cleans up his hastily spilled honey. But when Eddie returns, he has a beehive with him and throws it into the truck with the girl. The bees sting her mercilessly. He mouths "I love you" and draws a heart on the window—all mockingly, of course.

Meanwhile, Micki and Ryan head to Eddie's creepy boiler room "apartment," the kind of place that is normally not seen outside of a Freddy Kruger nightmare, and it leads to one of my favorite exchanges in the history of the series:

Micki: "I can't believe anybody lives like this."

Ryan: "Dracula lives like this."

Micki: "I meant someone real."

Ryan: "Are you suggesting Dracula isn't real?"

Eddie isn't there, and neither is the cupid, but they do find an obsessive collage of Laurie photos. (Eddie still has one with him, which, after he kills the bar girl, he kisses, ready to claim his real prize.) They return to Jack, who got a tip that if Eddie couldn't get a drink at the party, he was probably at the neighborhood dive bar. The bouncer there tells Jack he overheard Eddie going to Mason's Creek, and Jack starts searching the woods looking for signs of Eddie or the cupid. Instead, he finds Eddie's paramour's corpse. Drunken Bowser is also in the woods, looking for Eddie so he can pummel him for stealing his statue; instead Jack sends him to call the police.

Eddie has managed to find Laurie and her boyfriend having some wine alone in the woods. When the boyfriend goes back to the frat to grab another bottle, Eddie sneaks up on Laurie and scares her. She begs him to go away. Micki and Ryan, who have also been searching the woods, see Eddie hustling Laurie into his apartment. Ryan gives chase, and he leaves Laurie in order to make a faster escape. Micki checks on Laurie while Ryan follows Eddie into his room. Ryan knocks him out with a crowbar, grabs the cupid, and returns to Micki, who is trying to convince Laurie to come home with them. Laurie isn't too concerned, but Jack finds them, tells them about the corpse, and Laurie finally agrees to go with them. Before they leave, the campus cop comes by, sees the cupid and recognizes it as the one reported missing by Delta Lambda Chi. He takes it with him so he can check on the rightful ownership. (Apparently, he isn't there to check on the girl's corpse.) On his way back to the station, he sees Eddie and gives him the statue.

Back at Curious Goods, Micki puts Laurie in her room then joins Ryan and Jack in the kitchen. They overhear Laurie call Eddie to apologize for going with them, but she had to, or they would have "gotten suspicious." She agrees to come over and tells him she loves him.

Laurie sneaks through the night and ends up at Eddie's room where he has set up a candlelight dinner. He creeps up behind her, but when she turns around, we discover it isn't Laurie—it is Micki in a wig and Laurie's clothing. Naturally, Eddie is mad when he discovers the switch. Micki informs him he will have to kill Laurie, to which Eddie responds, "I don't *want* to kill them; I *have* to." He vows that girls will no longer make fun of him—they will all love him.

Ryan finally manages to break down the door, and no sooner does Micki inform him that she is fine than she is hit with cupid's arrow. "Don't hurt him! I love him!" she insists as she nuzzles Eddie. Eddie takes an axe to a steam pipe in hopes of slowing down Ryan, but the pipe knocks Micki out and gives Eddie a face full of steam. After checking that Micki is still breathing, Ryan chases Eddie through the labyrinthine rafters. Eddie slips off a pipe and falls to his death.

Status: The cupid statue goes into the vault.

* * *

Atom Egoyan is best known for his art house films *The Sweet Hereafter* (for which he was nominated for an Oscar) and *Exotica* (for which he won an Adult Video News award for Best Alternative Adult Film. How many directors can claim both?) but one of his first directing jobs was on *F13*. "I got the job based on some episodes of *The Twilight Zone* and *Alfred Hitchcock Presents* I had directed, which happened to catch the producer's eye," says Egoyan. "I had no agent at the time, so this was something of a miracle."

"Cupid's Quiver," though the third to air, was actually the first episode filmed. In syndication, there is no "pilot process." A series order is not based on one first episode. So, "The Inheritance" was actually the third or fourth episode to be shot (memories vary). This allowed the crew to gel, the actors to gain a rapport with one another, and production got the chance to find a routine so that, if the first-shot episode felt clumsy, it wasn't the first-aired, which risked scaring away the audience. Personally, I never noticed anything awkward about "Cupid's Quiver," but after finding out that "The Inheritance" shot later, I definitely saw more warmth and ease amongst the leads.

Egoyan says that, because this was the "production pilot," he was very involved with casting and worked directly with Frank Mancuso Jr. "I was given a lot of freedom, but we all understood that the series needed to have a certain tone. I felt that, while I tried to set a visual look, this became much more refined as the series progressed."

The seven-day shooting schedule proved challenging, especially since it was being shot on 35mm. Even more challenging was shooting on 35mm with bees. "The most vivid [memory] was being in the truck of the cab with all these live bees. The [camera] operator was terrified of being stung, so I was holding a 35mm camera for the first time in my life, trying to get the 'bee's eye' P.O.V. shot myself.

"I also remember being two hours into overtime on the first night, and *still* needing to do a unit move to another location. It was a miracle I wasn't fired!" In fact, Egoyan was asked to direct more episodes, but his film career began to take off.

Louise Robey remembers a steep learning curve. "It was overwhelming. I was completely green. I thought, *Hm. This is interesting. I worked all night, it's now daylight outside... that will never happen again.* [Laughs] And it did. All the time."

John LeMay got a kick out of the first episode. "I felt like I could do no wrong, even though I was fairly green—I had only done a few guest spots and had been in Hollywood for maybe three years. All of a sudden, to be put in this position, the lead of a television series, with the makeup people and the wardrobe people and the grips and the gaffers... everybody looks at you as the lead of a television series all of a sudden, which makes you feel like you can do no wrong. That feeling of people just putting their faith in you and trusting that you have the goods to deliver. You end up rising to the occasion because everybody believes in you. It was overwhelming but it happened so quickly, I didn't have a chance to be overwhelmed."

"A Cup of Time"

Written by: Barbara Sachs
Directed by: F. Harvey Frost
Original airdate: October 19, 1987
Cursed antique: Teacup

Homeless people in the park are turning up dead, strangled to death. A woman has been going to the park, offering people a hot cup of tea from her teacup with a hand painted ivy design. When the victims take a sip, the ivy comes alive and strangles the sipper. It's not long before we discover the woman with the tea cup is Lady Die (Hilary Shepard), Ryan's favorite musician of the moment.

Birdie (Maxine Miller), a social worker who has a crush on Jack, stops by Curious Goods to drop off some curtains she was hemming. While there, she mentions that one of her cases, a young runaway, was murdered in the park last night. She is not the first, but the police don't have much interest in solving a spate of homeless killings. Micki recalls another one of Birdie's cases being killed earlier that year, but Birdie corrects her: Sarah disappeared, she wasn't killed.

Ryan and Micki offer to look into the case and head down to the coroner's office. While Micki spars verbally with Lt. Fishbein (Richard Fitzpatrick) over what he is doing to prevent murders in her neighborhood, Ryan pockets a piece of ivy he finds on the floor. Back at the shop, Jack identifies it as Swapper's Ivy, thought extinct since the fourteenth century. Indigenous to Ireland, it was considered an evil plant. If you had it, you could trade for whatever you wanted. He does not specify if this was a spiritual/magical trade, or a simple barter item. Jack turns to the manifest, looking for anything decorated with ivy. He finds it: a porcelain tea cup, no mark, white with a hand painted Swapper's Ivy design along the rim. Lewis sold the cup two years ago to a man named Fat Eddie Burrell. When Micki and Ryan go looking for him, all they find is his pile of bones in his long-abandoned house

Lady Die is prepping for her concert to benefit the homeless, and her manager, Langley (Lubomir Mykytiuk), mentions she looks a little tired.

She immediately rushes off to find a victim, but tea time is interrupted by a young homeless girl named Kristen (Lisa Jakub). She wants some tea, but it is an "adult drink," so Lady Die offers up her expensive bracelet in exchange for her going away. Kristen accepts—but watches the adults while hiding in a bush.

Morning comes, and Micki and Ryan take Birdie to the park to identify the latest victim. She doesn't recognize him, but when Kristen asks her and Micki for some food, Birdie does recognize the bracelet she wears: it belonged to Sarah Burrell, Birdie's missing person—and yes, she is Fat Eddie's sister. Kristen tells Micki and Birdie what she saw, and that the lady with the man was pretty with "hair like fire." Birdie is distraught; she thought maybe Kristen saw her missing person, but Sarah was over seventy years old, with white hair.

After Birdie gives them a photo of Sarah, Ryan and Jack start to believe that Lady Die and Sarah Burrell are one in the same. Jack believes the ivy acts as a conductor, trading the victim's life force for the cup owner's age. (In other words, making the cup owner younger.) Birdie overhears this conversation when she comes to the shop to invite Jack to dinner. Seeing as how she is wearing something that looks like she took it from one of her young runaways, it is no surprise that Birdie, longing for her youth, is intrigued by what she hears. Jack turns down her invitation, and Birdie is frustrated, storming out.

Micki and Ryan head to the radio station, planning to confront Lady Die, who is doing press for her concert. Ryan goes as a reporter from Rock Icon Magazine, with Micki as his sexy chauffeur. (As someone who has worked as a journalist for over a decade, I can guarantee that magazine reporters *never* go anywhere in a limo.) They barge into the recording booth just after Langley mentions to Die that she is looking very tired. She's on edge and doesn't want to answer any questions about Sarah Burrell or a tea cup. Security drags Micki and Ryan out while Lady Die sneaks out the back door. In the alley, she runs into Birdie, who recognizes her as Sarah, now that the effects of the tea cup are wearing off. She is so distracted that she doesn't notice Kristen run by, stealing the cup from her bag. Micki and Ryan return to the car and argue about who is going to drive. Despite her chauffeur costume ("You look better in the outfit.") Ryan wins. They drive off to find Lady Die.

Die is in the park and wakes a man, desperate to give him a drink. She is horrified to discover the cup is missing and begins crawling through the park looking for it. But Kristen has it, and for whatever reason, she

The "witch" of "A Cup of Time." Photo courtesy of Hilary Shepard.

is holding on to it for dear life. She cradles it like a teddy bear when she crawls into the little nest she has made for herself in the bushes. But someone creeps into her nest and Kristen runs, clutching the cup. It turns out it is only Micki, who offers to trade her the cup for a hot meal, a real bed, and a cup that is almost as pretty. Kristen agrees, and Ryan and Micki take her home.

Jack and Micki take Kristen upstairs for potato chips (and, hopefully, something a little more nutritious). Ryan is tasked with putting the teacup in the vault, but he wants potato chips, too, and leaves the cup on the desk. Unattended. All for some potato chips. So, while Jack and Ryan are in the kitchen, and Micki is putting Kristen to bed, someone breaks in and snatches the cup from the desk. The guys rush down but find the robber—and the cup—gone. Ryan doesn't believe it was Lady Die who broke in. It was someone who moved slow, like Birdie's age. Jack suggests that the longer Die goes without using the cup, the older she gets.

The robber flags a cab, stocking still on her head. It isn't until she gets in the cab that we see the thief isn't Lady Die, as we are expected to believe. It is Birdie. Birdie is tired of being lonely and seems to think that youth is going to give her a social life—or at least make Jack want to date her. Apparently "not being crazy" and "asking another man on a date" never occurred to her. She went right for the cursed antique.

Following in Lady Die's footsteps, Birdie goes to the park and offers a wino a nightcap. He grabs eagerly for the bottle, but Birdie insists they be civilized and pours it into the cup. "Here is to happiness and health—and youth." The man eagerly takes the cup and starts to drink, but as the ivy comes alive, Birdie has a change of heart. She takes the cup away and gives him the bottle. The ivy returns to the cup and the wino offers her some booze through her tears. They drink through to morning, and Birdie feels much better. Nothing like staying up all night drinking in a park to make you feel young again. Birdie calls Ryan from a payphone and wants to return the cup. From a distance, Lady Die watches. She is horribly decrepit by this point.

The cops are watching as the Mercedes pulls into the park, but Birdie is not by the payphone.

That is because Lady Die, looking like a cartoon witch at this point, is chasing Birdie through the park. Birdie trips, Die hits her, and she tumbles down an embankment. This is where Micki and Ryan find her—and where the cops find them. Micki and Ryan are arrested, while Jack watches from a distance and sneaks away. I know that Jack has a plan, and that him getting arrested won't help anything, but it still feels a little sneaky—even traitorous—to watch him creep away.

Lady Die calls her manager and promises she will be there in time for the show. He is concerned because she doesn't sound like herself (of course not; she is now even older than she was before she got her hands on the teacup). Night falls, and Die makes one final attempt with the teacup. Shaking, obviously near death, she approaches a homeless man hunched over on a park bench. The man accepts the tea—then sits up, revealing himself to be Jack in a ridiculous wig. He spills out the tea and runs off with the cup.

It is show time, and Langley is panicked because Lady Die won't leave her trailer. Micki and Ryan show up, inexplicably released from jail (lets assume that Birdie woke up and exonerated them) with a plan to steal the teacup. Jack shows up and shows them that he got the teacup. Before they can head home, the door to Lady Die's trailer opens. "It's show time," hisses a decrepit voice. The door springs open and Lady Die is there, looking like, well, death. She looks like a mummified witch, and she keels over, dead. It is a strangely anti-climactic end to this episode.

Status: The teacup is vaulted, and Birdie takes Kristen to a new home.

Mentioned but not explored: All of these are seen as listings in the manifest. Harmonica; umbrella stand, oak, 1930; Garuda, Balinese, 1840; Cupid of Malek (not crossed off); cigarette case; "Italian" table (not sure why it is in quotes); Victorian table lamp, 1800; paperweight; jade earrings, dragon motif.

* * *

Actress Hilary Shepard played the memorable role of Lady Die, a role that she didn't think she had a chance at. "I was up against Moon Zappa and some other famous musicians, so I didn't think I'd get it!" At the time, she was part of a short-lived all-girl band, American Girls. "When I auditioned, the producers thought I might be too tough—that I was too bossy. I told them that all the women rockers I worked with had to be tough because we had to hold our own in a man's world. I think they really liked that take on things."

Hilary loved Louise Robey and John LeMay immediately. "They were very sweet and fun to hang out with. We all went to see a James Brown concert in the park," she says. Unfortunately, the prosthetics process was a little less awesome: "The makeup was a nightmare. The guys doing it were newbies and had no idea what they were doing. They were actually reading from a how-to book as they went. The first days they glued my prosthetics on and they couldn't get them off. It was agony. I remember them reading from the book and saying, 'Oops! We forgot to powder you first. From now on we'll powder the snot out of you.' The process would take hours. They would come to my hotel room at 4:00 a.m. and I'd sleep on my back as they applied it. Then they would follow me around all day saying, 'We gotta powder the snot out of you!'"

That makeup, however, was effective. "We were shooting in the park and I was in full old lady makeup. They told me to run and I ran down an incline full-tilt into a playground where some kids were on a swing set. I scared the bejesus out of those poor kids! I quickly ran back into the woods and I could hear the kids crying and telling their mother a witch was chasing them. The mother told them to stop telling tales. I wanted to go back and tell the mom the kids weren't lying, but I was afraid I'd scare her, too!"

"Hellowe'en"

Written by: William Taub
Directed by: Timothy Bond
Original airdate: October 26, 1987
Cursed antique: Amulet of Zohar

Ahh… Halloween night. A demented night to rot your teeth while zombies rot on the television. But when everyday is Halloween for Micki, Ryan, and Jack, what do you do on Halloween proper?

You throw a party of course.

Micki has misgivings about the party, but Ryan thinks it will be good for business. Lewis did not have a sterling reputation in the community (being in bed with the devil does have that effect on your social standing) so Ryan wants them to see "two upstanding citizens at the helm." Micki is worried, especially with the nonsense going on in the vault, but Ryan assures her: "Don't worry, I put a sign on the vault." This always amused me, because anyone who is rude enough to start snooping in your basement is not going to give two shits about a sign.

Micki is dressed as a witch; Ryan is dressed as some medieval poet—but with a demon face on the back of his head; and Jack is Merlin, delighting the crowd with sleight-of-hand magic and tarot readings. Unsurprisingly, a couple of Ryan's friends, Larry and Howard, slip past the sign. ("This isn't for us," Larry informs his nervous friend, "this is for the jerks upstairs.") They don't get into the vault, but they do turn off the electricity, scaring the partygoers upstairs. When Larry tries to turn it back on, the fuse blows. He leaves it and turns his attention to a crystal ball that is glowing blue. He decides to use it to contact Elvis, and mockingly calls the spirits. But in Curious Goods, the spirits always answer. The ball goes from blue to green, and smoke starts to billow across the floor. Ryan comes down to fix the fuse box and sends the guys upstairs with a stern lecture. On his way up, Ryan notices the crystal ball, the smoke, and the faint howling sounds.

He goes straight to Jack and admits someone had been playing with the crystal ball. A wind picks up in the closed shop, scaring the partygoers. When the walls start to crack, the party is over and the gang herds the guests out of the shop. At Jack's command, Ryan draws a pentacle around the desk, Micki gets his bag, and Jack retrieves the crystal ball from the basement. "Those friends of yours threw out a psychic line and hooked something," Jack informs them. "Halloween isn't a game. It's the one night of year when spirits can roam the earth freely." Jack chants, and all is still. They wait a moment, and Jack thinks it is gone. Ryan and Micki go upstairs to get celebratory drinks, while Jack checks on a delicate tap at the front door.

A little girl is sitting on a bench outside, sobbing softly. She lost her mom while trick-or-treating, and is scared. Jack offers to walk her home. They walk for awhile, and Jack starts to think they are going in circles. She prods him a little further, then turns a corner and tells him they are home. "Home" is a dead-end alley, and when Jack turns in, a gate drops down and locks him in. The little girl turns into an adult dwarf named Greta (Victoria Deslaurier) and laughs at him. Realization dawns on Jack: "Lewis!"

Micki and Ryan bring the drinks downstairs to find Jack is gone. Smoke billows up from the basement, accompanied by heavy breathing. A ghostly hand reaches for them, them fully materializes. Lewis Vendredi. "Not even a hello for your old Uncle Lewis?" he asks. Micki confirms it is him—she has seen his picture. Lewis promises he isn't there to hurt them. As a ghost, he can't even touch them. He is sorry, and is there to make amends. Lewis promises that he has returned to earth to undo the curse. "Curses aren't forever, they only feel like forever," he explains. He then tells them about his "final, secret sin." With a wave of his hand, a secret passage opens up in the shelves and the cousins move into a lushly decorated secret bedroom. It looks like a dusty 1920s brothel. He reveals a woman in the bed, his wife Grace. Lewis believes he killed her, not directly, but with his ambition and greed. Grace's soul was taken to hell, and he needs the Amulet of Zohar from the vault. With it he can free her soul and she will find peace. After he does that, he will undo the curse. But he only has until sunrise to do so.

Softies that they are, Micki and Ryan agree to do it—you know, "for his wife."

"I always imagined Lewis to be some kind of monster. But he's not if he would do something like this," Micki reasons naively.

Ryan thinks Jack would tell them to do it, and reasons that they have nothing to lose. "He can't even touch us."

I know that Micki and Ryan have only been at it for a month or so, but seriously, can they be that gullible? I guess they can be, because they bring the amulet back for Lewis. There is a flash of light, and suddenly Lewis is corporeal. He laughs at his niece and nephew and locks them in the secret room, telling them he must "attend to something before the night is out." In the garage, Greta has the car ready, and they steal the Mercedes. They have three hours and forty-one minutes before sunrise.

The cousins are irritated at their current predicament and start blaming each other. But they are both equally culpable, and they know it. At one point Micki actually says, "Why does this kind of stuff always happen when Jack's not around?"

Because, dear Micki, Jack would never be so stupid as to trust Lewis. Maybe it is because they never met Lewis while he was alive. Jack knows what an asshole he is. Clearly, Ryan and Micki's stupidity really pisses me off. The pair figure out they can escape through the fireplace, and they come out at the front of the store. Micki goes to the books, and immediately finds something on the Amulet of Zohar. It is in Ye Olde English, but as best as Micki can tell, Lewis is going to use the amulet to take over a body, one that died a peaceful death, not a violent one. They head out to check mortuaries, and Micki leaves a note for Jack, tacked to the wall with a knife (something that always tickled me).

Back on the street, a couple drunken frat boys in Halloween costumes decide to take a few minutes to pull over and taunt Jack like a zoo animal. Jack taunts them right back, and he gets their goat. The frat boys are so enraged and desperate to prove their manliness they wrap chains around the bars, then run their monster truck until the bars bend enough to let Jack out. The boys are ready to fight, but Jack throws a handful of flash powder and disappears into the night.

Lewis and Greta hit the Abraham Stark Mortuary, the closest one to Curious Goods. Greta asks if he has a preference: man or woman. "I choose to be alive!" Lewis affirms. "Nothing else matters!"

Inside, Lewis can only find bloody corpses, which means violent deaths. Time until sunrise: two hours, eighteen minutes. Luckily, as they are heading outside, they see a hearse roll up, carrying the body of a man who died in his sleep in a hospital. Lewis and Greta take the body inside and set up for their ritual. It is a pretty standard setup: the corpse at the center of a pentacle, surrounded by candles and chanting.

Micki and Ryan see their Mercedes parked outside, so they know they have the right mortuary. Ryan picks the lock ("Jack always makes this look so easy") and the two sneak in. Their working hypothesis is that if they take the amulet from Lewis, he will go back to being a ghost. Micki runs into the room, then runs right back out, acting as a distraction. Lewis is single-minded at this point, so he sends Greta after Micki.

After a brief game of cat and mouse, Greta traps Micki and puts her in a levitating trance. She floats Micki down the hall and puts her in a coffin. Back in the ceremonial room, Ryan tackles Lewis, but he is strong for an old man and throws him across the room. Ryan goes into the hall, runs right into Greta, and she gives him the same fate she gave Micki. With the coffins lined up on a conveyor belt, Greta pushes a button and the coffins head off to be cremated.

After seeing the note at Curious Goods, Jack gathers his bag of magical goodies and rushes to the mortuary. He finds Lewis pretty easily, but is more concerned with finding Ryan and Micki. He heads into the crematorium, sees the two coffins, and makes a huge assumption. Rushing to the one closest to the flames, he finds Micki and has to slap her to wake her from her trance. As soon as Ryan hears their voices, he yells from his own coffin and they release him. From there they have to hurry. Lewis is finishing the spell, and if they don't stop him, "we will find ourselves in the middle of a living nightmare." As long as Lewis doesn't complete the ceremony before sunrise, nothing will happen. Time until sunrise: eight minutes.

Ryan and Micki make taunts from the hall, and an annoyed Lewis sends Greta to finish them off. Jack enters, and Lewis's attention shifts. "It wasn't fair," Lewis protests. "If I had known, I wouldn't have done it." Apparently, in hell, you die forever, over and over. I assume when Lewis says he "wouldn't have done it," he means breaking the pact, not the deal itself. Lewis returns his attention to the ceremony, and Jack recites his own text in hopes of distracting him.

Greta's demented game of hide and seek with Micki and Ryan is not going well. She throws a chair at them, but they duck and it hits a wall. Things go (even more) horribly awry when she trips over a bottle of some sort and impales herself on the broken pieces of chair. It is a strangely anticlimactic, underplayed death for the little demon woman. Her body disappears in an explosion of smoke.

The cousins return to Jack and alert Lewis that it is sunrise. Lewis claims he still has two minutes, but Jack points out that the clock has stopped. It isn't clear, but I think that when Greta threw the chair, it hit a power panel on the wall, shutting off the clock. Anyway, Micki throws open the shutters and sunlight streams in. Like a vampire, the sun literally erases Lewis from the world. "I'll say this—the man can make an exit," Jack deadpans.

Status: The amulet is returned to the vault (I assume) and more importantly, Lewis is sent back to hell. Micki asks about Lewis' wife, Grace, and based on his poetic speech and dreamy look in his eye, it seems clear Jack was in love with her. When asked how well he knew her, Jack responds: "Better than I ought to but not as dearly as I wished." So, what is that, like second base? Strangely, Micki hopes that someone talks about her that way one day—but she's still engaged to Lloyd at this point. They don't break up for a few more episodes.

* * *

I wish *F13* had done more Halloween episodes. Three seasons, three chances to celebrate. Sure, I wouldn't want to see this particular story reproduced, but Lewis surely had other plots and schemes to come back to life. It's like our heroes never again celebrated Halloween. I guess when you are chasing down cursed objects, every day is Halloween.

The Amulet of Zohar is one of those weird, grey-area antiques. It's not clear if it was ever actually cursed, or if it was ever sold. If it was in the vault, then surely it has to have some evil in it. Maybe when Micki and Ryan moved in, they packed up *all* Lewis' stuff and put it in the vault… just in case. Seems like a wise idea to me.

And while it is not really a practical option, why didn't one of the guys move into that secret room? Ryan sleeps in an alcove in the kitchen; Jack sleeps somewhere in the cavernous basement. If you have a room (a secret passageway room, no less!) then dammit, you should use it.

The production of "Hellowe'en" was troubled. Director Timothy Bond shares a strange story about how he landed the episode:

"Did I do that one? What was it about? Oh yeah! The reason I don't remember much about that episode was that I wasn't supposed to direct that one. They got a guy, I don't remember his name. He'd done some great horror movies. He had done Hammer Films, a bunch of those. I was quite in awe of this guy when he came in. I was editing ["The Poison Pen"] while he was shooting. I met him. He seemed like a nice guy. I had heard gossip from the set that he was fast. All the directors were going, 'Oh shit, he's faster than we are! He's making his days, he's finishing early!' So, I wanted to go watch him work, see how he does it. But before I had the chance to do that I heard a rumor that they couldn't cut the footage. He wasn't covering anything; he did it all in one shot, then goes home because he is tired.

"The next thing I know, Jon Andersen comes into the editing room and asks what I am doing after lunch.

"I said, 'Editing this show.'

"He said, 'No you're not, read this.' He threw the script in my lap and said, 'You've got an hour. Read fast.'

"The cutting room was right across the street from the studio, and I remember looking out the window, and this limo pulled up. Jon Andersen walked this director out and put him in the car and the limo drove away. Jon told me later that they had gone to his hotel room and packed his bags and put them in the car. They drove him straight to the airport.

"So, I walked onto set after lunch and the whole crew was like, 'What are you doing here?' Nobody knew I was stepping in! I don't have much of a memory of the episode. I guess he had done two days and I did six. Eventually I got to see the footage he shot and do some prep, but I had to start shooting without doing any prep whatsoever, except having speed-read the script.

"When people ask me what my strangest story of directing is, I say, 'Replacing a director at lunchtime.'"

Line producer J. Miles Dale had forgotten all about the replaced director until I mentioned it to him. "That was a horrible experience," he told me. Glad I can bring the sunshine with me.

Composer Fred Mollin's experience with "Hellowe'en" traumatized him so badly it changed his work process forever. "At that point, in 1987, [the Kurzweil] had an internal memory that was on chips, not on hard drives. Digital chips. The deadlines were very tight. I generally had four days to write and record the show. Then, the fifth day would be the mix. It would be on the air two days later. It was stressful, but it was manageable. However, on 'Hellowe'en,' I had written a really cool score, very music-heavy. It was probably thirty-eight minutes of score in a forty-five minute show. It was very dense. I did all my work on the Kurzweil, overdubbed, built the sounds, built the arrangements, all me. I was literally on the last cue, and I was saving everything to the internal chips on the Kurzweil. I was not backing it up to a computer's hard drive. I was probably on the third day, twelve hours a day writing this stuff. I hit the save button on the Kurzweil, and I heard this—to this day, I can still hear that sound, like a little digital [thunk]. *What was that?* I looked at the readout on the Kurzweil, and it said 'Initializing version 7.0.' It had done a hard reset, which meant it wiped out everything I did. Since it was on chips, there was no back up, no way to recover it. It was gone in a millisecond. I found out that as you get near the end of the information you can put on those chips, it will automatically go back to zero and restart and erase everything. The Kurzweil wasn't that advanced, so it couldn't give you a warning. I was new to the instrument and under unbelievable deadlines. I lost everything. I was sobbing. I had a chair that was specially made for me, and I threw it against the wall and broke it. Then I started to sob. First of all, I thought I was going to be fired. And I was heartbroken. I had to make a call to Iain [Paterson], and I told him what happened.

"He said, 'Oh god, can you write it again?'

"I told him I don't use music paper, I write it in my head. I remember the themes, of course I can try to write it again, but we mix a day and a half from now. He called Frank to try to move the mix a day, but I had to write it in a day and a half. I spent literally twenty hours straight redoing the show. Most of it was not by memory because I didn't remember what I did, I really didn't. I remembered the main scenes, but that was it.

"Obviously at that point, something changed drastically in my life. I triple-saved everything every fifteen minutes to two different computer hard drives. I no longer do much composing for TV and film. I got burnt out and went back to record production. But it taught me a lesson. My engineers constantly are saving every vocal pass, everything needs saving twice. I just can't be traumatized again. I got lucky; I got an extra day and was able to write it again."

"The Great Montarro"

Written by: Durnford King
Directed by: Richard Friedman
Original airdate: November 2, 1987
Cursed antique: Magician's prop

Stage magician Fahteem the Magnificent (August Schellenberg) has a "death-defying" trick he calls the Cabinet of Doom. A coffin, propped upright, is rigged with nine steel swords. He steps inside, the swords swing down, and impale him—yet every time, he finishes the trick unscathed. Of course, that is because he has a little help from a cursed object. A huge marble box, called the Houdin box after a famous French magician, is kept in the basement of the theater. When a person is placed in the box, whatever damage that Fahteem might take is transferred to the unfortunate in the box. On stage, Fahteem emerges from his coffin, completely intact. Downstairs, the poor soul trapped in the box is sporting nine matching machete punctures. Of course, if there isn't anyone in the box, then Fahteem is going to get slaughtered by those swords. This is what happens one night when Fahteem is covering up the Coffin of Doom. An unseen person pulls the lever, drops the swords, and kills him instantly.

Jack finds Fahteem's death strange. He wasn't friends with him, but was floored by his sudden rise to fame. The Cabinet of Doom was what propelled him to the top, and no one ever figured out how he did it. Of course, a few had tried, but all failed. And when I say "fail," I mean they died. Fahteem's real name was Harvey Ringwald, which Jack finds funny. Micki doesn't—she recognizes that name. Sure enough, they find Harvey Ringwald in the manifest, as the original purchaser of the Houdin box. Micki and Ryan go speak to Robert, Fahteem's assistant, while Jack checks in with Monte (Murray Westgate), one of his friends from his Great Mad Marshak days.

Micki and Ryan find Robert (Martin Neufeld) to be a bitter prop builder who was Fahteem's flunkie. "I should have been the headliner," he seethes. Fahteem's secrets died with him and his equipment was auctioned off. But once Micki and Ryan leave, Robert makes a call to a mysterious partner, promising he didn't tell them anything.

The kids meet up with Jack at the Temple of Magic, where Monte is prepping a magic contest. The winners gain entrance into the Magic Stars Society. You'd think that magicians could come up with a better name than that. Monte remembers very little about Fahteem, other than he was a "sleaze bag," then excuses himself to prep for the show. Before Jack, Micki, and Ryan leave, they overhear The Great Montarro (Graeme Campbell) speaking harshly to his daughter, Lyla (Lesleh Donaldson). Monte asks them to leave; he has never heard of Montarro, and he is not on his list of performers. Then he reveals his trick: the Coffin of Blood. Same Cabinet, new paint job. It's not really clear if Monte recognizes it or not, but Micki is suspicious of him the moment she sees him yelling at his daughter.

Since they cannot be at the theater to watch rehearsals, Jack decides to revive his old magic act and enter the competition, with Micki as his lovely assistant. The Pendulum of Death involved Jack being strapped and chained into a straightjacket, then hoisted upside down over a bed of spikes while a flame burned through the rope. It takes some begging, but Monte finally agrees to squeeze Jack into the show. Now, the crew has a reason to be in the theater, but Jack is enjoying his return to magic a little too much. Micki times him trying to escape his straightjacket: it takes him eighty-five seconds. The rope burns through in just under a minute. "It's faster upside down," he insists. Ryan returns from the prop room, and found what appears to be Fahteem's box amongst Montarro's belongings. Jack goes to check it out while Ryan and Micki keep an eye on Montarro and Lyla. Once they are gone, Tommy, a magician wannabe, comes out of hiding. He had been spying on them the whole time.

Jack measures the Coffin of Blood, trying to match the dimensions listed in the manifest for the Houdin box. (That is one detailed manifest!) He hears someone coming and quickly hides inside. Montarro enters the room, followed by Ryan, who claims he is checking on their equipment. Montarro accuses Ryan of following him, which Ryan defends as being star struck, and asks for his autograph. While Montarro gives it, Ryan leans on the lever that drops the swords into the Coffin of Blood, alarming Jack. I'm not sure why one would store such a dangerous piece of equipment with the most dangerous part dangling precariously above, but I'll go along with it. Ryan lets go of the lever and everyone escapes uninjured. When our trio meet up to compare notes, Micki says Lyla is terrified of her father, and Jack confirms that the Cabinet is real; there is no way out of there.

It's show time (well, audition time). Micki and Ryan are in position, but Jack is nowhere to be found. They run off looking for him, with no luck. When they return to stage, Jack is already there, fully dressed in the straightjacket and hood. Micki starts her spiel, Jack is hoisted over the bed of spikes, and the rope is lit. All that is left is to step back and watch. And they watch. They watch as the key, hidden in a secret pocket of the straightjacket, snaps in the lock. They watch as Jack struggles. And they scream as the rope burns through and Jack is impaled on the bed of nails.

But Jack comes out from backstage and looks surprised by the hub-bub. Ryan pulls off the dead man's hood and discovers it is Tommy on the bed of spikes. He wanted his chance on stage so badly he locked Jack in the closet and took his place. They key was no accident either; it was filed through. Whoever did this wanted Jack dead. Micki thinks it is Miranda, the angry-looking magician who has been watching them like a hawk. But when they check on Miranda, they see she is hanging, dead. And "she" is really a "he"—it is Robert in a wig and dress. A stagehand comes by looking for Robert, but when he sees the scene before him, he runs scared. Ryan catches him, and the stagehand insists it was all Robert's idea. He wanted to blackmail Montarro into giving up the box that Fahteem used to do the trick. He doesn't know how the box worked, but someone has to be inside while the trick was performed.

Thirty minutes to show time. Micki is worried about Lyla and wants her to pull out of the show. Lyla can't do that—her dad can't do the show without her. Micki begs, insisting he is using *real* magic, and tells her about the Houdin box. Lyla thinks she has seen it and leads Micki to the basement. A huge marble obelisk stands there, and Micki is pretty sure this is it. The door swings open, and inexplicably, Micki gets in. "It's caked with blood!" she cries, to the surprise of no one. Lyla closes the door, sealing Micki inside. A red crystal on top lights up, and Lyla launches into her villain soliloquy: how she is the Great Montarro; how she made her father what he is; how he doesn't even know what is going on. She admits to killing Fahteem and Robert, and thanks Micki for saving her the trouble of finding a victim.

Jack and Ryan become concerned when they see Lyla on stage, but Micki is nowhere in sight. Lyla claims she hasn't seen her in a while, but the boys notice sawdust on Lyla's costume, the same sawdust that was on Robert's body. Ryan recalls seeing sawdust downstairs in the wine cellar. The Great Montarro is on. Montarro does the same patter Fahteem used to do but with an added evil laugh.

Downstairs, Ryan and Jack find the Houdin box, and hear Micki's muffled screams; they just can't figure out how to get her out of there. Jack tries to pry the crystal from the top, thinking that might be the lock. I still don't quite understand how the locking mechanism works (or doesn't) but the crystal turns green just as Lyla pulls the lever on stage. The box unlocks and Micki spills out. The curse needs a victim, and that victim is Montarro.

Status: The Houdin box is recovered, but who the hell knows where they put that thing. It was massive, it was marble, and there is no way it could fit in the vault.

*   *   *

There was a lot going on in this episode, and I think it weighed it down. There were too many misdirects that were never fully fleshed out. The whole Miranda/Robert and Tommy stories felt half-assed. Why did Robert feel the need to dress as a woman? Montarro didn't know him. How exactly were Tommy and Robert working together, and to what end?

It's too bad that logic seemed to be missing from this episode, because magic is such a good source of horror. This episode reminds me a lot of H. G. Lewis' 1970 gore classic, *The Wizard of Gore*, in which mutilation tricks performed on stage go off without a hitch, until later in the evening, when the female volunteers die suddenly of the very mutilations they had escaped on stage. Unfortunately, writer Durnford King doesn't remember what inspired him for this episode, but I like to believe the Godfather of Gore had a hand in it.

Lesleh Donaldson played Lyla in the episode, and she remembers the shoot as being a lot of fun. "They actually filmed it in a magician's theater in downtown Toronto, and they got a bunch of actual magicians to come out and be in the episode, doing their act. They were always doing stuff to keep us occupied between takes.

"I think they cast me because they wanted someone who looked really innocent and unassuming… the lovely little daughter-type character, and I guess I had those qualities," she continues. "Then I turn out to be the killer! I guess they wanted that naivety, like the last person you would assume was the killer. I guess I had that look. It was a challenge to act it, especially the last part, where I turn and get bitchy. And that crazy scream at the end!"

Fun fact: Donaldson originally auditioned for the role of Micki.

"Doctor Jack"

Written by: Marc Scott Zicree
Directed by: Richard Friedman
Original airdate: November 9, 1987
Cursed antique: Scalpel

A news article about a florist killed with "a small knife" catches Jack's attention because the killer is said to have made his getaway by slicing through iron bars with the same small knife. Jack finds a listing in the manifest for a nineteenth century scalpel, which was rumored to have belonged to Jack the Ripper. The scalpel was sold to Jim Morgan, an ex-con who now owns a knife shop. Jack, Micki, and Ryan pay Morgan a visit, and he insists he doesn't sell scalpels, never has, and has no idea what scalpel they may be referring to. Micki pretends to find the scalpel they are looking for, which causes Morgan to shout. "Impossible! I sold it-" He stops and realizes he has said too much. Jack produces negatives from 1979 that won't sit well with Jim's parole officer, and Morgan admits he sold the scalpel two years ago, to a Dr. Howlett (Cliff Gorman).

Once outside, Jack explains to Micki and Ryan that Dr. Howlett is a "miracle man," a doctor who has turned surgery into an art. He takes on hopeless cases and cures every single one. This alone should have been a warning to Jack. And the "photos" he has of Morgan? Just pictures of Micki and Ryan's trip to the zoo. "With a guy like that, chances are any year you pick, he's probably hiding something."

Howlett has become a superstar of surgery, something his former professor and current chief of surgery Dr. Price (Doris Petrie) isn't too keen on. Howlett has returned home to the local Ravenbrook hospital, and as much as Dr. Price doesn't trust Howlett, she needs him. The hospital has been buried under bad press, malpractice suits, outdated equipment and "minor scandals among the staff" (whatever that means). The hope is that Howlett, with his sterling record, can return some prestige to the hospital.

Micki, Ryan, and Jack wander around the hospital, looking for Howlett. But someone else is looking for Howlett, too—with a gun. She finds Howlett but before she can shoot him, Ryan tackles her to the ground until the orderlies have her sedated. Micki goes after Howlett with Ryan close behind. Jack goes to speak to the woman, Jean (Elva Mai Hoover). Jean believes that Howlett killed her daughter (though as far as I can tell, she has no proof, just a gut feeling). She was in medical school and she worshipped Howlett. When he came to town, the daughter went to visit him, determined to talk to him if it was "the last thing she did." And of course, it turned out it was. She was found in an alley, cut to pieces. The police had no clues, so Jean started following Howlett. Murders seemed to follow him, but they were "no big deal, back page stuff." Jean was waiting for him to slip up, but he was too smart and she decided she couldn't let it go on. When Jack asks about a weapon, Jean realizes he isn't a doctor (that is the question that brings her that realization?) and decides that Jack is in on it.

On the other end of the hospital, Micki has followed Howlett back to his office, where he is playing with his scalpel. She says she is an administrator, checking to see if he has everything he needs. She makes a hasty retreat, but not before seeing that he has the scalpel. Ryan finds her in the hall and promises to keep an eye on him while she meets up with Jack. Jack shares the information he learned from Jean, and the two take off again.

While Ryan follows Howlett into an off-limits area of the hospital, Micki and Jack search his office. The case is there, but the scalpel is gone. He isn't scheduled for surgery today, so Micki is confused—where did he go with it? Jack shares his theory. First, he agrees with Jean that Howlett is a "mass murderer," which drives me crazy. Jean never said that Howlett is a "mass murderer," but even if she did, that's not what he is. Howlett is a serial killer. For him to qualify as a mass murderer, he would need to kill four or more people at the same time. Anyway, Jack theorizes that Howlett uses the scalpel both to kill and to operate. It's like a battery that needs to be charged. If he doesn't kill for a while, he loses the ability to heal.

Ryan has seen Howlett with the scalpel, but when he trips, the noise catches Howlett's attention. Ryan hides in the morgue. Howlett assumes that he is in the drawer that was left ajar, but after stabbing the body in there several times, he discovers it is just the corpse of an old man. Moments after Howlett leaves, Micki arrives and frees Ryan. Jack is on Howlett's tail, and the two fight in an empty wing of the hospital. Howlett has the upper hand, and Jack plunges down an elevator shaft.

The next time we see Jack, he is being rushed into surgery. Micki and Ryan are sick with worry. To keep his mind off things, Ryan ducks out to search for the scalpel. Dr. Price tells Howlett that he needs to operate tonight. It's no one important, just "one of those patients who has no chance of living without one of your miracles." The press has a hold of this story, too, and they are hungry to see the miracle man in action. Despite Howlett's protests (he has no idea who he is operating on, but he hasn't "charged" his scalpel recently) he realizes he can't let his public down and agrees to the surgery.

While Howlett slips into the night, looking for a new victim, Dr. Price informs Micki of Jack's condition. There is a weakness in his artery that is almost always fatal. But don't worry, the best surgeon in the country agreed to the operation. "He's something of a miracle worker," Dr. Price assures her. Micki realizes what needs to happen for the surgery to be successful.

But the universe is conspiring against the surgery. Howlett finds a hooker to dice up, but he comes at her with the scalpel out, and she ducks

Chris Wiggins goofing off between takes. Photo courtesy of Louise Robey.

into a bar. Before Howlett can make a contingency plan, he is paged back to the hospital and reluctantly scrubs in for surgery. He sets the scalpel on the edge of the sink, and Ryan sneaks in, dressed in scrubs, and pockets the scalpel. Ryan rushes the scalpel to Micki like a proud toddler, and Micki explains the situation to him. Howlett is the only surgeon who can save Jack—and he needs that scalpel to do it.

Howlett is going ballistic, looking for his scalpel. Just as mysteriously as it disappeared, Ryan returns the scalpel to Howlett, claiming he "found" it. Howlett doesn't have time to interrogate him, as Dr. Price is breathing down his neck to get into surgery. He is nervous: does the scalpel have enough "power" to complete the surgery successfully? A nurse removes a sheet from Jack's face, and Howlett finally sees who he is operating on. He freezes, eyes wide in shock. He looks to the press (when have reporters ever observed a surgery?) and weighs his options. Howlett continues with the surgery. As he wraps it up, he insists that he personally take charge of his patient's post-op care.

During the surgery, Micki and Ryan pontificate about how much Jack means to them. Ryan indirectly refers to Jack as a father figure. "Me and my folks never got along, treated me like I had a screw loose. They never let me do anything important. Jack was the first one who thought I could do something important." Micki asserts that, no matter what happens with Jack, they can't let Howlett get away. "Jack wouldn't want it that way." Dr. Price tells the pair that Jack is out of surgery, and Ryan wants to see him, to "thank him" for taking on the surgery. Price directs them to Jack's room, informing them that Howlett will be overseeing his post-op care.

Howlett slips into Jack's room and moves to slice one of his ventilation tubes. Jean, who had tricked the guard into loosening her restraints to the point that she could escape, has found Howlett and pulls her gun on him. "You killed my daughter; now it's your turn." Howlett turns to Jean, the more immediate threat, and slices off the barrel of her gun with the scalpel. He attacks her, and Jean's screams bring Micki and Ryan rushing in. Howlett escapes, and Ryan and Micki give chase.

They chase him into the basement, but Howlett proves he is a worthy opponent. The cousins hide behind a heavy door, which Howlett cuts through with the scalpel. Jean knocks him out. Why didn't Jean just shoot him? Why didn't Micki or Ryan grab the scalpel? And when they run off, what happens to Jean? Micki and Ryan hit another dead end and look for weapons. The best Ryan can find is an old wooden crutch. He directs Micki to hide behind a crash cart and battles Howlett. It doesn't go well, and Ryan is knocked out cold. Micki taunts Howlett away from Ryan, but he assures her he hasn't forgotten about her. He moves towards her, scalpel at the ready, but Micki grabs defibrillator paddles, clamps them around the scalpel, and "clears" him to the ground. Ryan comes to and rolls Howlett over. The scalpel is embedded in Howlett's chest.

Status: Jack is allowed to go home and is already back to nagging Micki about putting the scalpel in the vault. Like an annoyed teenager, Micki assures him she put it away.

* * *

This was never one of my favorite episodes. As a kid, it just never hit the right chords, but as an adult, I can see why: the pacing is way off. Something semi-weird is reported in the news and Jack proactively checks the manifest, which is good because, really, how long does it take to flip through the manifest? But they make a lot of leaps in the storytelling (like Jean's assumption that Howlett was her daughter's killer without anything more than a mother's worry) that feel rushed. Clearly, the point was to get to Jack's injury and the ensuing moral dilemma of allowing him to be operated on with a cursed object. Frankly, Micki didn't seem that broken up over it, nor did Jack chastise them when it was all over. Yet in later episodes, where one of them has used a cursed object ("Shadow Boxer," "Tales I Live, Heads You Die," "Bad Penny") Jack is always careful to warn them about the dangers of dabbling in the black arts. Granted, none of them physically used the scalpel, but they allowed it to be used. I guess because it still had a "charge" in it, and no one specifically had to die before Jack's operation, the moral grey zone is a little lighter.

"Doctor Jack" was the first episode story consultant Marc Scott Zicree wrote under his own name. ("I never credit-jump, so any script I did a page-one rewrite on, I don't put my name on. I don't want to steal the residuals of that writer.") Zicree agrees that this script wasn't his best, but he has a good reason: his mother died unexpectedly the week before he was supposed to start his job on *F13*. They were extremely close, and the loss was devastating for him. But schedules were tight and Zicree had a job to do.

"'Doctor Jack' is going to be shooting, the machine is going, and [supervising executive for Paramount] Barbara Sachs said to me that I've got to write the script. She said, 'Well, you'll feel better. It will take your mind off it,' which was incredibly insensitive. She was not a people-person. I was devastated by my mother's death, but fortunately I am a professional writer, and I had those muscles, so I was able to just sit down and write it." One of Zicree's last outings with his mother was researching "medical stuff" with their friend, an X-ray tech. He noticed something was "definitely a little off" with his mom that day. "Normally I would have been much more on top of things with 'Doctor Jack.' Later, my friend was very surprised that the technical stuff wasn't correct. There were certain medical things that just weren't done properly. It's not one of my favorite episodes by any means, but I think it was competent. It was my first script for the show and I was certainly under duress."

I always wondered if the "Jack" in the title referred to Marshak or the Ripper. "I was a huge aficionado of Jack the Ripper and there were all these theories about who Jack the Ripper was," explains Zicree. Many theories maintain that Jack the Ripper was a surgeon or had medical training, so it seems fair that the scalpel could have belonged to him.

"Shadow Boxer"

Written by: Joshua Daniel Miller
Directed by: Timothy Bond
Original airdate: November 21, 1987
Cursed antique: Boxing gloves

Tommy Dunn (David Ferry) is a boxer—well, a wannabe boxer. He has a temper (served time for assault) and that makes him a risk in the ring. Manny (Jack Duffy), the gym owner, takes pity on Dunn and lets him hang around, sweep up, that kind of thing. Dunn thinks that his key to winning in the ring and beating gym "star" Kid Cornelius (Philip Akin) is to get his hands on a pair of antique boxing gloves in Manny's collection. He tried them on once and felt them ignite a fire within him. The gloves once belonged to Killer Ken Kelsey, a welter weight champ in the 1940s. In 1947, he unintentionally killed an opponent in the ring. Some say he went a little crazy after that, but either way, he hung up the gloves and never threw a punch again.

You can imagine what kind of curse Lewis (and Satan) could put on a pair of gloves with that background. When Dunn sneaks into Manny's office and steals the gloves, he feels his hand shake with the power of the gloves. The gloves seem to lead his hands to the wall, where Dunn touches gloves with his own shadow. The shadow boxes its way out of the locker room, all by itself. While Dunn is sparring with a punching bag in the gym, his shadow is out, roaming the streets. It finds Manny, and matches Dunn's punches as the shadow beats Manny to a pulp. With his dying breath (and his own blood) Manny tries to write Tommy's name. He gets through the T-O.

In the wake of Manny's death, his widow calls Curious Goods to see if they were interested in buying any of Manny's collectibles. Some were bought from Lewis. Jack instantly finds the boxing gloves in the manifest and remembers attending Killer's last fight. Micki is still engaged at this point and she is putting together a picture diary for Lloyd, "A Day in the Life of Curious Goods," so an old-fashioned film camera with a huge flash goes with her to the gym.

Jack can't find the boxing gloves among Manny's belongings. They are hard to miss—they have "Killer" stamped right across the them. Micki, being a pretty girl, has no problem wandering amongst the boxers on the floor, and none have any problem with her snapping their photo. Dunn swaggers up to her, all machismo and misogyny, and starts hitting on her. She politely—but firmly—turns him down. Kid Cornelius, aka Sam, scares him off.

Outside, Dunn spots Tony, a boxer Micki had been flirting with. Dunn wants to fight him, but what he really means is, he wants his shadow to fight him. Tony pays no mind to Dunn, who goes back into the gym to "prepare" for his real fight, in the ring. The crowd inside is surprised to see Dunn has, overnight, become a great boxer. Through her camera lens, Micki sees that Dunn is wearing the Killer gloves. Dunn wins the round, and someone runs in, yelling that Tony has been beaten to death. The perfect alibi. As the club clears out, Ryan rushes into the locker room to inspect "Terible" Tommy Dunn's locker. (Yup, that is how he spells it: terible.) He finds no gloves, but does find a medical report, citing Dunn as being unfit to box. Brain damage, no doubt. Sam scares Ryan off.

Micki, Ryan and Jack sit vigil outside Dunn's apartment. They have clearly been there for hours, waiting for him to leave so they can go looking for the gloves. Micki has an idea. "There are some things I can do that you two can't." She calls Dunn from a pay phone and invites him for coffee. He agrees, and moments later he leaves his apartment for the coffee shop around the corner. Jack and Ryan investigate his dumpy little apartment but turn up empty.

Dunn's already-thin patience is waning quickly as Micki stalls, picking at her pie, asking for more coffee, talking about the fight—anything to avoid the "nightcap" he desperately wants to have with her back at his place. He gets aggravated, calls her a tease, and grabs her arm. She warns him off her, and he storms out. Micki calls the apartment to warn Ryan, but Jack wisely reminds him not to answer the phone. Dunn walks in on them and realizes Micki was setting him up. He grabs the gloves from a hole in the wall, hidden behind a poster, and forces Jack into the hallway. Dunn comes at Ryan, but Ryan ducks and Dunn's fist goes through a brick wall. The shadow is outside, going after Micki, who isn't sure what she is looking at. So, she starts snapping photos. The flash blinds both Dunn and his shadow, but it is temporary. Micki snaps another photo without waiting for the flash to recharge. Dunn lands a punch on Ryan, which

Getting ready on location. Photo courtesy of John LeMay.

means the shadow lands a (light) punch on Micki. As she stumbles back, the flash goes off again. This one disables Dunn and his shadow, allowing Ryan to escape.

Back at Curious Goods, Ryan returns with the developed photos, lamenting that he had to trade in his *Green Lantern #3* to get these developed in the middle of the night. The photos reveal nothing, except in the one taken when Micki's flash didn't go off. Jack explains how the curse works, Dunn's shadow representing his literal dark side. In order for Dunn to win a fight, there has to be another murder.

The trio returns to the gym, and Sam overhears them talking about how they have no way of proving that Dunn murdered Manny. Manny was like a father to Sam, so he agrees to the fight Dunn has been begging for.

Before the fight, Jack confronts Dunn in the locker room, playing the shifty fight promoter, insisting on 70% of Dunn's winnings or he will call the cops and tell them he saw Dunn lift the gloves. Dunn plays along and tells Jack to wait for him in the parking lot. Micki is waiting for Jack outside—he took the bait, and Micki hides out in the bushes with her camera. As expected, the fight begins and Dunn's shadow comes out, looking for Jack. Jack signals to Micki, who has since ditched the camera in favor of a floodlight. The shadow fades; Dunn falters. The light blinks out, and Dunn—and his shadow—regain the upper hand. Shadow-Dunn knocks the light to the ground, breaking it. Jack lures the shadow away from Micki, who turns the car headlights on. This washes out the shadow completely, and Dunn loses any momentum he had. Kid Cornelius takes control of the fight and easily knocks Dunn out. While the crowd cheers on Cornelius, no one notices when Ryan steals Dunn's gloves and sneaks away.

But there are still ten minutes left in the episode.

Micki is mad that Dunn is getting away with murder. She goes to bed early out of sheer frustration. She wakes from an uneasy sleep with a meaty hand over her mouth. Dunn has sneaked in and holds a knife to her throat, demanding the gloves back. Ryan hears the commotion and investigates, with Jack following soon after. Dunn again demands the gloves or "your girlfriend gets it." Despite the fact that there is a knife to her throat, Micki still manages to clarify the situation: "I'm not his girlfriend." She isn't able to explain her and Ryan's relationship, for Dunn tightens his hold around her throat. Ryan heads down to the basement while Jack tries to reason with Dunn, and Dunn teases Micki with the tip of the blade. Ryan finally returns and hands over the glove—but just one of them. Dunn doesn't seem to notice at first, and pushes Micki to safety. When he does notice, he becomes enraged again, and Ryan reveals the second glove, hidden behind his back—and on his own fist. Ryan uses it to sucker-punch Jack, while his shadow strikes Dunn. He hits Jack again, and Dunn is knocked out. Ryan taunts Jack: "Get up old man! Get up!" Micki rips the glove off Ryan and breaks its hold on him. She collects the other glove and the knife (she's no dummy) while Ryan tries to justify his own guilt at using an object. "I had to! I had to save you! I didn't hit Jack that hard! Nothing went wrong."

Status: Gloves are safely returned to the vault. The official story is that Dunn broke into Curious Goods, started shouting, then just collapsed. Doctors weren't surprised; Dunn had years of scar tissue from being beaten the hell up. Jack is fine, other than a black eye and a damaged sense of humor. His threats of revenge against Ryan are only mildly playful.

* * *

"At one point, I think it was Bill who said, 'We'd like to do an episode about a boxer, but we don't yet have an angle,'" said episode scribe Josh Miller, describing a pitch meeting with story editor Bill Taub and story consultant Marc Scott Zicree. "I filed this away quietly and went home to let things percolate. Before the day was out, I started riffing on the phrase 'shadow boxer,' which is a boxer who practices his or her fight moves while watching their shadow on the wall. In the story, the twist was that the boxing gloves would be cursed, enabling the boxer's shadow to detach from him and murder people while he was engaged in public boxing matches, giving him an airtight alibi. From there, I beat out the plot, went back a few days later and pitched the story idea to Bill and Marc and I made the sale."

One of the strangest parts about re-watching *Friday the 13th: The Series* now are the leaps in technology. I was born in 1980, on the cusp of changing technology. My family had our first personal computer in 1986, but we still had a typewriter that my mother used almost daily. Vinyl records were being phased out in favor of cassette tapes around this time, and it was only a few years later that CDs replaced cassettes. It is strange because, on the one hand, I remember using cameras that needed film and flashes that needed to recharge; but on the other hand, I have spent more of my life using digital cameras. This odd disconnect takes place as I watch Micki waiting for her camera to recharge. I know that feeling, yet it feels like it was a different life because I more strongly identify with using a digital camera—or at least an always-ready flash.

This camera disconnect weighed on me as I re-watched "Shadow Boxer." But interestingly, I found the effects of the shadow boxer himself to feel completely natural. It didn't feel dated at all, and this is one of the most digitally-heavy episodes of *F13*. Director Tim Bond explains how they achieved the look in the early days of digital effects.

"I'm very proud of this episode. It was all done semi-live. The shadow was played by the same actor who played the boxer, David Ferry. I started by filming the scenes with the live actor. Then we went on a stage and dressed him in black and put him on a white background so there was a really good contrast for the computer to separate his outline. We had a monitor on the set and would take the feed from that camera and superimpose it over the footage I'd already shot of the live action, so we could move him around until he was in the right place in the frame.

"One of the big secrets of doing these things was that it has to look like it was shot by the same camera with the same lens at the same distance with the same level of inclination—all that sort of stuff. We had meticulous notes about all that. It took a lot of meticulous plotting to get us to the point where we could film—then we just went crazy with the shadow. It had to start with the shadow touching fists [with the actor], so we had to get that lined up carefully, and we had a white thing for him to punch so it blended in with the white background, and then he could go off and do whatever the action was. I could see the frame to make sure he stayed in it, and I could superimpose the original shot so I could say 'You have to walk around a garbage can there,' or something like that. Every shot was done like that, so it took several days just to film the shadows."

"When I saw the episode, I was blown away at what they achieved with the shadow effect," enthuses Miller, who didn't have any preconceived notions about how production would create the shadow effect. "I thought it would be achievable; I just didn't know how convincing it would be. But it was exactly how I had imagined it would look and that was a great thrill."

Producers brought in an old boxing pro to train David Ferry for the role of Tommy Dunn. He fought in Detroit as a flyweight during the days of Joe Lewis. "He was a little punchy," Ferry recalls. "While working on my body hooks, my glove barely touched him, and he punched me in the face—an automatic reaction." He assures me the incident was funny, not traumatizing.

"Root of All Evil"

Written by: Rob Hedden
Directed by: Allan King
Original airdate: November 28, 1987
Cursed antique: Mulcher

Jack discovers a letter addressed to Lewis that was never opened. Inside is a crisp, new $100 bill and an unsigned note, thanking Mr. Vendredi for the knowledge attained "from below." The postmark reads Temple Heights, and Ryan finds an item in the manifest sold to a Harley O'Connor (Tom Hauff) in Temple Heights. Item #27668, a fifty-year-old portable garden mulcher. Ryan picks up the phone to give a call, but finds Micki on the extension, talking to "him." With Micki gone for the last two months, it has put a strain on her and Lloyd's relationship. She insists that she still wants to marry him, and that she is not having an affair.

Micki and Jack visit O'Connor's house, to find it abandoned and boarded up. Micki, on edge after her call with Lloyd, gives Jack attitude as he suggests they look inside. "What's the point? Any fool can see he's left. One less curse to recover." She never wanted any of this, and Jack reminds her that none of them did, but they have a responsibility. She concedes and follows him into the house. Inside, Micki trips on some debris and knocks over a pile of abandoned nonsense. Underneath the junk, Jack finds a $5 bill, as crisp and new as the $100 found in the letter. A man sneaks up on them with a crowbar, demanding to know what they want. Jack hands him his business card and gives him the usual spiel. Crowbar man is a neighbor who looks after the place. O'Connor was an accountant. His mom went missing and the cops caught him with a bag of money. Some say he killed her, but the body was never found. (We actually see this murder in the cold open: mom was a horrible, droning nag, and Harley took a rake to her head before feeding her into the mulcher.) When the cops tried to question O'Connor, he went nuts and started talking about the teeth of hell, or the mouth of hell. He attacked the cops and was subsequently institutionalized. Later on, Jack discovers the mulcher was sold at a police auction to Robert Smith (not The Cure front man) who runs his own small gardening company.

Robert "Smitty" Smith (Jack Mather) is a kindly old man who loves his job at the Harrington Gardens. He has recently taken on a young apprentice, Adrian (Rico Colantoni), who works to live. He sees Smitty using the mulcher and is hypnotized by its spinning teeth. It calls to him. Even when Smitty sends him across the garden to work on the hedges, Adrian has a hard time focusing on anything but that mulcher. When he sees Smitty move on to another part of the garden, Adrian goes straight for the machine. His trance is broken when a vagrant approaches. He knew Adrian from the streets, where Adrian owes "too much to the wrong people." This "friend" of his wants $500 a week to buy his silence. Adrian doesn't have that kind of money and threatens to kill his buddy if he opens his mouth. The mulcher turns on, and Adrian knows what to do. He knocks out his friend and feeds him into the machine. Rather than blood and bits of flesh, the machine spits out money. Lots of money.

That night, Micki is getting ready for bed when she notices someone lurking outside her window. She immediately gets Ryan, who times his entrance so he can hit the intruder with the door. Ryan tackles the intruder and starts strangling him before Micki pulls them apart. It's Lloyd! Micki is thrilled to see him—for a moment. Then she is offended that he flew out to check up on her. He insists he was coming to town to take some depositions and agrees it is no excuse to spy on her, but he "had to make sure there wasn't another man in your life." After seeing Ryan, he isn't entirely sure there isn't. Micki is amused and disgusted by the insinuation, but Lloyd points out they are only cousins by marriage. "Stranger things have happened." "Nothing could be stranger than being involved with Ryan," Micki retorts. Lloyd insists that he just wants to help Micki with whatever odds and ends she has left to take care of, but clearly he can't. Micki promises to be home as soon as she can, but Lloyd isn't interested. "It's tough to marry someone who isn't 100% honest with you." He leaves the same way he came in.

The next day, Ryan and Micki head to Harrington Gardens to speak to Smitty. Micki is lost in her own world, until Ryan offers Smitty $2500 for the mulcher. Smitty wasn't interested in selling until Ryan gave him that figure; now he rushes off to prepare the machine for them. Adrian overhears this, follows Smitty, and knocks him out. He leaves Smitty in the shed while he hides the mulcher, but when he comes back, Smitty is gone. Not gone, but hiding. He tackles Adrian, but Adrian is ready for him, and stabs Smitty in the back. Dead for real, Adrian throws Smitty into the mulcher.

Jack visits O'Connor at the institution. He is off-his-nut crazy, and won't talk to Jack. Jack says he was partners with Lewis until Lewis went back on his deal with Satan and died for it. Jack wants to partner with O'Connor and split the yield from the mulcher. "How do I know you'll choose your investments wisely?" O'Connor asks. He details the system: bums and runaways are safe, but produce a low yield. He makes Jack promise a riskier stock portfolio like doctors and bankers. He has no other info to offer Jack, because O'Connor goes back to his insane laughter.

Micki and Ryan return to Curious Goods with no good news. Jack tries to tell them to watch what they say, but Ryan is already rambling about his suspicions of Smitty, that he "knows the mulcher is cursed and made cole slaw out of people." Lloyd stands, revealing himself, and Micki doesn't care what he overheard—she is so excited because he came back. Of course, Lloyd has returned with his suspicions and Micki finally takes him on a tour of the vault. She shows him a little statue that caused people to go blind; a lamp that burned down several homes. Lloyd takes particular interest in Veda: "You going to tell me this little doll tears people's throats out?" Micki is still sensitive about that one and makes him put it down. He does, and misses when it sits up and looks at him. Micki doesn't, and tells Lloyd he has to get out of there. He agrees. Lloyd leaves Curious Goods—this time through the front door. Micki locks herself in her room.

While Micki mopes at home, Ryan and Jack have gotten jobs as gardeners at the Harrington Gardens. No one has seen Smitty leave, which leads Jack to believe he may have become a victim. Adrian hears this and runs to the mulcher, but is sidetracked by Charles (Ian White), second-in-command to Amanda Harrington (Kay Tremblay). Charles is looking for Smitty, and Adrian directs him to the shed. Adrian beats him there, stabs him in the abdomen, and feeds him into the mulcher. He is still alive and flailing as the mulcher makes "cole slaw" out of him. Charles results in a great yield.

Lloyd returns to Curious Goods for the third time. "I don't want to lose you," he tells Micki. The two spend the afternoon together, clothed and in bed, drinking champagne. "I believe you—or rather, I believe you believe in this curse business." He wants her to come home with him tomorrow. "If you stay here, I can only assume you want to call off the wedding." Micki's face darkens a bit. Interestingly, Micki remains silent for this entire scene, which I think is meant to suggest she is drunk. Then the two start kissing delicately. "I'm coming home," she says and things heat up.

When Ryan comes home later, he is washing up in the kitchen when Micki comes out of her room. She is wearing a dressing gown and giggles when she sees Ryan. Lloyd comes out a moment later, reminding her he will pick her up at noon for a 2 p.m. flight. (Remember those days?) It's pretty obvious what was going on in there, and Ryan isn't happy about it, but he is more unhappy that Micki is leaving. "What about the pact we made?" Micki defends herself: she never made a pact with them, she didn't know they were selling cursed antiques. "Cut the crap Ryan—the only reason you're living here is because you like it. There are many problems in this world that I am never going to be able to solve, and that's the truth. Where is it written that I have to sacrifice my life and happiness for this place?" Ryan calls Lloyd "Mr. Snot Nose" (seriously) and Micki slaps him.

The next day, Jack and Ryan are back to working the gardens, but Ryan is having a hard time focusing. He gets frustrated and the two split up to search the grounds for the mulcher. Ryan spots Smitty's little golf cart, and finds a bag with stacks of cash just sitting in the front seat. He heads to the shed and finds the mulcher. Adrian is there, too. He tries to stab Ryan, misses, and gets his knife stuck in the shed. He leaves it to chase Ryan, but doesn't need it: Ryan trips and knocks himself out on the Harrington memorial stone. Adrian locks him up in the shed - he is after a much bigger fish.

Jack is waiting for Ryan when a cab pulls up. Micki is on her way to the airport and she couldn't leave without saying goodbye. But where is Ryan? Micki goes looking for him, with Lloyd following her, annoyed. "This is just a childish prank," he insists, while Micki reminds him that Ryan didn't even know they were stopping by. "I know he's in trouble."

Adrian brings the mulcher to the base of the stairs outside the mansion. He is so money-hungry that he has decided to mulch Amanda Harrington in the middle of the day. He doesn't seem too concerned with witnesses. I guess working with Satan fills one with a sense of entitlement. Amanda greets him warmly at first, but he quickly becomes hostile and Amanda's shrill screams draw Micki and Lloyd to the mansion. Adrian threatens them to stay back or Amanda "gets it," but she's going to get it anyway. Micki implores Lloyd to do something, but Lloyd doesn't know what. They just back up and watch Adrian leave with Amanda.

Jack confronts Adrian outside, but Adrian doesn't care what he knows—he's still a rich man. That is, until Ryan tosses his bag of money into the mulcher. Adrian tosses Amanda aside and dives in after the money. He gets mulched, and the attached bag fills with blood. "I guess he wasn't even worth a dollar."

Status: Lloyd and Micki are saying their goodbyes - their final goodbyes. Lloyd thinks she is staying because she saw a tragedy today, and "those two clowns" have gotten her involved in something very dangerous. She yells at him for calling her friends names, and reminds him that if he really cared about her, he'd try to understand. Clearly he doesn't, and he's not going to try. Lloyd leaves and Micki storms upstairs. Ryan tries to offer his support but Micki doesn't want to hear it. She comes out of her room a moment later to apologize, and see Ryan has hung up a handmade banner that reads "Welcome Home, Micki."

The mulcher is never mentioned, but I think it is safe to assume they got it back. I'm not sure where they stored it; they haven't discovered the vault "annex" yet.

*   *   *

The message of "Root of All Evil" is just so heavy-handed, I could see this even as a child: "a person's true wealth is judged not by their bank account, but by the content of their character." Louise Robey saw it as having a "dark comedy" to it. Writer Rob Hedden wasn't focused on a "message" with the mulcher; he was focused on the killing. "The inspiration for this story followed the general rule of coming up with a sinister object to launch the tale," explains Hedden. "I'd seen a mulcher grind up a tree in my neighborhood and immediately latched onto it as a candidate for Curious Goods. Although a huge grinding machine was not exactly a trinket that could sit on a shelf inside the antique shop, the visceral fear of it trumped that concern. The idea of being gruesomely devoured by a big, loud, remorseless mulcher was impossible to resist."

What always stood out to me about this episode was the insight into the personal lives of our characters (namely, of course, Micki). I like getting resolution on the Lloyd storyline. Between "The Inheritance" and "Root of All Evil," Lloyd isn't referred to even once. Micki never even wore an engagement ring. Barclay Hope, who played Lloyd, was never contracted for anything but the first episode. "I believe the writers and producers were still feeling it out and trying to find their rhythm," says Hope. "Nothing was etched in stone. Like they say on the casting breakdowns… 'possible recurring.' As young actor trying to find his groove, I, of course, would have loved to be written into more episodes but that is true for most actors and most roles. I sensed that this was it for the character Lloyd.

"My second appearance was memorable because I worked with Enrico Colantoni who was playing an addled gardener. I remember thinking 'I don't know who this guy is, but he's very talented.'" *Friday the 13th: The Series* was Colantoni's first role. He went on to star in a number of fan-favorite TV series, including *Just Shoot Me!, Veronica Mars,* and *Persons of Interest.*

Lloyd and Micki never "love" each other—it's a lot of "I care for you" or "I don't want to lose you" but never "I love you." I guess this was a byproduct of the 1980s motto "greed is good." Lloyd is the stereotypical WASP, and Micki, at this point, was WASP-lite. Ah, the 1980s. Hope remembers Robey as fun to work with. "She was quirky and inventive," he says.

"There was a moment where Robey was to open a door and hit me on the head," he continues. "I have always been athletic and ready for any stunts, but this was hardly what I would call a stunt. When I showed up on set, there was a guy dressed as me with his hair curled and looking every bit like Lloyd. This was the first time I met [stunt coordinator] Matt Birman. He and I have become very good friends over the years and occasionally laugh about the ridiculous 'stunt' he was to double for me. Over the years he used me as a stunt performer for nondescript driving and bar fights when I was hard up for money. We are still good friends."

"Tales of the Undead"

Story by: Alfred Sole & Paul Monette
Teleplay by: William Taub and Marc Scott Zicree
Directed by: Lyndon Chubbuck
Original Airdate: January 25, 1988
Cursed antique: Comic book

A young man, Cal (David Hewlett), pockets a comic book (no bag or board!) before he takes another book to the counter. While checking out, he sees a comic book in a display case. Charlie (Bob Aarrons), the shop owner, explains that it is issue number one of *Tales of the Undead*, featuring the first appearance of Ferrus, an indestructible robot monster. This issue also happens to be signed by the comic creator, Jay Star. It is one-of-a-kind, and will go up for auction in a couple days. Charlie suspects it will pull in $25,000. Cal just has to have it; clearly, he doesn't have the money to buy it. He stands off to the side, lusting after the comic book while Ryan comes in to pick up his weekly order. He is a little late, and Charlie asks if that "partner of yours" isn't pulling her weight. "Well, she's… you know… ." (No, Ryan, we don't. A girl? Spoiled? Hung up on her ex-fiancé?) Charlie shows off the rare comic book to Ryan, who reveals Ferrus is his favorite character. Ryan isn't hung up on the comic like Cal, and he leaves with his purchases.

As soon as he does, Cal tries to jimmy open the case. Charlie tries to stop him, and in his haste, Cal breaks through the glass case and grabs the comic book. Suddenly everything turns to comic book panels, in which we see Cal transforming into Ferrus. We return to live-action, and Ferrus is looming before Charlie, larger than life. He crushes Charlie's throat and tosses him aside. Ryan comes running back in, and stands face-to-face with Ferrus (well, face-to-sternum). Ferrus knocks Ryan out of the way and lumbers out of the store.

Ryan returns to Curious Goods and tells Micki what happened. Unsurprisingly, she doesn't believe him. "I know how it sounds—but I also know how it feels," Ryan says, referring to his bruised shoulder. Micki has seen a lot of strange things, but she's not going to believe a comic book came to life. (I wonder why that is where she draws the line?) According to Ryan, this is basically how Ferrus evolved in the comic book: a kid gets a hold of a magical book that transforms him into a robot. The book is absorbed into his body. Micki goes to the manifest. If what Ryan saw is real, it's bound to have something to do with one of the cursed objects. "Don't you think I would have noticed if there was a comic book in there?" he chides. But Micki finds it—listed as a magazine. Ryan points out that it doesn't matter who it sold to—he knows what happened to it. Luckily Uncle Lewis was a meticulous record keeper, and he wrote down who he bought it from: Jacob Staretzky. This piques Ryan's interest. That is the real name of Jay Star (Ray Walston). He created Ferrus and wrote the books for a few years, then disappeared. He was supposed to have died in poverty, but Micki sees it was purchased fairly recently—and his address is in there. Too good to be true. Ryan sends Micki to talk to the cops while he checks up on Jay Star.

Jay's caretaker, Mrs. Forbes (Michelle George), tries to get rid of Ryan when he turns up on the doorstep, but Jay overhears Ryan mention his real name, takes him as a "true" fan, and insists he be shown in. Ryan momentarily forgets why he is there, completely star-struck in the presence of the reason he started drawing. Ryan gets Jay's autograph and ogles his comic book award, which ignites Jay's bitterness: "It was supposed to be a passport to fame and riches." Ryan uses this rancor as a segue to ask about fans so obsessed with Ferrus they would kill for it. Jay isn't done being bitter, and Mrs. Forbes throws a little more gas on that fire. Peerless Comics cheated Jay out of his property and profits, and they got everything except a few old issues, some original art, and some censored scenes, kept in the basement because it pains him to see them. Jay rambles on, and after spouting off about how nothing surprises him, Ryan broaches the true reason he is there: "Ferrus has come to life." He explains Charlie's death at the hands of a cursed comic book. "Ferrus killed him?" Jay enquires before devolving into insane, old-man laughter.

Once Ryan leaves, Jay doesn't seem quite so feeble. He exchanges his afghan for his coat and heads out to the comic book store, where he finds an address for Cal. When he shows up at Cal's place, Cal is trying to arrange appearances with Ferrus to celebrate *Tales of the Undead*'s 40th anniversary. No one is biting. Cal is speechless when Jay introduces himself and offers up a prescription pill bottle as proof. But Jay is there for the comic book, stolen from him, and Cal isn't about to let it go. "Please don't make me do something I don't want to do," Cal begs, clutching the comic book. Jay knows what is coming, and he has come prepared. Cal becomes

Ferrus, and Jay kills Ferrus with his comic book award—quick and easy. When Cal returns to human form, Jay takes the comic and walks out.

Cal's photo ends up in the newspaper, and Ryan recognizes him immediately. He and Micki find no clues—and no comic book—at Cal's apartment, but Micki finds a note with Carmine DiMatteo's info on it. Carmine (David Clement) runs Peerless Comics, the company that supposedly cheated Jay out of millions and currently publishes *Tales of the Undead*. His account of what happened with *Undead* is very different: his father paid Jay a hefty sum for the comic, but Jay lost it all in a land deal. Jay was so mad he even wrote an entire issue where Ferrus (the indestructible) is killed off. Carmine didn't publish it, naturally—Ferrus is too big a moneymaker for him.

That night, as Carmine is alone at his office, signing off on some pages, he hears something and goes to investigate. Nothing there. Carmine returns to find Jay sitting in his chair, here to "stake his claim." He recognizes some artwork on the wall that should still be locked away in his basement. But he doesn't care about the stolen goods; he has "learned a new trick." Jay transforms into Ferrus and chases Carmine (slowly) through the office. Carmine tries to escape by way of freight elevator, but Ferrus just crushes through the gate and snaps Carmine's neck.

Micki and Ryan show up, just in time to see Ferrus leaving. The follow him outside, where cops are out in force. They pummel him with bullets, and Ferrus eventually drops, lending credence to Micki's theory that that is not the *real* Ferrus. As they approach, hoping to find the comic, Ferrus stands and lumbers away.

Ryan remembers what Carmine said about Jay killing off Ferrus in one of his books, and he and Micki return to Jay's house, hoping to find the missing pages. At this point, he still has no idea that Jay is now Ferrus. Jay is not happy to see him, yet is worried that Ryan will say something to the police. But what would he tell them? Ryan asks about the comic in which he kills off Ferrus, and Jay pulls out all the old man excuses: I'm sure I threw it away; I don't remember what happened. After Ryan leaves, Jay checks on his stash in the basement, where he is confronted by Mrs. Forbes. She admits she sold some of his artwork for the money, and offers to pack her things. Jay tells her that isn't necessary, but he does want to know who bought it. Mrs. Forbes is surprised that Jay isn't mad—but that's because he's about to go Ferrus on her ass.

Mrs. Forbes sold the artwork to a guy named Ted Haley, who was planning on selling it at auction. A trip to the auction house reveals that

Ted never made it in with the art, and a stolen Rolodex card leads Micki and Ryan to his house. They find Ted, halfway through his windshield, dead on his way to deliver the comic art. Micki searches through the art, but the pages depicting Ferrus' death are not there. Ryan finds something interesting: one of Jay's heart pills. The pieces fall into place, and the cousins rush back to Jay Star's house.

Jay has already started burning the "how to kill Ferrus" manual in his fireplace. Ryan breaks in and tries to rescue the pages from the flames. Jay tosses them back in, but is distracted when Micki grabs the cursed comic off the table. He comes at her with a fireplace poker. A well-timed trip sees Micki lose the comic and Jay uses it to transform into Ferrus. He charges towards Micki, but by this time Ryan has read enough of the comic book pages to know how to kill Ferrus. He grabs the comic book award and runs Ferrus through with it. Ferrus falls, and changes back into Jay Star. "Tell me boy," he says with his last breath, "how does it feel to be a hero?"

Status: The comic book is secured, and Micki now has a penchant for comic books. Ryan, however, has had enough. (For now... .)

* * *

With the comic book story, "Tales of the Undead" was really ahead of its time. Today, there are dozens of comic book-based shows on television, and every summer sees superheroes dominate the movie theaters. Especially unique was this episode's use of comic book panels representing the transformation of Jay Star into Ferrus. Sure, it was clearly an inexpensive way to represent the transformation, but it was effective and unique. Before *F13*, 1982's *Creepshow* used a similar tactic between segments, but the *Tales From the Crypt* television series, which utilized a similar technique, was still a couple years away.

The tale of Jay Star as a comic book creator screwed out of royalties is a tale as old as time. Jack Kirby and Joe Simon (co-creators of Captain America), and Jerry Siegel and Joel Shuster (co-creators of Superman) are among some of the biggest names who have faced the same predicament. Writer Marc Scott Zicree actually had Siegel and Shuster's situation in mind. DC Comics bought the character Superman from the pair for $130 and a promise of employment. A year later, when Siegel and Shuster realized the cash cow they had given up, they went to court in an attempt to gain partial ownership of Superman and a more equitable share of the profits. Their initial lawsuit failed, the pair was fired, and they ended up destitute.

"I was a voracious reader of comic books when I was a kid, and I loved DC comics," says Zicree. "Superman, Batman, The Flash, Green Lantern… the Silver Age of comics, when comics were 12¢. I knew about the story of Siegel and Shuster, the creators of Superman who got screwed over. I was thinking about how many of those comic book writers were ripped off by the system, and wondered what if one of them got a cursed object and could get retribution." He even named Carmine after Carmine Infantino, an artist and editor at DC. Not because Infantino was at all involved in the Siegel/Shuster incident, but because Zicree thought he was a terrific artist. He assures me that he has never written comics, so he didn't have an axe to grind.

One of the things I find fascinating about this episode is, for all the reverence given to comic books, *Tales of the Undead*, the comic book, is not treated very well. I can understand Jay crumpling it when he discovers its powers, but surely Cal must realize that when he grabs the comic in the first place, he is rendering it virtually worthless. What's more, what kind of comic store owner would not bag and board a comic of that value? I swear I saw my husband flinch when that comic was folded in half.

The comic book seems to be the first item that really "calls" to its owner. That is the only way to explain Cal lusting after the comic. His desire goes far beyond that of a normal comic book collector. I have known a lot of comic nerds in my life, and none would be driven to violence over a comic book. Then again, most of the comic nerds I have known aren't physically capable of being violent.

"Scarecrow"

Story By: Larry B. Williams and Marc Scott Zicree
Teleplay By: Marc Scott Zicree
Directed By: William Fruet
Original Airdate: February 1, 1988
Cursed antique: Scarecrow

Dave Meeno is a poor but hardworking farmer left to care for his son, Jordy, after his wife dies. The farm isn't doing well, but Dave intends on paying back every creditor. He's an upbeat, glass half full guy; the kind of guy that doesn't exist in real life (or at least not in Los Angeles). Dave puts Jordy to bed, and hears a noise at the door. Opening up, he finds a horrifying scarecrow come to life, wielding a scythe. He slams the door shut and turns to run, but the scarecrow magically appears behind him. The scythe comes down and lops off Dave's head. A woman, the scarecrow's "handler," shows up, collects the head, and leaves. Jordy sees the whole thing.

Micki and Ryan head into this small farming community a few days later. In response to one of the mailers, they got a letter from Charlie Cobean (James B. Douglas), which reads simply "Please come get that scarecrow!" Micki had packed a picnic lunch for the two of them, and brought along an old baseball. Ryan gets mad when he sees the baseball, which was inscribed with "To Ryan from Jimmy." He won't say anything further on the subject, and they continue to the Cobean farm.

Charlie claims he didn't send the letter and it must be a joke. His wife, Tudy (Norma Edwards), is all too eager to confirm that they bought the scarecrow, but Charlie insists it burned up in a crop fire three years ago. Micki asks to use the bathroom and whispers to Ryan, "Keep them talking." She uses this time to take a peek around the house. A rattling doorknob draws her attention, and when she opens the door, an angry young man, Nick Cobean (Todd Duckworth) bursts out. He tries to strangle her, but Charlie is fast, and beats him back into his room. "That's our boy, and that's our business. I didn't ask you to come, but I'm asking you to leave." Even when he is angry, he is being polite.

Clearly, Charlie Cobean is lying (and possibly abusive to his child) so Micki and Ryan start looking around the town. They try to peek into the barn next door, but Micki is drawn away to a large cross on a hilltop. Ryan explains that it is a crossbeam for a scarecrow—but where is the scarecrow? Marge Longacre (Patricia Phillips), the scarecrow handler, stops them suspiciously, but when she finds out they are just scouting antiques, she is all smiles and sends them over to her Longacre Inn. Marge meets them at the house and checks them in. While she readies their rooms, Micki tells Ryan she thinks Tudy was trying to tell her something. Marge listens from upstairs. We all know who is going to die next.

Sure enough, Marge takes the scarecrow outside and pins Tudy's photo to it. But Tudy has her own agenda. Once Charlie falls asleep, she slips out of the house—and runs right into the scarecrow. Tudy turns and runs. She heads to the inn, and makes it to the porch, but so does the scarecrow.

Micki hears Tudy's screams from inside and goes to investigate. All she finds is Tudy's disembodied head, twitching on the porch. Looking up, the scarecrow is standing there ominously. Micki screams and shuts the door. When Ryan opens the door, both the scarecrow and the head are gone. All that is left is Tudy's decapitated corpse.

When the sheriff comes to take Micki's statement, she tells him it was dark, she didn't see anything. When left alone with Ryan, she insists "it was the scarecrow come to life!" The sheriff hears this, and advises Micki to keep her "tall tales" to herself. But the next day, when the coroner's report comes in, it turns out that Tudy was beheaded with a "long, sharp blade" (like a scythe) and she had straw clutched in her hand.

Marge pays Nick a visit. She knows the non-verbal man-child has a thing for the redhead, and gives him some advice: "She's a wild filly. You've got to break her before you can ride her. Break her good." Despite Nick's clearly limited understanding, he seems to pick up on her innuendo.

Micki and Ryan buy a water pump from an old timer in town. (I don't think it was cursed; I think they just need stock for the store so they can buy groceries and fill the Mercedes with premium gas.) He tells them about the bad luck that has struck the community lately. Things haven't been good around here, except at the Cobean farm. It used to be that Charlie couldn't "raise fleas on a dog." Then overnight, his luck changed. Rainstorms that would wash out everyone else's crops would leave Charlie's untouched. He bought up a number of farms around him.

When asked about missing farmers, the old timer tells them about Dave Meeno. He and his boy have been missing for about a week.

Of course, the cousins visit the Meeno farm. There is a For Sale sign out front, but it looks abandoned. Ryan checks inside and finds fresh food on the counters, and the fridge wide open. Micki checks out back and finds the laundry still on the line. Then she sees blood. Fresh blood. Not seeing Ryan around, Micki investigates on her own. She follows the blood to a burned-out barn and spots what appears to be a canvas-wrapped body. She takes a deep breath and pulls back the canvas—to find a basket of mushy tomatoes. Micki's relief is short-lived when she turns around finds the scarecrow looming over her. She screams and dodges from the scythe.

Ryan made his own, slightly less disturbing discovery in the house: Jordy Meeno. He attacks Ryan, an intruder in his home, until Ryan calls him "tiger." Then he just gets sad. Micki's screams bring them both outside, just in time to see the scarecrow raise its scythe over Micki. Suddenly shots ring out and the scarecrow drops. The sheriff had come looking for Micki and Ryan; good thing he did. He unmasks the scarecrow and discovers he killed Nick Cobean. "I guess there was some truth to that scarecrow story," he says, without much sympathy.

Ryan offers to look after Jordy while they are in town. There is an instant bond that Ryan can't quite explain, but it seems Jordy feels it, too. Of course, Jordy still hasn't said a word to anyone. Ryan tucks the kid into bed and Marge pops in to check on them. She pinches Jordy's rosy cheek and asks if he has said anything yet. "If he pipes up, give a holler. I'll know just what to do," she offers ominously before leaving. The perfect veiled threat. Micki comes upstairs and Ryan finally opens up about Jimmy. Jimmy was his brother. One day, they were playing baseball in the street, and a truck came by, jackknifed, and killed Jimmy. "I saw it coming, but there was nothing I could do," he admits sadly. Something about Jordy reminds him of Jimmy. Sad story. But back to business. Micki found out that during every harvest, three people "go missing." This year, the town has only lost two so far, and there are only two days left in the harvest. Whoever has the scarecrow needs to find another victim. Micki left her purse downstairs, making her driver's license easy pickings for Marge. They don't know who has the scarecrow, but Jordy thinks he can help with that.

Jordy didn't see the face of the scarecrow's handler, but he was wearing a long black coat and a big black hat. Marge, ever the vigilant spy, smiles when she hears this. Jordy admits once he went to the Cobean farm

Louise Robey puts her modeling to good use between takes on "Scarecrow."
Photo courtesy of John LeMay.

and saw a scarecrow hanging in their barn. He didn't get a good look at it. Ryan wants Jordy to show them how to get into the Cobean barn, then duck out of sight. Micki collects her purse, and finds her license missing.

(I don't know about anyone else, but I can honestly say that I never open my purse, fish out my wallet, and check to make sure my license is still in there. Let's say Micki was just checking to see if she had… the Cobean address in there.) When Micki realizes her license is missing, Ryan decides it is safer to leave her at the sheriff station. You know, just in case.

Charlie is a wreck. He lost his wife and his son in two separate incidents, both in the same day. He checks some papers on his desk, then considers placing a phone call. Ultimately, Charlie stuffs the papers in his pocket and chooses to drink more. A noise rousts him, and he heads out to the barn, rifle in hand. Marge is there, with the scarecrow. He accuses her of killing his wife and son; she promises she "never meant to hurt you or yours." She made sure he got a good crop every year, and it quickly becomes clear that she is flirting with him. She comes in to kiss him, but has a huge hook hidden behind her back. It swiftly ends up in Charlie's back. There is an almost amusing pause before Charlie starts screaming.

Ryan and Jordy arrive at the Cobean barn, and find there are a lot of scarecrows there. Dozens, all hanging from the rafters. It is a horrifying tableau of dangling effigies, but none are the right horrifying effigy. Ryan notices blood on the floor and looks up—one of the dangling bodies is Charlie Cobean's corpse. Those papers that Charlie stuffed in his pocket? A contract. He sold his farm to Marge Longacre three years ago. The pieces start to come together for Ryan. Jordy runs to call the sheriff, but there is no answer.

There is no answer because Micki locked him in a closet. He went to get her a blanket, and she saw a long black raincoat and hat hanging on the door. Remembering what Jordy said, she thought it was the right thing to do. Micki runs back to the inn, calling for Ryan, but the only one there is Marge. "It's just us girls." She takes Micki upstairs and tells her to relax—Marge will take care of everything. There is a click, and Micki discovers she is locked in the room. But she is not alone—the scarecrow, hidden by blankets, sits up in bed. Micki's license is pinned to his jacket.

Downstairs, Marge is knitting peacefully. She smiles when she hears Micki scream. Ryan, Jordy, and the sheriff come in (Ryan freed him from the closet when he was looking for Micki) and Marge grabs a huge pair of scissors. She sneaks up on the sheriff and stabs him, then grabs Jordy and threatens him. Ryan freezes, then screams, "No, I'm not gonna let that happen!" He kicks the scissors away, tells Jordy to run, and starts fighting Marge.

Micki is doing her best to avoid the scarecrow's scythe. Luckily it works for her. He swings and stabs and manages to miss her, but hit the door. After a few swings, the door is sufficiently splintered enough for her to break through and run downstairs. But the scarecrow, with all its magical powers, appears before her, scythe at the ready. Ryan jumps on the scarecrow and the two try to fight it, but it is a demonic creature, after all. While Ryan holds the scythe at bay, Micki grabs her license off its shirt. The scarecrow instantly goes limp and falls against the wall. Marge comes from out of nowhere, knife in hand, *screaming* as she runs at Micki. Ryan swats her away, causing the knife to hit the wall and cut down a photo of Marge and her late husband. The photo lands on the scarecrow, and it rises once again. As Ryan backs away from Marge, the scarecrow makes its approach and cuts her head off. The photo falls off and the scarecrow goes limp one final time.

Status: The sheriff is injured, but alive. He's going to help find Jordy's next of kin. Ryan felt a real bond with the kid, clearly seeing something of his brother in the kid. He gives Jordy the baseball, signing it "To Jordy, from Ryan." Micki and Ryan leave with the scarecrow, but there is still one question Micki has: what happened to all the decapitated heads?

*   *   *

Indeed, what did happen to all the decapitated heads? Writer Marc Scott Zicree explains: "Micki says, 'I wonder what they did with the heads,' then the camera was supposed to pan past [Ryan and Micki], and it is raining. You see the field with the crossbeam for the scarecrow, and the water washes away the topsoil, and you see the tops of the heads. That was what it was supposed to be, but they wouldn't let us do that. The line is just there, hanging, and they wouldn't do it. I guess it must have been broadcast standards of some kind. The whole idea was these people were sacrifices to whatever dark god or Satan."

With the episode as it aired, my mind came up with a much more sinister back story for Marge. She killed—or tried to kill—an awful lot of people in this episode, without the aid of a cursed object. She killed Charlie to keep him from talking, and she set up his son to be killed. She tried to kill the sheriff, but that didn't quite work out for her, and she clearly would have no problem killing Ryan or Micki with her bare hands. It wouldn't surprise me if she was a killer before she got her hands on the scarecrow. I theorized that she kept the heads of her victims as trophies, lining a bookshelf in a secret room where she knits and stares at the heads like the Governor in *The Walking Dead.*

Actress Patricia Phillips, who played Marge Longacre, has her own idea of what happened to those decapitated heads. "I envisioned them buried neck up in the rotten pumpkin patch. The reason they were neck up was because I think most people have a fear of being buried head down and suffocating, so it was an extra tweak of torture. It was a lovely little secret for me to look at my field of heads, guarded by my scarecrow, knowing that they would suffocate in perpetuity." Since Phillips was expected to create her own back story and give depth to her character, this is just a deliciously twisted bonus. "I think I have a nice dark Irish side that allows me to revel in sinister feelings and enjoy the macabre, so that may have translated to the screen. Also, my big square face is suitable for unnerving people.

"I don't entertain the notion of a good character or bad character," she continues. "If an actor judges a character they are playing, they can't properly enter their skin. I found parallels in myself, which allowed me to empathize with her fundamental anger and fear, and I used them to find out who she was in the everyday world. I actual loved her as a character; she had great fierceness."

Zicree doesn't remember exactly how he came up with the idea for "Scarecrow," but he admits to being a huge fan of *The Wizard of Oz* and trying to think of "unlikely" cursed objects. "What I did with 'Scarecrow' was try to come up with all these twists and turns to make it different and challenging. I had fun with the idea of the scarecrow coming to life with the scythe. It was fun to write something that was just really scary. A friend of mine, a TV writer, said that episode scared the hell out of her. She really liked it. The scarecrow is creepy-looking. Any time you have a human figure that's not human, like scarecrows or dolls that come alive, it is all innately creepy."

The scarecrow was scary as hell—but it wasn't the only thing that was scary about that episode. "The truly scary thing was the old man's farm and the rotting pumpkin patch that was used as a location," Phillips says. "The house was horrifying inside, and walking through the field to set was curiously spooky. I remember freaking myself out one night, imagining all the upside-down heads with eyes wide open staring at me. I ran very quickly to the set that night." For Phillips, the location was more disarming than working with the scarecrow, played by stuntman Ted Hanlan. "I enjoyed his unrelenting obedience," she jokes.

Cinematographer Rodney Charters remembers a more human aspect about shooting at that farm. "We shot in this old farm on the edge of town, it wasn't that far from downtown; maybe twenty minutes, really. There was an old man in there, he must have been in his 80s. He lived alone in this house. He had so much fun with Robey. There was a rope swing outside, and whenever I saw him, he was pushing Robey in the swing. It was kind of a magical moment for him.

"The amazing thing [about the farmhouse] was in the sitting room, adjacent to the kitchen, there was a wood stove and a chair. There were piles of papers on either side of the chair. The whole place had the patina of smoke damage from fifty years, one hundred years of the smoke from the wood fire leaking out and browning everything. You can't make this stuff up; you have to see it and know it's the real thing. The top newspaper was about ten years old, browned a little bit. Underneath was another paper... there were about twenty-five papers on each side, and as you went down each stack, it went back ten years at a time. It went back to the 1900s. This guy's papers hadn't been touched for seventy years. Just crazy."

A number of episodes of *Friday the 13th: The Series* were set in farming or rural communities. "Scarecrow" was the first, followed by "The Quilt of Hathor," "The Sweetest Sting," "The Long Road Home," and, to a lesser extent, "The Pirate's Promise." "I was able to get into all that rural craziness," says Zicree. "Every gag about inbreeding and crazy farmers... it was very much inspired by *To Kill a Mockingbird* and Truman Capote, all that Southern Gothic stuff."

"Faith Healer"

Written By: Christine Cornish
Directed By: David Cronenberg
Original Airdate: February 8, 1988
Cursed antique: Single white glove

Stewart Fishoff (Miguel Fernandes) is a fraud. He runs a faith healing church and promises he can make the blind see, the paralyzed walk, the cancer-ridden be cured. He is exposed in the middle of a performance when Jerry (Robert Silverman), a professional debunker, comes up to the stage and "heals" the plant Fishoff was about to lay hands on. This "blind" man wore white contact lenses to simulate cataracts. The audience is shocked, and Fishoff runs from the auditorium. He is accosted by an older man in a wheelchair, who had been waiting for him. Fishoff goes the other direction, and encounters a trio of injured people, all trying to chase him down. Luckily for Fishoff, they are all on crutches. He turns down an alley and ends up tripping, falling into a dead end. He sees a white leather glove, shockingly clean amongst the garbage, and puts it on, intrigued. A woman on crutches, with heinous lesions all over her face, corners him. "You promised to cure me!" She comes after him, and Fishoff pushes her away with his gloved hand. She shudders, collapses, then stands—without the use of her crutches. Her skin is all cleared up. Fishoff is amazed, but sneaks away as the woman cries her thanks to her god over this miracle.

But now the glove Fishoff wears is infected with the disease it just cured. He tries to peel it off, but it just takes off layers of skin. It is swollen, bloody, pulsating, and eight different kinds of gross, and it puts Fishoff in immense pain. A cop wanders by and comes over to check on him. Fishoff presses his gross, gloved hand to the cop's face, and the disease is transferred. Fishoff and his glove are cured, while the cop dies a hideous, suffocating death, mutated beyond recognition from the skin lesions and whatever other disease that woman was carrying.

Some months later... .

Micki and Ryan are trying to fix the television (way back when most televisions picked up signal through antennae) and they get the picture to come in clear, but can't change the channel. Fishoff is on the TV, proselytizing, and Jack recognizes the glove he wears. To the books! Jack brought that glove back with him from Rome when he was a merchant marine. It was made for Antonio Sforza, an Italian alchemist from the 1500s, and was supposed to provide good health for the ruling families. Sure enough, it is listed in the manifest.

The trio waste no time in tracking down Fishoff. Jack is thrown out of the theater by a couple church tough guys who catch him trying to break into Fishoff's office. Jack heads back home and leaves Micki and Ryan to watch for Fishoff. If he leaves, they are to follow. Sure enough, after a few hours, Fishoff leaves—no goons in sight. Micki and Ryan lose track of him so they split up. Fishoff has found himself a woman, out walking a ridiculously froofy poodle, and transfers the disease to her. Micki and Ryan find the woman after following the whimpers of the scared dog, sniffing over the crusty puddle of her person. Returning to Curious Goods, Micki and Ryan can hardly verbalize what they saw. Jack thinks the glove absorbs one person's afflictions, but must transfer them to another. Maybe the glove even amplifies it. Jack has a friend who can probably help, but tells Ryan and Micki to stay at the store. "He's… a bit peculiar."

This peculiar friend is Jerry, the one who initially debunked Fishoff. He lives in a decommissioned ship at the docks, and the two men greet each other warmly. In the last twenty years, Jerry estimates he has debunked about four hundred "parasites," and not one was even close to being real. Jack wants Jerry to investigate Fishoff again, and shows him a tape from a recent television program/commercial. Jerry is suspicious— belief in the power of the supernatural is one thing the two friends have never been able to see eye-to-eye on. Jack insists that Fishoff is a fraud, but he has an item that lets him heal, truly heal people. "Where's the harm in that?" Jerry asks. "It has unpleasant side effects," is the best Jack can come up with. After some more bickering, Jerry finally gives in. "What do you want me to do?"

Jerry visits Fishoff, claiming to be impressed by his recent success and promising that if he is wrong, and Fishoff does have the power to heal, he is big enough to admit it. Fishoff accepts his new challenge, and Jerry returns to Jack on the boat. He has scheduled a private healing between Fishoff and a terminally ill patient. "If he can heal, let him heal." Jack is furious and explains the curse, but Jerry becomes angry: "You have no say in this anymore." Jack is taken aback, and Jerry finally reveals that he is the terminally ill patient. His chest is covered with huge, crusty black

With guest director David Cronenberg. Photo courtesy of John LeMay.

lesions that surely don't exist in real life. He pulls out a gun and ties up Jack before locking him in a closet. "You've never been a criminal before," Jack reasons. "I've never been dying before," he answers blithely.

Fishoff arrives and directs his chauffeur/muscle to stand right outside the door, but come in if he hears anything. Jerry asks him about the glove, and Fishoff is immediately suspicious. How does he know that is part of the healing process? Despite this, he puts on the glove, and asks for his patient. He balks when he finds out Jerry is his patient, but there is no turning back now. Fishoff goes through the whole rigmarole: making Jerry kneel, making him say he believes. Fishoff puts his non-gloved hand to Jerry's forehead, pushes him over, and starts to pack up. Jerry checks— the sores are still there. "Sorry Jerry, I must have used the wrong hand. Maybe next time." He puts the unsullied glove in his pocket and starts to leave, but Jerry threatens him with the gun. He fires it into the air to prove it is loaded, and the muscle rushes in. Jerry drops him immediately, but it has given Fishoff time to escape.

Jerry manages to get two shots into Fishoff as he climbs into his car; neither are immediately lethal. He puts on the glove and presses it to his wounds while he drives off, swerving wildly. Eventually he drives the car right down an alley, where it gets wedged in and craps out. On the upside, he is no longer dying from a gunshot wound; on the downside, he is dying from the glove. Jerry catches up with him, and in a last, desperate move, Fishoff reaches his gloved hand out a crack in the window, begging for help. Jerry laughs and waits for him to die, which happens very quickly: Fishoff is shot through by a half-dozen bullets from nowhere, the effects of the last "heal" he did, amplified. Fishoff is dead, the glove is clean, and Jerry takes it.

Micki and Ryan have been worrying over Jack for hours. Micki keeps seeing him with the same skin disease that killed the woman in the alley. As day fades into night, Ryan hits Jack's address book and finds the "peculiar friend." Since Jack has the car, they take bicycles down to the marina.

Jerry returns to Jack, glove on one hand, gun in the other. Jerry verbalizes the steps needed to heal himself and makes Jack sit on the bed. He sits across from him, gun still aimed, and reaches under his shirt with the glove. "It's working!" he rejoices. But now he has a diseased hand, and he comes after Jack with it. Jack dodges, holds him off, and eventually manages to force Jerry's hand back onto his own face. The disease transfers back to Jerry, and his face pulses, crusts, bleeds, all sorts of ick. "Pray for me, Jack," he begs with his dying breath. The glove is white and pristine; Micki and Ryan arrive just in time to see Jerry die.

Status: The glove is returned to the vault. Micki finds a cape in the manifest that sounds interesting, but she and Jack get into a fight about their work in the shop and leaving to lead normal lives… you know, all the stuff Micki bitched about in "Root of All Evil." Now, it is Jack's turn. Ryan interrupts before anything truly hurtful can be said, and they join forces to threaten Ryan with experiments to cure his head cold. All disagreements can be patched up when teasing Ryan is an alternative.

* * *

David Cronenberg was a big "get" for *Friday the 13th: The Series*. By the time he came in to direct "Faith Healer," he already had a string of hits and cult favorites under his belt: *The Fly, The Dead Zone, Videodrome,* and *Scanners* among them. But there isn't much story behind the "get:" Frank Mancuso Jr. was friendly with him, so he brought him in to do an episode.

Line producer J. Miles Dale remembers this episode as taking a little longer to shoot than the normal seven days allotted per episode. "Frank said to me, 'This is David Cronenberg. Maybe we should give him an eighth day.'

"But we ended up saying, 'Nah, fuck it, he can do it in seven, too!'"

"It was lovely to see David economize on what was a much more challenging schedule," remembers cinematographer Rodney Charters. "He's used to doing two pages a day, and we had to do eight or nine or something ridiculous." Perhaps that is why Louise Robey doesn't have fond memories of working with him. "He was kind of indifferent. He directed us, but he said he wasn't interested in the main characters."

Of course, he may have been distracted by a failed stunt—on Friday the thirteenth, of all days. Dale remembers the stunt, where Fishoff is driving his car after being shot. "When the front end hit the wall, we found out later that the brake line snapped. It turns out [the stunt driver] ran over a half million dollar camera. So, we had a really nasty insurance claim on that show with the camera." That camera belonged to Charters. "We had one of my 35mm Arris sitting on the ground on a ground plate with a high hat, between two steel containers that were roped together. We were on the other side; we were safe. Of course, the car came off the ramp too fast, exploded through the containers and rammed my camera, took out the lens and body. It was... it was an expensive night." Notwithstanding, Charters "had a lot of fun" with Cronenberg. "David and his blood... he wanted to put all his blood in."

Cronenberg is best known for his work in "body horror," which focuses on what happens when your body betrays you, whether it is because of disease or disfigurement. "Faith Healer" was the perfect episode for him: the cursed glove that heals the sick and kills the healthy. Cronenberg has said that he is more interested in things that happen inside a person, both mentally and physically, than an exterior threat. "To a certain extent, it is your own body that is the monster to your own existence."[1]

I can't help but wonder how Cronenberg came to direct this episode. He declined to comment for this book, and I was unable to locate the episode's writer, Christine Cornish. Cronenberg generally writes all the films he directs. Did he do a production rewrite of Cornish's script? Did he choose "Faith Healer" from the scripts that were about to go into production? Was it simply a happy accident? Regardless of the circumstances, "Faith Healer" is a worthy addition to Cronenberg's credits.

---

1. https://youtu.be/EL31jYevzTo

"The Baron's Bride"

Written by: Larry Gaynor
Directed by: Bradford May
Original airdate: February 15, 1988
Cursed antique: Cape

At the end of "Faith Healer," Micki mentions a cape in the manifest that she found interesting. Well, in "The Baron's Bride," our trio goes after said cape. This is one of the few times that one episode linked directly to the next (excluding two-parters, of course). When we come in on this episode, Jack has already located the cape, and has an idea of the curse it carries: it makes men irresistible to women.

Frank (Tom McCamus) answers an ad for a room to rent. Marie (Diana Barrington) is the homeowner, looking to rent some space after her husband's death. She is a strangely sultry woman, who shows Frank the room and leaves him to look around. Frank is taken by a cape lying on the bed, and can't help but try it on. Marie secretly spies on him, and her eyes widen in excitement when she sees him put it on. Frank is admiring himself in the cape when Marie comes back. She always believed the man who wore that cape would be the man who she spent the rest of her life with. There is a little poem she recites: "Now, you and I, through eternity will be bound; for with this cape, immortality is found; And with this clasp we can travel through time; Just a drop of your precious blood mixed with mine." But first, he must "become one of us." Marie reveals her vampire fangs and takes a big bite.

Jack, Ryan, and Micki are at the front door when they hear Frank's screams. They break in and rush upstairs. Marie uses her vampire-power to swat everyone away from her and her "beloved:" Micki is knocked out, Ryan is tossed into the hallway, and Marie starts to strangle Jack. Ryan returns with the "For Rent" sign from the lawn and runs the wooden end through Marie's chest. Micki rushes to Frank, but instead of wresting the cape from him, she falls under his spell. Ryan goes for the cape, but the blood from Frank's bite has mixed on the clasp with blood from a scratch on Micki's cheek. With Ryan holding onto the cape, the three of them disappear.

They reappear in what turns out to be London, March 12, 1875. Frank runs off into the night. A friendly young couple stop to see if Ryan and Micki need any help. The newlyweds introduce themselves as Abraham (Kevin Bundy), a writer, and Caitlin (Susannah Hoffmann), and invite them to stay with them. Back at their apartment, Caitlin cleans up Micki's wound. Despite claiming she is okay, Ryan can't help but notice something is off with her. He presses her, and she explodes. "How are we going to get out of here?" I suppose your first experience with time travel, especially when you aren't expecting it, can be rather traumatic.

Frank is busy running through the streets of London like a little kid playing Superman. But he is also hungry. He lures a streetwalker into a stairwell and drains her dry. A constable happens by, and Frank snarls and runs. The copper blows his whistle when he sees the dead hooker and soon a crowd of people are chasing Frank through the night. The mob literally is made up of people carrying torches and pitchforks.

Micki can't sleep. She slips from bed and tries to sneak out of the apartment, but Ryan stops her. She insists she is merely going to look for the cape, but Ryan reminds her that vampires are less powerful during the day. "Tomorrow could be too late," Micki implores. Ryan has an inkling of what is going on, and he doesn't like it. A commotion outside wakes Abraham and Caitlin. When queried, a man in the street tells them about the dead woman, and how people think it is the work of a vampire. Ryan and Micki join the chase, with Abraham tagging along, thinking it could make a good story.

Abraham doesn't buy the vampire story, and figures the murderer is just a man hiding in the city. He takes Ryan and Micki to check out some of the city's hidey-holes. They strike gold on the last location, a large warehouse with plenty of places to hide. Dawn has arrived, and they find the lock on the warehouse broken. Micki senses he is inside.

Frank is hiding out in the warehouse, waiting for the figurative and literal heat to die down. He practices swishing his cape around, but finds it choking him, so he takes it off. Unfortunately, this was keeping him alive. He begins to desiccate and starts looking like a gargoyle. He puts the cape back on, and instantly he is healthy again.

Micki is leading her team towards Frank. Frank appears behind them with a theatrical wave of the arms. He tosses the men aside and goes to Micki, who warns him of an attack from Ryan. He stops it easily and proclaims Micki is now his. They stare dreamily at each other until Abraham scares Frank away with a bulb of garlic. Ryan grabs Micki by the arm and drags her through the warehouse. She screams, like a child throwing a temper tantrum. Ryan throws open the door and Frank retracts from the sunlight, screaming. The three of them leave, but Ryan doesn't think to go back for the cape. He just wants to get Micki out of there.

Back at the apartment, Ryan knows she is going to be useless—Micki is under Frank's spell. Caitlin is worried about her, but the only way to save her is to get the cape back. He leaves Caitlin to watch Micki while he and Abraham go a'hunting.

Frank feels the same way that Micki feels about him, the "woman he wants to share eternity with." Micki is under a magical spell; Frank is just bewitched. He must find her, and licks her blood off the diamond brooch. This causes Micki to wake suddenly, as if in pain. Caitlin is mystified by this kind of love. Night falls quickly, and Caitlin thinks the boys must have stopped by the pub. Micki says "he" is here, she can feel it. Caitlin checks the window and sees nothing - but then Frank's face appears, *Lost Boys*-style, giving Caitlin a fright—they are on the second story. The face disappears, and Micki hears him on the roof. Caitlin is scared and decides they should leave, but when she throws open the door, Frank is there. Caitlin tries to protect Micki from him, but Frank easily pulls Caitlin away.

The boys have found another dead hooker in Frank's would-be lair. Realizing it is dark already, they race back home. When they arrive, there is a crowd gathered and police are everywhere. Inside the apartment, Caitlin is on the bed, dead. There is a hole in the roof through which Frank and Micki left. Abraham blames Ryan for turning his life upside down. He leaves sadly, takes a minute, then goes back to find Micki.

Frank has brought Micki back to the warehouse. He promises he won't hurt her, that he loves her. He thinks for a moment, then begins to recite the poem. (I suppose in this mythology the poem is necessary for creating a vampire?) Ryan comes running at Frank with a stake, and probably could have killed him if he hadn't entered screaming. Frank grabs Ryan by the throat, threatening him as he squeezes the life from him. Suddenly Frank is run through with a wooden stake. It is Abraham. Whatever his thoughts of Ryan are, vengeance for Caitlin is more important. With Frank dead and the cape in Ryan's arms (not around his neck), Micki's spell is broken. She and Ryan give their thanks, their condolences, and say their goodbyes to Abraham. They each put a drop of blood on the brooch, and disappear, leaving Abraham in wonder.

They reappear in the rental bedroom, where Jack has been waiting for them. "What happened to you two?" "It's a long story," is the best Ryan can offer.

Status: The cape is back in the vault and Micki is back to her old self. Jack desperately pumps Ryan for details of where and when they were, and is frustrated that they aren't "trained observers." Micki is offended and Jack apologizes, then shows them an early edition of *Dracula*. Jack is pretty sure that Abraham is Bram Stoker, and shows them the inscription: "To Caitlin, the only woman I will ever love."

* * *

Is it mere coincidence that the cape was owned by vampires, or was that part of the curse? Who is the titular Baron? I assume he was the first owner of the cape, but that aspect was never explored.

It is interesting that Jack thinks that Ryan is describing the Whitechapel area of London. First, Ryan doesn't really give any specifics; maybe Jack wanted it to be Whitechapel? When I think Whitechapel, I think of Jack the Ripper, which was his primary hunting ground. I am surprised Jack doesn't tie their adventure to the Ripper. I guess they already touched on him in "Doctor Jack." But when Abraham comments that Micki and Ryan have "fine Irish names," I imagine that to be a sly nod towards Bram Stoker's Irish roots.

Cinematographer Rodney Charters had a lot of fun with "The Baron's Bride." To start with, this was the first episode on which Charters was given a camera operator. "It was directed by Bradford May, an American director of photography, who worked in the Hollywood system. He immediately told the producers I would be dead if they didn't give me an operator because I was doing it all. There are a lot of cinematographers who operate their own work but you can't do it on a television schedule. There is just too much to do. So, [Bradford] forced them to give me an operator, and from that day on, I've always had one. It is the only way to do television."

"I remember it being one of the coldest winters in Toronto," says director Bradford May, "and of course we were shooting at night. It has been a long time since we made that episode, but I can still feel the cold. When I was able to get back to the hotel at the end of the night, all I wanted to do was lay in a hot bath and warm my bone marrow." Despite the freezing temperatures, May says "The Baron's Bride" was a very special episode for him. After nearly a decade as cinematographer, *Friday the 13th: The Series* marked his directorial debut. "I will always hold this moment in my career dear to my heart."

"He was tremendously excited and really happy to be shooting proper black and white," says Charters. "We were down at a location with old brick and eighteenth century architecture, and it doubled beautifully for smoggy London."

"Bedazzled"

Written by: Paul Monette & Alfred Sole
Directed by: Alexander Singer
Original airdate: February 22, 1988
Cursed antique: Brass lantern

This episode opens with Ryan and Jack in the middle of hunting down this week's object: a brass lantern. It is in the hands of treasure hunter Jonah (Alan Jordan), who uses it to shine a light on shipwrecks. A treasure chest always appears where the light shines, filled with gold and jewels. Of course, the diver who brings up the treasure dies: the light of the lantern sets him on fire. Ryan and Jack bust in on Jonah just after he sets his most recent diver on fire. Ryan tackles him and Jack tries to run out with the lantern, but Jonah's cohort, Tom (David Mucci), stops him. A ruckus ensues but Jack and Ryan finally get away—with the lantern.

Back home, the boys regale Micki with tales of their adventure—after the lantern is stowed safely in the vault. A huge storm is moving in, but the guys are due at an astrologer convention. Ryan wants to relax at home, but Micki and Jack convince him to go. The boys head out into the storm, leaving Micki alone.

Well, almost alone. Jonah and Tom tracked down Curious Goods and are hovering outside, waiting until Jack and Ryan leave. Just to be sure, Jonah calls the shop from a payphone, and is surprised when a woman answers. It doesn't matter, he assures Tom. They are still going through with their plan. Jonah heard Jack tell Ryan to "get the lantern into the vault," and he remembers a vault in the basement when he originally purchased the lantern. A phone repair man pulls up nearby to work on the phone lines. Jonah kills the repair man and takes his uniform. Perfect cover.

Inside, Micki has just agreed to baby sit for Richie (Gavin Magrath), a friend's son. She also talks to Ryan, and tells them they should get a hotel room. The storm has been upgraded to a hurricane. Shortly after she hangs up with Ryan, Jonah cuts the phone line. Jonah and Tom then come to the door, with a report that phones were down in the area. Micki doesn't think hers was affected, but checks anyway. Dead. She invites them in to fix it, but as they are heading down to the basement, there is another knock at the door. Micki lets the workmen go downstairs on their own while she takes in Richie. Richie is an obnoxious pre-teen who enjoys scaring Micki, reading Ryan's comic books, and picking the chips out of chocolate chip cookies.

Jonah and Tom are perplexed by the vault. There is no lock, no keypad, no dial. They assumed it was just a safe. Jonah suggests the blowtorch might work. It doesn't make a dent, and Tom, in frustration, knocks over some tools. Richie, alone while Micki checks the windows upstairs, hears the commotion and goes to investigate. He doesn't believe they are really there to fix the phone, and warns them against "fooling with the vault." Jonah tries to sweet talk the kid, make him an honorary repair man, but Richie doesn't buy it. He threatens to tell, and that's when things get ugly.

Micki comes downstairs and hears Richie's cries of help. She rushes to the basement and realizes they are not repair men. Micki tries to play dumb about the lantern, and about the vault. Jonah threatens her with a match (lit on his teeth!) and singes the edge of her hair. She gives in, kind of, telling them there is a secret entry, but she doesn't remember where it is. The instructions are written down in the manifest on the desk. Upstairs, Jonah tears through the manifest but is angry and frustrated when he can't find it. With his back turned, Micki comes at him with a heavy figurine, but Jonah catches her arm just before she can strike him with it. They return to the basement and Micki starts wiggling bricks, starting on the opposite side of where the real trick brick is. He eventually gets frustrated and starts wiggling the bricks himself. Jonah finds the correct one, and the doors swing open.

A cop doing his rounds notices the phone repair truck, but doesn't see the worker. He checks around and sees the phone cables cut. Further investigation reveals the dead phone man stuffed into a truck panel. The cop turns his attention to Curious Goods, and knocks. Tom deals with him, poorly, insisting that everything is fine and the phone lines are still working. Since the cop knows this to be untrue, he pretends to leave, but then kicks the door open. Tom lunges at him with a knife, and the cop drops him easily.

Jonah locks Micki and Richie in the vault, grabs something to use as a weapon, shuts off the power, and runs upstairs to regulate. He sneaks up on the cop, who is bravely trying to search the dark store, and impales the cop on whatever he has as a weapon. In theory, Jonah should "get" something in return; after all, what he used came from the vault, so it would stand to reason that it is cursed. There are deliciously disgusting wet suction noises as Jonah removes the weapon from the cop, then uses it to jam the front door shut. He checks on Tom (dead), takes some jewelry, and goes back downstairs.

The power is back on and Jonah opens the vault. Sitting front and center is the lantern. He doesn't question it; he just moves to grab it. As he does, Micki jumps out and hits him over the head with a figurine. She grabs the lantern and runs to the first floor with Richie. With the front door jammed, Micki decides the safest thing to do is fight. She and Richie hide in her room and push the dresser in front of the door. She strips the wires from a lamp, ties them to the lantern, and has Richie plug it in. Then they sit. And wait.

They don't have to wait long. Jonah creeps upstairs, jiggles the doorknob, and presses the doors (and the dresser) aside. Micki defiantly tells him he can't have the lantern, at which point, Jonah *should* have known it was a trap. The lantern is just sitting there in the middle of the bed. Luckily his greed outweighs clarity and he grabs the lantern. As planned, Jonah receives a huge electric shock that lays him out. Richie unplugs the cord and Micki can safely carry the lantern. They rush past Jonah, but he grabs Micki's ankle and pulls her to the floor. The two wrestle around the kitchen: he throws her over the table; she opens the refrigerator door in his face, then swings around a waffle iron and hits him on the head so hard he falls back onto Ryan's bed. Micki grabs the lantern, but trips on the landing. Richie throws the lantern off the landing, and Jonah sails after it. The fall to the first floor knocks him out briefly, but not long enough. He grabs the lantern and turns it on. Micki pushes Richie aside, ducks under the light, and grabs a mirror. Using it as a shield, she reflects the light back at Jonah, who drops the lantern when he is set on fire. Jonah is finally dead.

When Ryan and Jack return the next morning, Ryan complains unrelentingly about what a horrible night they had. Micki nods her head and rolls her eyes, trying to keep an amused/annoyed look off her face. When asked what she ended up doing, she replies, "Oh nothing." Jenny comes in to thank Micki for babysitting, but asks that next time she not tell Richie any ghost stories. "You wouldn't believe the tall tales he came home with: you guys were held captive by pirates pretending to be phone guys, then one guy gets burned to death by a magic lantern! It was the funniest thing I heard in my life!" Micki just smiles and saunters up to her room, leaving Jack and Ryan slack-jawed in disbelief.

Status: The lantern is back in the vault, and despite all the shenanigans that took place in Curious Goods, there is not a single bit of evidence that anything happened.

*   *   *

Jonah is the bad guy who wouldn't die. Like Michael Myers or Jason Voorhees, he just keeps getting up for more. He gets electrocuted, hit in the head multiple times (with the figure in the vault, the fridge door, and then a nice wallop with the waffle iron), *and* falls from the second story. But he is still ticking. It takes a cursed object to finally bring him down.

I love the sly little secret that Micki keeps of her very eventful night, but how did she and Richie escape without a tell-tale scratch? And what the hell did she do with three dead bodies? Why didn't the cops come around? At the very least, they should have come after their own.

An episode like this could very easily fall into the "woman in jeopardy" trap, where Micki is terrorized just because she is a girl. But she isn't portrayed that way. She doesn't make any dumb mistakes. Micki tries to get out of the store first and foremost, but she can't and decides she is better off fighting—not hiding. She sets up trap after trap to slow Jonah down (it's not her fault that they don't work), and thinks quickly when it comes down to the wire.

Fun fact: The mirror Micki uses to reflect the lantern light is the same mirror that Lewis appears in at the end of "Bottle of Dreams"—but it is *not* the same mirror that was used in "Doorway to Hell," even though "Doorway" was designed to open immediately after "Bottle."

"Vanity's Mirror"

Story by: Roy Sallows and Ira Levant
Teleplay by: Roy Sallows
Directed by: William Fruet
Original airdate: February 29, 1988
Cursed antique: Gold compact

Sylvia Unger runs a flower cart outside an swanky office building. Every night, Mr. Meniger, a wealthy, distinguished businessman, stops to buy a carnation. Tonight, Sylvia is feeling a bit testy, and she confronts Mr. Meniger, asking if he ever "sees" her. "I'm a woman, full of love and needs." She is a grizzled, unattractive woman with a crazy streak. Meniger swats her away and hurries past. She calls his name, and he turns. Sylvia flashes a gold compact in his eyes, and suddenly he sees her as she wants to be seen. "You are so beautiful. I never really saw you," he babbles. She takes him someplace private (an alley) and he promises her everything she could ever want, and promises to love her until the day he dies. She pulls a fire escape lever, dropping an iron ladder on his head. Meniger is instantly dead, and Sylvia runs back to her cart, laughing maniacally. Her laughter distracts her and she doesn't see the car barreling towards her. She is hit, and her compact rolls away. As cops and onlookers crowd around, high school student Helen Mackie (Ingrid Veninger) sees the gold compact on the ground. She slips it into her purse and casually walks away.

The next day, Helen goes to school with her beautiful older sister, Joanne (Gwendolyn Pacey), and Joanne's boyfriend, Scott (David Orth). Helen is, well, she's not a pretty girl. Acne-pocked skin, greasy hair, and a bad attitude make her a target for bullies. Scott defends her, quietly, telling his jock buddies that Helen and Joanne are a package deal.

After school, Helen sits on the school lawn and takes her first, long look at her new compact. Jock Greg (Zack Ward) approaches and asks her to prom, while his friends watch nearby, laughing uncontrollably. He returns to his friends, and Helen looks at herself in her mirror. "You can go to hell!" she screams. Greg turns around, and is flashed in the eyes by the compact. Suddenly his demeanor changes, and he approaches Helen, serious and sincere, and tells her how beautiful she is. Helen doesn't believe him, but he swears his love for her. That word clicks with Helen, and they walk off together, leaving Greg's friends stunned.

The next day, Helen and Greg walk through the school halls holding hands. Sometimes, Helen kisses him to prove a point to the popular girls, whose mouths are agape. But the bloom falls off that rose, and Helen quickly tires of the puppy dog act. She begs for just five minutes alone, and Greg agrees. "Anything you want. I love you. I'll love you 'til the day I die." Ding. Helen has an idea. She leads Greg to the enormous trash compactor and drops her hankie in. Greg promises to retrieve it and jumps in. Helen turns on the compactor, which worries Greg. But his love needs her hankie, so her hankie she shall have. He finds it and passes it up to her, and Helen shuts the lid. Greg begs for help, but Helen is unsympathetic. "I loved you too, Greg. Until the day you died." She dabs her eye mockingly with the hankie, then tosses it over her shoulder and saunters away. Greg screams as the compactor turns him into what I imagine is a slimy, bloody cube.

At Curious Goods, Jack is quite proud of the progress they have made: twenty-three antiques obtained so far. Micki is less proud—that is barely 10% of the stuff in the manifest. Ryan has a "highly scientific" way of deciding what antique they go after today: he closes his eyes and points. The winner: a gold compact, sold to Sylvia Unger. It doesn't take long for Micki and Ryan to find out that she was killed two weeks ago, and they return to the store with a news clipping on her death. In the accompanying photo, Jack sees a girl kneeling to pick up what is clearly the compact. She is wearing a high school jacket, and Jack finds her in the Lincoln High yearbook: Helen Mackie.

After Greg's tragic death, Scott and Joanne are in mourning at home, while Helen is perfectly unaffected, watching TV and eating an enormous sandwich. Joanne and Scott don't understand how Helen can be so blasé about her boyfriend's death. She is saved by a knock on the door. Micki is there, plays the "antique buyer" card, and asks about the compact. Helen is suspicious and tells Micki to "beat it." She slams the door and stomps up to her room where she can ogle the compact—and a photo of Scott.

While decorating the gym for prom, Russel (Simon Reynolds) confronts Helen and vows to find out what she did to Greg. She flashes him with the compact, and Russel's tune changes. He begs for forgiveness and insists he is in love with her. Helen leads the compliant boy through the basement into the wood shop. Between professions of love, Helen pushes his head into the table saw. Blood is everywhere and Helen is grossed out.

Ryan goes undercover as a high school student to track down Helen and get a lead on the compact. He sees Helen lead a star struck boy through the halls and follows them. He loses them momentarily in the basement labyrinth, but soon he can just follow the screams. He finally finds Helen, bloodied and hovering over Russel's corpse. She starts chasing Ryan, trying to flash him with the compact. He ducks, hides his eyes, and escapes through a door. Helen follows, and while Ryan avoids getting flashed, in all his dodging and dancing around, he tumbles over the railing and takes a grand fall onto the concrete floor below.

Helen goes home and starts preparing for prom. Joanne comes in for her eyeliner and gets excited when she sees Helen getting ready. Helen is ill-prepared for the trappings of traditional femininity: she doesn't know how to apply makeup and she teases her hair out into a rat's nest. Joanne offers to help; Helen declines. Joanne sees the gold compact and picks it up, complimenting Helen on it. She sits to gossip with Helen, but Helen is distracted, watching Joanne flip the compact over in her hands. Joanne finally takes the hint and leaves. She stops at the door to pass the compact back to Helen. She clutches it gratefully and returns to her preparations.

Scott arrives to pick up Joanne for the dance. Helen comes down a few minutes later, and Joanne plasters a fake smile on her face, biting back comments on her teased-out hair and whorish makeup. Helen is only interested in Scott's opinion of her. The best he can offer is that she will attract attention. They agree to wait until Helen's date arrives, but he never does. Joanne offers to leave them cab money. On the way out, Helen calls to Scott, flashes the compact, and he is love struck. Scott and Helen start kissing, leaving Joanne speechless. She pulls them apart and slaps Helen, which upsets Scott. He throws her against the wall, slaps her, and finally throws her over his shoulder in a true caveman move. They take Joanne upstairs to make sure she "never hurts us again." Joanne is bound, gagged, with a noose around her neck, supported only by a small stool on which she precariously balances on her tip-toes.

Micki and Jack are at the school, waiting for Ryan. He is a no-show. They get nervous and go inside to look for him. Traveling into the school basement, they come to the wood shop first. They see a male body with dark hair and Micki freezes. Jack is the brave one who checks—it's not Ryan. Micki isn't giving up on him and the two separate. Micki finally finds Ryan in a pool of his own blood. He must have been there awhile— the rats are already circling. Despite serious injuries (a concussion and

John LeMay makes new friends on the set of "Vanity's Mirror."
Photo courtesy of John LeMay.

surely a few broken bones, at least) Micki scoops him up and gets him walking. Meanwhile, Jack has gone to the Mackie house, hoping to find Helen and/or the compact. Instead, he finds Joanne, seconds after she slips off the stool. He cuts her down and promises she is safe.

Scott and Helen walk into the dance, among a flurry of whispers and gasps. Micki and Ryan burst in and push their way through the crowd until they can confront Helen. Helen is shocked to see Ryan alive. They taunt Helen: tell Scott how you're going to kill him; you're going to have to kill him like you killed the others. Scott punches Ryan and whisks Helen out of the gym. Micki and Ryan chase them across campus, but lose them in the woods. They continue on, and Helen and Scott backtrack to the school.

Helen takes Scott onto the roof. Scott proclaims his love for her, something she has waited so long to hear him say. They kiss, then dance on the edge of the roof. She holds the compact as they dance and Helen proclaims her love for Scott. A crowd gathers on the ground, and Micki and Ryan rush upstairs. Jack and Joanne have just arrived, and they follow. Helen is totally oblivious. She is lost in her love for Scott. "I don't want you to die. I don't want to lose you, but I know the only way I can have you is in death." As Micki, Ryan, Jack, and Joanne make it to the roof, Helen tells Scott once more that she loves him and they jump. Jack sends Micki and Ryan downstairs with the hysterical Joanne. Jack stays behind a moment to check Helen's purse. The compact is not there.

Status: For the first time, the antique o' the week is not retrieved, something Micki has a very hard time accepting. Back at Lincoln High, students go about their day normally. Helen jumped with the compact, and when she hit the ground, the compact rolled away. The final shot of the episode shows the compact sitting innocently under a bush… and a feminine hand picking it up.

* * *

After Jack and Micki find Russel in a bloody heap in the woodshop, Jack is worried about Micki being on her own. "The compact wouldn't work on me, would it?" she asks. My first thought is, "Why would she think that?" But it just goes to show that back in the 1980s, homosexuality was still virtually absent from American network television. And yet, the series touched on transgenderism (if obliquely) in "The Secret Agenda of Mesmer's Bauble." I have to assume it would work on any person, regardless of gender, but since all the antiques seem to have the ability to adjust their curses based on the person, maybe it only works on the gender you are attracted to.

"Vanity's Mirror" is the first time our heroes don't get their antique back. I appreciate that. They simply can't get every object, every time. Executive story editor Bill Taub was just trying to keep the show unpredictable. "Let's come up with a show where they don't get something back—it's still on the loose. It was just to try to mix it up," he says. "Then it makes the other [episodes] like, 'What's going to happen here?'"

Ingrid Veninger, as the awkward, unpopular Helen, always stuck with me. What kid hasn't gone through an awkward, unpopular phase themselves? I remember wondering why Helen would seemingly go out of her way to look so unattractive. Veninger remembers telling supervising producer Jon Andersen stories about being a loner in sixth grade. "I think that really intrigued him," she says.

She loved playing the ugly, unpopular Helen. "I didn't know how full-out they were going to go with the cold sore on my mouth and the greasy hair with the barrette and all that. I loved the getup for prom. I remember wanting my hair to be bigger and bigger and bigger. People kept saying that might be too much, but I said 'oh no, it's not too much because she is going *full on.*' I love playing character parts like that." Of course, sometimes playing the character part can have unexpected results. "During one night of shooting, a grip sat down next to me, and I could tell he was a little bit creeped out," Veninger recalls. "Then at the wrap party, that same grip came to me and said, 'Oh my god, you're actually not that ugly!'"

It was probably the fake cold sore, which the makeup department applied to Veninger's lip, that so disgusted that grip. It sure disgusted me—and Veninger. "The cold sore they made for me was this weird makeup, fake scabby thing. Shooting that scene where I was eating the sandwich, I kept eating the cold sore. It kept peeling off, which is really disgusting, because you never shoot something once."

Thoughtless grips and revolting makeup aside, "Vanity's Mirror" stands out to Veninger because it is where she met a lifelong friend and collaborator, Simon Reynolds, and she put his head through a band saw. Reynolds played Russel in the episode, and he didn't take it personally. Veninger produced his first two short films, and the pair co-wrote, co-directed, and co-produced her first feature film, *Only.* "I never expected that I would meet a life-long friend doing that episode. The guy whose head I put in a band saw."

"Tattoo"

Written by: Dan DiStefano & Stephen Katz
Directed by: Lyndon Chubbuck
Original airdate: Marc 7, 1988
Cursed antique: Set of tattoo needles

Tommy Chen (Leonard Chow) is a compulsive gambler. Like most gamblers (especially on *Friday the 13th*) he loses. A lot. And he owes money. A lot. After his most recent loss and a scary confrontation with bookie Frank (Harvey Chow), Tommy wanders into the basement of the club, where he sees the guy who just beat him tattooing a young woman in a platinum wig. She is bound and gagged, clearly not there of her own free will. "Tattoos are good luck," he tells the terrified young woman. "Well, maybe not for you, but for me." He tells her that the tattoo needle he uses is magic and lets him win. He finishes the tattoo (a scorpion on the girl's thigh) and returns to the tables. Tommy stays behind, watching from the shadows as the scorpion tattoo comes to life, bites the young woman, and poisons her instantly. Upstairs, the "artist" wins yet another hand. Tommy returns in time to see him scoop up his winnings.

Curiosity piqued, Tommy follows the gambler outside, into an alley, and stabs him dead. "You're luck is going to be my luck now," he vows. He steals the magic tattoo needles and a wad of cash, and returns home. He lives with his grandfather, Lum Chen (Keye Luke), a traditional herbalist with a small shop, and his sister Linda (Meung Ling). Lum and Tommy fight about his gambling, and about the blood on his hands. (Not metaphorical blood; real, actual blood.) While he washes up, Lum snoops through Tommy's room and finds the case of needles. He is concerned, but luckily Lewis left one of his cards taped to the bottom of the box. Lum calls the number, and finds Jack, not Lewis. Either way, he wants to get rid of the needles and gives Jack the address. Tommy catches grandpa and hangs up the phone. Lum says the writing on the tattoo case suggest a "great evil" and he will not allow it into his home. "They are your death," Lum warns. Tommy hits Lum, takes the needles, and leaves.

Ryan, Jack, and Micki visit Lum, but Lum is unwilling to talk about the tattoo needles. He claims a robber broke in and stole them. Linda asks them to leave. Micki and Ryan didn't notice any signs of a break-in, but they did see a photo of Tommy, and start to realize Lum is protecting someone. Ryan gets the scoop from another local shop owner: Lum has a grandson, a compulsive gambler who owes everyone in Chinatown.

Tommy heads to an opium den, selects a passive woman on an opium high, rips open her dress, and starts inking her belly with a huge spider. When the simple outline tattoo is finished, he heads to his game. The spider comes to life and bites the woman. (Yes, it is a harmless tarantula, but the producers aren't going to use a poisonous arachnid.) Tommy wins his game, tips like a high roller, and runs into Frank on the way out. Frank takes all his money, leaving Tommy with $10 to "play" with. He still owes Frank money. Tommy returns home, apologizes to Lum, and promises him lots of money. Lum doesn't want it.

When Tommy leaves again to go to the club, Ryan follows him. He hunkers down while he watches Tommy tattoo a huge, scaly claw on some guy's chest. Tommy returns to the game, and Ryan continues sneaking through the basement. He comes across the scorpion victim's corpse and stumbles backwards, which draws the attention of scaly claw guy. He accuses Ryan of killing the girl, and believes he is there to get the secret of the good luck. They fight, but don't get very far: the claw comes to life, pops out of the guy's shirt, and strangles him dead. Upstairs, Tommy is winning.

Micki and Jack, meanwhile, have gone back to Linda and Lum. Neither of them wants to talk about it, until Linda quietly asks Micki if Tommy is really in trouble. When Micki confirms he is, she tells them where to find him.

Tommy has won eleven hands in a row, which draws the ire of the house manager. He accuses Tommy of cheating. Tommy gets indignant, but doesn't fight the charge. There are plenty of other games in town. Frank wants the rest of his money, and Tommy promises he will get it soon. Ryan follows the blissfully unaware Tommy out to the street, where he finds Micki and Jack. He explains how the curse works.

Back home, Lum catches Tommy stealing a couple of priceless Ming vases. Lum tries to stop him, but only succeeds in breaking the vases. Next stop for Tommy is a payphone, where he calls everyone he can to get in on a game. No one will help him out. He calls Frank, who is not happy about another extension. Tommy swears he will take any kind of game, any action at all. Franks considers this and tells him they will be in touch. He informs his goons the game is on.

Tommy waits for Frank at home. And he waits. And waits. Finally, Frank arrives. He has found a game for Tommy, the "ultimate game of chance." He gives him an address then leaves, but on the way out Frank runs into our trio of heroes. He forces them into his limo at gunpoint, and stashes them at a warehouse. He promises to let them go when Tommy returns with the money he is owed. Jack makes a misguided attempt to scare Frank into releasing them, and ends up getting hit upside the head. Some snooping reveals a huge stash of fireworks (talk about a stereotype) and the trio rigs the fireworks to blow the door open. They get a nice little show, too. They return to Lum, begging to know where Tommy went. When they tell him that Linda could be in grave danger, he softens and gives up the address Tommy went to. Micki heads there to keep an eye on Tommy, while Ryan and Jack go to the gaming club he frequents.

On his way to his new game, Tommy hunts for a victim. He first attacks an elderly cleaning man at the club, but Linda walks in and the man gets away. Linda just wants to help her brother, but Tommy's idea of help is to bind her and set about tattooing her. Ryan and Jack arrive after the tattoo comes to life: a big poisonous snake.

Tommy arrives at the address, a dark abandoned warehouse. He asks what game they are playing; the answer is simply "life or death." Tommy sits at a table with a single opponent, and a revolver is revealed. Russian roulette. Tommy isn't worried. The game begins, and Tommy shoots first. Nothing. Opponent: nothing. Round two: Tommy is safe. Opponent is safe. Third round, fifth bullet. Tommy tries not to laugh as he prepares for the final round. But Jack and Ryan got to Linda in time. Jack blows a tiny dart at the snake with a straw, killing it instantly. Ryan flicks it off and helps Linda to her feet. She is shocked that her brother would try to kill her. Tommy confidently squeezes the trigger—and a bullet blows through his head, killing him instantly. Everyone in the club gathers around the opponent in congratulations, leaving Micki enough time to check Tommy's pockets. She finds the tattoo needles and disappears.

Status: Tattoo needles retrieved.

* * *

"Tattoo" never found a place in my heart. Even as I again watched the series for this book, I started to doze a bit. I also started to fall asleep while writing this chapter. Maybe I was just really tired when I started this chapter; or maybe it just didn't capture my imagination.

I actually really like the idea of tattoos coming to life. Sounds like a great horror movie franchise, with limitless possibilities. But the characters felt so flat and one-dimensional. Tommy is wholly unlikable. There have been several gambling-themed episodes in *Friday the 13th*, and none of the gamblers has been as unsympathetic as Tommy. He is angry and thinks the world owes him. Even when he is begging for his thumb not to be cut off in the opening scene, I was rooting for amputation. (To be fair, I also really enjoy gore.) Plus, I have no sympathy for someone who beats up his grandpa. On the other side of things, Linda is nothing more than a casualty. Her only purpose in this episode is to be Tommy's final victim. Linda as the victim is supposed to elicit more suspense, more emotion, and show just how far Tommy had fallen: he would kill his own sister. But the siblings *never* feel close, so Tommy's betrayal doesn't feel any more severe than if she was a casual acquaintance. Regardless, she wasn't a particularly interesting or sympathetic character to feel concern for.

Fun fact: Keye Luke, the actor who played Lum Chen, was the same guy who sold the mogwai in *Gremlins*.

"The Electrocutioner"

Written by: Rob Hedden
Directed by: Rob Hedden
Original airdate: April 18, 1988
Cursed antique: Electric chair

Evanclaw Federal Penitentiary, 1978. Eli Pittman's (Angelo Rizacos) stay of execution has been denied, and he is strapped into the electric chair, sentenced to die for killing his girlfriend. With his last words he proclaims his innocence, then the switch is flipped, and Eli fries. The doctor checks on him and discovers he still has a pulse, so they give him another round of juice. This time the doctor declares Pittman dead, and he is wheeled away. As they are removing Pittman, his hand twitches and the doctor checks him again—this time, he has a pulse. Problem is, Pittman was sentenced to die, and the doctor already pronounced him. Legally they can't just throw him back in the chair. Instead they send him to the hospital, to see "what it did to him."

Haverstock Reform School, present day. Pittman is now working as a dentist to wards of the state under the name Lindheim. Dentistry was something he studied in the 1970s before he was "sidetracked." He relates to the kids as an orphan himself. "No one cares if you live or die," Pittman commiserates. The kids give Pittman the juice he needs to go on living: he electrocutes the kids in his dental chair, which is the actual electric chair that failed to kill him. The kids basically evaporate, leaving a heap of smoking clothing, which Pittman brushes aside so he can take his place in the chair and absorb the kids' power.

Pittman is not actually using the kids to preserve his own life. Their "life force" gives him the power to electrocute people, like a comic book villain. He uses this power to kill the men responsible for his wrongful conviction and botched execution. On this particular night, he visits District Attorney Kendricks, under the auspices of getting a professional opinion. Kendricks doesn't recognize Pittman until he reveals who he is. At that point, Kendricks shows Pittman out. Pittman removes his rubber gloves and grabs the doorknob, electrocuting Kendricks. He leaves the D.A. dead.

He gets the chair! Photo courtesy of Angelo Rizacos.

When one of the mailers Jack sent out to Dr. Lindheim is returned with no forwarding address, he and Ryan visit the prison from where the electric chair originated. The chair was installed in 1937 and killed eighteen men successfully. After it failed to kill Eli Pittman, the chair gained notoriety, was sold to a private collector, and never used again. Another man confessed to the murder Pittman was accused of. Warden Hobbs (Frank Adamson) always believed Pittman. The case was a legal embarrassment and Pittman was quietly released from prison eight months after his supposed execution. No one knows where he is now.

Further research back at Curious Goods yields a photo of those involved in the Pittman case. Jack recognizes Kendricks from the news last night—he was killed. Jack also sees that Pittman was a fourth year dental student when he was arrested. He assumed Dr. Lindheim was a medical doctor, but he could easily be a dentist and comes to the conclusion that Pittman and Lindheim are the same person.

Next on Pittman's hit list is Judge Avery, who presided over his trial. He calls upon the judge as he comes home. As soon as Pittman pulls back his hood, Avery recognizes him and warns him not to come any closer. Pittman doesn't need to: he grabs the metal railing of the stairs—the same one Avery is holding—and zaps the judge. Avery drops just as Micki and Ryan arrive, a little too late to warn the judge. Pittman sees them and gives chase. Ryan and Micki make it to the car, but Ryan has dropped the keys along the way. He locks the doors and warns Micki not to touch anything metal. Pittman grabs the hood ornament and lets loose a current. The car's electrical system goes haywire, but the cousins are unharmed. Pittman keeps trying to electrocute them until he is drained of power. He stumbles away, barely able to walk upright.

The team splits up, and Ryan visits Warden Hobbs again to get an ID on some of the others in the photo. He recognizes the jury foreman, but invites Ryan over for dinner so they can look through his files on the case and identify the others. Jack and Micki, meanwhile, head back to Haverstock.

Micki and Jack pay Mr. Downing a visit. Pittman sees this, and to avoid being outed, calls Downing, claiming an emergency that brings him to the exam room. Pittman injects him with a sedative immediately, then straps him to the chair and demands to know what he told "them." Downey doesn't understand what is going on or what info Pittman is looking for, even after Pittman starts drilling his teeth. When it becomes clear that Downing has no information, Pittman changes tactics and turns on the chair.

The screams and the flickering lights draw Micki and Jack to the exam room. They put on rubber gloves (which match their stylish rubber boots) and peek in. Micki recognizes Downey's clothes, and Jack recognizes the electric chair, but Pittman is gone, escaped out another door. Micki wants to take the chair and leave, but Jack assures her it isn't going anywhere. Pittman, on the other hand, is: he is fully charged and has more victims.

Jack makes a crude compass by rubbing a needle on the electric chair, and it leads them into the basement, straight to a transformer. Jack thinks it is an error, but Pittman is there, hiding, waiting. When Jack and Micki come face-to-face with him, they hide in a corner. Pittman studies them, seemingly weighing his options. Something makes him turn and leave, without harming them. I guess he decides revenge is more important than a couple of nosy antique dealers.

Micki and Jack return the electric chair to the vault. Ryan comes home after identifying the final man in the photo, the jury foreman. He's dead, too, but he died ten years ago, of cancer. As far as Ryan is concerned, they got the chair back and there are no other victims. Seems like a win. Micki is upset that they can't bring justice to a killer. Jack is a buzz kill—maybe Pittman isn't just killing the guys in the photo. In a collective realization, they figure out who Pittman's final victim is: Warden Hobbs. A phone call to Hobbs doesn't go through due to a conveniently placed storm, so our trio heads out to the warden's home.

Pittman is already at the warden's house. Mrs. Hobbs assumes he is Ryan and lets him right in. Pittman goes to "surprise" Hobbs in his study. Hobbs doesn't immediately recognize Pittman, but he knows he isn't Ryan. Ryan is at the door with Jack and Micki, trying to explain the situation to a very confused Mrs. Hobbs. Jack sends the womenfolk to get help while the boys take care of the homicidal killer.

Jack warns Hobbs away from Pittman, and he hides in a bedroom. While Ryan runs to get the jumper cables from the car, Jack taunts Pittman away from the warden. "We've got the chair," he mocks, and Pittman turns his rage to Jack. Ryan returns, clamps one end of the jumper cable to the radiator, and Jack clamps the other end to Pittman's hand. He fries—for real this time—and plunks down in a rocking chair, cooked from the inside out.

Status: The electric chair is vaulted. I still don't know how they fit it in, or how they ever fit anything else in there.

*　*　*

I'd like to say that this episode inspired my fear and distrust of dentists. But no, it was just good old-fashioned bad experiences with dentists. Writer/director Rob Hedden was also traumatized by dentists, which unsurprisingly was the inspiration for this episode: "As a child, I'd had some rough visits to the dentist. I remember being terrified of climbing into his big creepy chair, which I equated with torture. I've always been fascinated by electric chairs, as well: a piece of furniture explicitly designed to exterminate lives. I thought, *Hey, why not put those two ideas together?*

"'The Electrocutioner' was my first episode as both writer and director—not just on the *Friday* series, but career-wise, as far as scripted drama," Hedden continues. "With only documentaries to my credit, the producers were uncertain of my abilities behind the camera. Hell, despite my outer confidence, *I* was uncertain. Obviously a lot was riding on it. Screwing up was not an option, so I decided to face my fears and really go for it. I shot the dentist's flashbacks and delusions in hand-held grainy

16mm black and white, which broke a few rules, and then spent several late nights warping the images in post until they were just right. I'm sure [the producers] thought I was a lunatic, but they ultimately liked the end result and I was invited to direct another episode."

"Rob was fairly new to directing so we actually got together for dinner to talk about the show and TV and films and art," says the dentist himself, Angelo Rizacos. "That was a luxury that did not happen in season two and three as the schedules ramped up."

"Brain Drain"

Written by: Joshua Daniel Miller
Directed by: Lyndon Chubbuck
Original airdate: April 25, 1988
Cursed antique: Trephinator

Harry (Denis Forest) has an IQ below 60. He is barely functional, and part of Dr. Robeson's (Francois Klanfer) study of the evolution of intelligence. A friend interrupts Robeson and Harry's session, and Robeson takes him to preview his super-secret new project. In a private lab set in the middle of a museum storage room is a gorilla's brain, floating in a tank of fluid. There are wires connecting the brain to computers. Robeson has figured out how to transfer intelligence to a computer chip, enhance it, and send it back to the brain. The gorilla brain in the tank is smarter than Harry. Harry is spying on them, and he is smart enough to understand he is being denigrated. Before he leaves, Robeson has one more thing to show his friend: the trephinator.

"Of all the things I have collected over the years, this is probably the most useless," Robeson says proudly. It was used to drain fluid off the brain and spinal column in order to relieve pressure. But this particular appliance had been modified by some quack who believed it could transfer intelligence from one person to another via spinal fluid—a brain transplant without the brain. The donor sits on one side, and the recipient on the other. A lever is pulled, arms swing down, and a needle drives into the base of the brain, sucking fluid from the donor to the recipient. Robeson sees Harry lurking about after his friend leaves. Harry doesn't want to be stupid anymore. He forces Robeson into the donor chair—even straps him down—then sits in the recipient chair and pulls the lever. The fluids exchange, and Harry declares it is "my turn to be smart." He picks up a nail file and begins working on his nails, something that Robeson had done during their sessions.

Mail call at Curious Goods. A letter comes to them from Africa, talking about the trephinator. Jack finds it in the manifest, sold to Vincent Robeson, and Ryan daydreams about traveling to someplace exotic. No dice. Robeson moved back to town and took a job at the museum down the street. The trio head down to the museum, where Jack discovers that Robeson died about a month ago. He wandered right out into traffic and was hit by a car. Before they leave, Jack sees a woman he recognizes: Viola Rhodes (Carrie Snodgress). They flirt for a few minutes before she runs off to a meeting—but not before setting a dinner date. Jack explains to Micki and Ryan: Viola is a top linguistic anthropologist, and she and Jack were engaged many years ago. But Viola went to Kenya, and Jack set off on his third trip around the world. They hadn't seen each other since. While Micki is advising Jack on his love life ("You don't have to be Romeo, just be Jack"), Ryan does a little digging and discovers that Robeson's assistant, Dr. Stewart Pangborn, has taken over his research

A visit to Pangborn reveals that he, unsurprisingly, is Harry. He is meeting with Dr. Verner (Brian Paul), a nutritional biologist to develop a plan to feed the aquarium brain. Pangborn is pissed to have visitors and assures Jack he doesn't know anything about a trephinator. Once they leave, Verner inquires about the trephinator, and Pangborn is only too eager to show it off. But in Pangborn's version of the story, the device is used to measure intelligence by measuring the size of the skull. Verner is only too happy to try it out, and Pangborn gets his brain upgrade. As Ryan, Micki, and Jack leave the museum, they see Dr. Verner stumbling like a zombie through the hall. He trips down the stairs, dead on impact. Micki sees a deep puncture wound at the base of his skull.

Jack has dinner that night with Viola. We learn a little bit about Jack's past: he was married, she couldn't take his traveling, and they separated a long time ago. Viola is married to her work. She would like to tell Jack what she is working on, but she can't. It's top secret, but very exciting. As we later learn, Viola is there to teach the tank brain how to speak. After dinner, Jack takes Viola back to her hotel and she invites him up for a nightcap. He hems and haws, and Viola makes the first move: "At our age, let's not pussyfoot around." The two go back to her room.

As dawn breaks, Jack sneaks back into the store, where Micki and Ryan "catch him" with his shoes in his hand. The ultimate walk of shame. They were worried about Jack, but he claims he was never better. Like kids responding to a parent, they decide to ignore the obvious and fill Jack in on what they found: Verner died before Micki had a chance to speak to him, but the doctors told her he had the mental capacity of a two year old. Ryan discovered that, like Verner, Robeson had a puncture wound in the base of his skull. They decide it all ties back to Pangborn. The museum doesn't open for a few hours, so Jack decides to catch a nap before they head out.

Pangborn and Viola are working with the brain. She is extremely excited about the project, but doesn't think she will be able to teach it basic speech for several months. That's not good enough for Pangborn, for he has to present at a conference soon. Viola is frustrated: you can't rush a project like this. Pangborn wants to show her something (the trephinator) but she is late for a lunch date, so Pangborn lets her go. At lunch, Jack inelegantly asks Viola to marry him—he even still has her original engagement ring (which she mailed back to him after their first failed engagement). She says yes.

Micki and Ryan snoop through Pangborn/Robeson's files, but they can't find anything on Pangborn—until they come across Harry's file and match the picture to the person. Pangborn returns and hears them as they try to leave. He thinks Viola is back, but it soon becomes clear that it isn't her. The cousins hide as Pangborn skulks around, a large wooden stick as his protection. Security pages him and he abandons his search, allowing Ryan to unlock Micki from the human-sized crate she chose to hide in, which, it turns out, also contains a mummified corpse. They pop into Pangborn's lab, where Micki is fascinated by the living tank brain. They don't spend much time in there before security scares them away.

Back at the shop, Micki and Ryan are stressed and taking their frustrations out on each other. Ryan wants to go back to the museum and find the trephinator, but Micki thinks they should wait for Jack. "Face it—we are alone on this one!" Jack rushes in with a goofy grin on his face, and announces his engagement. The wind is taken out of his sails when Micki explains that Viola is in trouble. "She's with him!" Jack exclaims. The ride to the museum is a tense one.

Viola has returned to Pangborn's lab and apologizes for her earlier reaction. She wants to be part of the project. Pangborn is pleased, but first wants to show her something. As they approach the trephinator, he knocks her out. He puts her in the chair, takes his seat, and WHAM! Viola becomes part of his crazy scheme.

Jack, Ryan, and Micki are trying to find a way into the museum. Unsurprisingly, all the doors are locked tight. (What museum *doesn't* lock up at night? You know that shit comes alive and runs amok.) They hear a door open around back, and Micki finds the victimized Viola lying in a heap of old boxes. The only way to save her is to reverse the process. They make it inside and Jack sits with Viola in a safe place while the kids go find

Pangborn. Without saying it outright, Jack is willing to kill Pangborn to save his beloved. Jack can't sit still for long, and he breaks into Pangborn's lab. He isn't there, but Jack does find a tiny pistol.

Jack finds Pangborn in the storage area—or rather, they are stalking each other through the storage area. Pangborn jumps Jack, holds a razor to his throat, and takes the gun. He taunts Jack with all the intimate things he knows about him, thanks to Viola's brain juice. "Viola would never shoot me," Jack points out. Viola wobbles in and knocks over Pangborn, allowing Jack to get a few punches in. Pangborn points out the trephinator to Jack. "Which chair does she go in?" Jack snarls, a bulging, maniacal look on his face. The two scuffle, and Jack knocks him into a chair. Without warning (what warning could she give?) Viola pulls the lever. No one is in the other chair, so the lever crashes into the lab, through the tank, and into the floating brain. Pangborn gets whatever negligible smarts the brain has, and Pangborn's stolen intelligence just disappears.

Status: The trephinator is presumably obtained, but it joins a growing list of antiques that are too big for the vault. Jack is oddly peaceful about losing Viola: "We were apart most our lives, now she has just gone someplace else without me. Again." To a photo of Viola, he says, "Wait awhile darling. Maybe we can be together after all."

* * *

I wonder how this episode played in 1988, when the science of artificial intelligence was in a much different place. Was the floating gorilla brain utterly ridiculous or a real scientific possibility? I don't know a whole lot about artificial intelligence, but it seems to me that teaching a disembodied brain intelligence would be less artificial and more... I don't know, planted intelligence? Maybe in the 1980s that was where AI was going; now it seems to rely almost solely on computers and code. Similar techniques are being worked on currently, but instead of transferring intelligence into a biological brain, science is working on transferring it to computer chips.

Who better to talk to about this than the screenwriter himself, Josh Miller, who says he didn't base it on any specific theory of AI: "I would say it was pure science fiction, yet plausible. My favorite sci-fi writer was a British novelist named John Wyndham, who was published in the 1950s. He wrote *The Day of the Triffids*, *The Chrysalids*, and *The Midwich Cuckoos* (filmed twice as *Village of the Damned*), among others. What was common to all of them was that they were so plausible, and because of this, they were also cautionary tales. I loved how one could posit a dystopian future by extrapolating from events in the present. If the internal logic held up, the stories were way more impacting, as they seemed to say 'this really could happen!' which to me made them even more frightening.

"'Brain Drain' came about as a result of some macabre research," Miller continues. "I don't remember what initially got me onto this topic, but I remember reading about something called trephination. This was a technique employed in the early days of medicine as a treatment for relieving excess fluid on the brain. Doctors would bore a hole in the patient's skull and use a metal tube to drain off the fluid to relieve the pressure. It was like tapping a maple tree and just about as sophisticated. From there, I developed the idea that trephination might be a way to capture someone's intelligence by transferring spinal fluid from one person to another. Of course, the unfortunate donor would die in the process! This led to the creation of the cursed object that was called a 'Trephinator' which ended up looking like a back-to-back double electric chair with tubing attached to a couple of enormous needles positioned about neck-high. I remember getting some positive fan mail on this episode, as it seemed to really creep people out, which, of course, was the DNA of the series."

Story consultant Marc Scott Zicree offers an anecdote about "Brain Drain" that taught him never to worry about plagiarism. "Before I got hired as story editor, I came in to pitch to [executive story editor] Bill Taub. I whipped up a story called 'Brain Drain.' It was about an evil scientist who wants to win the Nobel Prize, and the object is one that he can use to drain the intellect of his colleagues, leaving them blithering idiots and making himself a super-genius. I pitched this, and they didn't buy it, but they hired me as story editor. I started writing 'Doctor Jack,' which was one they bought from that pitch [meeting]. Then I had to fly to Thailand for a pilot and I told Bill I would be gone for two weeks. While I was gone, a freelancer came in and pitched an episode called 'Brain Drain.' It was about a scientist using an evil object to drain the intelligence from his colleagues, making him a super-genius, blah blah blah. And Bill bought it! I ended up doing the rewrite on that script. The funny part was that writer had no access to my material. It was just that we were all in the same pop culture stew, it was a total coincidence, including the title.

"I mentor a lot of young writers, and what they are most afraid of is that someone is going to steal their ideas. Many of them feel they have been ripped off. I always tell them that story. You would think, because it was that exact story, and that exact title, that I would have been ripped off. But I wasn't. It was a total coincidence. That lesson taught me to *never* worry about plagiarism. Ever. Even if people do rip me off—which has happened on occasion—I don't worry about it.

"The funny part is that Bill didn't even remember that I pitched it a few months earlier. Mine wasn't a trephinator, it was some other object," Zicree concludes. He doesn't recall the item.

One of the things that I discovered about this episode as an adult was that each time Pangborn gets a new donor, his affectation changes a bit, to reflect what he has "learned." With Robeson, it was filing his nails; with Verner it was taking on a touch of his German accent; with Viola, his voice softened a bit and he knew "intimate details" about Jack. It makes sense as an adult, but as a kid, it went right over my head.

"The Quilt of Hathor"

Written by: Janet MacLean
Directed By: Timothy Bond
Original Airdate: May 2 and 9, 1988
Cursed antique: Quilt

Micki, Ryan, and Jack get a visit from Sarah Good (Helen Carscallen) of the Pentitite colony. The Pentitites are a cloistered religious sect, much like the Amish: they live without electricity or modern conveniences, forbid music and dancing, and speak with a lot of "thees" and "thous." Sarah bought a quilt (innocently) from Uncle Lewis, one that "aroused dreams and feelings I didn't know I had." According to the manifest, it was sewn in the 1890s by Salem women following the occult. The quilt was stolen, and because the Pentitites are a secret and closed order, it had to have been taken by one of the followers. Micki and Ryan will go undercover as Sarah's niece and nephew to find the quilt.

The quilt is in the hands of the plain Effie Stokes (Kate Trotter). When she sleeps under the quilt, her dreams become someone else's nightmares. Her dream of choice is set in a French Revolution-era ball, where she dances with Reverend Josiah Grange (Scott Paulin), the leader of the Pentitites. In her first dream, the reverend's betrothed, Jane, falls from the second story onto the ballroom floor. In real life, Jane falls out of bed, breaks her neck, and dies.

The reverend is mourning Jane when Sarah brings Micki and Ryan into the community. The church is the center of the town, and their lives. Unmarried men and women sleep at separate ends of a dormitory, and the Pentitites don't take kindly to jokes about them "meeting in the middle." They are greeted by Laura Grange (Carolyn Dunn), the reverend's daughter. Ryan is instantly attracted to her, but she is (unhappily) engaged to the carriage driver, Matthew (Diego Matmoros). All marriages are chosen by the elders, and Laura's marriage was set when she was seven. The wedding will be in one week, when Laura turns twenty.

After an uncomfortable communal dinner, Ryan wants to search the rooms. With no locks on the doors, it should be easy. But Sarah warns that it is 7:00 p.m. Most will be in bed by then. Instead, Ryan decides to take a look outside ("Who can sleep at 7:00 p.m.?") He sees Laura slip into the stables and follows her. She is singing a lullaby while she feeds her horse. Ryan surprises her and they add a little bit of dancing to the lullaby. Suddenly Matthew attacks Ryan, throwing him into a pile of hay, a razor blade to his throat. "I saw the sin of lust in his eyes!" He has watched Laura, longed for her, his whole life (creepy) but Laura reminds him that they have laws, and murder is not their way.

Their way is a hearing before Reverend Grange. The reverend insists it is not a trial, but a "gathering of friends." It sure looks like a trial to me. Matthew testifies, claims that Ryan is an adulterer and should be banished. Neither Ryan nor Laura are married, so it technically can't be adultery, but when Matthew explains that they were dancing, the audience gasps. Laura takes the blame, admitting to the forbidden singing, a lullaby her mother sang to her before her death. Ryan admits he danced with her, and Micki jumps to his defense: "He didn't know it was wrong. In our world, everybody dances!" The reverend rules that, while here, Ryan must obey their rules, and forbids him to go near his daughter. I guess it isn't a trial because it is so blatantly biased.

The town elders hold their regular business meeting. There seems to be financial questions about the colony, and the heads of the Penitite religion want to do an audit. Reverend Grange is offended at the thought, so they switch to another, no-less-touchy topic: his wife. It has been six months since Laura's mother died, and a few weeks since Jane died. Next to the reverend, his wife is the second most powerful, important person in the colony, and should the reverend die, she would take over the colony. Effie suggests it should be someone around his age (Jane was his daughter's age) and who commands respect. If you haven't guessed by now, Effie is desperately in love with Josiah Grange. The reverend agrees.

Effie practices her engagement acceptance in her contraband hand mirror. "Those who shunned me will be at my beck and call." Micki targets Effie's room for a search; something about her "gives me the creeps." Effie is behind the door when Micki comes in, and she doesn't see her. Micki digs through her chest and finds the mirror, at which point Effie reveals herself, scaring the mirror right out of Micki's hand. Micki claims that she thought she was in Aunt Sarah's room, to help with her sewing. She apologizes for the mirror, but Effie is more concerned about being caught with a mirror. "If you tell, I will see you suffer." She throws Micki out of the room.

Dinner rolls around, and Reverend Grange stands with an announcement about who he plans to wed. Effie smoothes her hair, expecting to be a lock, but instead he asks Rebecca Lamp, the cook. Rebecca, naturally, accepts.

After dinner, Ryan finds Laura in the stables. Even though he was barred from seeing her, Ryan couldn't stay away. "Ever since I first saw you... ." His voice trails off, but Laura agrees. Matthew calls for Laura, and she buries Ryan in a haystack before he comes in. Matthew offers to help feed the horse, totally missing out on the fact that Laura bonds with the horse while feeding it by hand. He digs a pitchfork into the haystack Ryan is buried in, and shovels a ton of hay into the stall. "She's had enough," Laura insists. Matthew, satisfied that he has helped his wife-to-be, stabs the pitchfork back into the hay, and they leave. Matthew vows not to leave her alone until they wed. Just what Laura wants to hear.

Blood oozes from the hay stack.

Effie goes to sleep and dreams that she and Josiah are feeding one another. But Rebecca is there, making eyes at him, so Effie pours a vial of poison into her drink. As Rebecca sputters and foams at the mouth in the dream, Effie and Josiah dance. In real life, Rebecca foams at the mouth and dies.

Micki rushes through the colony, looking for Ryan. She finds him in the stable, still buried beneath the hay. She helps him out and removes the pitchfork (which went through his arm) and gives him the "I told you so" bit, but Ryan is smitten, so it doesn't sink in. Bells go off in the community, and the two rush to the center of town, where they discover Rebecca has died in her sleep. Ryan's first instinct is to go check on Laura; Micki reminds him they are there to get the quilt.

The reverend buries his second fiancée in as many weeks, and Micki assumes it has to be the quilt. "Someone who hates the reverend enough to kill his fiancées," Ryan suggests. Micki, with a woman's touch, adds: "Or loves him." Ryan catches up with Laura, but for once he means to talk to her about business: who might want to marry her father. Many would like to, Laura muses, but admits Effie Stokes has been infatuated with him for as long as she can remember. Ryan leans in and kisses Laura, timidly at first; more passionately when she doesn't pull away. Matthew jumps out of nowhere, tackles Ryan, and threatens to bash his head in with a rock. The reverend sees all this and decides they will settle this the old way: with a cleansing.

A wooden platform is built in a triangle shape above a flaming pit of coals. The men will fight, and the loser will fall into the coals. Micki finds it barbaric, but as Sarah points out, "the colony will be cleansed." They are both given long poles and dance around, American Gladiators-style. Ryan doesn't want to hurt him, but Matthew baits him. Ryan nearly falls in, but gets his bearings and starts whomping Matthew with the flaming end of the stick. (Surely that cannot be regulation.) Ryan knocks Matthew off the platform, and leaps down, the victor. Micki thinks he is coming to hug her, but instead he throws his arms around Laura, and the two walk off together.

Sarah saw Effie's disappointment when she was passed over to marry the reverend, and her delight at the funeral. She goes through Effie's belongings and finds the quilt in a secret compartment at the bottom of her chest. Effie catches Sarah, kicks her out, and lies down to sleep. Micki finds Sarah, who recommends she be complacent about Ryan. She does inform Micki that Effie has the quilt, but she was caught before she could take it.

Effie dreams of Sarah as a scrubwoman, who she tosses a candelabrum on, engulfing her in flames. In real life, Sarah leaves a candle burning on her nightstand. In the throes of a nightmare, she knocks the candle over, setting her drapes alight. The fire is put out before too much property damage occurs, but Sarah is dead. After hearing this, Micki goes straight to Effie and demands the quilt. "Quilt?" she asks innocently, while waving her arms over the bed, where the quilt is laid out. Micki grabs the quilt without a fight, which drives me crazy. She is way too smart to fall for such a blatant move. Accusations fly (Micki is called a thief; Effie is called a murderer) but Ryan drags Micki out of there. "Who do you want to call as a witness, the sandman?"

As soon as morning breaks, Micki is packing. Ryan comes to her room and tells her he is staying. She doesn't believe him at first. "This place is all wrong for you. You love hot dogs and Saturday morning cartoons." (Who doesn't?) Ryan has found something more important—and not just Laura. Yes, he is in love with her, but he also loves the way of life, the sense of purpose he has with the Pentitites. Realization sets in, and Micki grows mad. Ryan tries to hug her; she pulls away. "I can't do it alone." "You're strong. You don't need me anymore," he insists gently. She grabs her bags and the quilt, and runs from the room. At the doorway, without turning around, she says "I'll miss you." She runs to her carriage and rides away without looking back.

Micki is a mess when she returns to Curious Goods. Jack comes downstairs, welcomes her home—then realizes Ryan isn't with her. "He's not coming home," she explains. Jack is flummoxed, but he tries to rationalize that if that is what Ryan wants, he has to follow his own path.

To change the subject, Micki proudly informs Jack that "We... I got the quilt." He spreads it over the desk while he tells her about the curse on it, then picks it up. The corner catches on the desk, and there is an audible rip. "Oh no," he murmurs, then pulls out his lighter and sets the corner of the quilt on fire to test his theory. "The real quilt can't be destroyed," he reminds Micki. "It's a fake!"

Ryan is now a full-fledged Penitite. He is approached by Elder Florence, looking for the reverend. Seeing as how she is speaking to "Sarah's kin," she tells him that she has seen the quilt with her own eyes. This doesn't shock Ryan at all, even though Micki was supposed to have left with the quilt days ago. She confirms Effie has it, and Ryan insists they get it. Florence will only give it to Reverend Grange, which is fine by Ryan, just so long as Effie doesn't have it.

Florence makes Ryan wait downstairs while she pilfers through Effie's belongings. She has no trouble finding the secret compartment in her chest, but Effie walks in on her taking the quilt. There is an argument, and Effie wrests it out of Elder Florence's hands. She throws her out, then curls up beneath the blanket right there on the floor (even though her bed is inches away).

In Effie's dream, Florence is serving Effie big chunks of ham from a huge buffet. Florence drops the two-tined serving fork, and Effie picks it up for her. Rather than handing it back, she taunts Florence with the utensil until finally jabbing it her eyes. In real life, Florence has collapsed in the hallway and claws her own eyes out. Ryan is the first to respond to Florence's screams, and before he can get to Effie, a couple men drag him back downstairs.

The reverend can't catch a break. Brother Fraser has just returned from the main Penitite colony, where the council has concerns over Reverend Grange's leadership. Among their problems with him are his inability to choose (and hold on to) a wife, the fear that he has let witchcraft into the town, and that he has promised his only daughter to an outsider. (So, I guess Laura and Ryan are betrothed at this point.) Then he has to deal with Elder Florence's death.

The reverend takes Ryan into his office. "Since you arrived, four of our own have died," Grange points out, then says some are accusing Ryan of witchcraft. "They are right—it's the power of Satan." The reverend thinks he is being mocked, and Ryan explains the curse, and that Effie has the quilt. The reverend seems mystified; why would she kill? "She loves you, always has," Ryan explains. The reverend is not apt to believe Ryan,

On the set of "The Quilt of Hathor." Photo courtesy of John LeMay.

whom he has known for two weeks, over Effie, whom he has known since they were children. The reverend promises to consider all the options, and forbids Ryan from discussing it with anyone else.

At dinner that night, the reverend has an important announcement: in an effort to stabilize the colony and and stave off the death of yet another betrothed, he was secretly wed this afternoon. To Effie Stokes. This seems to be the reverend's solution to his problems with the council: he gains stability for the colony *and* gains access to a nifty magical weapon.

That night, Effie spreads out the quilt, to ensure dreamless sleep. She waits anxiously for her first night of wedded bliss, and is highly disappointed when the reverend goes right to sleep. Effie feels slighted and decides to retreat into her dream world.

In her dream, Effie and Josiah dance, a formal Victorian dance, spinning in circles. Effie grabs a knife off the buffet and holds it, threateningly, to Josiah's back. Suddenly the two of them are dressed in their plain Penitite clothing, spinning outside in the snow. It is dream world versus dream world—and Josiah wins. In his dream, Effie drops the knife and the reverend dips her, breaking her back in half. The same happens in Effie's own dream. The reverend wakes suddenly. He ended up under the quilt, in a chair across the room. Effie is still in bed, her back broken and her head dangling off the bed. He wraps Effie in a non-cursed quilt and hides her in the shed beneath his house.

Ryan is waiting for the reverend the next morning. Reverend Grange had hoped taking Effie as a wife would mean she would reveal where the quilt is. He actually had it in his hands, but when he woke, Effie and the quilt were gone. Later, when Ryan and Laura are feeding the chickens, he voices his concerns about her father's story. Laura, naturally, is offended.

Inquisitor Holmes arrives early for his inspection of Reverend Grange's colony. Matthew meets with him first, and tries to pin the blame on Ryan. Holmes isn't buying it: council policy is to encourage converts, and he suggests Matthew do the same. The reverend comes in, and Holmes asks about a quilt. Apparently it is all anyone can talk about. The reverend blows off the question, claiming it wasn't stolen, but mislaid. He leaves nervously.

That night, the reverend tells Ryan that the inquisitor has ordered his expulsion. He has one hour to leave. Laura comes by to check on him. They have since made up. Checking to see that no one is in the hallway, she shuts the door (harlot!) and promises to write him often. They exchange pretty words, and while the question is still on Ryan's lips, she tells him she could never leave the Pentitites. Matthew interrupts their kiss to tell him that Holmes wants to see Ryan.

This is clearly a plan concocted between Matthew and the reverend, for when Grange sees Ryan head to the inquisitor, he wraps himself in the blanket. At the hall, where Holmes has been working, he struggles to stay awake. It is no use, and he slumbers. He is struck by nightmares, and Ryan comes in as he is screaming. He tries to wake the elder up, but Holmes grabs a letter opener and stabs himself with it. Fraser and other elders enter the hall in time to see Ryan pulling the blade from Holmes' chest. "It was you!" Back in his house, the reverend wakes to the sound of the bell. "Try to unseat me, inquisitor? Witchcraft here? Never!"

Micki and Jack have been trying to make their way to the Penitite colony, but problems with the fuel pump on the Mercedes kept them away. It is now that they arrive, to find an utter circus. Ryan is put on trial before Reverend Grange, but it is less of a trial than Ryan's first hearing was; this is more of a sentencing. When Micki and Jack try to speak out in defense of Ryan, the "outsiders" are removed. Ryan maintains he did not kill Inquisitor Holmes, and instead accuses the reverend. Grange rages and sentences Ryan to death: burn at the stake, of course. As he is being dragged outside, he begs Laura to go look for the quilt.

Ryan is tied to the stake, and a woman sings a hymn (I guess they do allow *some* music in the colony). The townspeople ready their torches, as any good mob should. Laura, meanwhile, rummages through her father's house, looking for the quilt. In a last-ditch effort, she checks the storage shed.

The fire is lit, and flames lick at Ryan's shoes. Micki and Jack beg for mercy. Laura comes running out, a bloody quilt in her arms, and wastes no time tossing snow on the fire while she explains. The quilt was made by her mother, and she found it wrapped around the corpse of Effie Stokes, and shoved into the shed under Reverend Grange's house. Ryan is removed from his stake, and Fraser leads a team to check out the shed. All the while, the reverend rants, nearly hysterical, and calls for Ryan to be burned. At this point, no one listens to him. He gallops off on horseback; he is going to get the quilt.

Ryan and Laura take the horse carriage and follow the reverend back to the mill. Grange barricades himself inside and goes upstairs, where he has hidden the quilt. Ryan breaks in and finds Grange trying to take a nap. He grows weak and collapses, but has enough strength to grab the quilt away from Grange. The men have an actual tug-o-war over the quilt. Laura urges Ryan to let go, and he does. The sudden change in tension causes Grange to fall backwards, through the window, and land on a pile of wood below. He is dead beneath the quilt.

Status: The quilt is returned. Ryan returns to the store with Jack and Micki, and responsibility for the colony falls to Laura. I can't help but wonder, if she gets married, does the primary responsibility for the colony remain with Laura, or fall to her husband?

*   *   *

My first time seeing "The Quilt of Hathor" was actually when the two episodes aired together, as a TV movie. It was one of those Saturday afternoon matinees that are usually a zero-star affair that the network can get for next to nothing. I found it by accident, flipping through channels and seeing someone who looked suspiciously like Ryan in quaint clothing. I decided to watch it for a little bit—I was deep into my *F13* obsession at this point. A woman who looked awfully close to Micki appeared. That couldn't be a coincidence. A quick check in the *TV Guide* revealed that I was not wrong.

Director Tim Bond remembers shooting it like movie. Instead of the normal eight days prep he had per episode, he got sixteen, then shot both episodes straight through. Of course, this was still a TV series with TV budgets and timelines, so had roughly fourteen days to shoot a "movie" under $1 million. "I think it did pretty well for Paramount, because I'm still getting residuals," remarks Bond. "They must be selling it somewhere."

The Pentitites are, surprisingly, not a patriarchy. I am not a religious person but one of the things that always pissed me off was the almost universal patriarchy of traditional religion. The female Pentitites—or at least what we see of them—are not just baby machines. They are equal to the men in the business meetings, and the reverend's wife is the second most powerful person in the sect. Of course, they are also forced into arranged marriages at a young age, and their honor can be won in gladiator fights, so…

This strong female point of view is largely due to a woman scripting the episode. Writer Janet MacLean took pride in being one of the first female writers on *Friday the 13th: The Series*. "There is a persistent bias that women can't write action or suspense/horror as well as male writers," MacLean told me. "It didn't offend me—it was part of the air we breathed at that time.

"The story idea was mine from the start," says MacLean. "I'd just spent time in Cape Breton admiring quilts, so my thoughts turned that way when I was coming up with cursed objects. The quilt seemed to me a very feminine object, and one that allowed for a female villain, which interested me. I also liked the idea of a gothic Puritanical sect that repressed sexuality so deeply it erupted into unconscious explosions of violence. [For example, Matthew.] And I liked the chance to set up a *Witness*-style romance between Ryan and a chaste member of the sect.

"The Pentitites weren't based on any sect in particular," MacLean continues. "I was raised Catholic, so the penitential elements—the guilt and sexual repression—were very familiar. The rest was a hodgepodge of Mennonite, Amish, and Puritan, laced with gothic."

Actress Kate Trotter, who played Effie Stokes, had some familiarity with playing someone from a puritanical sect. Early in her career, Trotter was in a play about the Amish in World War I. "I was young and brave then. I would drive up the driveway and their buggies would be there, and I would just say, 'I'm doing this play and I wondered if I could talk to some people about what it feels like to be Amish,'" says Trotter. "I can't tell you how wonderful they were. One woman I am thinking of in particular showed me her clothing and how it was made. So, I had a real insider's look, a warm and intimate knowledge about the Amish. I didn't feel like they were cultish or spooky or scary or any of the things that I think sometimes those religious sects can evoke in people.

"I didn't have a sense of playing some kind of weird person. I had a sense of playing a real person, in a real situation, even given the oddity of the show—which was quite odd," continues Trotter. "I had no problem flinging myself into the 'truth' of it. I guess I felt a kind of loyalty to a world that had thoughts about religion and reasons for doing things that were different from mine."

Scott Paulin, who played Josiah Granger, also had some experience playing this kind of role. "I tried to base the character on another character I had played on stage, an obscure play by Albert Innaurato called *Wisdom Amok*. Father Wisdom was a grandiloquent and loony priest much like Josiah." Looking back, Paulin was never sure he did the role justice, but "it was really fun trying." He remembers Trotter being very supportive and encouraging.

One of the most difficult parts of shooting *Friday the 13th*, a comment I have heard over and over, was how damn cold it was while shooting. "Quilt of Hathor" was no different. Most of the shooting took place in a Shaker community that was a tourist attraction in the summer, but closed in the winter. "The place is just as it would have been in the nineteenth century with no electricity or running water," Paulin recalls. "During the filming it was bone-snapping cold in Toronto and no amount of underlying warm clothing could keep out the chill. I'm sure my years in Southern California hadn't properly prepared me for Toronto, and no doubt the locals thought I was a real lightweight, but I mainly remember trying desperately to keep my mind off the creeping numbness in my extremities while ranting and raving."

Story consultant Marc Scott Zicree has but half a memory of this episode: "I remember, in-house, Bill [Taub] and I were not pleased with 'Quilt of Hathor,' but I don't remember why." MacLean was pretty surprised when she saw the final cut on television. "I'd written a fight between Ryan and Matthew, but it hadn't included a fiery pit! I remember watching that scene in total amazement."

"Double Exposure"

Written by: Durnford King
Directed by: Neill Fearnley
Original airdate: May 16, 1988
Cursed antique: Camera

A murderer has the city on edge. He has killed eight victims with a machete, and not left a shred of evidence. He does, however, call local news reporter Winston Knight (Gary Frank) during his live broadcast—which he takes on air—to tell him where to find the bodies. This drives Knight's ratings through the roof, and he dreams of a Pulitzer.

Of course, Winston Knight is the one behind the murders, and one of Uncle Lewis' objects is helping him out.

Knight has an antique camera. He takes a photo of himself, then when developing it in his private darkroom, an exact humanoid duplicate crawls out of the bubbling, frothing chemicals. Knight gives it a task, which is normally to kill, then has him call him on-air at a specified time. Knight gets the recognition and notoriety, and has a perfect alibi should there be any witnesses. Of course, there weren't any witnesses for the first eight victims. The ninth, that's a different story.

Ryan is on a date with Cathy (Catherine Disher), a girl he picked up when she came into Curious Goods. He takes her home, then is walking home himself when he hears a scream. Heading towards the noise, he sees Winston Knight machete-ing a woman to death in an alley. The murderer lunges at Ryan, who fends him off with a crate. "Knight" can't stick around too long; he has instructions to follow. The clone calls into the news desk to tell Knight where he can find the body. After the show, Knight burns the film negative. His double turns into a charred outline of a human form on the sidewalk.

Ryan returns to Cathy's house and gives a statement to the police. He swears the murderer was Winston Knight, even though he was on the air at the time. The detective calls the news station, and Knight is still there.

Ryan returns to the store, waking Micki and Jack. She confirms she watched Knight on the eleven o'clock news, and the killer called in. She suggests the person Ryan saw was wearing a mask or makeup. Ryan wants to check the manifest, but Jack waves him off; he would have recognized Winston Knight's name. Besides, "What kind of object could it possibly be?" (Jack, you've been doing this long enough. You should know the answer is pretty much *any object*.) After a nightmare-filled sleep, Ryan is all dressed up, in what Micki refers to as his "asking for a loan" clothes. She fixes his tie while he explains that Knight has agreed to meet with him.

Knight summons a new double, but when Ryan and Cathy arrive early, he hides the duplicate in his darkroom. Knight is glad that Ryan called: "We belong to a select club that no one wants to join." He wants to work with Ryan to catch the Machete Killer; he will even give Ryan full credit. Ryan still can't get over how much the killer looked like Knight, who vaguely suggests the killer had plastic surgery to resemble him. He cuts the meeting short but insists on talking to them later.

Outside, Ryan offers to give Cathy a ride home, but she has some shopping to do. If being Ryan's girlfriend didn't do it, this decision guarantees her death. They kiss goodnight and Ryan leaves. Cathy barely takes two steps before she realizes she left her purse in Knight's house. Through the window, she sees Knight talking… to himself. Literally. She spies on them as the clone asks why Knight must always destroy him. "Because that's how it is, it's either you or me. You have five hours to exist," Knight tells him. Knight sees Cathy watching them. She runs in fear; Knight empties her purse and passes her keys on to the clone.

Micki and Ryan are watching the nightly news while they wait for Jack to come home. Ryan can't get over how creepy Knight was, blowing off his every question. Jack returns from "prospecting." He made a list of all the manifest items that could create a duplicate: mirrors, prisms, paintings, etc. He came up with a camera, and found one sold to Kahn. No first name, no address. It took him awhile, but he finally realized it wasn't a name; it was TV station call letters. Sure enough, when the camera was purchased, Knight worked at the TV station KAHN. The trio leave the shop.

Cathy attempts to call for help from a payphone, but Clone-Knight attacks the box, so she hops into a cab and goes home. She keeps a spare key under the mat and calls Ryan. Ryan isn't home, so she leaves a panicked message telling him what she saw. Clone-Knight clicks on the TV and reveals himself to Cathy, who tries to slow him down by throwing vases at him. She hides in the closet, but machete beats wooden door and

Cathy is slaughtered. The clone wanders around in a haze for a little bit. When he is nearly hit by a car, the driver angrily yells, "You trying to kill yourself?" The clone considers this. "No. I want to live."

When they return to the store, Micki plays the message from Cathy. Jack and Ryan rush to her house, which is now a crime scene. Ryan sobs and Jack reminds him that, like always, "we are on our own." They return to the store, where Micki tries to comfort Ryan, but he is there for a few minutes when he decides he is going to get Knight.

Outside the TV station, Ryan jumps Knight as he is about to burn the Cathy-killing clone. He threatens the reporter, who is worried that he dropped the negative. Ryan grabs the negative and takes off back to the shop. He is as proud as he can be under the circumstances, for retrieving the negative. According to Jack, his research on cameras and the

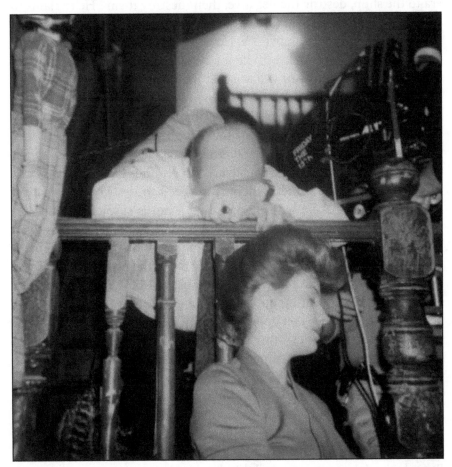

Working 18+ hour days means you nap wherever you can. Photo courtesy of Louise Robey.

occult revealed that a duplicate, living in a photo negative, can only exist for about five hours. If the negative isn't destroyed before then, the original dies and the clone takes its place. Jack wants to use the negative to blackmail Knight into giving him the camera: they literally hold his life in their hands. Ryan doesn't care about getting the camera back; he just cares about sending Knight to hell. When Jack points out that killing Knight doesn't necessarily mean the killings will stop, Ryan agrees to let Jack set up a hand-off.

Jack arrives at Knight's house. His associates have the negative, and they will destroy it the minute he returns with the camera. Knight plays along—then knocks Jack out and snaps a photo of him. When Jack wakes, he is bound and staring at an exact duplicate of himself. In typical bad-guy fashion, Knight reveals his plans: he tells Clone-Jack to take the camera to the shop, destroy the negative, then "destroy them." He explains to Jack that his duplicate will kill two more people (Micki and Ryan), then confess to the murders on live TV. He will stay alive long enough so that Jack dies, then Clone-Jack will die for being the Machete Killer. (Watch this scene closely, and you will see that the Clone-Jack, just slightly out of focus, is Chris Wiggins' stunt double.) He calls his producer and tells him and a crew to meet him at Curious Goods. Clone-Knight is watching through the window and overhears the diabolical plan.

"Jack" arrives at Curious Goods and Micki takes the camera straight to the vault. But he wants the negative. Ryan reminds him they have both the negative and the camera; there is no need to destroy the negative. Jack is insistent that he have the negative. Ryan is suspicious, but goes to get it while "Jack" rips the phone cord from the wall. Jack meets Ryan downstairs, and Ryan tells him "Good thing you didn't break the camera on the way over here." "It was the only way to get the negative back. I was extra careful." Ryan kicks the clone away, just as Micki comes in, and he explains why he is beating up "Jack." Clone-Jack gets the negative, but before he can leave he is set upon by the now-sentient Clone-Knight. The two duplicates battle each other with their machetes. Clone-Knight cuts off Clone-Jack's hand, and from his stump oozes a pale greenish goo, the same goo that bubbles out of Clone-Jack's torso when Clone-Knight stabs him. Ryan grabs the negative from Clone-Jack's amputated hand, but before he can burn it, he sees Clone-Knight has his weapon to Micki. Ryan moves forward slowly, negative proffered in his outstretched hand, then stabs Clone-Knight with an awl. He leaks the same liquid, but Micki and Ryan don't stick around to watch his demise.

Outside, Knight's film crew is set up, despite producer Phil's concerns that they should call the cops and let them handle it. Micki and Ryan race out, taking Knight by surprise. He tries to cover by saying he didn't know anyone was inside, but when his duplicate stumbles out, Knight tells the camera crew to cut. Phil insists they keep rolling. Knight demands the negative from his clone, but the clone is no fool. He crumples it in his hand, and the real Knight slowly fades from sight. The duplicate is ecstatic. "I'm alive!" he exclaims proudly. But he is still injured, and the goo from his stab wound has been replaced by blood. He collapses, dead.

Status: The camera is safe in the vault. I guess Knight really did give Clone-Jack the correct camera.

*　*　*

Well, that was fast. Last week Ryan was betrothed to Laura Granger; this week he is dating the adorable Cathy Steiner. He cried more about losing Cathy than he did Laura. Then again, Laura wasn't brutally slaughtered. "I can't keep a girlfriend!" laments John LeMay. "It became a running joke. Pity the poor girl who got cast as my love interest, because she was not long."

This episode is a good example of *Friday the 13th* being ahead of its time. In 1988, reality television was virtually non-existent; *TMZ* was entirely non-existent; and the news was actually fact-checked and relevant. In 2015, not only do people like Winston Knight exist, they are even making Oscar-nominated movies about them. In *Nightcrawler* (2014), Jake Gyllenhaal plays a news stringer whose attempt to get the bloodiest footage ends with him eventually staging the violence so he can be first on the scene.

Director Neill Fearnley explains how he got some of the effects shots in the episode: "The double climbing out of the developing tray was done practically. First we built a set that had a table with a false bottom and placed a tray that had an opening in the center but a lip around the edge, into which we could put the dry ice. An actor hid below the table and was brightly lit from down there and simply had to stand up. This way it appeared as if he was coming out of the tray. For the wide shot we also took away the table to shoot the legs of Winston Knight standing behind the table and the room beyond. Using a split screen we made it appear as if it was a normal table.

"In another shot, done in one take without any cuts, I wanted to have Chris [Wiggins] and Gary [Frank] appear both as themselves and doubles, by moving the camera to find each of them as needed in the story. To do this we built the set that played for Knight's house with hidden doors. We had a double for Chris to play out of focus for a moment when they were both in the shot, and a double for Gary to answer the phone. Then, as the camera moved, the two actors, with the help of crew members, quickly dashed from spot to spot. We had to untie and retie Chris quickly, then swap out Gary with a double answering the phone as he raced around the set to appear in the window as the phone call is made. That shot was a lot of fun to design and pull off."

"I think I looked like a good victim back then: long hair, big eyes," says Catherine Disher, who played Cathy. She certainly remembers her death scene. "It was very closely choreographed. To achieve that slightly 3D effect, they had me throwing objects as close as I could to the camera lens. I was very worried about actually hitting the camera, or Gary Frank, whose point of view the camera was filming. I think it was all done in one shot, too, which was also nerve wracking. I liked the fact that my actual death was off camera. For me, that made it much more frightening.

"When I went to do ADR, I had to do some screaming for my off-camera death, I guess," Disher continues. "The sound engineer thought that I was such a good screamer that he asked me to do a whole bunch of extra screaming that they could use in future episodes."

Of the three episodes he wrote for the series ("The Poison Pen," "The Great Montarro," "Double Exposure") Durnford King liked "Double Exposure" the most. "Primarily because of the visual treatment—but as with children it's very hard to chose one over the other." This was also one of story supervisor Bill Taub's favorite episodes, which he also likens it to *Nightcrawler*, "but we did it twenty-five years ago!"

"The Pirate's Promise"

Written by: Carl Binder
Directed by: Bill Corcoran
Original airdate: June 27, 1988
Cursed antique: Foghorn

Joe Fenton (Cedric Smith) takes a date out to his old, creepy lighthouse. She finds it spooky; he says it is part of the charm. Inside, Joe has a huge collection of weapons from sailors and pirates, but what he really wants to show her is the light. What he doesn't show her is the knife he hides behind his back. Upstairs, he blows an antique foghorn. Through the mist, a ship appears. It seems to just be sitting there, waiting. Joe claims he doesn't see it, then stabs her. He delivers the girl to a guy in a dinghy in the name of Abel Mercer. The guy tosses Joe a few gold doubloons before returning to his ship with the girl.

Micki and Ryan roll into Whaler's Point after town historian Dewey Covington (Thomas Hauff) calls them in response to their mailer. He sold an old foghorn to a man who ran the lighthouse. He died last year; Joe Fenton has taken up the mantle. Micki enjoys leafing through the old history books, so Dewey gives them a quick history lesson: Whaler's Point was settled by pirates, who decided to give up life on the high seas and become whalers. Rumors of buried pirate treasure continue to this day. On their way up to the lighthouse, Barney (Bernard Behrens), the town drunk, warns them against going up there. Barney lived at Whaler's Point his whole life, and one of his ancestors was part of Angus McBride's crew. McBride was one of the founders of Whaler's Point in 1717. In 1720, it was said that Angus cut off the ears of the ship's cook, salt and peppered them, and made the cook eat them. The crew mutinied, and set Angus adrift, effectively killing him. "I bet he's the one who done in those pretty young things," Barney slurs. Four girls in the last six months have disappeared. Micki and Ryan continue on to the lighthouse, where Joe says he sold the foghorn when he moved in, but he promises to check with the buyer if he sees him again.

Day turns to night, and Joe meets with a buyer who is shocked to see his mint-condition doubloons are authentic. Her company will help him find a reputable buyer, then starts in on the boring business talk. Joe strangles her mid-sentence. Like with his date, he blows the foghorn, then meets a dinghy on the beach. In exchange for the woman, Joe gets more gold, this time delivered in the name of Edward Donovan. Back in the lighthouse, he marks off the name in the book. "Just one more," he murmurs.

Barney had been drinking on the beach and sees the entire transaction. He races to tell Dewey, who promises to listen to him in the morning. He then goes to the bar, where Micki and Ryan are having dinner, ranting about what he saw. The manager throws him out, but not before Ryan hears Barney say he heard the foghorn just before the pirate ship appeared. Ryan and Micki race to find Barney, but he is gone, so they return to their hotel.

In the morning, Micki and Ryan return to the lighthouse. Micki intercepts Joe and keeps him busy with chit-chat while Ryan snoops around the lighthouse. Her questions about foghorns bore him, so Micki tries to get flirty with him. He has no interest and won't invite her in. Luckily Ryan hears Joe enter and races to the top of the tower. Joe heads up there too, walks around the platform, then returns to Micki, who is concerned—where is Ryan? Ryan had dangled himself over the side of the lighthouse. Luckily Joe didn't look down, otherwise he would have seen fingers. Clearly, after Joe had swept the lighthouse for Ryan, he was feeling more comfortable, and invites Micki back anytime. Micki and Ryan meet up further down the beach, where Ryan finds a gold doubloon.

Apparently Barney couldn't find anyone to listen to his story because he goes to the lighthouse, angrily accusing Joe of dealing with Angus Mc-Bride. But he is perhaps more angry about the gold than anything else. Barney claims to have been digging for McBride's gold for thirty years and seems to think Joe has an inside track to it. Joe shows Barney the log from McBride's ship, the Corrianne. The last name on the list, Frederick Williams, is Barney's ancestor. Joe shows him some of the gold and admits it rightfully belongs to Barney, then suggests they call McBride. Joe doesn't need to kill Barney before the ghost dinghy shows up; Barney wants to be there. He meets McBride and begs for some of the gold. "My people were with you when you took it, so some of it is rightfully mine," he begs. Joe takes an axe to Barney, then announces proudly that Barney was the last one. McBride disagrees. There is one more. Joe argues and wants his treasure, but McBride simply sails off. He won't reveal who that "one more" is.

Ryan and Micki bring the found doubloon to Dewey, who is certain it came from McBride's treasure. He leaves the cousins looking over an informal history of McBride's ship while he takes a phone call. The pieces all start to fall into place. Micki asks Dewey if the missing women were descendants of McBride's crew. "They were!" Dewey exclaims in a "eureka" moment. Ryan goes looking for Barney while Micki goes to the hall of records. Dewey takes a look at a book and realizes Barney was an ancestor.

Ryan finally finds Barney, in a cave off the beach… with an axe in his head. There are a dozen other corpses in the cave, in varying stages of decay. Ryan screams like a little girl. Micki is having better luck at the hall of records. She finds something that makes her go, "Oh my god!" but leaves quickly when Joe arrives. He doesn't see her, but he does see the book she left open, and smiles.

Both Micki and Joe look for Dewey at the museum (separately, of course) but he is not there. Micki finally runs into him on the beach, where she reveals what she found out: Dewey is a McBride descendant. His mother died giving birth to him, and he was adopted by the Covingtons. Dewey remembers McBride's curse, that he would return to avenge himself, and sail to hell with his crew and their descendants. He will continue looking for Barney while Micki goes into the lighthouse for the foghorn. Since she isn't a descendant, Joe would have no reason to kill her—at least, not a reason to satisfy the curse.

Micki sneaks into the lighthouse, and Joe sees her flashlight shining through a window. He catches her and attacks her with a sword. He misses, of course. Dewey comes in and tells Micki to run before he starts fighting Joe. Joe ends up impaling Dewey.

Meanwhile, Ryan is fighting his own battle in the cave. It's not just corpses in there; the ghost of Angus McBride has taken shelter there, as well. Ryan finds a knife for protection, though I'm not sure how much help that will be against a ghost. Luckily the hideous sound of the foghorn rings out, and McBride recedes. Micki and Ryan meet up on the beach, both frantic and out of breath from their encounters, and fill each other in.

Joe meets McBride on the beach, dragging Dewey's corpse with him. McBride insists there is *another* descendant, and raises his hook hand menacingly (because a pirate is not a pirate without a hook hand).

With Joe distracted by McBride, the cousins scour the lighthouse looking for the foghorn. Ryan finds it, wrapped in sheets. They run into Joe as they are leaving, who begs for the foghorn. "He's going to kill me!"

McBride explodes through the wall, hooks Joe, and raises him up as he bleeds to death. Both Joe and McBride disappear.

Status: The foghorn is returned. Ryan reveals that there was one, final McBride descendant: Joe Fenton. He was less than a year older than his brother, Dewey. Joe was the final descendant.

* * *

"The Pirate's Promise" was a last minute idea from writer Carl Binder. "Initially I was asked to come in and pitch some ideas to them. I came up with four pitches, typed them up and was ready to go. Then, while waiting in the parking lot (I always get to meetings early), I thought of another pitch involving the ghost of a pirate, jotted it down in pencil, then went in and pitched my five ideas. They only like one of them: the freshly hatched pirate pitch, which became 'The Pirate's Promise.'" Angus McBride was not based on a real-life pirate, though McBride is Binder's best friend's last name.

Problems arose when it came time to shoot the episode. There was only one lighthouse in the Toronto area, and according to director Bill Corcoran, it was not very "shootable." He encouraged the producers to broaden their search for a location with "more production value," which took them to a lighthouse on Lake Erie, which mean an out-of-town shoot and hours of travel. "It was a fun trip for the crew because they got to stay in hotels, got extra per diem, and had a night or two of partying," Corcoran remembers. "It was a disaster for my shoot because everyone was tired, and worse, my episode got shortened from seven days to five and a half of actual filming." Travel time was deducted from the shoot days. Corcoran thought the episode turned out okay considering, and ultimately it was worth it to find a better location. "The interior lighthouse scenes were shot after the episode was filmed, on a small studio set with a very limited crew and no sound." The audio was dubbed in later.

The foghorn's curse is finite. Once all of the descendants of McBride's crew are killed, the treasure is revealed. So, then what does the foghorn do? Does it pick another pirate treasure to reveal, slowly, as descendants are killed? Will it only work when used by a secret pirate descendant? The curse is very specific, so I assume the foghorn was on McBride's ship. It's a great curse and a great story, but it doesn't seem to have a lot of juice in it. Can an antique's curse "run out?"

"Badge of Honor"

Story by: Roy Sallows
Teleplay by: Roy Sallows and Jim Henshaw
Directed by: Michelle Manning
Original airdate: July 5, 1988
Cursed antique: Sheriff's badge

Detective Sharko (Val Avery) is staking out a counterfeiting operation with a few other detectives. They are waiting for backup, which is slow to arrive. Sharko gets impatient and rushes into the trade. Gunshots are exchange and the backup arrives, but a female detective is shot dead. The counterfeiters are arrested and Sharko is put on suspension for nearly ruining the whole operation. Sharko packs up his locker and turns in a box of department property. As he does, a silver sheriff's star falls on the floor. He pockets it.

Sharko falls asleep in front of the TV, which is playing a news report about "local entrepreneur" Victor Haas (David Proval), who was picked up in the sweep and released from custody. Sharko has a nightmare in which his wife Gwen is blown up from a car bomb installed by two of Haas' underlings. He wakes up screaming, then rushes to the bedroom to apologize to Gwen. Gwen remains unseen, tucked away in an oxygen tent.

An extended scene introduces us to Hass' nightclub. Lots of neon, lots of dancing, lots of couples making out—all the usual nightclub stuff. Fun fact: the song playing over this scene is "Killer Instinct," performed by Louise Robey herself. Outside, Sharko marches right up to a bouncer, one of the two men directly responsible for Gwen's car bomb. The men fight, and as the bouncer tosses Sharko around, the sheriff's badge drops. Sharko hits the bouncer with a wooden plank, he falls onto the badge, and starts convulsing and twitching wildly before he dies. A burn in the shape of a star appears on his chest, and the badge magically returns to Sharko's hand. Sharko returns home to his beloved Gwen and excitedly tells her that he can get Haas, he just has to be careful and patient.

Next, Sharko meets with a CI named Raoul on the docks to find out where Haas is. Raoul only knows that Haas is going to leave town until things cool down. He doesn't know when he is leaving. Sharko doesn't like that, thrusts the badge into Raoul's chest, and he spasms into the water. When the badge reappears, Sharko strolls away.

At Curious Goods, Ryan is reading a comic book, hidden behind the newspaper. I'm not sure why, since he seems to be home alone and his fandom is not a secret. All reading materials go away when a handsome yuppie enters the store and asks for Micki. She enters a few minutes later and is surprised, yet pleased, to see Tim Ayres (John Stockwell). Ryan takes an immediate dislike to Tim, not helped by the fact that he is looking for a place to stay and she volunteers the store—then volunteers Ryan to take Tim's bag. Micki is very coy about her relationship with Tim. Clearly they were lovers, but Micki just refers to him as an "old friend." She does this same coquettish bit with Calvin in "Wedding in Black." Is it so hard to just say an old boyfriend, or a former flame? Tim has to run out for a little bit, and later on, Ryan and Micki fight about Tim.

"Couldn't he afford a hotel? Aren't all your friends yuppy success stories?"

"If it were your friends it would be different?" she counters.

"Hey, at least my friends need the help," Ryan retorts.

It backfires when Micki remarks, "You said it, not me."

Ryan does have a point: he and Jack are literally living in alcoves of the store; it's not like there are a lot of places for Tim to bed down—except in Micki's room.

Tim returns to the store, interrupting any further argument, and while Micki goes upstairs to make him tea, he uses the phone. Though he speaks quietly, Ryan overhears the suspicious phone call, with key phrases such as "made the connection," "ready to deal," and "couldn't find me if they tried." He goes upstairs to check on his tea, and Tim and Micki start kissing passionately, reminiscing when they come up for air. The tea forgotten, they stumble into bed together.

The next day, Micki is singing to herself, basking in the post-coital glow. Ryan is less cheerful and tells her about the phone call he overheard. He wants to go through Tim's bags, which Micki naturally opposes—until Ryan finds a handgun, equipped with a silencer. "What else is in there?" she asks, now fully on board. There are some surveillance photos of Haas in there, too. Ryan recognizes him from the news.

Tim is meeting with Haas at his club, trying to strike up a deal for his counterfeit bills. The deal is interrupted when Sharko marches in. Fists fly, gangsters scatter, and Haas and Tim jump into a car whose license plate literally spells out "STOLEN." Micki and Ryan are outside, keeping tabs on Tim, but they see something much more interesting. Sharko comes out into the alley, following the younger guy who blew up Gwen's car, and badges him in the chest. Micki and Ryan come out of hiding as Sharko walks away. They are just in time to see the badge disappear.

Back at the store, Micki and Ryan's attention is turned from Tim to a new antique they need to recover. Ryan finds the sheriff's star badge in the manifest. Research into Jack's files shows that it was sold to a Herbert Cooter, who was thought to have committed a series of bizarre murders with no clear cause of death, but all the victims had a distinct, star-shaped brand on them. Cooter believed he was the reincarnation of Jesse James, and was killed in a police shoot-out, dressed in western wear. Tim interrupts the research, and Micki takes her anger out on him. He won't reveal why he was at the club, and claims he doesn't want her or Ryan involved. Micki thinks he is lying to her, using her, and tells him to get the hell out.

Micki and Ryan try to speak to the police captain about the Cooter case. He was the one who killed Cooter. They tell him about the shoot-out outside Haas' club, and describe seeing Sharko out there with the badge. The captain doesn't know anything about it, but he does recognize the description of Sharko. When the captain heads out to Sharko's house, Micki and Ryan follow.

The captain confronts Sharko, drawing a correlation between the victims in the Cooter case and a few corpses that have shown up in the past few days, all with star-shaped burns. Sharko blows him off, but the captain informs him there was a witness tonight. Sharko changes his stance, defending himself. To him, vigilante justice is still justice. To the captain, killing is still killing. The captain wants to bring him downtown, which doesn't go over very well. The captain reaches for his gun, and Sharko reaches for his badge. Sharko is faster. The captain stumbles down the hall in spasms like all the other victims. He collapses onto Gwen's bed, pulling down down the oxygen tent and revealing that Gwen has been dead for some time, looking like a stunt double for Mother Bates. Sharko runs in, fusses over Gwen, and when the badge reappears, he rushes out.

Everyone converges on the docks. Haas is there with a couple of goons, getting ready to leave town. Tim is there to close the deal for the counterfeit bills. Sharko is there to kill Haas, and Micki and Ryan are there to get the badge.

Tim meets Haas, who wants him to come closer. Ryan knocks over a pile of palettes, which draws all the wrong kinds of attention. Haas runs, Tim pulls out his gun and announces he is with the FBI. Haas shoots Tim twice: the first one knocks him down; the second one hits Micki in the shoulder when she moronically jumps in to take the bullet. Haas then shoots Sharko, who, with his last bit of life, badges Haas to death.

Status: Tim is dead, Haas is dead, Sharko is dead. The badge is safely vaulted.

*   *   *

I never liked "Badge of Honor." I was actually dreading watching it again for this book. I always remember it as being my least favorite episode. Guess what? That honor still sticks.

There are a few things I didn't dig. I'm not a big fan of mobster storylines on TV shows. Never liked them on *Law & Order*, either. But with *Friday the 13th*, I wanted to get back to the horror. This episode never comes off as horror; rather, it feels like an episode of *Miami Vice*: gangsters, bars with lots of neon, slutty club girls in skin-tight dresses, and cocaine everywhere. Story consultant Marc Scott Zicree remembers that the story came from writer Roy Sallows' background as a cop.

As director Michelle Manning explains, "I think that I had just directed a music video using those techniques and I had wanted to put them to use on the show. The producers were fine with it—the style of the show was laid out with different items going to the shop in each episode, so the producers really didn't tell you to shoot with any specific look."

Sharko is not relatable. He is made out to be an anti-hero, someone who assumes the end will justify the means. But keeping the mummified remains of his dead wife in his bed and talking to her, that is both weird and icky, and smacks of *Psycho*. (A similar subplot was used in "The Long Road Home," to much better effect.) On top of that, Sharko comes across as a bumbling idiot who should have retired long ago, not some supercop who is ready to go against the city's biggest organized crime family. Plus, that hideous plaid jacket that he wore in the opening gun battle was a joke, and Sharko was pathetic for wearing it. If he has "conversations" with his wife, then why didn't "she" tell him it was heinous?

What was interesting to me was that the badge was one of the few items that didn't actually "give" you anything. It basically allowed Sharko to kill without leaving any physical evidence. It didn't allow him to bring anyone back to life; he didn't gain youth or health; it didn't bring his wife back to life; he wasn't promoted. It was just a way for him to kill. Did he really need a cursed object to kill?

Manning has one of the best anecdotes about shooting this episode. "This was my first experience shooting in Canada. We were shooting nights in an alley and had dressed the alley up to be sleazy, like New York City. We broke for lunch and came back and the alley was pristine, just as it was before we dressed it! I found that to be a lasting impression of how proud the Canadians are." Proud, or just how damned helpful they are!

"Pipe Dream"

Written by: Marc Scott Zicree
Directed by: Zale Dalen
Original airdate: July 11, 1988
Cursed antique: Smoking pipe

After an inventor's seminar, Ray (Michael Constantine) chats up a young go-getter, Keith Fielding, and convinces him to share his invention with him. Keith reveals blueprints for a laser sight that controls a miniature guided missile. It explodes on impact, and has 100% accuracy at up to a half-mile away. Ray wants to form a partnership, and to celebrate, he lights up an old, wooden pipe with a charmingly terrifying demon face carved into it. A rich uncle gave it to him, and he has never smoked it before. (I know that Ray's "reveal" is supposed to be a surprise until the end of the first act, but doesn't the "rich uncle" part kind of give it away?) Ray lights the pipe and orange smoke billows out, chases Keith, and smothers him. Ray seems surprised—I guess this really was the first time he smoked it—and watches as Keith's face melts like a chemical burn. Then Keith disappears altogether. Ray pockets the pipe and Keith's blueprints.

Later (months, I assume) Ray is demonstrating Keith's gun as his own for Mr. Clemens (Nick Nichols) and his team of weapon scientists. Clemens loves it, puts Ray on the payroll, and makes his weapon the number one priority, thoroughly pissing off the (former) head scientist, John (James Kidnie). Ray heads home, to a dumpy apartment in a bad part of town, and gives a huge bouquet of roses to his girlfriend, Connie (Marion Gilsenan). He promises her a better life.

Mail call at Curious Goods. Ryan gets a letter from his father, and is surprised to see he is getting married—again. Micki is excited for him, but Ryan isn't. He and his dad don't get along. They haven't spoken in years because Ryan was always a disappointment. Micki wants Ryan to go and make peace with his dad, and he agrees, but Micki will have to be his date.

Ryan is concerned when they pull up to the address on the wedding invite: the house is far too nice to be his father's; he never had any money. But there are balloons outside, the international sign for "there's a party in here." The door opens and dum-dah-dum—Ray is Ryan's father! (Come on, we all knew this.) Ray is not happy to see his son. He didn't send the invite, Connie did, and she welcomes them in warmly. Ryan introduces Micki as "cousin Katherine's daughter." Connie convinces Ray to take Ryan to the factory while she puts Micki to work preparing for the wedding.

Ray shows Ryan around the factory and explains that he isn't home free until his final demonstration tomorrow, right before the wedding. He then shares a story that apparently Ryan had never heard before. Ray's father left the day he was born, but he did have a strong male figure in his life: Lewis Vendredi. This gets Ryan's attention, and Ray explains it was "between us," which sounds dangerously close to what a pedophile tells his victim. When Ray was four years old, he fell and split his chin open. He ran to Uncle Lewis, who puts something there, healed him instantly, and made the blood disappear, "like magic." Lewis was dirt poor, but struck it rich overnight. He never understood how that little store could make so much money, but "if my Uncle Lewis can do it, I can do it."

While showing Ryan the firing range, Ryan is surprised that this weapon came out of his dad's head. It is not clear if it is because his dad doesn't have the science/engineering background necessary, or simply because it is a destructive weapon. Either way, Ryan refuses to try the gun out, and this antagonizes Ray. He's mad that Ryan dropped out of college to run the shop. "Why Uncle Lewis left that shop to you, I'll never know," Ray says, suggesting that maybe a teeny-tiny bit of Ray's distaste for his son is jealousy. Ray keeps comparing Ryan to Lewis, telling him to man up, do something with his life, yadda yadda yadda. Ryan finally erupts: "Uncle Lewis made a deal with the devil, that's where he got all his money! I've been running all over hell trying to get back his cursed antiques." Ray is stunned, more at the outburst than at the demonic revelation. Ryan tells him to forget it, and John comes in for Ray, adamant that they meet in his office, immediately.

At the homestead, Micki knocks over a box and finds Ray's old photo album. Connie shows her some old pictures of Ray, including one with an older man, whom Connie identifies as Uncle Lewis, the only person to give Ray a Christmas present as a boy. Micki's jovial mood becomes clouded, and she asks if Lewis ever gave Ray a gift later in life. The only thing Connie can think of is an old pipe that Ray considers his good luck charm. Micki is concerned and heads to the factory.

John expects Ray to sign over his invention to him and walk away from the company. He has proof that Ray stole the invention from Keith Fielding. John's plan, apparently, is to steal the invention from the man who stole the invention to keep the world from knowing the invention was stolen. Okay, I'll roll with it. John gives Ray some time to think it over, but Ray really doesn't need time. He pulls out his pipe, starts smoking it, and the orange smoke chases John down the hall. Unfortunately, Micki is coming down the hall at the same time. She sees John "on fire" in the orange smoke and starts screaming. Ryan rushes to her aid, but by the time he gets there, John and the orange smoke have completely disappeared. Ray is concerned that Micki may have seen something, but Micki insists she just let her imagination get the best of her.

That night, the cousins chat. Ryan feels like a kid again, trying to please his dad. "I just wish he would be proud of me for me," he laments. Success isn't just a big deal for Ray—it is the only thing, and it got worse after Jimmy died. Ray dragged Ryan and his mom from town to town, from one grungy apartment to the next. Micki steers the conversation back to what she saw today, which Ryan dismisses as a lab test or a practical joke. He gets defensive when Micki reveals that Uncle Lewis gave Ray a pipe. Ryan jumps to his dad's defense, and Micki backs off. But once everyone is asleep, she calls Jack and asks him to check the manifest for a pipe.

A visitor stops by in the morning: Jack. Ray is suspicious until Ryan introduces him as Lewis' friend. Jack is quick to mention that he is also a friend of Ryan's, and that he owes his life to him. Like with Micki, Connie welcomes Jack and puts him to work. Jack and Micki break away for a minute to talk. There was an eighteenth century pipe listed in the manifest; Lewis received it but never sold it, leaving plenty of room for it to be gifted. Jack suggests they keep Ryan out of it until they are absolutely sure Ray has the pipe, and it is cursed.

Ray and Ryan are having a father-son bonding moment. Ryan insists that he is only there to see his dad, and that he wants nothing from him. When asked, Ryan confirms that he saved Jack's life before, and "he's saved mine." Ryan doesn't expect his dad to believe that they recover cursed antiques, but that is what they do, and Ryan does it because his father taught him the difference between right and wrong. The tender moment is ruined when Ryan can't find the car keys and Ray flips out, thinking Ryan was sent to distract him while Micki and Jack left to sabotage him. I'm not really sure why Ray thinks that the three of them are engaged in some sort plot against him, but I guess coming across a million-dollar idea illegitimately makes a person paranoid. Anyway, Ray jumps in his car and races to the factory. Connie and Ryan follow closely in her car.

Micki searches Ray's office while Jack works at picking the locked drawer. They hide behind the door when they hear Ray coming, and once he takes the pipe from the locked drawer, they jump him, all three fighting to get the pipe. Micki wins, and she runs with it while the men fight for another minute. She goes all the way down to the firing range, followed by Ray, who is followed by Jack. The men fight some more, allowing Micki to escape upstairs. Ray grabs a fortuitously-placed taser gun and zaps Jack into unconsciousness, then props him up behind one of the firing range targets.

While Ray deals with Micki, Clemens has brought their guest of honor, General Abelar, into the firing range, where they toast. The general wants to try the weapon, and he starts aiming at the targets. One shot, two shot, all is well. Ryan and Connie rush in, looking for Ray, but no one has seen him. Ryan takes a long hard look down the firing range... and sees a human hand behind the target. The general is taking aim, so Ryan rushes him, grabs the gun, and points it up. He rushes down the firing line and sees that it is Jack who nearly got blown up. Jack weakly informs Ryan that his father has been using a cursed pipe, and that Micki is in trouble. Ryan grabs the weapon, action hero-style, and runs to save her.

Micki is trying to find somewhere to hide. Ray catches up with her and manages to wrest the pipe away. He lights it up and she ducks into a storage closet, taping up the cracks in the door to keep the smoke out. She isn't fast enough and it starts leaking in. Ryan rushes in and demands to know where Micki is. "I am not your son!" he screams when Ray tries to mollify him. Ryan moves towards the sounds of Micki struggling, despite the fact that she warns him away. "It always takes a life," Ray informs him. Since the smoke is having a hard time getting to Micki, when it "sees" Ryan, it changes its track. When Ray sees his son fighting the smoke, he finally asks himself, "What have I done?" He pushes Ryan out of the way and lets the smoke take him.

Status: The pipe is returned, and our heroes let Connie believe her almost-husband disappeared. Jack comforts Ryan by telling him that Ray, like Lewis, renounced the curse and paid the price. "But, unlike Lewis, he did it for love."

* * *

The pipe is the second cursed item in a row to offer nothing specific in return for its use; just untraceable murder.

This is just a guess… but I think Clemens is selling Ray's super-gun to a foreign government. Probably not a democratic one, either. After all, the demonstration is for *General* Abelar and I can't think of any democracies run by generals.

It took writer Marc Zicree seven months to get the approval to write "Pipe Dream." It was a very personal episode to him, as it was largely autobiographical (except, of course, for the stuff about a magic pipe). "My father and I had this very stormy, loving, but very troubled relationship. I was trying to get his approval, and he was a very damaged man. I really wanted to write about that relationship between me and my dad, that sense of disappointment, where a father and son are disappointed with each other, where they are longing for connection. There is love there, but somehow they can't get to it.

"When I was a kid my dad worked in aerospace. It was during the Vietnam era, so it was very much about weapons procurement and weapons systems and all that. He always had these get rich quick schemes. He always believed they were million dollar ideas; that he'd be rich, that his ship would come in. Finally, in later years, he came up with this thing called the Mommy Medic. He was sure this was it, and he bought the equipment to manufacture it—and it was a huge disaster. A total failure. So, all of my dad's dreams of making it big suddenly came face to face with reality, and he realized it was a pipe dream, his whole life. My father so wanted to be important, to matter. I was trying to come up with an object that would be good. My dad was a smoker—he smoked cigarettes, not a pipe, but I had known people who smoked pipes. I came up with the idea of the pipe as the cursed object, the idea being that the smoke would kill people. It seemed like a very cool visual.

"I was very proud of the script. It had so many moments of genuine connection between Ryan and his father, and that thing of wanting to be there for each other, being disappointed in each other, loving each other, hoping to communicate with each other. I could identify with what Ryan was doing in the show, and I could understand the corners the father had cut, because he was a little man who wanted to be a big man, wanted to be a hero to his family, but what he was doing was causing great harm to the world. It's not that you start a monster, but that's where you end up, because of those small compromises you make that ultimately become big compromises. That is what I was writing about in 'Pipe Dream.'

"I told Bill that I would do as many rewrites as it takes, but I didn't want other people to rewrite me. He honored that, so my scripts weren't rewritten, unless it was production draft. [Story editor] Roy Sallows, for some reason, put one line into 'Pipe Dream' that wasn't mine but I really liked. Ray looks at Ryan and says, 'You're not the little boy I was mad at.' I think Roy had a very troubled relationship with his dad, too, so he got it."

Director Zale Dalen remembers hearing that this episode was semi-autobiographical and was quite amazed at that. "I'm more a reality guy, so I found it strange that there was some kind of allegory as a base for the story." Dalen was most interested in the design of the pipe. "I thought I had made it clear to the props department what I wanted, which was a pipe that had a demonic face on it that would be visible when the actor held the pipe in his hand and smoked it. The design the props people presented to me didn't work at all. It was too small and impossible to hold in a pipe-holding way without completely covering the face.

"I ended up designing the pipe myself, making it out of plasticine," Dalen explains. "I modeled it on the faces of European gargoyles and made sure that the base could be held with the face looking out above the fingers. That worked great, but I'm pretty sure I didn't make any friends in the props department. I really liked that pipe design, and when I got home I made a slip cast from the plasticine in plaster. A friend with a kiln glazed and fired it. I still have that someplace in my memorabilia collection."

Response to "Pipe Dream" was great. Zicree remembers doing a radio show where someone called in and told them he was in tears at the end of the episode. "I thought, *Well, I've done my job!* To be able to do that with a horror show is really something." Another kudos came from an elderly orthodox Jewish woman who lived in his building. "She said, 'We saw your episode. It was wonderful. Better than Exodus!' I didn't know if she meant the movie or the biblical chapter! Then she said, 'It's funny, that lead actor didn't look like you at all, but I felt like it was you speaking to me. It was like you talking through the screen.' In that episode, she saw Ryan as me, speaking my voice, and my heart."

"What a Mother Wouldn't Do"

Written by: Bruce Martin
Directed by: Neill Fearnley
Original airdate: July 18, 1988
Cursed antique: Baby cradle

After years of trying, Leslie Kent (Lynne Cormack) is finally pregnant. Unfortunately, it is a high-risk pregnancy, and the doctor advises her to terminate it. The baby will not survive, and Leslie's life will be at risk. Husband Martin (Michael Countryman) says nothing, but is clearly on the doctor's side. Leslie is appalled at the idea and rushes from the doctor's office. As she walks through the city, trying to clear her head, she sees an old wooden baby cradle in the window of Vendredi Antiques. It's like it calls to her, and she goes inside for a closer look. Lewis greets her and sees she is crying a little. He tells her the cradle is special, and offers her to tell the fascinating story over a cup of tea. "Don't worry about the money," he hints. "Things have a way of working out."

Six months later, Leslie is still very pregnant and her friends throw her a baby shower. They all chipped in for the cradle, and Leslie is overwhelmed with the gesture.

A post-pregnant Leslie is at the park with the baby pram, pretending to read a book. In reality she is keeping her eye on a jogger. When he is just close enough, she kicks the pram down a small hill, and it rolls into a pond. Leslie screams for help, and the Good Samaritan rushes in to rescue the baby. When he peeks in, he sees the pram is empty. Martin jumps out from behind a bush and whacks him in the head, killing the jogger dead in the water. "That is number four," Leslie breathes. About the same time, baby Allison, laying in the cradle at home, goes from screaming to giggling.

When Leslie and Martin come home, babysitter Debbie (Robyn Stevan) gives them the report: Allison seemed to have been sick for awhile, but then she was all giggles the rest of the afternoon. Debbie leaves and Leslie gives Martin an "I told you so" look. Martin is clearly feeling guilty over killing people to save his only daughter.

Let's talk about the curse. We find out bits and pieces of the curse over the course of the episode, but it is pretty involved, perhaps the most involved back story of any object in the series. A mother was taking her baby to New York on the Titanic. When the ship went down, the woman tried to get on a lifeboat, but it was full. She then tried passing her baby—in the cradle—to them, but the people wouldn't take her. In the ensuing struggle, the lifeboat tipped over. All seven passengers in the lifeboat died, while the baby floated to safety in her cradle. The curse dictates that, if seven people die in water before the anniversary of the Titanic's sinking, the baby in the cradle will be healed of whatever maladies it possesses. However, the baby cannot be removed from the cradle, for any reason, or it will succumb to its disease.

That night, Leslie wakes to the baby coughing and the cradle rocking. It needs to be "fed." Martin refuses to partake, so Leslie will do it herself. She calls the building super, Mr. Johnson, for an emergency leak. Leslie hits him over the head with a candlestick when Johnson arrives. She goes in for a second whack when Martin stops her and reminds her he has to die in water. (If you are going to do it, may as well do it right.) The two drag him to the toilet and drown him. As they drag him, his keys fall off his pants and catch in a corner. The baby stops crying, the cradle stops shaking, and Martin dumps the super into the swimming pool.

The Curious Goods team is cleaning up in the vault when they find a letter, thanking Lewis for the cradle. Handwritten, no signature. The manifest reveals two names in the "sold to" field: Everly and Kent. Ryan takes the former; Micki, the latter. Micki goes straight to the Kent apartment, where Debbie is babysitting, and offers to buy the cradle. Debbie explains that Mrs. Kent would never sell it, but Micki leaves her card, just in case. Debbie tears it up after she leaves.

When the Kents come home, Debbie tells them about her visitor, which makes Martin anxious: "Someone knows!" That night, Debbie reads about Johnson's death, and remembers seeing the keys in the Kent apartment. She goes up there, casually mentions Johnson's drowning, and Leslie plays the shocked acquaintance to perfection. Once she leaves, Martin sees the super's keys on the floor and goes into a whole new level of panic. "She said she loves the baby," Leslie coos. "Isn't that nice?"

Debbie draws a bath. Micki and Ryan are staking out the apartment from the Mercedes. A masked intruder sneaks into her apartment from the balcony, which brings Micki and Ryan running. The intruder struggles to drown Debbie in her tub, but she fights back like crazy. Maybe the bubble bath made her slippery, because after a prolonged struggle, the intruder rips down the shower curtain and tries to use that to keep her beneath the water. Ryan breaks into the apartment, scaring the intruder out the way he came in. The intruder is, no surprise, Martin. Leslie tells him not to worry; they will get Debbie later.

Ryan and Micki take Debbie to the store to keep her safe. While they discuss the implications of the curse, Debbie listens through a vent from upstairs. She makes a phone call and plans a meet about Allison's well-being. Debbie tapes a note to Micki's bed and sneaks out. (You'd think that room belonged to a teenage girl for how often people sneak in and out of there.) Ryan finds the note, and the trio rushes to follow. They arrive at the apartment, in time to see Leslie drive by. Ryan goes after her while Micki and Jack go into the apartment to get the cradle.

Debbie meets Leslie at a boathouse, and tries to convince her to let her take Allison—Leslie will get caught and then Allison will have no one. (Yeah, except for her father.) Both women speak of their love for Allison, and how both want what is best for her. But for Leslie, what is best is if she cracks Debbie on the head with a crowbar. Ryan arrives to see Leslie toss Debbie's lifeless body into the water, and he jumps Leslie. Leslie, in turn, tosses him into the water, excited that she has her seventh victim, and uses a pole she finds on the dock to knock him out. Leslie is overwhelmed with relief and rushes home to hold her baby girl for the first time.

Back at the apartment, Micki and Jack have found the cradle, which is rocking a fussy Allison. Micki, who spent the whole car ride over worrying about Allison's safety, takes the baby from the cradle, but as soon as she does the baby cries, and the cradle shakes like it is throwing a tantrum. Micki puts the baby back, reasoning to Jack that she couldn't let her die in her arms. Martin appears with a gun. "Neither could we."

Martin moves everyone into the living room, where Jack tries to undermine the family unit and insinuate that Leslie always planned on making her husband the seventh victim. Leslie bursts in with the happy news, but the cradle is still rocking the screaming baby. Leslie is nearly hysterical: "I gave you seven!" In a panic, she grabs Martin's gun and shoots at Micki, who darts out of the way. Martin finally stands up for what is right. "She has suffered too much," he reasons. "I want to hold my daughter, and maybe she will know I tried to ease her pain." Leslie shoots Martin and he falls dead, never making it to the cradle. She turns her attention Jack and Micki and makes them go out onto the balcony, intending to push them over, into the courtyard fountain. Ryan bursts in (of course he isn't dead), which shocks Leslie. She shoots, but is out of bullets. The baby is screaming, time is running out, and Leslie knows what she has to do. She throws herself off the balcony, landing in the fountain. Dead in water. Ryan, Micki and Jack go back inside and return to the cradle, but see the baby isn't there.

Status: The cradle is returned. Micki is concerned that the cradle somehow absorbed baby Allison. What happened is that Debbie didn't die that night at the boathouse, but when Martin died, Leslie's bullet shattered the fish tank, dumping water over Martin—technically, he died in water. Debbie sneaked into the apartment, and while the adults were busy on the balcony, she slipped the baby from the cradle. The last scene of the episode is Debbie taking a happy, healthy Allison out of town, to start a new life.

* * *

Leslie Kent is one of the most sympathetic curse-users in the series. Yes, most use the curses for their own greed and always personal gain, but Leslie was using it for someone else: her daughter. And when push came to shove, she gave her own life to save her child. No other antique-owner in *F13* ever sacrificed herself to the curse for the benefit of another.

Actress Lynne Cormack, who played Leslie, remembers that the episode had a great script. "It really was about finding that deep-rooted want and need to do anything to save your baby. I think I was able to find the love. You can never judge your character or else you can't play it."

Cormack didn't do any of her own stunts, but she did lay in the fountain for her after-death scene. "It was 3:00 a.m. and they gave me a wet suit underneath my costume. I am intensely claustrophobic, so I hated being taped into that little suit, but it was *very* cold. I remember they laid me in the water and they were getting shots. I told the first A.D., 'Okay, you've got one more shot, then I'm outta here.' It was just horrible. They knew they had to get me out of there."

"Bottle of Dreams"

Written by: Roy Sallows
Directed by: Mac Bradden
Original airdate: July 25, 1988
Cursed antique: Canopic jar

As the first season comes to a close, Jack decides it is time to celebrate. With Jack in a tuxedo, Micki in a red cocktail dress, and Ryan in a ridiculous bolo tie, the trio partakes in a champagne toast: "To the most successful hunters of cursed objects in the whole wide… neighborhood!" Their toast is cut short when a mysterious man enters the store in a swirl of mist, dressed in Middle Eastern robes and carrying a large parcel. "I have come to return something. It belongs to you. Take it." He leaves without another word.

Beneath the old cloth and straw wrappings is an urn. Micki checks the manifest and finds an Old Kingdom Canopic jar, the kind that was used to preserve internal organs during mummification. "This is the easiest we've ever gotten anything back," Ryan says and takes it to the vault. Micki goes to help ("It's getting crowded in there"), while Jack double checks the entry. He doesn't remember that entry, and there is no customer name.

The vault is a mess. Micki is still creeped out when she sees Veda. Ryan asks her what's wrong, and the urn flies out of his hands and lands dead-center of the vault. The Anubis head stopper pops out and green smoke fills the vault. When the shop starts shaking, Jack comes running—in time to see the vault seal shut.

While Jack calls his friend Rashid (Elias Zarou), we watch Micki and Ryan writhe in panic as we relive "The Inheritance" finale.

Rashid arrives and Jack fills him in. The urn wrappings look like they may be 5,000 years old. He shines a black light over the cloth and discovers Egyptian hieroglyphs, punctuated with Horace, the hawk-headed god who escorts souls through the halls of the dead. According to all of this, Rashid diagnoses Ryan and Micki as experiencing an epic death dream. They will be forced to relive the most horrifying experiences of their lives, over and over, until the terror causes their hearts to burst. Rashid estimates they have until midnight to save them. It is 9:00 p.m.

In the vault, Micki and Ryan relive the finale of "Cupid's Quiver."

Jack and Rashid mix up some powerful potions. Rashid chants, commands the vault to open, and the potion bubbles up—and fizzles out. Jack has a suggestion: send him into their nightmare. Rashid tries to remind Jack of the danger involved, but Jack is resolute. "It's their only hope."

Down in the vault, the cousins relive scenes from "Scarecrow" and "Tattoo."

10:00 p.m. More potions. Before Jack can drink, the men are visited by an old friend: Lewis (as a ghost, of course). "My niece and nephew are paying a price for interfering, and it will keep on until they die. Then the forces of darkness will take over the store, and once again Satan's toys will flow across this world like an unholy tide." Lewis always enjoyed theatrics. Rashid gets rid of Lewis with a spell and glowing Superball. Jack drinks the potion.

Next up in the trip down horrifying memory lane is "Dr. Jack" and "Tales of the Undead"

11:00 p.m. Rashid prepares to send Jack into the dream plane, promising that Lewis will attack where he is most vulnerable: his love. Jack must cause Micki and Ryan to disbelieve, turn away from the dream. Then they can break through the barrier and Rashid will pull them out. Of course, if they don't break through the barrier, and Micki and Ryan die, Jack will die, too.

Jack appears in a black room, screams all around him. The guillotine blade from "The Poison Pen" flies by. A young boy in a hospital bed appears, Lewis at his side. Jack calls him by name: Peter. And Peter calls to Jack by the only name he knows him as: "Dad." Lewis taunts him, telling Jack that his only son is at his mercy; that Peter will burn forever unless Jack agrees to take his place. Jack swears he won't be distracted. "Peter is dead!" It is with difficulty, but necessity, that Jack moves on.

Micki and Ryan are now in the opening of "The Baron's Bride," fighting vampire Marie.

Lewis returns to the shop to annoy Rashid, but he cannot be distracted. "Hell must have made you slow and stupid if you think I'm going to believe you." Rashid lights another candle, and Lewis—either dejected or bored or magically evicted—disappears.

Jack has found the barrier, an orange digital test pattern-looking thing. Through the barrier, Jack can see Micki and Ryan living out the black and white portions of "The Baron's Bride." Lewis tries one more time to trick Jack, this time by offering to save Ryan and Micki if he takes Lewis' place in hell. This is a much easier option to say "no" to.

Just a few minutes before midnight…. .

Micki and Ryan are now in the finale of "The Baron's Bride," where Abraham stakes Frank. In well-styled reshoots, Micki and Ryan hear Jack yelling for them, and they return the call. As Rashid chants faster on the outside, they finally make out Jack on the other side of the barrier.

The clock strikes midnight.

Jack reaches them on the second ding of the midnight chimes. Holding them close, he calls for Rashid to get them out of there.

Jack returns to the ceremonial circle. Ryan and Micki are not with him, and shortly after he arrives, Rashid passes out. Jack rushes to the basement and pulls the secret brick on the vault doors. Nothing happens. Suddenly they burst out of the vault, and collapse into Jack's arms.

Status: The jar is, presumably, still in the vault. Jack admits he saw Peter in the dream plane, and when asked who Peter was, he simply answers "My son." Jack, wearily, heads upstairs, and Rashid explains to stunned, clueless Micki and Ryan. Peter was a gifted psychic child, with "an infinite capacity to love." He tried to help a friend of his, a young girl whom doctors said was insane. Peter knew she was possessed. While reading one of Jack's books, Peter discovered the existence of the dream plane. He went in, alone, with no psychic anchor, and he died there. Peter was only twelve.

As the episode ends, we see Lewis one more time, as a reflection in a mirror, laughing demonically. The mirror cracks. A sign of things to come? (Yes.)

*   *   *

Yup, a clip show. After only twenty-five episodes, *Friday the 13th* has resorted to a clip show. It was purely for practical reasons: in March of 1988, the Writer's Guild of America went on strike, so Bill Taub and Marc Zicree were on the picket lines. It was the longest strike in WGA history, going on for six months. Because *F13* was a Canadian co-production, the show went on, but according to Bill Taub, "going back was not easy." Marc Zicree agrees. "When we came back, it felt like we had been gone a long time.

"Without Bill and myself, the machine was still running, and they found other ways to do the show," Zicree laments. "So, my job didn't really exist anymore. [Supervising executive] Barbara Sachs said, 'Why would we have you back?' They hired Bill back for a very short time. I went in to pitch to Bill a few times, but I wasn't really in the mood anymore. I pitched a bunch of stories but nothing really clicked, and I was not that unhappy about that. The writer's strike interrupted what we were doing—I think we were on a very good roll—but that's the way it goes."

Jim Henshaw had originally been offered the job of executive story consultant as season one staffed up, but was already on an espionage show for CBS called *Adderly*, so he turned it down. When *Adderly* finished its second—and final—season, *Friday the 13th* still had a few episodes to go on its first season. "I was available and just called to see if they needed help with anything," he remembers. Since Henshaw wasn't WGA, they called him in to do a rewrite on "Bottle of Dreams." "I went down to L.A. and met various people, and they pulled me in for the second season."

Because it was basically a clip show, "Bottle of Dreams" was an unexceptional episode. The one bright spot in this episode was the introduction of Rashid, played by Elias Zarou.

At a time when U.S. production was still relatively new to Canada, Zarou believes that, because he had just come back from three years working in the States, therefore proving himself in an American market, it gave him a leg up on the competition. "I have worked most of my career clean shaven, but at the time I just happened to have a beard, which gave an appropriate look to an Egyptian, white wizard," Zarou recalls. "Though Canadian born, I had found that my olive complexion required an ability to do accents and I had become know for an accurate Middle East sound." For *Friday the 13th: The Series*, Zarou says he modeled his accent on Omar Sharif. "I was told at the time that the sincerity and warmth of my audition delivery had been factors in the casting choice."

Season 2

JIM HENSHAW (executive story consultant) – When I got to *Friday the 13th*, what I discovered was you had to write differently for the personalities that were there. There were three very different acting styles.

I think season one had been a bit of a bear for them. It was a really ambitious show for the time and I think they burned out a lot of the first-season crew. When I came in, they decided they wanted to go with a change of direction, not do so much splatter stuff. They wanted to do more psychological horror. We didn't back off on the gore, but we found a lot more "logic"—if you can call it that—in the stories. We used to refer to all the stuff that went on with the cursed objects as "the mystic shit." We just found more ways to make "the mystic shit" more believable, or to base it more in character, as opposed to, "here's a cool way we can kill a bunch of people this week."

TOM MCLOUGHLIN (director, story editor) – Frank reached out to me again and asked if I would like to do some episodes. I can't remember what came first, whether he offered me an episode to write and direct, or the story editor job. They had Jim Henshaw up there, but they didn't have anyone down [in Los Angeles]. Frank wanted to be more hands-on. So, I came aboard and basically oversaw the rewrites of certain scripts.

FRANK MANCUSO JR. (creator, executive producer) – I remember doing a test, where I said to Paramount, "Let's just go out there and put an alternate title on the show, and show two focus groups the same show. One with the *Friday the 13th* title, and one with another title." Just to see how the two of them react differently to the show. It would tell us if "Friday the 13th" was a big part of the reason why people are watching the show. What it kind of told us was the reason why people enjoyed the show called *Friday's Curse* was the narrative and the stories. And then when pushed, a lot of the reason people didn't sample the show was because they thought it was the movies. I went back to Paramount and said, "Look, it seems to me that this is the best news you could have gotten. What it says is, you could change the show's title and position it differently and perhaps expand the audience."

JIM HENSHAW – Apparently during the first season, they had done a lot of test audience stuff. At one point, they had two episodes: one they really like a lot, and one they really hated. They played them both for a group of people in L.A. The test audience loved the episode that everyone [on the crew] had hated and they hated the show that everyone loved. So, they had a discussion afterwards to decide if they were going to make the show they wanted to make, or if they were going to be pushed by the audience. So, at that point, I think they stopped doing the test screenings.

FRANK MANCUSO JR. – In some ways the LeMay-Robey parts were… thankless is the wrong word, but they were the more "gumshoe aspect" of what we were doing. I felt like both of them worked off each other well. In a lot of the episodes we featured one or the other, some both, but I never really felt like we had to steer towards certain kinds of things. I didn't feel like they wouldn't be able to do this, or she can't do that. I didn't feel limited in that way.

LOUISE ROBEY (Micki Foster) – The regulars were only given one take. The co-stars were given more takes, but we were expected to land it in one. Most of the time, we did.

ARMAND MASTROIANNI (director) – *Friday the 13th* was all shot on 35mm film. They allowed us the luxury of going into overtime and stuff like that, if we needed it. They wanted a quality show, and I think they got it, for TV. TV was always quick and down and dirty. Get in, get out, finish it off.

JIM HENSHAW – This is going to sound kind of weird, but we had a kind of quality control. It was "The Frank's Mom Rule." Basically, Frank would show an episode to his mom, and if his mom went, "Oh, Frank," we would pull back. If she wasn't offended or if she understood and appreciated what was going on, we would continue in that direction. So, somewhere in the back of my mind, I'm thinking, "Is she participating with the dark side, or fighting it?"

FRANCIS DELIA (writer, director) – My older brother Alf was a real *Friday the 13th: The Series* fanatic, oddly enough. It was practically a coincidence that I just happened to be directing some episodes, because it was later that I found out he was an inveterate fan of the series.

LOUISE ROBEY – I remember having an argument with a director. One director said "the girl"—he actually made the mistake of calling me "the girl." The whole crew went silent! I'm just standing there, watching. Rodney Charters said, "Hey mate, she just saved somebody's life last week. I wouldn't call her 'the girl' if I was you."

I said I'm driving the Mercedes this week.

He said, "It's not your's—it belongs to the store."

I said, "The store is mine."

He threw the keys at me—didn't hand them to me, he threw them at me. So, I got to drive it. I drove it quite a lot. I love the Mercedes. It was a really great car.

There was one time when they gave me a walkie-talkie in the car. It was freezing cold out, and I was out of sight of any of the crew, around the corner. I had to rush down the hill and just hit the sandbags, so the car would end up on the bags. I *thought* somebody had said action… but they hadn't. So. I came roaring around, headlights on. I stopped right on the sandbags. But the camera crew was gone! They ran in all different directions!

TOM McLOUGHLIN – So many of us went up there kicking and screaming, "Why do we have to do this in Canada?" But the crew was so loyal, and every director pushed these guys with consistent eighteen hour days. What always stuck out to me was that they were so tired, but they never complained. They always moved forward. There was one point where the boom operator was absolutely asleep on his feet, with his head down and the boom up. It was like he was using the Force: as the actors would move, he would follow them. So, he was operating off some sixth sense! I sat there, watching this, wondering if I am really seeing this. His eyes were absolutely closed, and when the mixer nudged him, he snorted awake! He did not realize! I thought, *There is a craftsman.*

It was the beginning of me falling in love with the Canadian experience, and the fact that these people were so new to doing this on a regular basis, but not complaining like the Hollywood crews. They didn't know what to demand yet!

RODNEY CHARTERS (cinematographer, director) – We went up on top of the building one night, during winter. We'd been inside shooting, and we went onto the roof—it was actually snowing. In those days, the assistants would check the [camera] gate at the end of every take to see if there was any dirt on the edge of the gate that would show up like those little hairs you see on film when you screen it. It was dark, so this guy put the little Maglite flashlight in his mouth so he could look down the lens. He finished checking, and he tried to take the flashlight out of his mouth and he couldn't get it out. It had frozen to his tongue! He was standing there, trying to figure out what to do, and we're all staring at him. He kind of yanked at it and he pulled a piece of skin off his tongue! It started to bleed of course, and he's standing there with this red patch of skin on his flashlight.

LOUISE ROBEY – When we got bored, we used to go up to the office at four in the morning—me, some of the crew—and we'd fax our bums to Paramount.

But there was an awful lot of waiting around. I'd read a lot of books, study art, wrote children's books with my paintings in them that I hope to have published one day. There was loads of time. You are waiting around for ages. On a show like that, there was so much beautiful . . I called it "painting the air." What the camera team did, the lighting, the sets... if you study them, they are really works of art.

MARC SCOTT ZICREE (story consultant) – They gave us these great crew jackets. They were black and had an enormous "Friday the 13th" logo on the back. Very lurid—it looked like a gang member jacket, so I almost never wore it out in public. One day, I am walking down the street with my wife in Studio City. Suddenly, a seven foot tall black guy runs up behind me, grabs me by the shoulders and says, "They made a series out of that? I can't believe it!" He spins me around, and it turns out it was Kevin Peter Hall, the guy who played Harry in *Harry and the Hendersons*. He was one of the great "suit" actors. He was a really nice guy. But there was that moment where it was like, "I shouldn't have worn this jacket!" Ultimately, I put the jacket on eBay and sold it to one of the fans of the show. It was a great jacket.

ELIAS ZAROU (Rashid) – I can't be sure exactly what went on behind the scenes. I know that Chris was exhausted from the sixteen to eighteen hour shooting days that frequently occurred. I heard a rumor that he was being tough with regard to negotiations for the next season. The rumor further suggested that my character was introduced in the final episode of season one in order to show Chris that a replacement for him was readily available. I think, once the negotiation with Chris was settled, they brought me back for the opening episode of season two and then, perhaps their intent was to have me show up from time to time.

"Doorway to Hell"

Written by: Jim Henshaw
Directed by: William Fruet
Original airdate: September 26, 1988
Cursed antique: Wall mirror

The episode opens with a recap of "Bottle of Dreams," ending with Jack saying, in voice over, "Lewis seems closer now, we can all feel it." An actual door to hell blows open, somewhere. Wherever it is, Jack feels it, or hears it. Lewis appears in a mirror. (Interestingly, not the mirror from "Bottle of Dreams," but it has the same cracked glass as that one did.)

Jack puts Ryan to work looking for the mirror in the manifest. The two are getting frustrated when Micki walks in and tells them they won't find it in the manifest; she found it in Lewis' room and moved it down here when they were restocking the store. This makes sense to Jack: it is one of Lewis' personal belongings, that's why he could see Lewis in it. Lewis was a practitioner of the occult, and mirrors that have reflected occult ceremonies become windows into realms of darkness, the dimension between here and hell. It seems that Lewis has found a path through mirrors to try to come back to life. He decides to go find Rashid for help. While Ryan and Micki are waiting for Jack, Ryan examines the mirror and finds one of the shards loose. Beneath it is a piece of paper, a deed. Lewis owns a house. Over Micki's fervent protests, Ryan insists they go investigate the house.

Eddie (Justin Louis) is a kid on parole, working at a filling station, and basically trying to get his life on track. An old criminal consort of his, Buddy (Charle Landry), rolls in and robs the place, forcing Eddie to help him. Before they leave, Buddy shoots the station owner Mike dead, all because Eddie told him Buddy's name. With few options, Eddie hops in Buddy's car and the two drive off.

Buddy has been holed up in a large house that hasn't seen occupants in years. In case you haven't guessed, this is Lewis' house. They return there, with Eddie marveling at how a house with no electricity can be so hot. They are totally oblivious to Lewis, laughing in the mirror. As Eddie shaves and Buddy cooks breakfast, Eddie hears the laughter and Buddy finally decides to investigate. What he finds isn't Lewis, but Ryan, snooping around. Micki stumbles upon Eddie, who holds a knife to her throat. She kicks her way free and runs to find Ryan. He's not in a better situation: Buddy has a gun aimed at him.

Buddy and Eddie tie up the cousins, but Buddy is very curious as to what they are doing there. He asks Micki, whose response is dripping with disdain and mockery. "What are you doin' here?" she says in her best mobster accent. Eddie just wants to bail, so Buddy sends him to finish shaving. Strangely, that's what Eddie does. It seems so weird for him to do, but it does allow Uncle Lewis to grab him by the neck and drag him into the mirror. Down the hall, Buddy hears the screams and asks Ryan if there is someone with them. "I'm afraid so," he responds in a moment that is endearingly cheesy.

Eddie is wandering around the shadow realm when suddenly he collapses inelegantly in spasms. Jack and Rashid are back at Curious Goods, using one of the mirror shards as a window into what is going on at the house. Rashid, as usual, is doing a spell, which is what caused Eddie's collapse. Rashid is concerned: an immense force has taken over the entire dimension. Jack suggests it is Lewis, but Rashid doesn't think that a single spirit could possess that much power.

Back in the shadow realm, Eddie wakes up, with a strange, mixed-up demonic look to his face. He has war paint of some sort on his face, and his teeth are worn down to meth nubs. Goo drips from his mouth, and he laughs. Buddy hears this and decides to send Micki to investigate. Eddie returns before she can leave the room, and the house starts to shake. Eddie moves like a cartoon Frankenstein's monster: stiffly, with arms extended, and a blank look in his eyes. Micki dodges out of the room while Ryan unties himself. Electricity shoots out of Eddie's hands, forcing Buddy to lift the gun to his own mouth and squeeze the trigger. Blood explodes, blocking Jack and Rashid's view. Ryan joins Micki downstairs, trying desperately to find a way out—the doors are sealed tight and the windows can't be broken. Upstairs, Eddie collapses onto a pile of mirror shards, and Lewis uses this opportunity to jump back into the mirror. (Or maybe he didn't have a choice. Maybe the mirror pieces act like a sponge.)

Jack is frantic back at the store. Rashid theorizes that there is so much negative energy, it is causing the realms to twist and bend, which is why they can see into the house, not the dark realm. I see we are bringing a touch of physics into the proceedings. Lewis appears in the mirror and

Louise Robey and John LeMay warming up between takes on "Doorway to Hell."
Photo courtesy of John LeMay.

threatens that he "needs Micki and Ryan for a little task he has to complete." The link shuts down, and Jack decides he can't wait any longer—he has to go get them. Rashid reasons with him, threatens that it is suicide to go, all of which Jack ignores. "We mustn't lose the connection" is Rashid's final ploy to stay, so Jack hands him the shard of mirror. Off they go.

Ryan and Micki have a new danger to face: Eddie. Lewis is out of his body at the moment, and Eddie is confused. He thinks they killed Buddy and is mad that he can't leave the house. Ryan and Eddie struggle, with Eddie falling into another mirror, breaking it. Lewis returns to Eddie's body, and Micki and Ryan barricade themselves in a room without mirrors. Micki finds a calendar, and realizes that today is the one year anniversary of Lewis' death.

Rashid and Jack arrive, and Rashid approaches the house and starts chanting. Lewis, in Eddie's body, laughs and with a wave of his hand knocks Rashid away. Jack rushes to help his friend, and it is at this point that Rashid decides Lewis has somehow opened the doorway. "The doorway… to hell??"

Inside, the house is coming down all around Micki and Ryan. A door opens and a white light blinds them. As scary as it seems, they have no choice but to jump. They land in the dark realm, in a mossy swamp-like setting, with zombie arms reaching up at them from the ground. They run, and hear Jack calling for them. Micki urges him to look at the date, but before she can give him the pertinent information, Lewis pulls them out of the realm, drops them back into the house, and breaks Jack's connection with them. Lewis-in-Eddie's-body threatens to kill Micki, so Ryan chokes him. Lewis taunts him: kill him, and you will send your soul right to hell. Micki separates them and realizes that Lewis is going after Jack, and there is something he doesn't want them to know.

Jack is getting pretty frantic, even suggesting they ram the house with the car. Rashid is worried that the power of hell would then spill over into the real world; I am more worried about that beautiful car. Jack finally pieces together what Micki was saying about the date, and they rush back to the store. There, in one of his books, Jack finds what Lewis is up to: "From midnight on the first death date, to the rising of the sun, those drawn to hell may purchase freedom from the evil one. Eternal life is granted to he who serves the devil right and draws three corrupted souls into the endless night." Micki, Ryan, and Jack. Rashid suggests waiting out the sunrise: if Jack is not in that house, nothing can happen. Lewis appears in the mirror and promises that even if Jack does nothing, he gets to kill them anyway! He blows out the mirror. Jack heads back to the house while Rashid stays behind. With the proper incantations, Jack can enter the dark realm through one of those mirrors and close the door to hell.

The door swings open readily when Jack returns to Lewis' house. Micki and Ryan hug him gratefully. He tells them to give him five minutes, then start breaking every mirror in the house except the one he goes through. It is purely to distract Lewis, make him think they are trying to trap him, while Jack is actually shutting the door to hell. Jack enters the dark realm easily and heads through the swamp, armed with a big silver crucifix. Vines grab him, garrote him; the crucifix burns through the vines. Lewis is busy chanting, begging to release the beast. In the light, we can just barely make out a huge demon figure. Micki and Ryan begin smashing mirrors, which enrages Lewis. With Lewis distracted, Jack manages to shut the doorway to hell, just as the "master" is barreling towards the door. He seals the door shut with the cross.

With the door to hell closed, the door to the house opens. Micki and Ryan rush out, dragging Eddie with them. Lewis separates from Eddie at the doorway—he can't leave the house. Like any villain, he shouts the empty threat, "You haven't heard the last of me!" In the dark realm, Jack holds up the shard of glass, begging Rashid to get him out of there. He seems to be trying to match the mirror shard in his hand with the space where it belongs in the mirror Rashid put back together.

The house has stopped shaking and is back to normal. Micki rushes back in, looking for Jack. There is no sign of him, and the mirror they left for him is shattered. Micki sobs on Ryan's shoulder: "We lost him."

Status: Micki and Ryan return to the store, despondent. But once they arrive, Jack comes downstairs, fresh out of the shower. They jump on him like puppies. The mirror is in the vault, and Jack thinks they have seen the last of Lewis. But then, they hear something shatter.… .

Of course, they need not worry. Lewis will only appear in one more episode, "Night Hunger," and that is in flashbacks. He never tries to come back again, which I think is for the best. There are only so many times a person can try to crawl back from the underworld before it starts to grow tired. (I'm looking at you, *Supernatural*.)

* * *

I remember loving this episode as a kid, and watching it all the time. But as an adult, I don't know what I saw in it. It was a fine episode, but nothing really stood out about it to me now. Maybe it was the play on the haunted house trope. It made this episode, more than most, feel like a little horror film. At this age my parents still monitored my movies pretty closely, but somehow, if it was on television, it was okay.

Though Rashid only appeared in two episodes, it always felt like he was in more—or at least supposed to be in more episodes. "Towards the end of season two they asked me to come in and work on an episode," says actor Elias Zarou, "but I was shooting a TV movie in Halifax that week so they simply renamed the character and went ahead without me. And that was the end of that." If I had to guess, I would say the role of Gareth in "Coven of Darkness" was originally meant for Rashid. It would make sense that he would come back and help Micki harness her witchy power.

"The wild premise of *F13* meant that we were constantly walking a fine line between the normal and the paranormal, both on and off set," says production designer Stephen Roloff. "I didn't want to create any cult how-to guides, so when episodes dealt with Satanism, witchcraft, voodoo, black magic, and the like, the art department did meticulous research… and then made changes to the iconography and ritual elements."

"The Voodoo Mambo"

Written by: Agy Polly
Directed by: Timothy Bond
Original airdate: October 8, 1988
Cursed antique: Voodoo mask

There is a big "Solstice Festival" taking place right outside Curious Goods. Jack's old friend, Hedley (Joe Seneca), is coming down for the festival and stops in to visit Jack. Hedley is a Legba, a high priest of old African religion. Legbas channel energy between people and spirits, guiding it back and forth between this world and the next. There are four Legbas, one for each of the four elements, and they are protective but can be dangerous if not fed. They seem to feast on a diet of music and dancing and sacrifices. Hedley is a fire Legba, and his granddaughter, Stacy (Rachel Crawford), will be ordained as an air Legba. The two give Micki and Ryan a bit of history on voodoo as a misunderstood religion. Most importantly, they talk about the loa, the voodoo soul, believed to live in the throat. Voodoo is part of Stacy's family. Her parents were priests, but both died when she was a baby. After enjoying the carnival for a little while, Stacy must go to her ceremony. The first part is private; the rest can join her later.

Across town, spoiled rich kid Carl Walters (David Matheson) is having a spat with the executor of his father's will. Jeremiah Walters made a fortune from Haitian coffee beans, but Carl has squandered the family money. Property, stocks, cash—it's all gone. Carl rushes to his massive family home to find a "For Sale" sign in the yard. (Come on, no multi-million dollar estate would put a "For Sale" sign on the lawn.) Inside, Valerie Sands, a high-end realtor, greets him—then tells him he has one hour to vacate the property.

While Carl is in the basement getting a suitcase, he notices an unopened crate of his father's personal effects. It is mostly desk clutter, but one item interests him: a ceremonial mask. Inside the crate, beneath packing material, in a cloud of smoke, and oozing glowing gold liquid, Carl finds a ceremonial mask. He puts it on and it seems to almost fuse with his face. An exasperated Valerie comes down to check on Carl, and is startled by the mask. He moves towards her, and she threatens to call the cops. He grabs her, holds her still, and snake lunges out of the mouth of the mask and rips her throat out before retreating back into the mask. Carl is scared—he clearly didn't realize what he was getting himself into when he tried on that mask. But the "mask" begins speaking to him, identifying herself as Laotia (Suzanne Coy), his servant, who wants to show him how to claim his "true inheritance." She claims she was the one who made his father's plantation flourish, and promises no one can hurt him when they are one. "Let the mask taste the light. That is its life force. Then it will do your bidding. Kill the guardians of the elements, and all the universe will be at your command."

In the first part of Stacy's ceremony, she dances with abandon with a number of other girls while a priestess chants. A breeze picks up, gets stronger, brings with it sand and dust. The priestess commands the spirit to leave, claiming this land is holy. Carl, wearing the mask, steps into view, and the snake darts out and rips the throat out of the priestess. Jack and the rest of the team hear the priestess's strangled cries and head in that direction. It looks to Micki like an animal attack, but Hedley is more concerned. No animal can know the voodoo lore. Someone has stolen her soul.

Reconvening at Curious Goods, Hedley and Stacy fill in the team on more voodoo beliefs, as well as their own family history. Hedley thinks it was Ghede Nibo, or the god of death. It is believed that the dead can be reborn if four souls are gathered. The more powerful the soul, the more powerful the reborn will be. Twenty years ago, in Haiti, a powerful priestess named Laotia was hired by plantation owner Jeremiah Walters to claim she could steal the souls of the workers if she wanted to. She terrorized them into working harder. Laotia was finally killed, but not before she killed many who opposed her. Jack suspects there is more to the story (there is) but Hedley insists on taking Stacy to finish her ceremony. It doesn't take long to find a Haitian snake mask in the manifest, sold to one Jeremiah Walters. Walters died fourteen months ago, so Jack sends the kids to check his home while he goes after Hedley, determined to dig out more of the story.

At the Walters house, Ryan and Micki head into the basement. Drops of blood on Micki's arm alerts her to Valerie's corpse in the rafters. Ryan finds a card for David Rhodes, Jeremiah's attorney, and they hurry out of the house. Carl watches them leave from the shadows, and Laotia tells him to let them go. "But they saw the body!" he exclaims.

"You still don't understand," Laotia soothes, "there is no danger." She explains that the soul they took makes the mask stronger, and that he now has power over air. To prove it to him, she directs him to draw a bird in the dirt. Carl does, and it lights on fire before turning into a real crow and flying away. "Three more souls, and you will have command of man and matter for all eternity," she assures him. All she wants in return is one small reward, which she won't reveal until they are done. Nothing suspicious about that.

Stacy goes through the last ceremony and the elements welcome her. Hedley and Jack congratulate her. Micki and Ryan rush in and fill them in on what they have been up to. Stacy insists it is Laotia, but Hedley insists he saw her die. Laotia created the snake mask to enslave her people; Stacy's parents died battling her; and Hedley "drove her into the sea." (He drowned her.) The mask vanished with Laotia. Jack tells him about Lewis and the store, but Hedley refuses to believe. Ironic, seeing as how he believes so deeply in the spirits of his religion, but the spirits of someone else's religion are impossible. Either way, it's time to pass out the assignments: Stacy and Micki go alert the guardian of water; Ryan goes to speak to the attorney; and Jack takes a voodoo priest back to the store. Though not an official "assignment," Hedley visits the Walters house and scrapes up some of the golden goo in the basement.

The girls go to the beach, where Dyzon Legba is confident that Ghede Nibo would not dare hurt her. Of course, she speaks too soon, and Carl, in the mask, pops out of the water. He kills Dyzon and Laotia appears like a ghost over the water. The girls run, and Laotia advises Carl to follow the Haitian girl; she will lead them to the third guardian.

Ryan pays attorney David Rhodes a visit, and he doesn't tell Ryan much that we the audience don't already know. He does suggest Ryan check with Carl, Jeremiah's son, then goes back to bed. This scene is important, though, because on his way back to the car, Ryan is dive-bombed by the crow that Carl and Laotia summoned.

Jack and the earth Legba are back at Curious Goods, and the Legba suggests an herb that Jack can take to prevent Laotia from possessing his spirit. The girls return with the report of the water Legba's death, and Hedley comes back with the glowing goo, which he says is the residue the spirit leaves when it comes to this plane. He also has one final chapter of Laotia's story to share: Laotia was his wife, Stacy's grandmother. "Your father died fighting his own mother," he admits sadly. The plan seems to be that Laotia will take Hedley's soul, then inhabit Stacy's body forever.

Goofing off on the set of "The Voodoo Mambo." Photo courtesy of John LeMay.

Ryan comes in, shaken and bloody and warns them about Carl. The shop starts shaking and Carl makes his grand entrance, exploding out of the floorboards. He instantly kills the earth Legba, and Laotia appears (in spirit form), asking if Hedley can kill her again. Carl carries Stacy out of the store, and Jack reminds Hedley that if Laotia doesn't have his soul, there is nothing she can do to harm Stacy. Ryan suggests they put Hedley in the vault for safe-keeping, but that's not Hedley's style. So, they all head back to the Walters house.

At the house, Carl has already tied Stacy up. Laotia advises him not to harm Stacy - she is the wish he will grant her. "Through her, I will live again. The moment it is done, I will be gone forever and you will be the master of earth." She asks to borrow the mask, only for a moment, which

Carl naively turns over. She puts it on, lassos him with orange light, kills him, and takes his power for her own.

The sun is coming up and Laotia forces the mask onto Stacy. Jack and the crew break in, but Laotia immediately whips out a voodoo doll and collapses Jack in pain. Micki stands up to her, and Laotia threatens to drain the life from her. She forgets about Micki when Ryan and Hedley come in. Hedley offers his life to her, if she lets their granddaughter go. To aggravate her, Hedley talks about murdering her, relishing every detail. Laotia is angered and takes the mask off Stacy and holds it up in the sunlight. "I'll have you both!" she insists. Ryan comes in with a sneak attack and knocks the mask from her hands. Unfortunately, the Ghede Nibo has already been called and he won't leave without taking a soul. It strikes Laotia, who turns into a desiccated old woman before disappearing. The mask drops harmlessly to the ground.

Status: Micki buries the mask deep in the back of the vault, where sunlight will never hit it (not like anything even remotely resembling light has ever gotten near the basement) and the group goes outside to enjoy the rest of the carnival.

* * *

I hardly ever watched "The Voodoo Mambo" when I was a kid, and watching it again now, I remember why: the damn snakes. Why does it always have to be snakes? In episodes like "Tattoo" and "And Now the News," the snakes were limited to just one or two scenes. But the serpents are scattered throughout this entire episode, and it really gives me the chills. Even as an adult, watching the throat-ripping scenes, I can see now that the snakes (in those scenes) are not real, but it doesn't give me any less of the heebie-jeebies. It's kind of fun, though, almost like watching an episode I have never seen.

Director Tim Bond commiserates over the fear of snakes with this hilarious—if terrifying—story. "I have a lifetime fear of snakes. When it came time to make the shots of the snake shooting out of the mouth of the mask, I spent a night with the second unit, staging the shots. The second unit cameraman, Rick Wincenty, brought his own six foot long rat snake for the shots. He told me they only eat once a month, and he had not fed his pet for about five weeks.

"The snake was a finicky eater. He liked mice, but only if they're peeled! So, Rick had brought along an egg carton full of skinned, recently thawed dead mice. We mounted the mask on a black wall, a hole behind the mouth with a plastic pipe leading to the hole. Rat snakes like to travel down narrow tubes. For greater impact, I had the camera very close to the mask so I could use a super wide lens. That way, when the snake lunged out of the mouth toward the camera it would get very large in the frame, very fast. And to extend the fear, we ran the camera at high speed, which means the shot would end up in slow motion.

"I stood well back while Rick called the snake. We rolled the camera, which sounds like a demented Kitchen Aid mixer when you're shooting slow motion. Rick operated, watching the snake through the eye piece while he dangled a peeled mouse just off camera, close to the lens. Wham! The snake snaffled the mouse and hauled ass back into the pipe to get it down. But, when you're looking through the viewfinder with a very wide lens, you lose all sense of depth. Rick missed moving the camera to hold his pet in the frame.

"We tried again. And again. And again. After six mice the snake was getting full. Even moving more slowly, it was hard for Rick to frame the shot using one hand, while dangling a dead mouse from the other. He suggested I hold the mouse! No fucking way. So, I ended up operating the camera while Rick fed the snake. There's nothing like watching a snake lunge at you when you have no perception of depth. By mouse number nine we had the shot and it was a killer. The snake came right at the lens, mouth super wide, incisors slicing the air.

"So, we stopped shooting. Rick called the snake back out of the pipe. It obediently began its retreat—and got stuck in the pipe. He was too full, bulging in the middle with nine mice. He tried to come out through the mouth, but he couldn't get out that way, either. Then I noticed the snake was afraid. I had no idea a cold blooded snake could feel emotions! My fear of reptiles vanished. All I felt now was compassion and an overwhelming desire to free the poor snake. Careful work with a hacksaw over thirty minutes and we got the poor guy free. He curled up around Rick's arm and went to sleep. And I went home, cured forever of my fear of snakes."

In my admittedly limited research on voodoo traditions, it seems that the legbas referenced in this episode would be more properly called loa. Loa are the intermediaries between humanity and the spirit world. Legba appears to refer to Papa Legba, a specific loa who (according to Wikipedia) helps communicate between humans and loas.

Actress Suzanne Coy, who played Laotia, has a better understanding of voodoo tradition. Coy was born in Jamaica, where they have a derivative of voodoo called "Obeah." "It seemed to combine herbal healing with mystic influences and spell-making or cures. All I knew about voodoo was it involved possession by the ancestors, though everyone in Jamaica has some experience with ghost, also known as duppies."

Friday the 13th: The Series was Coy's first foray into the horror genre. "When I was four my parents took me to see *The Wizard of Oz.* I was petrified and spent most of the show screaming under the seat. See, I thought there was a door on the side of every screen where the characters could get out. So, this was my first horror show and it was good to see how things were done. I thought it was a great way to de-mystify how scary stuff was made.

"I remember shooting seventeen hours one day," Coy continues. "It was the day they did an eight hour makeup job on me for the horrible old face that my character turns into as she is dying. It was also the day we did matching black and white shots where my husband was supposed to drown me. Nothing like being drowned in a bathtub for fun."

"And Now the News"

Written by: Dick Benner
Directed by: Bruce Pittman
Original airdate: October 10, 1988
Cursed antique: Radio

The Maseo Institute for the Criminally Insane. An inmate, Mary (Wendy Lyon), is *screaming* because Dr. Finch (Kurt Reis), head of the department, is holding a tiny little snake out to her. I don't blame her; I would probably have the same reaction. Her father poured snakes on her while in bed, just to torture her, and she killed him for it. Finch sees this as a breakthrough, and believes Mary will eventually be released. If he can break the phobia, he can break the criminal tendencies.

Dr. Carter (Kate Trotter), the other psychiatrist there, brings an antique radio into Mary's room, a "treat" for her breakthrough with Dr. Finch. It plays music—without being plugged in. Mary goes to sleep, listening to old fashioned music, but the music is interrupted with an announcement: "And now the news." The "news report" is about thousands of snakes filling the Maseo Institute. Mary is scared, but she isn't just imagining the invasion—she is seeing it. Her room is flooded with snakes, slithering all over her. She screams, and Finch comes running, but by the time he and a support team arrives, Mary is dead and there is no evidence that there was even a single snake in her room. As Mary is wheeled out, the radio wraps up: "… and that's the news." The phantom announcer promises to return with news about Dr. Carter discovering a cure for serial killer Craig Eddy, a paranoid schizophrenic.

Micki and Ryan get pulled into this case when a response to one of their mailers comes in. Joe Damien bought the radio, but this letter is from his lawyer. He died one year ago at the Maseo Institute. He was admitted on a Friday; died on a Sunday. Hanged himself. Jack is out of town, so the cousins head off on their own to the institute.

Nurse Bradley (Fran Gebhard) explains that Dr. Finch is currently in charge, working with impulse killers who kill because of childhood phobias. He is not having much success and will probably be replaced by

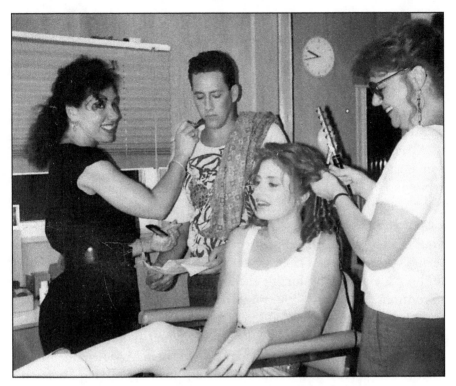

Getting pretty for "And Now the News." Photo courtesy of John LeMay.

Carter as the head of the department. Finch is not very helpful: he is not familiar with Damien, and he doesn't want them looking around. But he does keep their card. Micki is easily frustrated and suggests they call Jack. Ryan doesn't want to go running to him every time they hit a brick wall. He plans to "visit" after hours.

Craig is "cured," and Carter sees him out. Another patient, John Gibson (Stephen Black), wants the same miracle cure. He knows someone is helping her, and he threatens to tell. Finch is already suspicious of her methods, but doesn't believe she is curing them overnight. Of course, for most psychoses, there is no cure; the best one can hope for is that it be well managed.

Micki drops Ryan off outside the institute, and promises to return in an hour. Ryan examines the fence and gives it a climb. He is cautious when he gets to the barbed wire at top, but doesn't realize it is electrified. He is shocked and collapses. Some of the nurses find him and bring him in on a stretcher. Ryan is still twitchy from the volt. Nurse Bradley runs for Finch, but he is deep in the middle of a session with a pyrophobic patient. So, instead Carter examines him. He is fine, but Carter won't let him leave until Ryan explains why he was climbing the fence. He makes up some story about it being a frat prank. Carter buys it and won't call the police. Ryan returns to Micki and suggests the radio might not be in the hands of a patient, but a staffer. Carter has been doing a lot of press lately, so Micki will go in tomorrow as a magazine reporter.

And now the news: Dr. Carter will begin treatments with John Gibson. If she succeeds, it will lead to a Nobel Prize. Gibson is a sociopathic rapist and murderer, the kind of shit that can't even be managed.

Carter pops in on Finch during another session with his pyrophobe, Clarence. She needs access to the Gibson file. "No woman is safe with him!" Finch insists. He doesn't trust her, but he's not going to endanger people's lives, not even her's. Carter throws it back at him, blaming him for his patients' deaths, forcing them to confront fears they are not ready to confront.

Orderly Swanson has left Micki outside the restricted, high-security zone while he goes looking for the doctor. When another orderly leaves the ward, Micki takes the opportunity to sneak in. A violent, demented man (who we later find out is a cannibal) pops up, scaring Micki and sending her right towards Gibson. "Don't be afraid," he assures her, "I'm not like the rest of them." Micki, somehow, believes this and moves a couple steps closer (I guess, in the moment, he seemed like a better choice than a cannibal) before Swanson warns her away. Carter comes in, reprimands Swanson for the lapse in security, and whisks Micki away.

After Clarence's session, Carter had brought in the radio. So, while Carter is speaking with Micki, Clarence believes he is burning alive, thanks to a news report about the institute being engulfed in flames. Clarence panics, rips the bars from his window, and hurls himself to his death. Ryan is outside, pacing nervously, waiting for Micki. He sees this frenzied suicide—but no fire. Not even a wisp of smoke. Finch enters Clarence's room a few minutes too late to save him. Understandably, this death caused Carter to cut the interview short. Micki will return tomorrow to finish.

Before anyone can search Clarence's room, Carter has taken the radio back to her office to get her next cure. The radio tells her that Gibson responds to treatment when a doctor approves of his actions. She is also told that Clarence is the first of three who must die before midnight in order for her to cure Gibson and get her Nobel. Finch pays her a visit and accuses Carter of taking the radio, the one those antique dealers said could be used to hurt people. He also remembers her being the only doctor to work with Joe Damien. As he starts to draw the correlations, Carter knocks him out with a lamp.

Finch wakes, strapped to a gurney, and discovers Carter is depositing him into the cannibal's room. The cannibal violently tears into Finch, leaving blood and gristle on the tiny plexiglass window in the door. Carter seems shocked at the violence. "Feels good, doesn't it?" asks Gibson, watching from his own cell. Carter ponders this as she picks up Micki's card from the floor.

Micki gets a call from Finch, claiming he has the radio, and tells her to meet him in the Thompson wing. But of course, it's not Finch—it is Gibson, calling at Carter's behest. Carter assures him that he can use Micki to cure himself. "We never *want* to hurt them, but sometimes we need to." Gibson has never been spoken to like this, and he wonders if it is a trick. "So, it is okay if I do this?" Yes.

Micki heads into the darkness, into the clearly abandoned Thompson wing. While Micki heads off to certain doom, Ryan has learned his lesson, and climbs the fence again—this time with thick rubber gloves. He makes it over safely.

Micki calls for Finch as she explores the abandoned wing. She has a flashlight, not sure where she got it, but she has one. Suddenly she is grabbed from behind. Gibson. He throws her down on a filthy, bare mattress, the kind from the most disturbing rape nightmares. She fights him off; he grabs her back; she fights more; he slaps her. Ryan's break-in has set off alarms, which momentarily distracts Gibson, long enough for Micki to run—just not far. Gibson tears off her sweater, but she has grabbed the flashlight and knocks him out with it. Micki runs, without looking back. Ryan has made his way into the Thompson wing and comes across Gibson, who is just getting up. Ryan sucker punches him, but he in turn is knocked out by Carter. "Forget the girl; he is your ticket out of here," she tells Gibson. Sure, that's easy for Carter to say—she wasn't the one looking forward to raping the girl.

Once a safe distance away, Micki finds a room to collect herself in. She vomits and takes a minute—until she peeks out a window and sees Ryan being carried into the hospital.

Ryan is strapped to a gurney and Carter brings in the radio. Gibson is eager to break his neck, but the doc insists it look like an accident. She will electrocute him with the shock therapy tools and pretend he got electro-

Director Bruce Pittman and assistant director John Board flanked by the series stars on the set of "And Now the News." Photo courtesy of Bruce Pittman.

cuted on the fence. As Carter prepares to zap him, the power goes out—thanks to Micki. Carter goes to find out what happened, and Ryan sets to work trying to free himself. Carter returns, closely followed by Micki, who gives Gibson a shove. He falls into the electric paddles and fries to death. Micki frees Ryan and Carter comes at the two of them with the paddles. She is distracted by a new news report on the radio, announcing her own death. Carter is shocked, and the radio continues: she was unable to complete the requisite accidental deaths by 11:55 p.m., which has "forced this station to cancel its commitment to her." She grabs the radio and is starts burning her from the inside out. Oozing blisters appear on her face, and she explodes into ash. "We'll be back with a new offer to listeners, right after this," the radio announces before clicking off.

Status: The radio is vaulted, but before Micki can lock it up, the radio springs to life with one, final offer: a way to retrieve cursed objects quickly and safely, then render them useless—if certain conditions are met.

* * *

This episode is one of my five favorite episodes. It is well-paced, with plenty of action and interesting characters. It is also the only episode that genuinely scared me. I am severely phobic of snakes, and this episode opens with big, nasty room full of snakes. I still can't watch that scene. Story editor Jim Henshaw shares a great anecdote about that scene: "We called virtually every snake handler in Toronto. They brought in hundreds of snakes to shoot this scene. We had the studio set up on a Saturday so we could do minimal crew, no one else around. These guys show up with their snakes, and they were a pretty odd collection. The most immediate concern was, how do we tell everyone's snakes apart if they are all going to be in a pile? The actress, who was also a stunt woman, had no idea it would be like this. Anyway, what someone decided was that we would color-code the snakes. We used the little round stickers that you put on files and put them on all the snakes' bellies. One person's snakes got a red sticker; another person's got a blue sticker. We threw the snakes in this pit and we did the scene and it went really well. No one got hurt, and no one got eaten. That was one of the big concerns: that some of the bigger snakes would eat some of the smaller ones. These are the kinds of things you never take into account when you are doing it. All of this ends, and we forgot how hot it would get in this pit with these snakes. All the stickers had come off, so the final image of the day was all these guys standing with a handful of snakes saying, 'I think this one's mine, but I think this guy is yours.' It was absolutely ridiculous. Hysterically funny."

Director Bruce Pittman's snake anecdote is a little more terrifying. "I was wearing sandals. A snake got wedged in my sandal during the take." He had to ask actress Wendy Lyon, who was covered in snakes, how the take went. Pittman admits shooting that scene helped him get over his fear of snakes, even if the snakes didn't really do anything. "They just kind of laid there," he says. "I think the studio was too hot, the lights were too hot… they weren't doing anything. We sent the props guy to the dollar store to get some rubber snakes. So, the snakes that are really effective are rubber snakes. We shot some inserts with a snake coming through a vent, and stuff like that. But most of the really good snake stuff was rubber snakes." One of the snakes was venomous, but the herpetologist on set promised you would basically have to step on it for it to bite you. Small comfort, I'm sure, to those on set. Of a hundred snakes, only one got away. "We have no idea, to this day, where it is. Somewhere in that studio there is a snake. Not venomous, but it is exotic."

Cinematographer Rodney Charters has a coda to this story. "They thought they got them all. Everybody was happy. They got all their snakes back. But about a month later, we came into work and there was a shed skin on the ground. So, obviously, there was a snake living on the set, somewhere in the bowels of the set. It gave a little edge to crawling in dark spaces. No one ever found it. It had gone feral by then; it was on its own. I'm sure it kept the rat population down."

Actress Kate Trotter, who played Dr. Avril Carter, didn't have any interactions with the snakes, but she was attacked by a rolling bin. "I had to stop a big bin from hitting a wall. We rehearsed it at half-pace, and then we did it, and he pushed that bin so hard. My finger was between the wall and the bin. I thought, *Well, if I stop now, we'll never get the scene because as soon as I release the bin, I know the pain will just shoot through my body.* So, I just kept going. My adrenaline was really high so I could do that. And then of course it hurt a lot when [Bruce] called cut and they pulled the bin away. I said, 'I think I hurt my finger.' They sent me to a doctor and I got it wrapped up and within a couple hours I was back and we just shot without my hand showing."

"And Now the News" was shot at Lakeshore Psychiatric Hospital in Toronto, which was operational from 1889 through 1979. "It was a huge property with all kinds of buildings that had dark corridors and large rooms where you could build sets. It was almost like a film studio," Pittman said of the location. After its closure, Lakeshore was a popular place to shoot. Several *Police Academy* films were shot there, and *War of the Worlds* was in production around the time *Friday the 13th: The Series* was shooting. "Occasionally we would want to use a part of the space, and we would pull up and find they already parked their truck there to shoot in the same spot." As with most old hospitals, rumors persist to this day that Lakeshore (which is now Humber College) is haunted. No one that I spoke to from *F13* ever mentioned the place feeling haunted.

One thing that always struck me about "And Now the News" is how Micki is *not* a "scream queen." She has never been a "woman in peril," but this episode really highlights it. Micki is put up against a psychopathic rapist/murderer (yes, she should have thought twice about meeting the "doctor" in an obviously abandoned portion of the hospital, even if she thought she was retrieving an item from storage) and she saves herself. Ryan doesn't come in until Micki is out of harm's way, and he is the one who ends up needing to be saved. It is one of the few episodes where the direct danger is not at the hands of a supernatural entity, but a real, live human being who was evil without benefit of a cursed antique.

"They were always human beings," says Trotter of the characters in *F13*. "No matter what their problems were, or what cursed objects they were dealing with, they were human beings with real needs." In reference to her own character, Trotter saw her as being "just on the edge of insane." "What does this character want and what does this character need? That determines how you are going to play a scene, what you are going to do physically. That's when you have good writing. A good writer gives you that underbelly and gives you that drive, so you can form those intentions. I felt that with that woman. I always knew what she needed and why."

The final offer that the radio makes to Micki and Ryan is antithetical to its very existence—or it could be paving the way to being the *only* curse in town.

"Tales I Live, Heads You Die"

Written by: Marilyn Anderson & Billy Riback
Directed by: Mark Sobel
Original airdate: October 17, 1988
Cursed antique: The coin of Ziocles

Graveyard. Night. A couple hooded men dig up a grave, while an older man, Sylvan (Colin Fox), looks on. The groundskeeper confronts them and threatens to call the police. "The call's on me," Sylvan says, tossing him a coin with a ram's head on it. The coin flashes and glows, seemingly hypnotizing the groundskeeper before a beam of light zaps the guy dead. He is left with a ram's head branded into his forehead. A harried reporter, Tom Hewitt (Bill MacDonald), is hiding behind the tombstones, snapping frantic photos.

Sylvan and his followers bring the coffin to their underground Satanic coven, which is exactly as creepy as it sounds. "We are gathered here to invoke Satan's will," Sylvan begins the ceremony, which is intended to summon "the best, the strongest of us" from the "hindrance of death." Hewitt is watching from the shadows. The coffin is the centerpiece of the ceremony. Sylvan places the same ram's head coin on the head of the corpse and pronounces "So mote it be!" The coin glows, disappears, and the corpse's eyes open. His mouth opens slowly, gruesomely, and he sits up. Sylvan kisses his hand and welcomes him.

At the shop, our trio is enjoying their first peaceful evening in a long time. Ryan is sculpting a bust of Micki, when the phone rings. It is Hewitt, and he is frantic. He was told Jack was an expert on the occult, but it is too dangerous to meet. He left him an envelope in the basement locker of Union Station, with the key left separately, and begs him to retrieve it as soon as he can. Hewitt promises to call back, and leaves Jack with a little teaser: "I think I just saw a man come back from the dead." No sooner does he hang up than the cult members grab him.

Hewitt is brought back to the ceremonial bunker and confronted by Sylvan. As is typical of a villain, Sylvan explains his evil plan before killing Hewitt. The one who they brought back from the dead is the first of three to be revived. He is Carl Naft (hardly a threatening name for a Satanist), and is skilled in calling spirits. The other two are Tiriel, the most powerful Satanist of the last century, and Hiberia, the witch queen of Salem. "Together, we will call our master to regain his throne." With his soliloquy finished, Sylvan and a couple cult members lead Hewitt back to the graveyard, where he kills Hewitt with the coin and leaves him in a grave. I could swear that I could still see Hewitt breathing after his "death."

Jack and Ryan retrieve the envelope and take it back to the store to look through. Inside are photos of a witch's coven, undeveloped film, news clippings on the death of Carl Naft, and a mini cassette. When played, it sounds like gibberish, but Jack recognizes it: the Lord's Prayer chanted backwards, which is the opening prayer in a black mass. The next day, Hewitt's obituary appears in the newspaper. Jack had the film developed and sees that the resurrected corpse is indeed Carl Naft. Micki draws the connection quickly to a cursed object, suggesting someone dies, and another is resurrected. Jack sends Micki down to the coroner's office while he and Ryan visit a taxidermy shop that Hewitt photographed.

At the taxidermy shop, Ryan and Jack see a couple guys unloading a human-sized crate from the museum of natural history. They enter the shop a few minutes later, and are surprised to see no sign of the crate. Sylvan is there, behind the counter, and Ryan inquires about stock for the store: "lion's heads, tiger rugs, those umbrella stands they used to make out of elephant feet." Ick. Sylvan insists they have nothing like that; they do custom work, no leftovers. The guys leave, but Sylvan is suspicious. As soon as they are gone, he slips into a trap door behind the counter, which takes him into his labyrinthine coven. Carl is waiting for him by the crate, and asks about the visitors. Sylvan identifies them as the people who picked up Hewitt's package, but he isn't worried about them. They have Tiriel, and by tonight they will have Hiberia. Then they will be too strong to be stopped.

Reconvening at Curious Goods, Micki learned from the coroner that the victims had ram's heads branded onto their foreheads. To the manifest they go, and Jack finds the Coin of Ziocles, sold to Sylvan Winters, the taxidermist. Ziocles was a fourteenth century alchemist and powerful warlock, who minted his own gold coins, then used them to decide if his enemies would live or die. I guess he was the original Two-Face.

Jack and Micki head back to the taxidermy shop. They hear the Satanic chanting and follow it through the trap door, down the tunnel, and settle into a hiding space on the stairs. Sylvan is leading the ritual to revive

Tiriel, a decayed corpse covered in bugs. (The museum curators should be ashamed of themselves.) Jack points out the coin as it is placed on Tiriel's forehead, and identifies a low, grumbling sound as the voice of Satan. Tiriel sits up, and Sylvan assures him they are on his side, and are set to revive Hiberia.

Micki knocks something over and the clank draws the attention of the cultists. Jack tells Micki to run upstairs while he draws their attention away. Only a handful of cultists follow Jack; Micki is left to face Carl and Tiriel. She tries to go the opposite direction, but comes face-to-face with Sylvan. The best she can offer is that she didn't see anything. Sylvan says nothing, just flips the coin. It lands in front of Micki, hypnotizing her… then it zaps her, slams her against the wall, and leaves its mark on her forehead.

Micki is dead.

Jack returns to the store, out of breath, having run the whole way. Ryan thought Micki was with Jack. Jack gives him the broad strokes of what went on, and Ryan is pissed. "She's still down there?!" "I'm afraid she isn't," Jack laments as the two race out.

But Micki is dead.

Arriving at the taxidermy shop, Jack and Ryan find the car still there… but there is also a police cordon. They force their way through and find Micki lying on the ground, dumped outside by Sylvan or his minions. Ryan falls apart, cradles her, stroking her hair, repeating "she can't be dead, she can't be dead." He cries unashamedly and refuses to leave her. Jack talks to the cops for a minute, then returns to Ryan, insisting they go. "We can't do anything more here." Ryan relents. He kisses her forehead, closes her eyes, and lays her down oh-so-gently.

Micki is dead.

Back at the shop, Jack researches to keep busy, but Ryan can only stare at his sculpture of Micki, lamenting that she didn't deserve this, then turning his anger to Jack. "Why did you run out on her? Why did you let them get their hands on her, you bastard?!" He tries to hit Jack, but Jack catches him and Ryan collapses into tears on Jack's shoulder. "I loved her, too," Jack says, his voice breaking. "I know this wasn't her job, it's not yours, and it certainly isn't mine, but who else is going to stop what began here? If we don't do it, what happens to all the people other people love?"

Despite all the pretty words, Micki is still dead.

Returning to the books, desperate to keep their minds occupied, Jack finds out more about Cameron Tiriel, a Satanic priest and warlock from the nineteenth century. He published a tome called "The Region of Shadows," which was purported to have been dictated by Satan himself. The combined powers of Tiriel and Hiberia are said to be enough to bring the devil himself to earth. Legend has it that Hiberia, the queen witch of Salem, was said to have been Satan's lover. The witches of Salem were hanged and thrown into a swamp, where the mud preserved them. The men prepare to head back out to Sylvan's headquarters tonight, to stop him from bringing back Hiberia. Ryan informs Jack that when this is over, when they get back the coin, he is out. Finished. Done. Jack seems like he is going to try to talk Ryan out of it, but then Ryan says, "I don't want to go through this when you die." As they leave the store, a pair of cultists attack them with a dagger.

Micki is still dead.

Sylvan dresses Hiberia with oil. The two cultists slip into the ceremony, but it is really Jack and Ryan in the cultists' robes. Jack holds the knife to Sylvan's throat and threatens him. Sylvan claims the coin is "down there," and Ryan gets rid of Hiberia so at least they won't be able to bring her back. Sylvan tries bargaining for his life, and Tiriel attacks. Jack warns that they better not kill him if they want to know where Ryan took Hiberia. "Save him for the coin," Sylvan decrees sadly. They leave Carl guarding Jack and find Ryan, dragging Hiberia through the tunnels. He has no choice but to give up the mummy.

Micki is still dead.

The ceremony begins again. Hiberia is placed on the altar, and Satan is called upon to bless the ceremony and the rebirth of his mistress. Ryan and Jack are locked in a closet, and the voice of Satan echoing through the caverns scares Ryan. Jack just focuses on picking the lock. Sylvan produces the coin, like sleight of hand, and places it on Hiberia's forehead. He commands her to rise, and slowly, slowly, the mummy sits up. But the clay mask breaks.

Micki is alive!

It was Micki beneath all that mud. She looks way too pretty to have been dead for the last few hours, and her hair way too silky to have been caked in clay. Sylvan is shocked. Satan is pissed, and starts bringing the building down. As Sylvan begs for compassion from his dark master, Jack throws a still-dazed Micki over his shoulder and Ryan digs around for the coin.

Our heroes are on their way out when they are stopped by Sylvan, who really wants that coin. So, Ryan flips it behind him as they continue outside, the rumbling growing worse. Jack wonders why the coin didn't work on Sylvan, and Ryan reveals that it was just a silver dollar. "I've got the real coin right here!" he announces proudly—then promptly drops it. Why the hell would he pull it out of his pocket in the first place? Jack tells him to leave it as the roof collapses. The three of them make it out alive.

Back at home, Ryan and Jack tuck Micki into bed and explain the whole cunning plan. Ryan sneaked her body out of the morgue while the coroner was having a midnight snack. He made a mask of Hibera to put over Micki's face, then switched the bodies while Jack was keeping Sylvan busy. Micki asks why they didn't just use the coin themselves, and Jack laughs. "We didn't have the coin. Our one chance was to get Sylvan to do it for us, and that is what destroyed the coven," he explains. Also, they are not supposed to use a cursed antique, no matter how altruistic it may be.

Status: The coin is not returned, but Jack seems to think it is as safe beneath a hundred tons of rubble as it would be in the vault. "I think we can say we won this one," Jack says. Ryan "wouldn't want to go on doing this stuff" without Micki, an admission that surprises Jack—and makes him proud.

We get one final look at the coin, among the rubble, and a cultist's hand, making a desperate, if fruitless, attempt to grab it.

*   *   *

Our heroes have always been in danger, but this is the first—and only—time that any of them have actually died. Modern horror shows, like *Supernatural* or *The Vampire Diaries*, kill off characters on an almost weekly basis, but death is never final on those shows. I have lost count how many times the Winchester brothers have died. In *Friday the 13th: The Series*, death is a little more finite. But no one was going to let Micki die. Hell, they wouldn't even kill off Ryan when John LeMay wanted off the show.

And yet, they almost did let Micki die. Marilyn Anderson, who co-wrote this episode with her then-writing partner Billy Riback, remembers the story producers joked that they'd like to "keep" her dead. "Basically, they loved the idea of killing Micki—and I think that probably sold them on us, then and there; they loved the idea and the story we created with it."

Neither Anderson nor Riback had any experience with the horror genre; both were comedy writers and met as stand-up comedians. In fact, the only writing sample the pair gave the *F13* producers was a spec script for the show *Cheers*. "Marilyn was really the brains behind our little operation," says Riback. "She was very aggressive, and back then being a woman writer and being aggressive was not looked on particularly fondly, but she didn't care—thank god!" Anderson met Bill Taub and Marc Scott Zicree at a WGA event and they mentioned they were looking for Canadian writers. Riback is from Montreal, so she pitched them as a team. "They read our *Cheers* spec and they said they really liked it, but it was a comedy so they didn't really know if we could write in the horror genre. I convinced them that we could definitely do it and asked if we could please come in and pitch," says Anderson, who was pretty sure they only agreed because Riback was Canadian, and half the writers needed to be Canadian. Ironically, they ended up filling one of the American "slots" since Anderson was WGA and would get a better deal.

Both writers remember Zicree's warning to them: "'No comedy. Don't even think about it. The whole show is going to sound like a set-up to you, and it is. Avoid it at all costs. It's not tongue-in-cheek, there is no irony,'" Riback remembers. "He was right, because as we were writing, the jokes *leaped out* and there was *nothing* I could do about it. It took tremendous restraint on my part."

Even still, Riback managed a little joke with the title, "Heads I Live, Tales You Die." "I remember a great line in 'The Honeymooners' where Ralph is trying to screw over Norton, and they were betting something. He said, 'Heads I win, tales you lose.' I always loved that. I think the episode sort of followed from that, believe it or not."

"Symphony in B#"

Story by: Peter Mohan
Teleplay by: Carl Binder
Directed by: Francis Delia
Original Airdate: October 31, 1988
Cursed antique: Violin

Janos Korda (James Russo) is one of the greatest composers and musicians of the generation (according to Jack). Unfortunately, he died five years ago in a car accident. And yet, every year around the anniversary of his death, a new Korda recording is released, presumably from previously recorded, unreleased tapes.

But this is *Friday the 13th* so we all know the most logical answer is not even close to the real one.

Korda didn't die in that accident, but he was horribly burned and his hands were crippled beyond use. The night of his "death," his girlfriend and student Leslie (Ely Pouget) gave him an antique Guarnerius violin. When Korda kills someone with the violin, it temporarily repairs his hands so he can play. The bow of the violin has a hidden knife, which Korda uses to stab his victims to death. I can't help but wonder at what point the knife was added to the violin. Was the violin crafted with the knife? Did Uncle Lewis add it? Or did Korda install it when he learned of the curse?

Micki drags Ryan with her to the symphony. He is bored senseless, until he takes notice of the second chair violinist, Leslie. While he is busy flirting with her backstage, Micki sees the police outside. The janitor was killed during the show. Unbeknownst to the audience, Korda was playing along with the symphony from his *Phantom of the Opera*-esque lair in the basement.

Leslie blew off Ryan after the concert, but he is smitten, so he takes to stalking her. But "gentle" stalking—Ryan's not a scary-stalker, though it is a little questionable when he bumps into her on the street as she leaves a music store. Anyway, he again pursues her for a date, and is turned down at ever chance.

During rehearsal, first chair violinist Phil (Christopher Britton) scolds Leslie for her sloppy playing. Korda, always watching from the shadows, follows Phil up to the roof on his smoke break, lures him in with his torturous strains on the violin, and stabs him through the heart. Ryan just *happens* to be walking down the street shortly thereafter, sees the cops, and goes inside to check on Leslie. She tells him about Phil's murder, and despite having known Ryan for a grand total of five minutes, turns, and cries on his shoulder.

He finally gets a dinner date, and she admits to feeling better after the meal. Even still, Ryan walks her home and she goes inside without so much as a handshake. But once inside, Leslie hears the ghostly violin, unmistakably that of Janos Korda, that has been haunting her the last few days. She investigates, calling Korda's name, and the music stops. She panics and runs.

Outside, she just *happens* to run into Ryan, who was bringing her the music she forgot. She is afraid and doesn't want to spend the night alone. Ryan is happy to stay with her, and the two end up in bed. Come morning, Leslie seems a lot more relaxed.

This is about the time that Micki starts to get concerned. Ryan didn't come home that night (hard to bring a girl home when you don't actually have a bedroom) and he seems to have fallen for Leslie very quickly. Add with that the two murders in as many days at Leslie's symphony, and Micki and Jack turn to the manifest. The Guarnerius is listed, having been purchased by a Frank Macklin, who bought it as a gift to Korda from one of his students. Leslie was one of his students. Jack speaks to another student, who confirms it was Leslie who gave Korda the violin, but denies it could be her on the new Korda recordings. "Leslie's good, but she'd have to sell her soul to play like Janos." Furthering suspicions is the discovery that there are murder sprees every year around the release of a new Korda record.

Leslie notices a pocket watch on her music stand, one she gave to Korda with an inscription on it. (She gave him an awful lot of gifts.) Her fear now replaced with curiosity, Leslie follows the phantom violin, down into the basement, and into the Phantom's lair. She doesn't seem particularly shocked to see him, despite the fact that he is completely wrapped in bandages, *Invisible Man*-style. She is upset that he essentially faked his death; he would rather be dead than left like this, unable to play. She sobs into his chest and he begs her not to reveal his secret.

Ryan visits Leslie, but she wants to be left alone. He refuses, so she leaves, and he promises to wait there for her. While she is gone, an intruder breaks in. Ryan sneaks up on the thief—but it is only Micki. Ryan doesn't want to hear any wild accusations, and seems surprised to learn that Leslie and Korda were lovers. I can't help but wonder how he couldn't have known that. Oh right, he's known her for two days. He sees the pocket watch and leaves.

Leslie, meanwhile, had gone out looking for Korda. Unfortunately, she finds him, just as he kills a drunk off the street. Korda grabs her and drags her back to his lair, where he forces her to play with him on his newest recording. Somehow Leslie's whimpers don't make it onto the recording. Ryan follows the music and finds Leslie tied up in the lair, Korda nowhere in sight. She begs him to leave, but Ryan won't and Korda appears. Leslie defends Ryan, claiming he is just a friend. We have a dramatic burned-face reveal (that sadly just doesn't live up to the pinnacle of burnt faces, Freddy Krueger) and Korda throws Leslie to the side and makes a lunge towards Ryan. Leslie jumps between them and takes the stab meant for Ryan. Korda's howls can be heard throughout the cavernous, empty theater.

Korda races through the tunnels, carrying Leslie, with Ryan giving chase. The whole thing has a Gothic romance feel to it. Korda lays Leslie out on the stage then runs into the rafters. After checking that Leslie was, indeed, dead, Ryan continues after Korda, who laughs evilly, a true villain laugh. The men fight up in the catwalk, and Korda has the upper hand. But then he sees Leslie below them, dead, and decides life isn't worth living without her. He throws himself to the stage and ends up dead atop her.

Status: The violin is safely vaulted, and Ryan mourns Leslie's death. He is not comforted by the idea that Leslie had nothing to do with the killings.

Mentioned but not explored: All seen in the pages of the manifest: door knocker (Victorian); letter opener; maple chest of drawers.

* * *

"Symphony in B#" was undeniably inspired by *The Phantom of the Opera*. For the episode's Phantom, director Francis Delia wanted James Russo, an actor he had worked with in an earlier film. "I had to do a little bit of selling with Russo because I don't think [the producers] knew who he was," admits Delia. "We wrapped Russo's face in toilet paper, with little slits for the eyes, because we knew that was the model. I think that helped him get into character. He brought a lot of pathos and of course, it's always a little bit of a collaboration. [The Faustian bargain] eventually came into play as we evolved the character. Essentially, that little screen test led to the model of the character we actually filmed." Delia remembers using those tapes to give the wardrobe and makeup departments an idea of what he wanted Janos Korda to look like.

Delia did what amounted to an unaccredited, page-one rewrite of this episode, during which he thought it would be a good idea to light Korda's head on fire in a dream. "T.J. Scott did the stunt. We covered Korda's mask with some kind of fire retardant material, then put flammable gel over it. We did a lock-off shot where we could match-dissolve the head of the character on fire. They said once I was ready to go they would light him up, then we would have about twenty seconds to roll before they would want to put him out. This is one of those shots that you really wanted to get in one take. It wasn't that they were unable to do it again, but it was a messy thing. I wanted an ambulance on scene and a medic standing by. I knew our guys knew what they are doing, but I wasn't going to do this without professionals standing by in case of a mishap.

"We were ready to go, but our medical guys weren't there. So, I said we were going to sit and wait until they got there. We [as an industry] had learned from the Vic Morrow incident on *The Twilight Zone* movie. [In 1982, actor Vic Morrow and two child actors were killed on the set of *Twilight Zone: The Movie* when a pyrotechnic effect caused a low-flying helicopter to crash.] For me, there is no shot worth injuring someone, let alone losing a human life. It was a no-brainer. It would have been too difficult to set for another shot, so we literally sat around for an hour while we waited for the medical people to show up. They did, I was happy, and we executed the shot without incident. I think it brought an added visual dimension to the storytelling. And nobody was any worse for wear when we called cut."

There was one thing that Delia did dangerously: his first shot for his first episode was done in a "oner." One camera, one angle, no coverage, and no options in the edit bay. "In the very first shot, we had our heroes looking at the album cover of Janos Korda. We started in a wide shot, there was some dialogue, then the camera moves past certain things that had some visual import in the scene. It wound up pushing from the widest possible shot you could do on that set [Curious Goods], into a close-up of Janos Korda, the cover of this record album. I remember Frank watching, like an eagle, his new director, watching the camera, watching it move, watching the way it timed… it wasn't brain surgery, but it did have to time rather well. I remember calling cut and Frank just looking at me, his eyebrows raised, with a somewhat prolonged nod of approval. The inmate was unleashed on the asylum. Frank actually circulated a memo to the whole crew after the edit was done, saying, 'This is always what I imagined the series could be.'" Delia owes it all to his obsessive need to pre-visualize a project before walking onto set.

Ely Pouget played Leslie in the episode, and she had two days to learn the violin—or at least fake it. "I think there were three or four of us who were working with this guy to fake it, the song. They gave us the song to practice. It was Tchaikovsky we were 'playing,' so it made Tchaikovsky my favorite classical composer." The orchestra that Pouget played with was the Toronto Symphony Orchestra. "I had a silent bow so they didn't hear how bad I was and I certainly didn't pretend to be a musician. You have to keep up with the orchestra. It's not just faking it, because it's not a single [shot] of you. You have to be at the same [pace] as they are."

Leslie dates Ryan in this episode, so of course, she dies. "It was the last shot of the day, like five or six in the morning. I had fake blood all over my chest, it was all gross. They asked if I wanted to hose off in the makeup trailer. I decided to go home. I just had so much fun. So, I drove back to the hotel with this bloody chest, and people were staring, doing double takes, absolutely horrified. It was very, very funny. When I walked into my hotel, everyone went 'Yeagh!'"

Watching this episode as an adult, I had a lot of problems with it; mainly (as you can probably tell) the relationship between Ryan and Leslie. He goes from a stranger stalking her to her lover overnight—not even overnight! Over dinner. According to Delia, John LeMay and Ely Pouget had an actual, off-screen romance. No one ever wants to talk about failed romance, especially one from nearly thirty years ago, but Pouget admitted to me that she had a crush on LeMay. "He's a wonderful guy. It was wonderful to talk to him. He cared very much about his craft. We had a great time working together." As a kid, I didn't think anything of Ryan's pursuit of Leslie. As an adult, I found it kind of creepy and strange that Leslie would give in so easily, turn to him as if he were her protector after knowing him all of five minutes.

"Master of Disguise"

Written by: Bruce Martin
Directed by: Tom McLoughlin
Original airdate: November 11, 1988
Cursed antique: Makeup kit

Curious Goods is entering a new venture: renting out (non-cursed) antiques to be used as props on a local film set. Micki is excited because the film stars William Pratt (John Bolger), one of the biggest, dreamiest movie stars in the world. Jack and Ryan see her primping and tease her about it. Micki takes it in good humor because, frankly, like every other woman in the country, she does have a crush on him.

Before they even arrive to set, there is trouble. A young extra stays behind after wrap to find her purse. She is "haunted" by someone who is stalking her across the stage. A Klieg light tumbles down on the starlet, killing her, and a gnarled, monstrous hand soaks up her blood with a sponge, filling a little jar with it. The director, Sandy (Hrant Alianak), doesn't need this trouble. He is already dealing with a leading man who will disappear in the middle of a shoot, and a leading lady, Tanya (Chapelle Jaffe), whom he calls the "Dragon Lady" because of her horrible temper.

Micki and Ryan bring the props to set and watch a take in which Pratt seduces a pretty ingénue. Micki is absolutely transfixed. Sandy calls cut and Todd, the P.A., shows them where to put the props. As Micki follows Ryan, Pratt locks eyes with her. He is smitten and immediately introduces himself to her—while completely ignoring Ryan. Pratt literally cannot take his eyes off her. Todd comes back for Pratt, and alerts him that gossip reporter Foster Geary (Aaron Schwartz) is on set, looking for an interview—one that Pratt will not grant.

Pratt finds Geary in his trailer, wanting to know his history. "Up until three years ago, no one had ever heard of you," Geary muses. He plans on going on the air with what he has—which is nothing—until he starts asking about the name William Pratt. Pratt insists it is his name. "Then who is J.W.B.?" he asks coyly, opening a drawer where Pratt keeps his cursed makeup case. Pratt finally kicks Geary out, but soon notices some blemishes starting to peep through his makeup.

Back at his hotel, Geary draws himself a bath, when the concierge delivers some champagne, courtesy of William Pratt. He is too distracted by his own television segment to pay much attention to the delivery man, and promises he will "take care of him later." Geary slips into his bath with a glass of champagne and watches his report on actor Dale Miles. (Fun fact: this is clearly a nod to line producer J. Miles Dale.) If this were a slightly different show (or on HBO), Geary would be jerking off to himself. The concierge moves into the bathroom and tosses the television into the bathtub. Geary is electrocuted. The "concierge" puts out the "Do Not Disturb" sign and wheels out the room service cart, carrying a champagne flute full of blood.

Pratt and Tanya are shooting a confrontational scene in which Pratt is supposed to strangle Tanya. She breaks character, screaming that Pratt is hurting her. "I was trying to help your acting," he says innocently, earning a slap. She throws her wig at him and storms off the set. Sandy is none too happy, so Pratt suggests Micki fill in for Tanya, at least until she calms down. Sandy isn't thrilled with the idea, but they have some time, so they might as well.

Micki is overwhelmed. The makeup artist, Joanne (Joyce Gordon), remarks that she has worked on every Pratt film and never seen him come on to anyone like he has to Micki. Pratt comes to whisk Micki off to wardrobe, and Joanne mentions he is looking a little shiny. Ryan asks her about this, and Joanne tells him that Pratt does all his own makeup. "He has his own makeup case—says it is his good luck charm." She shrugs it off though: "All actors have their quirks."

The next take of the scene includes Micki, and she does an excellent job. The shot goes past where Tanya had her freak-out, and ends with a passionate kiss between the two that leads the crew to applaud. Tanya, unfortunately, sees all this and places a phone call. Sandy has to tell Pratt that Tanya will sue if they recast her, but maybe we can use her in the next picture. Pratt promises to deliver the news himself. But first, he has someone else to visit.

Tanya. Tanya is stewing in her juices in her trailer when Pratt comes by, claiming to need her tonight. She tells him to go to hell; he comes in anyway. He keeps to the shadows, hiding his grotesque visage while she tells him to go make his movie with that "redheaded bimbo." This angers Pratt: "Don't talk about Diana like that!" He reveals himself, terrifying Tanya, who doesn't believe he is Pratt. Doesn't matter who he is—he bludgeons her to death with an award on her vanity. Drizzling blood on his makeup case, it magically clicks open and he mixes the blood with some pancake makeup inside. As he leaves the trailer, it explodes.

Micki is getting ready for her date with Pratt, but Ryan doesn't think she should go. "This guy is William Pratt. He could go out with any woman in the world; why would he choose you?" He apologizes immediately, and Micki tells him to let her lead her own life. Ryan points out that someone has died on every one of his movies. Micki sees he has been checking the manifest and storms out. Jack comes upstairs and Ryan tells him about his concerns. He couldn't find William Pratt in the manifest, but Ryan off-handedly mentions that Pratt does all his own makeup, and Jack remembers a makeup kit in the manifest. He finds it, once belonging to John Wilkes Booth, sold to a Jeff Amory, no address listed.

Jack visits an old friend, Sig (George Sperdakos), an agent, and asks about Jeff Amory. Sig remembers him, an "ugly son of a bitch" who only got bit parts in horror movies. He finds Jeff's headshot and shows it to Jack while he relates the sad story of Jeff Amory. He made a movie with an actress, Diana Lamb, a "gorgeous little redhead," who was nice to him and spent time with him. One night, she went up to the Hideaway Cabins at Evergreen Lake with another guy. Jeff followed them and, in a jealous rage, killed the guy with an axe. Diana ran off into the night, slipped, fell down a cliff, and broke her neck. The next day, police find Amory just sitting there, holding Diana's corpse. He had a mental break and was institutionalized. For all Sig knows, he is dead. Jack returns to Curious Goods and relates the tale to Ryan. Jack stays at the store, in case Micki calls, while Ryan goes to check Pratt's trailer for the makeup kit.

After a fabulous date with Pratt, in which he relates to her the version of *Beauty and the Beast* he has always wanted to do (the Beast doesn't change; Beauty loves him for who he is), Micki leaves the shop early to meet up with Pratt. He takes her to set, but when they get there, shooting has been suspended due to Tanya's death. Rather than shock and concern over the death of his co-star, Pratt reminds Sandy that they have a perfectly good star in Micki. Sandy rejects the idea: there are too many deaths, insurance is through the roof, and he is going back home to Europe. Pratt stomps away, into his trailer, where Ryan is snooping around, looking for the makeup case. He hides in the bathroom while Pratt tosses some toiletries into an overnight bag and grabs the makeup kit from a locked drawer. He returns to Micki, waiting for him in his Porsche, and takes her someplace where "no one can find them."

But first, they have some sex to get to. They make love all night. Micki wakes first and kisses Pratt awake. He returns the kisses, and she feels a huge boil on his forehead. He rushes to the bathroom, leaving Micki concerned and begging to help. The boil pulses angrily as Pratt cleans it up. He comes out of the bathroom, scaring Micki with a playful "boo." "Afraid I'm not the same man you went to bed with?" he teases, before revealing the boil is gone; just an allergy thing he gets sometimes. Pratt suggests they escape to Evergreen Lake. Micki loves that idea.

Ryan and Jack return to Curious Goods, and are concerned that Micki still isn't back—the note they left for her is still there. None of her friends have heard from her, and it isn't like her to be missing for twenty-four hours. Yet the guys are strangely calm. They check the answering machine, and find she left a message: "We are going up to Evergreen Lake for a few days. Be happy for me—I think I love him."

On the way to Evergreen Lake, the couple stops at a gas station. Pratt is not looking well and escapes to the restroom for a touchup. He is out of blood; there is not even a drop left to open the makeup case. His boils and growths are becoming worse every minute. The gas station attendant, a star-struck kid, volunteers to go check on Pratt when Micki worries he has been gone along time. "Please don't make me do this," Pratt whispers when the kid knocks on the door. But of course, he has to. As soon as the kid comes into the bathroom, Pratt throws him against the wall.

Micki decides to go check on Pratt herself. Her knock startles Pratt, and he drops his jar of blood. Before Micki can walk in, Pratt comes out, fresh-faced and vibrant. He confirms he saw the kid, gave him an autograph, and surmises that he "probably went to sell it." As they leave, blood leaks ominously from beneath the bathroom door.

It is night when they finally arrive at the Hideaway Cabins. Micki wakes, disoriented, and asks where they are. "I thought you loved it up here," Pratt answers. Micki doesn't question the strange remark and goes to check in—as Mr. and Mrs. Foster, of course. Pratt specifically requests room number five. The moment she is gone, he starts writhing in pain. By the time Micki returns, the Porsche is empty. A light flicks off in one of the cabins, presumably number five, and she heads towards it.

Pratt is scurrying around in the dark when Micki comes in. "Stay away, Diana, please," he begs. "Who is Diana? What is going on?" She moves further into the room, insisting she loves him for who he is, not the way he looks. He continually calls her Diana, which Micki, likely sensing that this is a mental break, does not question, even when he identifies himself as Jeff Amory. She assures him there is no reason to be afraid and insists he stop hiding. He finally reveals himself, shocking Micki into taking a step backwards. "You said you wanted to hold me," Pratt insists. "You lied! You said you loved me!" Micki finally returns to the Diana thing, asserting she is not her. But Pratt is too far gone. "You'll never love me," he laments and starts strangling her. Micki insists she loves him, really and truly, and Pratt loosens his grip. He will only let go if she kisses him. Micki considers this for the briefest of moments (perhaps trying to figure out where his lips are on his gruesome face) before pulling him in to a deep, passionate kiss. Pratt collapses into tears. "You really do love me," he weeps.

Jack and Ryan, who have been racing to the lake to "save" Micki, burst in on cabin number five and see they are too late—Micki has saved herself. They find the two on the floor, Pratt sobbing into Micki's lap, Micki sobbing with him. "It's okay," she whispers to her friends, and continues rocking Pratt.

Status: The makeup case is returned to the vault. Micki is crying over Pratt, but angry at herself for it—he's a murderer. Jack promises it is okay. She saw him for who he was (who he was before all the murders, that is). Jack also has a theory as to why Amory chose to go by the name Pratt: it was the real name of Boris Karloff, a "great actor who made his living playing monsters and ghouls, yet was the gentlest, kindest man" Jack had ever met.

* * *

"Master of Disguise" was the first thing Tom McLoughlin directed that he hadn't written. "Kubrick never wrote his own stuff," McLoughlin defends, "because you don't have that moment of discovery, that way of saying, 'I think I can add another layer to that.'

"It was such an interesting piece. The more I read it and the more I lived it, the more it felt like mine," recalls McLoughlin. "To me, it was a wonderful collaboration of taking someone's really good story idea and script and developing it into something I could see. The way I work is that I kind of have to live it through every department, but particularly the actors. I had to somehow feel what it was like to be this guy. It was easy for me because I grew up with the Universal monsters. They were always misunderstood monsters: Dracula saying 'To be dead must be glorious.' The Wolf Man did not want to be a werewolf. Frankenstein's monster did not want to be brought back to life. They all had this underlying empathy. And here this guy was so ugly, and this [makeup case] allowed him to be a star. At the bottom of this whole thing was this chance to do something but you just don't have the looks, so you sell your soul. All that to me really, really rang true."

This is the kind of episode that would be submitted to Emmy voters on behalf of Louise Robey. This is her story. It starts with a fairytale romance: the instant attraction; the doting attention of a rich, handsome, famous actor; the kind of dates that only happen on television. Things get intense very quickly, but when things start to go wrong, it is Micki who saves the day, saves herself. Sure, the boys are rushing to save her (not because of any notion that Micki is a girl and therefore needs saving, but because they love her and care for her) but when they get there, they find that Micki has already neutralized the situation.

"Robey really needed a lot of hand-holding," McLoughlin admits. "There is a charisma about her. I would never want to compare anyone to Marilyn Monroe. If she worked within her limits, she was really good. But if she tried to go beyond that, or if the role was written beyond that, she struggled with it. It wasn't her fault; she knew what she could do well." McLoughlin wanted to push the envelope with the love scene between Robey and John Bolger (who played Pratt) and they were both willing to go for it.

"When we were casting, in walked this guy that had that Timothy Dalton/James Bond quality to me," says McLoughlin of Bolger. "He was the perfect movie idol-type. And a really, really nice guy. Really terrific actor."

"Wax Magic"

Written by: Carl Binder
Directed by: William Fruet
Original airdate: November 14, 1988
Cursed antique: Handkerchief

Marie (Susannah Hoffmann) helps her husband Aldwin (Angelo Rizacos) run his wax museum exhibit at a traveling carnival. She is beautiful but sickly, frequently falling victim to debilitating migraines. Aldwin seems to have little sympathy for her maladies—at least, that's how it looks to Danny (Yvan Labelle), the dwarf who runs a nearby game stall, and Marie's only friend. Aldwin might be angry, but he does everything he can to ease Marie's suffering—like using a cursed object to help her. Aldwin has an antique handkerchief that he pins to his Lizzie Borden wax figure, causing her to come to life. The figure kills victims with her no-longer-wax axe, and Marie's migraines disappear.

Ryan is annoyed that Sally canceled their date to the carnival that night. With Micki gone until Monday, Ryan tries to talk Jack into coming with him. Jack would rather check up on old newspapers. "Must be awful getting old," muses Ryan. This lures Jack to the carnival, but this doesn't mean he will have a good time. When asked if he wants to go on something called The Annihilator again, Jack responds with "I'd sooner go for do-it-yourself brain surgery." Ryan goes for some junk food (another offer Jack turns down) and bumps into Marie, spilling her drinks. He buys her new ones and she offers to take him through the wax museum. Jack is forgotten; Ryan is in love.

Marie introduces Ryan to Aldwin, who seethes when he sees his wife fraternizing with another man. Jealousy and paranoia bubble over when Marie takes Ryan into Aldwin's workroom. He tries to physically throw Ryan out, but is distracted when Marie collapses with another one of her "spells." Aldwin casts Ryan out with an angry bellow, then sends Lizzie out to kill. She finds a couple drunk townies in the parking lot and hacks them up to pieces. One of the drunks manages to pull off Lizzie's finger before he dies.

Worried about Marie, Ryan heads back to the carnival the next day. He finds it crawling with police, investigating last night's beheading. Ryan claims he works there and is just let through (because Ryan looks so much like a carney). On his way in, he finds the wax finger. He pockets it, but doesn't think much of it.

Ryan and Marie get coffee in the mess hall. Aldwin tells her that the fainting spells will pass, but she can't remember much, other than the nightmares about Lizzie Borden. Aldwin interrupts: time for Marie to start work. Jack comes in and tells Ryan it is time for them to get to work, too. His research revealed that murders have followed this carnival everywhere for the last two months, and all were killed with an axe. Ryan shows Jack the wax finger and they make a plan to check on the wax museum. Danny is hiding under the table, listening to their conversation, which seems like a strange, vaguely offensive place for a dwarf to hide—and it's not particularly well hidden.

While Jack keeps watch outside, Ryan sneaks into Aldwin's workroom. He observes body parts, molds, mannequin heads... all weird and creepy things, but nothing out of the ordinary for a wax sculptor. Danny sneaks in, as well, and wants to talk to Ryan, just not here. Aldwin, meanwhile, has led the tour into the tent, and catches sight of an unidentifiable figure sneaking out the back.

Back at his tent, Danny gives Ryan and Jack the lowdown on Aldwin and Marie. Aldwin has been with the carnival for a long time, but Marie is a "rube," a townie. Aldwin had a crush on her, but she wouldn't give him the time of day. Then, a few days after the carnival leaves town, Marie follows, and she has been devoted to him ever since. This was about two months ago.

Aldwin hears all of this. Later that night, Danny is butchered by Lizzie Borden. But this time, we can see through her thin veil, and we see it is Marie. The police arrive, and Marie is devastated to learn about Danny's death. She has no memory of wielding the axe. Aldwin, in his usual postmurder, Marie-is-well pattern, comes onto his wife, but is turned away. Aldwin becomes enraged. "Everything you have is because of me. What gives you the right to turn me away?" He accuses her of having an affair with Ryan, which she denies. "If you don't stop acting so strange, I will give you the worst headache you've ever had," he promises her. "I made you want to love me. Why aren't you the way you used to be?" Seems like you answered your own question there, Aldwin.

Ryan sees Danny's death in the newspaper and wants to nail Aldwin, cursed object or not. Jack, who had no luck finding anything in the manifest that could fit the case, finally finds a listing with a tenuous link: a handkerchief belonging to Louis XVI. Famous wax sculptress Marie Tussaud escaped Paris during the French Revolution and cast a death mask of Louis XVI. She was paid with that handkerchief.

Back to the carnival. Marie grieves for Danny, her only friend. She has nightmares of Danny's death, and doesn't remember anything before the carnival. She married Aldwin because he promised to heal her. She appreciates that Ryan truly cares what happens to her. "It's a nice feeling." Aldwin threatens to call security on the guys, which scares them off. Aldwin slaps Marie, holds up the handkerchief, and warns her, "your boyfriend is going to wish he never laid eyes on you."

Lizzie attacks Ryan and Jack at the shop. Lots and lots of antiques are broken, and a chandelier nearly crushes Jack. Ryan runs at her with a

Getting ready for stunts on "Wax Magic." Photo courtesy of John LeMay.

blow torch (what antique shop is without a blow torch?) and melts Lizzie's hand into a waxy clump. He throws up her veil—and discovers he has just torched Marie. She rests at the shop while Jack explains that she was alive until Aldwin killed her and preserved her in wax. The more she kills, the more alive she becomes, and the more aware she becomes. Marie wakes and wants to go home. Ryan refuses to remove the handkerchief, fearing Marie will die. He stomps upstairs like a petulant child, and Marie begs Jack not to hurt her. Before he can unpin it, Aldwin charges in, shoots Jack in the arm, and takes Marie back to the carnival.

Aldwin sets about repairing Marie, but Marie has questions. She realizes that her nightmares are real. "Why did you do this to me?" Ryan sneaks in and tackles Aldwin. Marie tries to intervene but Aldwin throws her back, into the stove where the wax melts. A huge fire erupts and Marie steps into it. "It's the only way, Ryan. The only way." She melts, in a grotesque combination of wax and flesh.

Status: Ryan has a difficult time coming to terms with Marie's death. "She knew no one life was worth that much death," Jack explains. The handkerchief is safely vaulted.

* * *

Never in the history of film has a carnival not seemed creepy. "Wax Magic" is no exception. Growing up in Los Angeles, less than an hour away from Disneyland, Magic Mountain, Knott's Berry Farm, and Universal Studios, we didn't get much opportunity for the creepy little traveling carnivals from "Wax Magic" or *The Funhouse* (Tobe Hooper's underrated 1981 horror flick). And that always disappointed me. I love those big, flashy amusement parks, but that wasn't what I wanted out of a carnival experience. I wanted the ill-lit fairway; the creaking rides that seemed certain to give way at any moment; the strange drifters who ran the attractions. I remember the one time a cheap little carnival set up near my house. I never did work up the courage to go on one of those death-rides (I wanted to be scared, not dead) but just being amongst the cheap gaudiness gave me the chills.

Writer Carl Binder added the wax museum attraction to the carnival because he has "always loved wax museums—totally creepy." But he wasn't entirely pleased with the episode. "I thought 'Wax Magic' could have been creepier. I wanted the wax museum to be darker, more moody and spooky." I kind of feel like the curse could have been thought out better. Would the handkerchief only work on a human/wax hybrid? Could it eventually turn a full wax figure human?

Actor Angelo Rizacos, who played Aldwin, remembers "Wax Magic" as a fast shoot, faster than normal. "I remember being in a studio on the first day and they set up a chair in the middle of the studio and applied makeup because they needed me in a hurry. Jon Andersen was sitting in a chair opposite watching and at one point said, 'Ok that's fine. Angelo, you'll remember this makeup right?'

"I replied, 'Remember it? I haven't even seen it.' The makeshift makeup area did not include a mirror so I had no idea what the woman had done. Jon and I both laughed.

"He yelled, 'Can somebody bring a mirror so that Angelo can see his makeup?'"

Whenever Marie returns from one of her kills, Aldwin immediately wants to have sex with her. Is this when she, as a human/wax hybrid, is at her most human, her most vital? Or is it simply that the murders turn Aldwin on? I like the latter notion; it makes Aldwin seem even creepier, and gives the whole episode an extra splash of seediness. Not like it needed anything to make it more disturbing.

"Read My Lips"

Written by: Peter Lauterman and Angelo Stea
Directed by: Francis Delia
Original airdate: November 21, 1988
Cursed antique: Silk flower

Micki gets an unexpected letter from her best friend from high school, Gabrielle (Linda Griffiths). She is getting married and wants Micki to be her maid of honor. Gabrielle is living in town with her fiancé, Edgar Van Horne (Billy Drago), a ventriloquist. Ryan turns down an invitation to go to the show, echoing a feeling I suspect most of us have: "I don't feel comfortable around people who talk to themselves for a living."

Edgar is performing a series of sold-out dates at a local supper club. Like many ventriloquists, his act consists of a smart-ass dummy (this one is named Oscar) who cracks wise and insults the audience. One night, towards the end of the performance, Oscar announces it is "time to pay the piper," a phrase which fills Van Horne with dread. He tries to drink the problem away, but that doesn't help. After the show, that same chant lures the doorman into Van Horne's dressing room, where he stabs the man to death.

There are no murders on the night that Micki attends the show, but Oscar seems to take a special interest in denigrating Gabrielle, to the point where the audience is uncomfortable. Edgar literally clamps his hand over Oscar's mouth to keep him from finishing another joke at her expense. Gabrielle brushes it off, claiming it is all in fun. "Sometimes Oscar gets a little carried away," she excuses; Micki corrects her: "You mean Edgar."

The girls go backstage so Micki can meet Edgar. He is "auditioning" a ventriloquist named Travis (John Byner), and Oscar can't wait to announce that he will go on the road with Travis while Edgar is "honeymooning." Edgar and Oscar argue, for what is probably the millionth time, over the impending nuptials, and Travis slips away. When the argument escalates to the point that Edgar is yelling at Gabrielle, Micki takes her exit, too. Edgar insists that he doesn't want to cancel the wedding and that he is not hiding behind Oscar. Gabrielle is adamant that he get some help and get rid of Oscar.

The next day, Edgar meets with his manager, Bernie. (Why are all managers named Bernie?) Edgar wants to quit, which doesn't have Bernie too pleased: he was with him when he was nothing; now that he is something, he wants to throw it all away. But Bernie is not just a manager, he is a friend, so he makes a deal with Edgar: finish the club dates, and he will see what he can do. This is amenable to both Edgar and Gabrielle.

Next stop on the Edgar Van Horne Road to Recovery is a visit with a shrink. She insists on meeting Oscar, and as soon as he comes out of his case, he starts railing against Gabrielle. The doctor makes him put Oscar outside. Edgar obliges, but it isn't long before he hears Oscar chanting, "time to pay the piper." The doc starts analyzing Edgar while he paces, ending up right behind her. Knife in hand, he is about to kill the doctor when she spins around and he swiftly pockets the knife. She wants to see him as often as possible for the first few weeks. Edgar agrees, and leaves without murdering.

Ryan investigates a crime scene in an alley, where a guy had been cut up into sixteen pieces. He finds nothing but some blood stains, but discovers it is about fifty feet from the club where Edgar is performing. Ryan goes straight to the manifest, but doesn't find anything. Micki tells him that Edgar has promised to see a psychiatrist and get rid of Oscar, which surprises Ryan. He decides to stop by the bachelor party and meet Edgar for himself.

The bachelor party is a stereotypical shindig: poker, booze, blue movies (played on a projector!), and plenty of strippers. Ryan mentions that he was hoping to meet Oscar tonight. Bernie encourages a drunken Edgar to take him out, "he is the life of any party." Edgar stumbles away, and Bernie mentions off-handedly that ventriloquists are all the same. Their dummies are a part of them. "But lately, it's like they can't stand each other." Edgar has given in and removes Oscar from his case. Oscar immediately starts in on the anti-Gabrielle smack-talk. Edgar slaps Oscar, and Oscar retaliates by biting Edgar on the hand. Edgar locks the dummy in his case and bails on his own party.

Ryan tells Micki about the bite, and she is still in denial, believing it to be an illusion—after all, Edgar is an entertainer. Chopped up bodies seem to follow Edgar's club dates but as Micki points out, there is no dummy listed in the manifest. Maybe it is something else. "Maybe it's like these Nazi souvenirs Jack is tracking down," Ryan suggests. Jack is out of town, searching for Nazi paraphernalia, so Ryan has been helping him with research. (It is unclear if these are cursed antiques or just stock for the store, but it seems more than likely they are cursed.) The Nazis were really into the occult, reanimation, and giving inanimate objects life. They were convinced that a certain amount of killings could give something life.

No time to follow that lead for now—it's wedding time. Oscar is sitting in one of the front pews, and somehow, no one finds this strange or creepy. When the priest asks if there is anyone who has any objections to this wedding, Oscar is the only one who speaks up. It turns into a complete melee, with Edgar choking Oscar, promising to kill him. It takes Ryan, Bernie, and two more guys to carry a flailing Edgar out of the church. Once outside, Edgar calms down enough to be let go, but as soon as they do, he runs into traffic and is hit by a car.

Inside the church, Travis picks up Oscar, who innocently asks, "Not exactly a marriage made in heaven, is it?"

After spending time with Gabrielle and Edgar at the hospital, Micki comes home with a status report: Edgar will live, but when he came to, he was still yelling about Oscar. The two of them realize that no one thought to check on Oscar—but maybe they should.

Travis has teamed up with Oscar, and will take Edgar's place in the remaining shows. The crowd loves them; Travis loves the spotlight. "This is just the beginning," Oscar whispers to his new right-hand man. "Stick with me, we are going to the top." After the show, Travis takes his dummy into the alley.

Oscar tells him he might have to "climb over a few bodies" to get ahead. "Get what I'm saying?"

They bump into a big, beefy dude who is looking for a fight. Oscar instigates things and hands Travis a knife. He doesn't seem to have a problem stabbing the guy dead, though afterwards he looks a little bit shocked; not that he did it, but that he had the power to do it.

Ryan visits Edgar, now strapped to a bed in a sanitarium. He is quiet, until Ryan asks about Oscar. Then Edgar gets angry, and starts screaming to keep him away.

"What are you so afraid of?" Ryan asks.

"He just started doing stuff on his own! You don't know what he would have done to me... he made me kill all those people. I said no," Edgar rambles. "Look what happened—he destroyed my life." He then starts singing, in a crazy, sing-song voice, "I'm in here, he's out there... ."

As Edgar devolves into The Joker, Ryan quietly leaves. Ryan next visits Bernie and insists that Oscar belongs to Edgar—Travis just can't take him. Bernie makes a deal with him: let him finish tonight's show, and he will get him back.

After the show, Bernie suggests Travis get a new dummy, one that is more "him." Travis refuses. Oscar springs to life, and all on his own knives Bernie in the belly. Travis cleans up the mess, and Oscar is now a "real boy" (played by Ed Gale), talking in his own, distinct voice. "If Gabrielle is dead, and Edgar is in the looney bin, they won't separate us," Oscar reasons. "We'll go right to the top."

With no word from Bernie, Ryan heads to Travis' house to search for the dummy himself. He finds a reel-to-reel recording of the last conversation Bernie and Travis had, and plays it while he explores the house. He finds blood in the kitchen. He opens the little fridge, then opens the freezer section—and there is Bernie's head. Ryan is pretty freaked out and calls Micki (who answers "Yeah?" which, for whatever reason, just tickles me). Before Ryan can say anything, she fills him in on what she has found: a pink silk boutonniere. Hitler's occult advisers told him if he wore it, he wouldn't die; he would be reanimated. The collector in Miami Jack had visited sold it Edgar. Ryan fills her in on Bernie and tells her to call Gabrielle and warn her.

Micki can't get through to Gabrielle—a small gloved hand has cut her phone line. Gabrielle is in the middle of making tea when she hears someone enter the house. She finds Travis and Oscar and wants them out of there. Oscar stands on his own. "It's show time!" He hands Travis the knife, and Gabrielle throws her kettle of hot water in his face. He screams for help, and Oscar helps him—by killing him. Then he turns to Gabrielle. Oscar attacks her, sending her tumbling down the stairs as Micki and Ryan burst in. Micki goes to help her friend while Ryan wrestles with the little dummy come to life. I know this is horrible, but I really just wanted Ryan to punt him across the room. Oscar must be imbued with Satanic strength because he pins Ryan easily. Ryan goes straight for the flower on Oscar's lapel, and the moment he pulls it away, Oscar goes limp and turns back into a lifeless wooden dummy.

Status: The silk flower is returned to the vault. With Jack out of town, Micki delivers the end-of-the-episode wisdom: "So innocent, yet so powerful." This is why they let Jack do it.

*　*　*

There is a long history of killer ventriloquist dummies in films and television, from *Dead of Night*, a 1945 British anthology film (which is likely the first appearance of a killer dummy on screen) to 1978's *Magic* starring Anthony Hopkins to 2007's failed slasher flick *Dead Silence*. Dummies also featured into episodes of *American Horror Story, Tales from the Crypt, Alfred Hitchcock Presents*, and *The Twilight Zone* (which did *two* separate episodes on different dummies). So, director Francis Delia had a lot to work with, which is good and bad. "I felt this is very cool," he says, "having grown up on stuff you are now being allowed to take part in. But I felt there was that sense of, 'Wow, better do your best on this one!'"

After the success of the "oner" shot from "Symphony in B#," Delia decided to up his game and take a four page scene (approximately four minutes of screen time) and shoot that as a oner. "That really involved quite a lot of preliminary thinking," Delia admits. That scene was the bachelor party scene. "I was able to design it in a way where we began with a close-up on a projector. Then, we began moving the camera. Of course, we have our ventriloquist. Along the way I remember we designed some dialogue... your biggest responsibility as a filmmaker is to keep the frame alive."

Although Delia didn't write the script, he made the decision to make Oscar the dummy a misogynist. "I thought it would add a fun dimension to that half of the story. Edgar is very dedicated to his lovely, much younger fiancée, but any time he has the dummy on his lap, the dummy is shooting nasty wisecracks at her. To this day, I still think it's funny because psychologically, this guy is talking out of two sides of his mouth. For reasons that don't really need to be explained, when he is talking to his fiancée through the dummy, he's letting out the side of him that really, perhaps, has issues with women. The rest of the time, he is this very dedicated, caring fiancé."

Did Edgar ever understand that there was an otherworldly evil afoot? He was a ventriloquist before he got the silk flower. Was he already a little nutty to begin with? I imagine you'd have to be nutty to be a ventriloquist. It's an old trope, the ventriloquist who has a psychotic break and believes his dummy is a real person. When Oscar started talking to Edgar directly, did he even realize something had changed? Was he already having conversations with Oscar? Clearly, Edgar did not want to kill. I feel like he would have stopped if he only knew how, or thought that he could. Delia suggested to me that there was a duality that actually existed in his personality that would ultimately drive him to some sort of breakdown.

I always felt they should have put Oscar in the vault—or burned him, because that little fucker is creepy. There is just no way he isn't at least a little bit evil, all on his own. As a kid, the idea that the dummy itself wasn't evil confused me. How would the silk boutonnière work if it were worn on a man's suit? Or decorating a woman's hairdo? I couldn't separate the evil dummy from the evil flower. It didn't help any that the credits normally roll over a still of that week's cursed antique, and for this episode, it was Oscar sitting there, the flower barely visible on his lapel.

I asked Delia if it wouldn't have just been easier, more direct, if Oscar was the cursed antique as opposed to the boutonniere. "I couldn't agree more," he said. "In a way, I'm glad I didn't have credit for that—credit or blame." The director remembers a production meeting in which they had to get casting done so that they could create the dummy to look like whoever they cast as Oscar when he comes to life. "I don't remember how close we came, but I remember that being a concern." The part ended up going to Ed Gale, who played the titular *Howard the Duck* in the 1986 flop.

"A ventriloquist dummy may seem like an easy enough thing for your prop department to generate, but I will tell you, after filming for days on end, with Billy Drago trying to work the mouth on the dummy…." Delia recalls, "I remember him having some difficulty with it, and him even complaining. He said it was really damaging his hand because the mouth was not very easy to operate. We had someone off-camera reading the lines while Billy worked the mouth. That was the part that really did demand a bit of accuracy on Billy's part."

Fun fact: The role of Travis, which was played by John Byner, was originally meant for Richard Belzer. Then mainly known as a stand-up comic, Belzer is best known now for his role as Det. John Munch on *Law & Order* (and its spinoffs) and *Homicide: Life on the Streets*.

"13 O'Clock"

Written by: Rob Hedden
Directed by: Rob Hedden
Original airdate: January 2, 1989
Cursed antique: Pocket watch

Reatha Wilkerson (Gwynyth Walsh) is more than just a trophy wife. She's a thieving trophy wife. Her older husband, Henry (Ron Hartmann), brings her expensive trinkets in exchange for her doting attention—and a creepy daddy/princess role play game. Reatha, meanwhile, pawns her expensive gifts and brings the cash to her boyfriend, Eric (David Proval), in the dumpy little apartment he can barely afford. Eric is under a lot of stress, facing an indictment for real estate fraud, and doesn't believe Reatha's stories of a magic watch.

Reatha suspects her husband is up to something, so she follows him to a subway station in the middle of the night. Henry finds a street musician playing in an alley just outside, and kills him with a hammer. Returning to the subway station, Henry waits nervously. The watch begins to glow, and as it hits 1:00 a.m., a three appears beside the one. Everything turns to black and white, frozen in time like an old photo. Everything except, of course, Henry.

In the morning, Reatha is poking around Henry's desk and she finds the watch. I'm not sure how she figured out that it stops time, but I imagine this is the last leg in a long investigation. Henry catches her and threatens her with a spanking. She turns on the little-girl charm (so creepy) and he relents and gives her presents. The first comes in a jewelry box, but Reatha is disappointed to discover that inside is an engraved letter opener. She doesn't care that it is solid platinum; she wants another present. Luckily Henry has one for her: a shiny new sports car.

Micki and Ryan are on their way to pick up the Chalice of Sacmar when the car breaks down. This leads to a fight between the two: Ryan blames himself for letting Micki drive, which infuriates her—then he asks for money for a cab. With the money comes the power, and Micki decides it is time to take the subway.

They retrieve the chalice, which takes them much longer than they expected, but clearly wasn't interesting enough to share with the audience. They are taking the subway home when they spot Skye (Ingrid Veninger) and a group of street kids messing around on the edge of the platform. Skye cartwheels along the edge, then slips and falls onto the track. Ryan jumps in to save her, but it was all a gag: she is fine and jumps out unharmed. Ryan has a closer call, and Micki pulls him out in the nick o' time. He yells at those no-good kids like an old man yelling at kids on his lawn, and Micki hurries him into the train.

Another night, another chance for an extra hour. Reatha follows Henry again, but this time she confronts him. He is mad, until Reatha confirms she knows *everything* about his evening activities. "I only did it for you, princess," he assures her. She promises not to tell, but wants to know how it works: you have to "take care of" someone, then be in the Castle Hill subway station at exactly 1:00 a.m. and time will stand still for one hour. Henry is about to hammer her to death, but she beats him to the punch and stabs him with his own letter opener. Skye sees the whole thing from her hiding spot in the alley, and runs from the scene. Reatha must decide: go after Skye, or go claim her reward. She chooses the reward.

Reatha makes it back into the station in time, and the curse works just as promised. Everything freezes except her. She snatches a bracelet right off a woman's arm. No repercussions. Outside, she finds a cop standing in front of a jewelry store window. She takes his baton, smashes the window, grabs a watch, then places the baton back in his belt. No repercussions. As her hour winds down, Reatha is loaded down with packages, jewels, furs. The world returns to normal, but Reatha has a ton of new goodies—and no repercussions.

The paper reports on the murder at Castle Hill station, which took place just after Micki and Ryan left. There were also burglaries reported at a jeweler, drug store, and furrier, all around the same time. There was another murder a few days ago in the same area, followed by a rash of inexplicable burglaries, all taking place around 1:00 a.m. You know what that means: a cursed antique. They turn to the manifest, not sure what they are looking for, but Jack finds an interesting listing. Last night's victim was Henry Wilkerson; well, Bart Wilkerson purchased a pocket watch from Lewis three years ago. He sends Ryan and Micki to meet the widow while he checks up on Bart.

Eric has moved into Reatha's house, and she promises she is going to kill the little old woman who is the only witness to Eric's real estate fraud.

She has been in a coma, with a guard on her door twenty-four hours a day. Eric doesn't believe her. "Why not?" Reatha asks. "I killed Henry." Ryan and Micki come to the door, and Reatha is quick to fall into the role of grieving widow. She knows nothing about the watch they are looking for, but takes their card. Other people asking about the watch seem to lend credence to Reatha's story, and Eric is starting to believe her.

Ryan and Micki decide to try a new approach. They head back to the subway, find Skye and her brother Johnny-O (Jason Hopley), and ask for their help. Skye demands $20; Micki hands Ryan her wallet without a word. "It was dark, I didn't see nothing," Skye snickers. Ryan is pissed, but Micki still uses a gentle approach and leaves her card with them.

Meanwhile, Reatha has been busy looking for a new sugar daddy. She finds Bob, a man who is flattered by her attention, but nervous about the way she is being so forward. He suggests they go to a hotel, but Reatha insists they don't have enough time. She takes him to her car and stabs him. She goes back to the subway to await her thirteenth hour, and Micki and Ryan spot her. Ryan grabs her as the clock strikes thirteen, and he watches the entire station freeze. Reatha throws him onto the tracks, and he is knocked out cold. Seems safe enough to leave him there; she only has an hour to go kill a little old lady. She does so easily, with a little injection of poison into her IV.

Ryan wakes just as the world is coming back to life. He rolls under the subway platform, narrowly avoiding being crushed to death. Back at Curious Goods, Ryan describes the event as being frozen in time like a black and white photo. Micki saw nothing, and had no sensation of time stopping. Jack explains that Ryan was "drawn into Reatha's force field." He was moving through time as she was, in what is known in the occult as thirteen o'clock. Jack also discovered that Bart Wilkerson was a switcher at the Castle Hill station. He was fired for drinking on the job, and vowed revenge. He pawned the watch after being fired, but bought it back a year later, this time with a bonus gift of a demonic curse.

Reatha pays Skye and Johnny-O a little visit. They swear they saw nothing, but that's not good enough for Reatha and she stabs at them. Skye is cut, but the two make it out of the alley in one piece. Reatha isn't worried; she will get them during her hour. Of course, this is the point where Johnny-O decides enough is enough, and calls Curious Goods.

At the shop, the kids are treated warmly. Micki dresses Skye's wound and feeds them. Skye admits what she saw, and Ryan tells them about the pocket watch and what it can do. "As long as she has that watch, we are all targets," Jack worries. Skye offers to help however they can. With the help of their friends, they should be able to cover all the ins and outs of Castle Hill.

Jack will take the rear entrance; Micki and Skye will cover the front entrance, and Ryan and Johnny-O will cover the platform and incoming trains. Reatha strikes again, this time stabbing a man in the alley, who then stumbles out onto the street. Micki rushes to help, and Eric and Reatha grab Skye and force her down into the subway. Micki notices Skye is gone and races into the subway.

Reatha and Eric sit with Skye wedged between them. He is getting antsy and wants to kill her now, but Reatha doesn't want to chance any more witnesses, so she will kill Skye when time stops. Skye sees Johnny-O across the station, weighs her options, then grabs the watch and runs onto an outgoing train. Reatha and Eric give chase. It takes about a minute and a half to get to the next station; Ryan and Johnny-O rush for the emergency stop.

Skye didn't work out the finer points of her plan. Now, she is being chased through a metal tube by a pair of psychopaths. The subway is fairly empty, and the few old ladies or homeless drunks she finds are not about to help. She gets to the end of the train and is cornered. Luckily, Ryan has pulled the emergency stop, so the train screeches to a halt. Skye tosses the watch at Reatha, knowing it won't work anyway. Reatha's only focus now is getting back to Castle Hill. She and Eric hit the track in a full run.

Ryan is running towards them, and tackles Eric. The guys fight, and Ryan is knocked out *again*. Less than one minute left. Micki and Johnny-O see them racing down the tracks as the seconds tick by. Five seconds left. Ryan chases after them. Two seconds left. He grabs the watch. Reatha *screams* and she and Eric are frozen in time, black and white photos in a world of color and motion.

Status: The pocket watch is returned to the vault, and Skye and Johnny-O return to the streets. "We are at home on the streets," Skye insists.

Mentioned but not explored: The Chalice of Sacmar. Returned to the vault.

* * *

"I loved H.G. Wells' *The Time Machine* and all the *Twilight Zone* episodes dealing with time," says writer/director Rob Hedden on the source of "13 O'Clock." "The manipulation of time has always fascinated me; the challenge was to do it in an original way. The episode title popped into my head one night—that was the genesis. It played on the series title and it just sounded cool. I imagined a crooked number three burning in beside the one on a watch face to create the magical hour of thirteen o'clock, at which point time stops and evil ensues."

This episode always captured my imagination because I loved the idea of an extra hour, all to myself. As a kid, I would always daydream about what I would use that extra hour for. I don't remember what I came up with, but I think the part I liked the best was an extra hour in the middle of the night.

Gwynyth Walsh, who played Reatha, had a good working relationship with Hedden. "He told me that the main reason I got the part was because I was the only actress who understood that the line, 'Oh, a letter opener!' was not an indication that she was pleased with it, but rather that she was covering up because the gift was so disappointing to her."

After the "success" of Hedden's first directorial outing for the series ("meaning I didn't get fired"), he decided to up the ante with "13 O'Clock." "I pitched the idea of having the world turn black-and-white whenever time stopped, with a twist: what if the holder of the watch remained in color as they moved through a frozen monochromatic world? At this point in time, no TV series had done anything like that, and there was no such thing as CGI. Equally daunting, it involved painstaking frame-by-frame rotoscoping, which consumed both time and money. We did a lot of trial and error to get it just right; it's to the producers' credit that they allowed us to experiment with no guarantee of success. The payoff came when the episode got an Emmy nomination for visual effects."

"Night Hunger"

Written by: Jim Henshaw
Directed by: Martin Lavut
Original airdate: January 9, 1989
Cursed antique: Silver chain necklace

Mikey Fiorno (Richard Panebianco) is an angry young man. His father, Dominic (Nick Nichols), who owns the hardware store next to Curious Goods, was physically and emotionally abusive. As we see through numerous (perhaps too numerous) flashbacks, Dominic is constantly telling Mikey he is a loser, a wimp, worthless. Dominic thought that if he was tough on Mikey, he would really turn into something. On his sixteenth birthday, Mikey wanted a car; Dominic gave him a blank key and suggested he "come back when you are worth something, maybe you will have a car to go with it." In Dominic's mind, having a car was a sign of manhood. Mikey started spending a lot of time with Lewis, and as we later find out, Lewis gave him a silver chain to wear the key around his neck, making it a "real" gift.

On the eve of Mikey's twenty-first birthday, Dominic comes into Curious Goods, hoping to get him a gift and rebuild the strained relationship. Jack doesn't know why Mikey would be interested in anything from the shop, and Dominic reveals that Mikey used to hang around a lot when Lewis ran the place. While Jack shows him some stuff in the back, Micki and Ryan go through the manifest. They find nothing, but that doesn't rule out a gift.

Mikey is a car guy. He works in a garage and he races at night. Dominic used to be a street racer, as well, so Mikey is both trying to impress his father and show that he is better than him. More than anything, Mikey wants to race Deacon (Real Andrews), his childhood rival. Deacon runs a gang of street racers and insists that Mikey race his guys before he gets to the boss.

First up is Dead Boy (Elliott Smith). Mikey beats him easily, thanks to his cursed key-and-chain. Mikey kills someone, then dips the key in their blood. He uses the key in his ignition, and wins the race. Dead Boy is furious that Mikey won, and thinks he cheated. After some pouting and foot-stomping, Dead Boy turns over the keys. The next night, Mikey tries again to race Deacon, but he insists he race Chang first. The race is set for 2:00 a.m. Micki and Ryan stop by to see him and ask him if he ever bought anything from Lewis. Mikey is reasonably friendly, yet aloof. He says he never bought anything (which is true) and invites them to watch him race tonight.

Mikey returns to his shop. Dominic pays him a visit and makes a weak attempt to make amends, one which Mikey sees right through. He throws his dad out. Dead Boy comes in, again trying to get his car back. Mikey is so perturbed that he tosses Dead Boy his keys and tells him to get out. Dead Boy goes for his car, but comes upon a chain link dead end. Mikey appears, in his car, and crushes Dead Boy between the car and the fence. He charges up his key and prepares for tonight's race.

Ryan didn't think anything seemed out of the ordinary at the street race, but when Jack finds an article about a serial hit-and-runner, Ryan goes back to the race while Micki helps Jack go through Lewis' paperwork. At the race, Deacon sheds a little light on Mikey's background, including that he only got a car last year, right after his mother died. Mikey shows up at the race, this time driving Dead Boy's car. Mikey and Chang race, and Mikey beats him handily. Chang accuses him of cheating because he always beat Dead Boy. "I'm not Dead Boy," Mikey deadpans. Ryan notices that Mikey's car actually glows while he is racing.

Chang breaks into Mikey's garage and starts poking around under the hood of Dead Boy's car, certain that Mikey is cheating. Mikey grabs him from behind, knife to his throat, and Deacon enters. He is "building something special" and wants Mikey's help. "You want to be one of my people? You're in."

The next night, Micki and Ryan head to Mikey's garage. They see him leave and Micki turns off the headlights so they can follow more discretely. Mikey is heading down a winding road, and Ryan gets nervous. He makes Micki put the headlights back on, even if it means they have to drop back a bit.

Mikey meets with Chang in the middle of nowhere. The meet was meant as a chance for Chang to buy his car back, but Mikey uses the opportunity to run over Chang. He puts Chang in the passenger side of his own car, then climbs into the driver's seat. Going back the way he came, he passes Micki and Ryan. Luckily Micki is observant, because she recognizes Mikey in the driver's seat and changes direction quickly. It is a low speed chase, but Mikey loses control of the car, flies over an embankment, and crashes, hard. Both he and Chang fly through the windshield. Micki stops just in time, and she and Ryan race to help Mikey. With his chest ripped open, the key and chain have snaked their way into Mikey's chest, settling among the blood, like a leech setting up for a big meal.

Everyone meets up at the hospital. Mikey is just coming out of surgery, and Dominic goes to check on him. Micki and Ryan fill in Jack and tell him they couldn't find the chain. That is because, as a doctor will soon show them in Mikey's X-rays, the chain is wrapped around Mikey's heart, with the key snuggled up against it. Removing it now would surely kill him, so they are just going to have to monitor the situation. Ryan is hopeful that, even though they can't get the key back, Mikey can't use it, but Jack isn't so sure: "That key is in his possession now more than ever."

Dominic visits with Mikey. "I always knew this would happen," he tells his unconscious son. "Kids were always getting hurt when I drove. Maybe I never treated you right, but I always cared." Mikey wakes suddenly, his eyes aglow. Out on that empty highway, Mikey's car starts up, glowing red, and drives itself away. Mikey seizes violently for a minute, then settles into maniacal laughter. His chest pulses in waves, suggesting the key is alive and well.

Three weeks later... .

Ryan and Micki are frustrated. They can't find Mikey's car, and Micki doesn't think they ever will. Mikey was released from the hospital this morning, so the kids split up: Micki goes to check the garage; Ryan goes to the drive-in, a popular spot for racing.

Mikey looks pale and demonic as he approaches Deacon that night. He walks with a bad limp, aided by a cane. Deacon is surprised that, even in his condition, Mikey still wants to race. Deacon finally gives in. They will race in three hours. Ryan pulls up to Mikey and quits pussyfooting around. He knows about the key. "People can't keep dying so you can keep winning races." He tries to relate to Mikey over their crappy fathers, but Mikey can't be swayed. He is going to race.

Micki is at the garage where she is surprised to find Mikey's car. "Maybe it drove itself," Mikey laughs, creeping up behind her. His eyes begin to glow, and his car starts on its own. She runs. Luckily Ryan is happening by, so she jumps in the Mercedes and they zoom out of there. Mikey's car returns to the garage. Dominic is there, waiting for his son, and he asks how he did that. Mikey taunts him, suggest he go tell the cops, and reminds his dad that if he doesn't like who he is, he has no one to blame but himself. Mikey jumps into his car with the parting words: "I owe you one. For the first time in my life, I like who I am."

Reconvening at the store, Jack doesn't know what they can do. They can't get the chain from Mike without killing him, so Jack suggests a more psychological approach, in the hopes of convincing Mikey to stop playing *Christine* with his car. Dominic comes in and admits that he was tough on Mikey as a kid, telling him that the other kids were better than him, especially Deacon. "Now, if he beats Deacon, he also gets back at you," Jack surmises. Even though Lewis had a hand in it, it was Dominic who turned Mikey into who he is today.

Micki and Ryan arrive at the race. They are too late to stop it, so they watch nervously as Mikey and Deacon race. Suddenly, Dominic appears out of nowhere, in his truck, and races towards Mikey. The two cars collide at full speed, exploding into a massive fireball.

Status: Micki and Ryan find the key and chain amidst the wreckage; it was about the only thing left. Ryan gives it a good polish before it goes back into the vault.

* * *

While the cursed object in "Night Hunger" may not be the most interesting antique (okay, a chain is flat-out dull), its curse certainly is. This is the first time an object has adapted to its situation. The chain gets sucked into Mikey's chest cavity? No problem, the chain can still work. It is the only cursed object that actually becomes part of the owner's body. The hearing aide from "Stick it in Your Ear" sort of becomes part of Adam Cole, but it's a hearing aide that's supposed to go inside the body. A chain is not supposed to wrap itself around your heart.

The other interesting part of this curse is that it is like a communicable disease. The curse actually extends to the key. Would it have done that no matter what hung off it? A heart, a peace sign, a religious icon? The key survived the wreckage, suggesting it was made impervious by a curse.

"'Night Hunger' was the episode that most disappointed me, for a lot of reasons," says episode writer Jim Henshaw. "It just didn't work, and we were so disappointed. On the page, it looked great, but when we got out there, it just didn't come together. We worked on it in post, and we did a lot of extra second-unit stuff, but it was one of those episodes that almost made me want to quit writing and go on vacation or something. Somewhere I got something very wrong. Ultimately, I don't think it was anyone's fault; it was just a combination of four or five different things that just didn't gel."

"The Sweetest Sting"

Story by: Rick Butler
Teleplay by: Rick Butler and Roy Sallows
Directed by: David Winning
Original airdate: January 16, 1989
Cursed antique: Bee hive

A man named McCabe (Art Hindle) runs a very special roadside stand, selling honey from his own apiary. When he "accidentally" drips his special blend on customers, he releases his bees to "clean it up." Of course, the bees sting the customer to death. McCabe brings his hive of killer bees back to his apiary, where he has a second business set up, hidden in the shadows of his barn. His new client, Ben Landis, is an elderly man in failing health. McCabe promises that the world will think he died in a car accident, and his family will be well taken care of. Ben sits down and puts his hands through something that resembles medieval stocks, set into a wall. McCabe goes to the other side of the wall and unleashes his killer bees on Ben's hands. Ben screams in pain and collapses, but does not die. When the bees are away and McCabe checks on him, Ben is now a young, strapping man, the man who McCabe killed on the side of the road, Bob Tucker (Tim Webber). Weekly touchups will be required to maintain this transformation, and he promises that his blood will be used to make a "very special blend."

Norman Hendricks (J. Winston Carroll) is having the worst day of his life. The sixty-something tractor salesman was just diagnosed with cancer. The doctor estimates he has six months, maybe a year left. Norman returns to work and is immediately laid off by a new, young boss, Fred Marr (David Palffy), whose slick suit and stony expression are trademarks of the Stereotypical 1980s Guy (except this isn't Wall Street). To top it all off, when Norman leaves work, he thinks he is being mugged when young Bob Tucker rushes up to him. Bob insists that he is Ben Landis, Norman's old friend, and offers an anecdote to prove it. Bob/Ben tells him about his second chance at life and gives him a note: Sweet Life Apiary in Crawford Corner.

With his life rapidly going down the shitter, Norman visits McCabe and doesn't balk when asked to sign his life insurance over to him. McCabe promises that he will make sure his wife Joanne is taken care of, but once Norman is transformed, he must never see her again. McCabe then goes on the hunt for Norman's new body. I'm not sure if Norman made the suggestion or if it was just a lucky coincidence, but McCabe ends up in the elevator with Mr. Marr, who ignores his offer of honey, forcing McCabe to wipe it on him. The bees swarm, and Marr is dead.

Bob/Ben takes Norman back to McCabe for his actual treatment. McCabe takes Bob/Ben aside and sends him to find a body that matches Norman's so he can "close out the file on Norman's life."

"You want me to kill someone?" Bob/Ben asks incredulously.

"Unless you know a better way. I'd hate to keep your taste of honey from you," he teases.

Bob/Ben's hands are starting to wrinkle. He will need some honey soon. Ben doesn't want to lose his new, perfect life, so he finds a hitchhiker who roughly matches Norman and chops him up beneath a spinning combine while McCabe transforms Norman into Fred Marr.

Micki has been up in this neck of the woods on her own, looking for the beehive. According to the manifest, Lewis sold it to Duane Purdy, and Jack is particularly interested in this piece because it is one-of-a-kind, and he has no idea what the thing does. Micki arrives at the Purdy farm, and is greeted by an old angry man with a shotgun and a guard dog. This Purdy is Duane's brother. Duane died, and a beehive was not among his belongings. As Micki heads out, Purdy warns her that it's "not safe around here come nightfall." Micki reports back to Jack and tells him she is going to stay another day or two, check out some other apiaries. Ryan finds Duane's autopsy report—he had so many beestings the coroner couldn't count them all. He died right after he bought the beehive from Lewis, but there have been no other bee sting deaths in the area since. Jack and Ryan will borrow Rashid's car and join Micki in the morning.

Jack meets with McCabe as part of his tour of apiaries. Ben arrives during this meeting, old again. "You've gotta help me. I need that honey!" McCabe laughs it off, promising his shipment is boxed up. Inside, McCabe is furious. "If you ever put my operation in danger again you will wish you died a hundred deaths." Micki and Ryan's visit back to the Purdy residence wasn't of much use either, other than Purdy being terrified of the hive.

When the trio meets up later, they compare notes: fear of bees, desperation for honey. Jack mentions that Ben looked prematurely old; his body didn't look "used." Micki remembers from school that Egyptians believed honey could restore youth. Jack returns to the store and leaves the kids to keep an eye on McCabe's farm. "He's the key to this, I'm sure."

Ryan and Micki return to McCabe's farm for a little snoop. They set off a silent alarm as they examine the transformation room. Micki finds the blood honey and collects some of it while Ryan checks out the loft. Micki has a taste of the blood honey (why why why?!) and Ryan gets a visit from McCabe and his bees. Ryan yells for Micki and the two run for the car. McCabe is close behind. Micki trips as they approach the car, and the bees set upon her fast. She rolls around, swatting the bees off as best as she can, until Ryan grabs a fire extinguisher from the trunk and sprays her down. The two escape into the car and drive home immediately.

Jack is looking at one of the bees under a microscope. Its little pollen sac is full of blood. Had they overwhelmed her, she would have been drained of blood. Jack can't be sure until he checks the sample of honey she brought back, but he thinks the bees are making honey out of blood, and eating the honey keeps you young. There is still a piece of the puzzle missing and tomorrow, Jack is determined to make Purdy talk.

Sure enough, Jack, Micki, and Ryan surprise Purdy, take his shotgun away, and demand he talk. "You can't fight that hive. The bees come straight from hell!" Purdy finally gives in and admits that McCabe is his brother. "First he stole the hive from Duane, then he stole his body." Jack fills it in for us: "The bees drank Duane's blood, then transferred it to McCabe." In other words, it is Duane's body, McCabe's sparkling personality.

"Marr" has been checking in periodically on Joanne, and promises to look into Norman signing over his pension. One of these calls is interrupted by McCabe, who is furious that he has been dodging his calls. "I gave you what you wanted; now I am hear to collect my debt." He is always in need of bodies, and wants "Marr" to kill for him. He hands over Jack's business card, and instructs him to kill those three visitors. "You won't get a taste of honey until they are all dead." As added incentive, McCabe later kidnaps Joanne. When "Marr" decides he just can't kill anyone, he goes looking for McCabe and discovers Joanne. "I'll let her go, but only if you kill them." McCabe threatens to otherwise drain Joanne dry, or turn her old and ugly. "It's an interesting dilemma," McCabe muses. "Tell someone, and they won't believe you. Do nothing, and you both die."

Micki, Ryan, and Jack pull up at the Sweet Life Apiary as Marr is driving away. They sneak in and start packing up the honey. McCabe is in a transfer body, so he will need the honey himself. Maybe they can use it to force him to take them to the hive. While Ryan takes a case to the car, Micki hears Joanne's sobs and unties her. Unfortunately, McCabe sneaks up on both of them and takes the opportunity to strap Micki into the chair and make her a feast for his bees. But Marr has had a change of heart, and he comes back to the apiary with a gun aimed at McCabe. "If I die, you die," McCabe warns. "I'm already dead," sighs Marr. Ryan and Jack race back in to the barn to find McCabe knocking out Marr, and use this chance to get the ladies out of there. McCabe goes for the honey, but Marr comes to and shoots McCabe. He misses McCabe—but his shot hits the honey jars. The bees swarm McCabe.

Marr stumbles weakly out of the barn. He is aging rapidly and is clearly near death. He calls weakly for "Jo-Jo," and collapses in her arms. "Forgive me," he moans. As he dies, he physically returns to Norman.

Status: The bee hive is vaulted—without the bees. Jack explains that the bees were "smoked out" and sent to another hive. Without the hive, they are harmless.

*　*　*

I remember seeing the promo for this episode, which featured the scene with Micki getting attacked by the swarm. That scene sent me into a panic. Cursed objects couldn't be destroyed; could the bees? I wasn't sure if the bees were now indestructible, and if they were, what did that mean for Micki? How could the bees be called off their intended victim? Remember, I was about ten years old when I first watched saw the "Next week on" promo. I didn't understand the basic economics of television, which is that a lead character would not just randomly die in the middle of the season without some sort of buildup. Hell, Micki actually did die a few episodes prior, in "Tales I Live, Heads You Die," and she came out of that. I think the only show to get away with randomly killing main characters nowadays is *The Walking Dead* (and even that, you have a rough guideline with the comic books). Of course, I waited on pins and needles for that scene, and when Ryan blasted the bees with a simple fire extinguisher, I was relieved—and mad at myself for getting so worked up about it.

For director David Winning, "The Sweetest Sting" was his first foray into directing for television. "In 1988 I was twenty-six years old and still finishing my first feature film, *Storm*, a labor of love I'd dedicated my twenties to making. I was a brand new, really green member of the Director's Guild of Canada. Producer J. Miles Dale was apparently in need of a director after one recently dropped out. He was literally flipping through the DGC member guide, stopped on my name, said 'WINNING? Sounds positive!' and hired me on the spot." He was completely "freaked out" and "unprepared," but certainly wasn't going to turn down a directing gig, so he headed from his home in Calgary to the set in Toronto. "In retrospect, I had absolutely no idea what I was doing," Winning admits. "They asked me how old I was, and I lied and said thirty-four. Being tall helped."

Being green didn't have an affect on the actors, at least not Art Hindle, who played McCabe in the episode. "I came away impressed with the director, David Winning," Hindle says. "We have tried time and again to work together but it hasn't worked out."

Hindle remembers, like most episodic television, there was not much time to "prepare" and "find" the character. "For that role, I remember deciding to part my hair on the opposite side I normally do, and slitting my eyebrow on that side in two. It had the desired affect for me. When I looked in the mirror, the face looking back seemed 'odd' and 'evil.'" Hindle is careful to qualify that statement: "I've played many roles that people call 'bad guys' but an actor can't go into a character believing the character is bad—no one really think themselves 'bad' no matter what they do. I choose to call them good guys who do bad things."

The "stars" of the episode were, of course, the bees. Hindle knows they were around but doesn't remember working directly with them. "We had bee handlers on set," Winning recalls. "When we used real bees, the stuntman was completely insulated with protective gear under his costume. I remember them dumping two giant hives on this poor guy; a total of 50,000 bees, for the scene where Bob Tucker is writhing on the road after the first attack in the episode opening. Pretty sure we did it twice, too. We had a nurse on set with an adrenalin shot at the ready, and on the second take, the bees got in through a rip in the costume. I have a clear memory of the nurse pulling the stingers out of his bare, welted back. More than seventy stings! Stunt guys earn their money."

"The Sweetest Sting" shot in the middle of the night on a Mennonite farmer's field. "They'd been kind enough to lend us a combine," remembers Winning. "It was a bit awkward when they showed up to watch: good religious folks watching as their combine was spewing fake bone and blood all over their field. I saw their faces sag. Memorable. I'm not sure they had been given the script to read. This was the quick and dirty eighties."

Looking back, the most important lesson Winning learned on his first TV show was to get to set early to meet the crew. "I stayed in the office prepping my show and making my little storyboard drawings all that first week. I was too scared to go to set. Then on day one, I show up, not knowing anyone. It's a mistake I made only once in my career—on *Friday*. Ever since then I make friends early. It is incredibly important. It makes the set more comfortable and it establishes the creative relationships as early as possible."

"The Playhouse"

Written by: Tom McLoughlin
Directed by: Tom McLoughlin
Original airdate: January 28, 1989
Cursed antique: Playhouse

Mike and Janine Carlson (Robert Oliveri and Lisa Jakub) are forgotten children. Their mother Sylvia (Belinda Metz) only remembers they exist when she is angry and can use them as a punching bag. They are dirty and underfed and frequently left alone for days at a time while mom runs around with one of her many loser boyfriends.

Luckily they have the playhouse to take care of them.

Given to them by one of mom's former loser boyfriends in the hopes of keeping them quiet while he banged their mom, the playhouse is a Victorian-style house with big stained-glass windows. Mike and Janine take neighborhood kids inside the playhouse, promising them their heart's desires. The kids are easily duped (remember this is the 1980s, when it was still "safe" for kids to play in their neighborhoods unsupervised, at least until the streetlights came on) and never think twice about going with a couple friendly kids their age to play with an amazing new toy. The kids generally get a little nervous when they enter the playhouse and discover it is completely empty. But Janine and Mike look at each other and a wind picks up in the sealed playhouse. White light engulfs the children and they are transported out of the playhouse into an *Alice in Wonderland* setting (as envisioned by Tom Petty in his "Don't Come Around Here No More" video). Anything Mike or Janine—or their guests—ask for, the playhouse makes it appear. Candy, worms, ponies, toys, costumes, the playhouse provides it all. But of course, it comes with a price. Mike and Janine must profess their hatred for their new playmates, and the house sucks them into the wall. Then Mike and Janine are free to play—until the house gets hungry again.

As the episode opens, Mike and Janine befriend Danny, a young boy down the street. A later news report reveals that he is the ninth missing child from the neighborhood in the past five months. The Curious Goods crew does not initially make the connection, but while following a lead on the playhouse (Ryan's assignment of the day), Micki realizes the most recent owner, Brad Farrell (Wayne Best), lives in the neighborhood of the missing kids. The connections start lining up. Ryan checks in with Brad, who says he can get it back—for a price. Ryan agrees to the $5,000 ransom Brad is asking, even though he knows they can't afford that. Jack will keep an eye on Brad while Micki and Ryan check in with the parents of the missing children.

Brad gives Sylvia a call, and she is happy to let Brad take the playhouse back, if only because it will hurt the children more than a slap across the face would. Frantic, the kids race out to the playhouse—it will know what to do. Around this time, Micki and Ryan come to the house after Danny's mom points the way. They go straight into the backyard, where the playhouse sits serenely beneath a tree. Sylvia barges outside and Micki and Ryan take refuge within the playhouse. While in there, they try to dismantle the playhouse, but it is as solidly constructed as a real house. Janine and Mike are "downstairs" (I don't know how else to describe the central play area) playing military when the house gives them a window to its "foyer." Mike has the house bring them to him and his sister, where the grown-ups will play by "our rules" before turning them over to the house.

Ryan and Micki wake in Wonderland, tied to chairs. "We are having a party in your honor," Mike informs them. There is a clown, a juggler, costumed mascots, and an enormous cake. But then a monster jumps out of the cake, and the other characters turn into evil versions of themselves. (Except the clown—adding bigger teeth to the clown doesn't make it more evil than a clown normally is; it just means it needs a trip to the dentist.) The kids are distracted by another vision from the playhouse: Brad is outside, trying to dismantle the house. They abandon Micki and Ryan to protect their beloved house.

Despite the fact that Danny's mom told Ryan and Micki where they can find the Carlson house, she is weirded out by their seemingly random interest in the case, and she alerts the police. While the police officer is taking a statement from her, he hears screams from the Carlson house and rushes over. He finds Brad caught up in a fight with Janine and Mike, who are defending their home. The kids immediately rush to the officer, and Brad is arrested.

Jack stumbles upon the scene and gives a statement to the police. Brad had seen him watching him and knocked Jack out to prevent him

Lisa Jakub and Robert Oliveri just being kids on the set of "The Playhouse."
Photo courtesy of Lisa Jakub.

from following him to the playhouse's location and cheating him out of the money. The cops don't spend much time with Jack; they think Brad might be the kidnapper, so all focus is on him. That makes it easy for Jack to slip into the yard and crawl into the house.

The kids have returned to their Wonderland, dressed in black robes. Micki and Ryan are now tied to stakes. But before the burning can begin, Janine "senses" another intruder upstairs. Jack seems to sense her, as well, and begins to concentrate. The house shows the kids Jack on the intruder-cam, and Mike wants to teach him a lesson. Again, Micki and Ryan are left alone. (The playhouse has seen more visitors than a whorehouse.)

Jack tries to convince Mike and Janine that he, Micki, and Ryan are simple antique dealers, but Mike is convinced they want to steal their power. Micki chimes in, insisting they care about the kids. (Why would a trio of strangers care about these kids when their own mother doesn't?) Mike insists that only the house cares. The children in the walls begin to wail. The house is hungry. Micki and Ryan are untied and the kids begin their "I hate you" chants. Nothing happens. The house doesn't want adults; it wants the innocence of children. So it goes for the closest thing it can: Janine.

Janine, through all of this, has been relatively quiet. The more children they feed to the house, the more the resistance shows on her face. She keeps up with the facade because of her brother. So, when the house wants Janine, Mike is faced with a difficult decision. "You know the deal Mike. Hate keeps it alive," Jack eggs him on.

Mike can't do that to the only person who loves him. He refuses, grabs Janine, and hugs her fiercely. "I love you," he insists.

Just your typical day on the set of "The Playhouse." Photo courtesy of John LeMay.

The house begins breaking down, and Jack encourages this line of action. "You robbed the house of its power. You have to tell those kids you love them. You can't be afraid to give love if you ever expect it back."

Janine isn't afraid. She chants "I care! About all of you! I love you!"

With a little encouragement, Mike joins in. In a flash of light, the children wander out of the walls, completely unharmed.

Outside, Sylvia is fighting with a cop, who has multiple reports of child abuse and neglect on her. She insists she is a good mother, but that doesn't really follow when Mike and Janine crawl out of the playhouse and she starts screaming at them. Jack assures them the courts will find loving foster homes for them. The cops are stunned when all the missing children file out.

Status: The official story (the one the cops seem to buy) is that the kids were all hiding in the playhouse. The playhouse is in police custody for the foreseeable future, which is just as good as the vault in Jack's mind. (Plus, how the hell would they fit that playhouse into the vault?)

Mentioned but not explored: Top hat; Indian sacrificial knife

* * *

"The Playhouse" was the first episode Tom McLoughlin both wrote and directed for *Friday the 13th: The Series*. "I felt like I really 'owned it.' It was really like I was making a feature film. Frank Mancuso, as he was with my *Friday the 13th* movie, gave me such creative control. If he ever had a note, it was always a good note and easy to do."

The impetus for "The Playhouse" came from the birth of Tom's son. "My son had just been born, so I suddenly became very impassioned about children's rights," he explains. "What if you were a kid and you had something to empower you in some way? 'The Playhouse' came out of that. To this day, I still think I didn't accomplish [the style of the playhouse] as visually as I could."

Lisa Jakub, who was ten years old when she played Janine Carlson, begs to differ. "The set for the playhouse was visually incredible—the set decorators did a wonderful job. Those stairways to nowhere were so intriguing and the crazy aspect ratio really created a dream-like setting."

"I was lucky enough to get two very gifted kids, so the whole experience was great," Tom says of Jakub and Robert Oliveri, who played Mike. "The separation [from my son] gave me a more emotional connection to the kids. They sort of became my surrogate family [in Toronto]."

Lisa also loved working with Tom. "He was really great to us and always made sure we were comfortable, especially during the more emotional scenes. It was so nice to work with a director that understood how to work with kids. He never talked down to us or treated us differently than the adult actors. We were all there to do a job and we had fun doing it."

She has high praise for her co-star, too. "Robert and I got to be great friends, I adored him. He took his job seriously and even looking back on the show now, he was a really talented actor. But we also had a great time off set, playing cards and just hanging out and doing kid stuff.

"When we worked together, Robert was already doing some acting in Los Angeles and had a manager out there. He said that his manager was interested in meeting me. I'm from Toronto and had only ever worked in Canada, but on Robert's recommendation, my mom and I went out to L.A. for a three-month stay. I started booking acting jobs and ended up moving to L.A. several years later. If it weren't for Robert, I'm not sure that I would have ever made that leap.

"Unfortunately, at some point, Robert and I lost touch. It was hard for young actors to keep up consistent friendships since we were traveling so frequently for work. I'll always be grateful for the influence that he had on my life and my career. "

I tried to track down Robert for this book, but he has retired from acting and I could not find him.

"Eye of Death"

Written by: Peter Jobin and Timothy Bond and Roy Sallows
Directed by: Timothy Bond
Original airdate: January 30, 1989
Cursed antique: Projector

Atticus Rook (Tom McCamus) is a "picker," specializing in Civil War antiques. A picker is someone who seeks out antiques for collectors and shop owners, the kind of thing Jack used to do for Uncle Lewis. Jack is acquainted with Rook, but has no reason to believe that he might be in possession of one of Lewis' antiques: pickers never hang on to their picks. Of course, the name Atticus Rook is like a bad guy calling card. Jack should have seen it earlier. Rook is listed in the manifest as being the buyer of something that Lewis called the "Eye of Death." This was one of the earliest projectors, named so because it was primarily used to show the carnage from the Civil War battlefields. It was the first time many people had ever seen such brutality.

Rook's scheme was simple. By killing someone, the Eye of Death would allow him to step back into the past, into the scene of the antique slide he had, depicting the Battle of Antietam. Once there, he would pilfer what he could from the dying soldiers, then kill someone to open the portal back to modern day. The stolen goods would instantly become mint-condition antiques and fetch a huge profit at auction.

Jack has been trying to track down Rook for months, and finally catches him at a Civil War auction. Rook insists he never bought from Lewis, but Ryan follows him home after the auction, just in case. Rook takes his date home and shows her the magic lantern: "This one is really magic." His talk of death and magic frightens her, but he snaps her neck and disposes of her in the dumpster outside his apartment building before she can run. Ryan sees the body dump (who the hell dumps a body where they live? Did that stuff fly in the 1980s?) and sneaks into the apartment. He tackles Rook as he steps through the portal, and Ryan travels back to 1862 with Rook. Ryan is startled by his new surroundings and Rook takes this opportunity to knock Ryan out. The portal is only active as long as

On the set of "Eye of Death." Photo courtesy of John LeMay.

the candle on the lantern is burning, which is about three hours at a time. Rook sees this as a death sentence for his stowaway and heads out to steal his batch of soon-to-be antiques.

Micki and Jack are concerned that they haven't heard from Ryan, and head to Rook's apartment to find him. Micki realizes that all the antiques Rook sells are from the same year, the same battlefield. It isn't much of a leap to believe the magic lantern is taking him to that point in time. By the time they get to the apartment, the police are there, collecting the body. Jack claims he is Atticus Rook and Micki is his daughter in order to gain access to the building.

Once in Rook's apartment, Micki immediately goes for the lantern, until Jack stops her. It is in operation, and if the object works the way they think it does, and Ryan time traveled through it, if they shut it off he would be stuck. Jack finds some fresh blood and tries to wipe it on the wall, but nothing happens. There is nothing they can do, so they leave—without the lantern. "If Ryan has entered the past, that's his way out, too."

In "the past," Ryan wakes in the home of a Southern nurse, Abigail (Brooke Johnson). Her father, Murphy (Al Kozlik), thinks Ryan is a Yankee spy, but she thinks he is a bounty hunter. This sounds less likely to get Ryan killed, so he agrees, and promises the man he is hunting, Rook, is the same one who killed Abigail's husband. Ryan snoops around, then sees Rook kill Murphy. The light window opens, and Rook escapes through it. Ryan, stuck there, hides from the soldiers who think he killed Murphy.

Things start to get a little *Back to the Future*-y when Micki finds a picture of Ryan with General Lee in a history book. The caption reads "Union spy, just before his execution." "We know Ryan couldn't have died in the past," Micki insists, "he was alive tonight!"

"No. We know he *was* alive. This might be his last night in the past *and* the present," Jack corrects her.

Meanwhile, my brain explodes.

Rook returns home and finds the detective is there, waiting for him. The same detective who spoke to Jack less than twenty-four hours earlier, who doesn't seem to notice that Atticus Rook is now a completely different man. Doesn't matter anyway: Rook kills him, but in the struggle, his slide breaks. In a panic, Rook calls Edward, another Civil War collector who has a similar slide in his collection, and offers a trade: the slide for General Lee's sword. He takes the lantern with him to see Edward, and Jack and Micki follow.

Meanwhile, Ryan convinces Abigail that he is from the future. Whether or not she *actually* believes him doesn't matter. She agrees to turn Ryan in to General Lee as a Yankee spy so he can get close to Lee and be there when Rook returns to consult with him. General Lee is having his photo taken when Abigail presents him at gunpoint—this is the photo that Micki found in the history book. Now, Ryan just has to remember enough history to stall him until Rook shows up. If it were me, I would have been dead in seconds.

Micki and Jack sneak into Edward's apartment just in time to see Rook kill him. Micki charges after Rook and falls into the past with him. He doesn't seem too concerned about her, which allows her to snoop around for Ryan.

General Lee has listened to Ryan stumble through high school history for over an hour, and he hasn't given him anything useful. Rook shows up with important battle details, and General Lee decides to listen to Rook and imprison Ryan. All Rook wants in exchange is Lee's sword. Abigail sees the exchange, and follows Rook.

Micki comes in on horseback, using the element of surprise to startle Ryan's captors and allow him to break free. He hops on the horse and they escape under a hail of bullets. Micki and Ryan find Abigail just as she is shot by Rook. Ryan is ready to kill Rook out of anger when Micki points out that the light window is open: Abigail's death gave them a way out. They race for the light, with Rook right behind them. As soon as Micki and Ryan come out on the other side, Jack blows out the candle. Like Han Solo in carbonite, Rook is frozen halfway through the wall.

Status: The lantern is returned, and Ryan has a permanent place in history. As Jack points out, he is the oldest living veteran of the Civil War.

* * *

Timothy Bond co-wrote and directed this episode. "I used to work with a writing partner named Peter Jobin and we came up with that idea, and pitched it," Bond explains. "We went through all the steps of delivering a script—and they hated it." The producers had the episode rewritten by Roy Sallows. Bond was already set to direct, and he offered to bow out. The producers still wanted him to shoot the script, and they asked him to have a look at it first. "I went into a meeting with Jon Andersen and Jim Henshaw and started asking questions about why this happened, or that happened.

"After about two hours of that, Jon said, 'We may as well just shoot your script.'

"I said, 'No comment.' So, Jon turned to Jim and said, 'We're shooting his script.'"

"Eye of Death" was shot in February, and Bond remembers it was *freezing*. Pretty tough when such a large part of the episode was shot outside. One of the set pieces of the episode is the soldier's camp. "We hired these Civil War re-enactors. At that time we had a hard-nosed production manager, and some dispute came up while I was shooting. These guys didn't like what they were getting paid. I think they were being paid as extras, but they weren't being paid for their costumes and guns and all that. This dispute came while I was shooting at three in the morning, and [the producers] told me about it. I said, 'Well, if you want, I can go on shooting without them. You can send them home and I'll just shoot the tents and the camp and say everyone is asleep. I can make that work.'

"The A.D. said to me, 'Tim, they own the tents!'

"So, I sent word back to the office that they better pay these guys, quick! I guess it all worked out, because they were still in the show and they seemed pretty happy.

"We had all these generals on horseback with torches. Rodney [Charters] starting lighting them, and it just didn't look exciting, so he went and turned off all but one light and shot it. So, they were basically lit by the torches, which was harder to do then than it would be now because of the slower film stocks. He kept saying, 'Don't set fire to your beard!'

"The other fun thing I got to do was a field hospital. I had a few young guys [extras] who had amputations. There was one guy in particular, who had lost his leg in a motorcycle accident, and we had a bloody stunt with a blood pump [as a soldier who lost his leg in battle] and I told him I really wanted him to scream, just really scream. He said, 'I know how to scream when your leg comes off.'"

"I tried to do as many stunts as I could—stupidly," admits John Le-May. "I would end up getting hurt. But I was just trying to save shots." He recalls one such attempt at a stunt on "Eye of Death." "I was handcuffed, and Robey was driving the horse. I was supposed to jump on the horse's butt and she was supposed to ride up into the shot, with cameras facing us, and we both dismount at the same time. The horse was to come around the corner of this barn. I was going to do it all in one. I was tired and just wanted to speed things up. These were long, long hours we were working, and it was always in the middle of the night, and we would work until the sun came up. Robey kicks this horse into gear and we don't make it twenty feet and this horse bucks me right off his ass and I fall onto the hard, Canadian tundra. I had the biggest bruise on my buttock that lasted forever. The right buttock. They put me up in a local hotel and were just hoping I wouldn't die from my injuries. My butt injury. They told me to sleep it off; hopefully the internal injuries won't kill you."

Post-production was a bit tedious back in those early days of computer effects. Bond talks about creating the effect that sent Rook back in time. "I had to shoot the slide and start with [Rook] being still, though we could doctor it with the computer if we had to, then have him come right up to the lens in the slide. In the computer, they isolated him, because he was the only thing moving—well, the people in the slide were trying not to move but not doing that good a job. So, they would isolate him, and draw an outline around him for every frame—at twenty-four frames per second—so that he could be isolated from the rest of the image. Then what we did for the rest of the image was just use one frame, so it was a still. When he ran up to the camera, we cut. On the set, I had projected the slide onto a screen, rolled the camera for a little while, kept it locked, and stepped him in and lined him up with the image of himself as he was about to run up to the camera. I could project that on the wall, line him up, pose him, then roll the camera and tell him to burst through the wall. He'd throw himself forward and we would finish the scene, with the projected slide still behind him. That was fun to do, and fun to figure out how to light him, so the light didn't splash onto the slide, because then you wouldn't be able to see it.

"That was the gimmick of it, and the technical challenges are fun," Bond continues. "But the most fun was the idea that he was robbing the dead and selling the stuff in the present day as antiques. I loved that."

"Face of Evil"

Written by: Jim Henshaw
Directed by: William Fruet
Original airdate: February 6, 1989
Cursed antique: Gold compact

Joanne Mackie (Gwendolyn Pacey) is back. After her ill-fated prom in "Vanity's Mirror," Joanne has graduated high school and is working as a photographer's assistant at Degage, a high-fashion magazine. At the end of "Vanity's Mirror," her sister Helen (Ingrid Veninger) dove off the top of school with Joanne's boyfriend, Steve. Both died, and the compact rolled away, hidden beneath a bush. Joanne was the one who picked it up, and even though she knew what it did, it was the only keepsake she had to remember Helen, so she kept it. She thought it would be safe with her, in her bag. But she is wrong. *Dead wrong!*

Tabitha (Laura Robinson), once a top supermodel, is starting to show her age. Her live-in boyfriend, Emory (Barry Greene), is a photographer who is not-so-subtly fooling around with Sandy (Monika Schnarre), the young model who is next in line for Tabitha's crown. Tabitha was the one who recommended Joanne for the job, so she thinks nothing of telling Tabitha to look through her bag for a tissue. She does, and also finds the compact. Tabitha is just casually dabbing her eyes when the mirror shows her images of Helen, and how the compact worked. Tabitha snaps it shut and slips the compact into her own bag. Joanne doesn't realize that the compact is missing until that night. She searches everywhere and comes up empty. In desperation she calls Curious Goods, but when Ryan answers she chickens out and hangs up.

Tabitha pays a visit to her plastic surgeon, desperate for something to return herself to her former glory. The doctor tries to talk her out of it, but Tabitha is obsessed. She also can't stop examining her crow's feet in the compact. The doctor is temporarily blinded when the compact reflects light into his eyes. Tabitha sees the doctor's bloodied face in the mirror, and when he tries to leave, Tabitha grabs him by the arm. The doc tumbles over the banister and goes through a glass table. Tabitha's first instinct is to race down to help him—but then she remembers his bloody reflection in her mirror. She looks again, and sees her crow's feet are gone.

Joanne finally swallows her pride and goes to Curious Goods. She explains what happened, and Jack is annoyed that she kept the compact, even after she knew what it did. "It was all I had to remember Helen by," she explains. (Apparently Helen's bedroom contained nothing pocket-sized.) Micki and Ryan head to work with Joanne to investigate.

Today's shoot is set in a boxing ring, and Sandy is all set to be this year's cover girl. Tabitha isn't scheduled for the shoot, but she shows up anyway, to "wish Sandy her best." Cora (Lynne Gorman), the magazine's editor-in-chief, greets Tabitha and mentions that she looks stunning. "Emory's photos haven't been doing you justice." She tells Tabitha to come to tonight's shoot, and if she looks this good, she might just push Sandy's cover debut to next year. Joanne casually asks Tabitha if she has her compact. Tabitha becomes slightly defensive, but Joanne assures her she doesn't think she has it; she's just asking everyone.

Tabitha returns for the evening shoot, and Joanne mentions the lines around her eyes are "starting to peek through." Not only that, but they are getting worse. Tabitha dons huge sunglasses and rushes to find her next victim. She goes straight to Sandy, who is smoking and fluffing her hair. Tabitha tells her she has a "very unique look" and flashes her compact in her eyes. The reflection the mirror delivers is Sandy's face melting off. "Your face is worth a fortune," Tabitha purrs. "It will get you everything you deserve."

She slips away, and Sandy picks up a big can of 1980s aerosol hair-spray. The highly combustible nature of the hairspray plus the lit cigarette is not a good combination, and the hairspray turns into a flamethrower. Sandy *screams* and everyone comes rushing. Tabitha's lines disappear. Cursed object or not, it seems to me that the fireball outcome is unavoid-able if you are smoking while using hairspray. This is possibly the least-suspicious injury in the entire series.

As Sandy is wheeled out by paramedics, weeping about her face, Emory wants to call it a night. Tabitha is understandably mad and wants to keep going. "This is my issue, my cover, my spotlight. This is not a business for the faint of heart. Sandy wasn't right for this spread any-way." Everyone is horrified at Tabitha's callousness—everyone except for Cora, who seems proud of Tabitha's work ethic. But this directness causes Joanne to flash back to Helen's own indifferent attitude to Greg's death, and she starts to worry.

Laura Robinson and Barry Greene on the set of "Face of Evil."
Photo courtesy of Laura Robinson.

Emory takes Tabitha home and is hurt that she doesn't invite him in. "Oh, is that how it is? I'm back on top, so you think you should be too?" She lets him in and runs herself a bath. Before he makes them some drinks, he makes a phone call to Kamichi (Sandrine Ho), the other model on the shoot (aka Emory's backup bang). He tells her he is stuck at work, but she will be doing the runway show with Tabitha. Tabitha overhears this, and doesn't like it one bit.

Back at Curious Goods, Jack has done some research on the compact. The first time around, it gave Helen love and respect. Tabitha already has all that. But her career is her face. Both the doctor and Sandy only had injuries to their faces. The compact feeds on the vanity of whoever has it.

It's time for the runway show, and Emory is shooting the rehearsal. He wants Kamichi to go out first: she is younger, fresher, and virginal. Tabitha, somewhat surprisingly, agrees: "I'm just glad to be a small part of it all." But Tabitha checks out her reflection and sees the lines are back, and worse than ever. Joanne sees her with the compact and flashes back to when she first found the compact on Helen's vanity. Joanne does the wide-eyed scare so well.

Tabitha is busy trying to get a moment with Kamichi, who is constantly surrounded by hair and makeup people. This gives Joanne a chance to look through Tabitha's belongings, but of course she wouldn't leave the compact behind. Tabitha makes her move when Emory and Kamichi go back to the runway for photos. She flashes both of them with the mirror, and moments later, the massive light grid drops on both of them. While Tabitha admires her handiwork, Joanne snatches the compact out of her hand and runs.

Tabitha corners Joanne backstage. Joanne tries to convince her that it destroys people, it destroyed her sister. Tabitha insists she needs it to stay on top. Micki and Ryan rush in, and the distraction allows Tabitha to grab the compact. She then chases the girls with the mirror reflection, but Ryan herds them away. Ryan tries to bounce the light from the compact off a mirror of his own. It doesn't work and he hides, so Tabitha returns her attention to Joanne.

Micki tries the mirror trick and it works for her. She gets Tabitha twice, and she drops, shrieking. Tabitha ages very rapidly, turning into some terrifying combination of a witch and a mummy: sagging grey skin, warts, wrinkles. She reaches one last time for the compact but dies before she can get it. Joanne doesn't resist when Micki finally takes the compact.

Status: The compact is finally secured in the vault, and Jack absolves Joanne of any wrongdoing. "You can blame Lewis for this."

* * *

The first eight minutes of "Face of Evil" is basically a compilation of scenes from "Vanity's Mirror," organized as flashbacks. Frankly, I think this is a better way to fill in new viewers than to just make the characters give stilted exposition. You would think that eight minutes would be enough to catch people up on what happened in "Vanity's Mirror," but there are still another five minutes or so of flashbacks scattered throughout. Even still, I loved this episode. I think it was the glamour and sexiness of the modeling world, juxtaposed by violence and disfigurement. Not in any sort of feminist-statement way; I just like watching pretty things being destroyed. Plus, I found this episode to be one of the more graphic episodes of *F13*. The victims aren't just shot or drowned, but are mutilated and, in most cases, left alive to live with their mutilation.

The compact is one of two items to be featured in two individual episodes. But unlike the coin in "Tails I Live, Heads You Die"/"Bad Penny," the curse changes. Episode writer and executive story consultant Jim Henshaw: "We wanted to use Ingrid Veninger a second time. She was in the original compact story ["Vanity's Mirror"]. She didn't have much to do in the second one ["Face of Evil"] but she's a terrific actress and we wanted to use her again. So, we thought we would revisit that story and have her associated with the compact and see what happens. But we couldn't tell the same story, so we did something else." However, Ingrid's only appearance in "Face of Evil" was archival footage. I think Henshaw may have meant Gwendolyn Pacey.

"Face of Evil" was Monika Schnarre's first acting gig. Before that, she was a print and runway model, with the cover of *Vogue* and a spread in the *Sports Illustrated* swimsuit edition all before she turned eighteen. The role of supermodel Sandy seems a good role to cut her teeth on. "It's unwatchable for me," laments Schnarre, "but working on it did inspire me to study acting." Laura Robinson, who played rival model Tabitha, assures me that there was no rivalry off-screen. During the scene where Sandy's hairspray turns into a blowtorch, she is supposed to scream, "Tabitha, don't!" "I was being really nice and encouraging to her, but she got really comfortable with me and kept calling me Laura," Robinson says. "If I hadn't helped her so much she would have been even better in the role!"

Schnarre loved wearing the prosthetics for her big burn scene. "I loved wearing the prosthetic home and scaring my mother! I think that I also wore it home on the subway which was fun." Unfortunately, Robinson's experience with her comparatively minimal wrinkle prosthetics was not as good. "I hated doing the prosthetics. I think it was really hard on my skin. They did it with hair spray and spirit gum and toilet paper. They put it on me and dried it with a blow dryer, and it made all these wrinkles. After I took it off, I was wrinkled for a long time after. I thought I should have never done that stunt. It should have been a proper prosthetic, but they did a jury-rig on it and I think it really gave me wrinkles."

Fun fact: Both Laura Robinson from "Face of Evil" and Hilary Shepard from "A Cup of Time" invented board games. Robinson created "Balderdash" and "Identity Crisis;" Shepard created "LIEbrary" and "Love It or Hate It."

"Better Off Dead"

Written by: Bruce Martin
Directed by: Armand Mastroianni
Original airdate: February 13, 1989
Cursed antique: Silver syringe

Dr. Warren Voss (Neil Munro) is trolling for a hooker. He picks one and takes her back to his impressive mansion. He sends her to fix herself a drink while he checks on his daughter, Amanda (Tara Meyer). Though you can't hear it from downstairs, the hall outside her bedroom is filled with her screams. Instead of going into her room, Voss checks on Amanda through a peephole. She is struggling against the restraints that have her strapped to her bed, Linda Blair-style.

Returning to his hooker, Lesley (Bonnie Beck), Voss takes her by the hand and drags her to his lab. "Come on, let's get this over with." While she likes the monkeys he has, she warns him she doesn't do anything "weird;" he promises that he doesn't either—but he does want her to lay down on his medical table and put her into restraints. Fully clothed. She does so, but isn't amused. Voss launches into a villain's soliloquy. He is studying a condition known as hyper-violence, and seeking the section of the brain that controls the desire to hurt one another. He removes a huge antique syringe from its case, and assures her that no *animals* suffer in his lab. With one hand over her mouth, Voss plunges the needle into Lesley's neck and withdraws a clear, yellowish liquid. Voss takes the syringe to his daughter and injects the liquid into her neck. Almost immediately, Amanda's writhing stops. She quiets down and her father unstraps her. Amanda is calm and responsive; a regular, sunny child.

Dr. Henry Chadway (Lubomir Mykytiuk), a friend, comes to visit the Vosses. While Voss insists his daughter is getting better, Chadway thinks Amanda should be committed. As proof, Voss calls Amanda over. She is all smiles, pleasantly playing with a stuffed bunny. Chadway is in disbelief when Voss tells him the disease is in remission.

That evening, Voss is going over his notes. The fluid "donors" lapse into hyper-violence, and as more liquid is extracted, the stronger they get.

Monkeying around on the set of "Better Off Dead." Photo courtesy of Louise Robey.

Lesley is still alive, kept in a cage, and is quickly descending into a feral state. "What did you give me?" she growls.

"Nothing—I just took something away," Voss says simply, then opens the cage to take another sample. Lesley knocks Voss over and races out of the house, into the woods.

A piece in the paper notes that Lesley is the fifth prostitute to disappear in the last month. Jack decides to file it away, as there is not enough to suggest this is a "case" for them. (After all, disappearing prostitutes is, sadly, not a new or unique occurrence.) Besides, they have a houseguest: Micki's college roommate Linda (Camilla Scott) is staying with them while she looks for an apartment.

Ryan and Linda are heading out to dinner at the same time Lesley escapes from Dr. Voss' House of Horrors. She comes out of nowhere, running into the road, causing Linda to hit her. Voss had been following, but when he sees someone else has taken care of his prostitute problem, he quietly retreats into the woods. After checking that Linda is okay, he rushes to Lesley. She is not dead; in fact, she grabs him by the throat and begs for help. He runs to a nearby phone box, where Voss knocks him out. Linda has ventured out of the car, but she sees Voss and rushes back to the car. She can't start it in time, and Voss drugs her and drags her home. Ryan sees this as a blurry haze before passing out.

Back at his lab, Voss has Linda strapped to the table. She begs to be let go; he hopes she will be the last. He jams the needle into her neck. After the extractions, Voss hopes to remove that special part of her brain and put it into Amanda.

Micki and Jack pick up Ryan at the police station. Lesley is dead, but the picture they have of her is not the girl they hit, even though her prints and dental records match. There are needle marks on Lesley's neck, and evidence she was kept in a cage. There is a good chance Linda will meet the same fate.

Back at the shop, Ryan sticks with his story that the woman they hit looked more animal than human. "I wasn't in shock; that's what I saw!" He doesn't know how someone could change so much in two days, but does remember the man who took Linda was wearing a lab coat. Jack goes

Director Armand Mastroianni and Neil Munro try to warm up between takes on "Better Off Dead." Photo courtesy of Armand Mastroianni.

straight to the manifest, and finds a good potential antique that could have been used by someone in a lab coat: a silver syringe. This particular syringe once belonged to Thomas Neill Cream, who Jack explains was a Chicago doctor arrested for murder in London. He claimed to be Jack the Ripper before he was hanged for a string of murders. The syringe was sold to Henry Chadway, who Micki finds in the phone book under Chadway-Voss Institute for Clinical Psychiatry. Jack and Ryan will go visit Chadway while Micki investigates the scene where Linda disappeared.

Voss gets an unwelcome visit in the morning: Nurse Shiller (Barbara Franklin). She was sent by Chadway and the courts to make sure he doesn't administer any unapproved treatments or medications to Amanda. Upstairs, Amanda's treatment is wearing off. She goes from playing quietly in her room to breathing heavily, eyes bulging, and ripping the head off her stuffed bunny.

Voss pays Chadway a visit, furious with his meddling. He insists he is one step away from a cure and that he has found the physical seat of the human soul, a part of the brain that doesn't exist in animals. "If I can transplant this into Amanda, she will be cured!" Voss insists.

Luckily, Chadway doesn't counter with questions of where he is getting these extra chunks of brain. He does, however, refuse to give Voss the requested/demanded few extra days. He will have the hospital collect Amanda in the morning. "Hasn't she suffered enough? She's like this because of you!" Chadway accuses.

Nurse Shiller is trying to feed Amanda when Voss comes in. He throws the nurse out, not wanting Amanda to be antagonized. But it's too late: she throws her dishes at her father and hides under the bed. Amanda tries to jump on her father, but he pins her down and injects her. The nurse is horrified when she sees this, and runs to the phone. Voss interrupts her and throws the nurse down the stairs as Micki rings the doorbell. Voss leaves the dead nurse on the floor, shuts off the lights and unlocks the door. Micki hears the lock slide, and enters the house. (Oh Micki.) She rushes to help the nurse, and Voss knocks her out with a vase to the head.

Micki wakes in a laboratory cage. Linda is strapped to the table, but she is no longer the Linda Micki knows—she is feral and growls at Micki, who shrinks back into the cage. Voss comes in and extracts from Linda again. Micki begs him to let them go, but he explains that some have to die so others can live. Micki insists it is the curse that is making him kill, but Voss is adamant that after tonight, he will never need to use it again. "I'm going to go look for her soul," he says, marking Linda's forehead with a pen. Micki again pleads with him to let them go. "This will cure my daughter—or would you rather I kept using the syringe? Kept killing people?" He thinks that saving hundreds of children is worth one more life. Micki is still annoying him, so Voss tapes her mouth shut. He then returns to Linda and apologizes for not being able to use anesthetic—it will weaken the brainwaves. He turns on a circular saw.

Jack and Ryan surprise Chadway in his office and introduce themselves as the new owners of Vendredi Antiques. They ask about the syringe, explaining that it may have been used in a series of murders. Chadway has a large collection of medical antiquities, but scoffs at the idea that it was used in a crime. He goes to his cabinet to prove it is still there—but of course, it is not. Chadway last remembers seeing it a month ago, and explains that Voss was the only one who had access to it. He and Voss were studying hyper-violence syndrome, a rare childhood disease in which the victim deteriorates into a violent, animalistic state. He isolated the virus, but left a used needle out. His daughter found it and became infected. Voss became obsessed with finding a cure, and Chadway had to fire him.

After the commercial break, Linda is gone from the bloody table. Voss was right: the source of our humanity was there. Amanda can be normal again as soon as he replaces the tissue the virus destroyed. He uses the needle on Micki, then goes for Amanda, already prepped for surgery. He puts Micki on the table, marking her forehead. He estimates a five hour surgery.

The boys arrive at the house and seeing the Mercedes in the driveway, waste no time breaking in. They split up, and Ryan finds Amanda's room, complete with restraints. Jack calls Ryan back downstairs when he follows the sound of the monkeys. He picks the lock to the lab door, but Ryan becomes impatient when he hears a drill start up, and bashes the door with a shovel.

Voss is alarmed and he stops the drill. "I had hoped you'd be the last, but at least you can help me and Amanda make our escape." He extracts once more from Micki, then scoops up Amanda as the guys break in. They are too worried about Micki to see Voss and Amanda hiding. Micki goes nuts, kicks Jack and attacks Ryan. The cousins wrestle and Micki shoves Ryan into a cage. Voss has gone upstairs, with an aerial view of the "operating theater" and puts his daughter in a chair and picks up a gun.

Down in the lab proper, Ryan slugs Micki, knocking her out and allowing him and Jack to get her back on the gurney. Voss takes aim, but before he can fire, he sees Amanda foaming at the mouth. She has reverted to her animalistic self and attacks her daddy, biting and scratching him.

Taking temper tantrums to a new level on the set of "Better Off Dead."
Photo courtesy of Armand Mastroianni.

He tries to give her another injection, but she throws him over the railing. Voss crashes to his death below.

Ryan runs upstairs and finds a bloody, snarling Amanda on the balcony; he shuts and locks the door. Jack collects the syringe off Voss's corpse and looks up to find Amanda's face pressed against the banister, growling and gnashing her teeth.

Status: The syringe goes to the vault; Amanda goes to a mental hospital. Micki is recovering slowly, showing signs of emotion and tears.

* * *

Another favorite episode of mine, likely because this one was quite violent. In fact, I remember that this episode opened with one of those "viewer discretion advised" title cards. It was the first time I had ever seen that on a television show, and in fact, it may have been one of the earliest examples of a TV content warning. Naturally, as an eleven year old, when you see something that says "viewer discretion advised," you stick around! Watching the episode, it is not hard to see why this one got a warning: violence at the hands of a child always touches a nerve.

"Better Off Dead" was the first episode Armand Mastroianni direct-ed for the series, and he wanted to push the envelope right out of the gate. "Initially they just injected the girl with something," Mastroianni recalls. "But I wanted to make it more horrific, like it had to go into her brain to control her seizures. Being influenced by *The Exorcist*, I loved the idea of the child being restrained and looking horrific and demonic, rather than just being sick all the time. [Jim Henshaw] said we should go for it. I remember getting very detailed about where the needle had to go, in the fleshy part because it couldn't go through the skull. They had to get me different needles because [the prop] needle would only compact so much before it would stop. I had to make it look like it was going in completely, so we would cut to the girl squinching her eyes or something, then use a second needle that compacted even more.

"I remember asking where they were going to get candidates for this cursed needle that helps cure his daughter. Jim said [Voss] would go pick up prostitutes. I thought, *What man would pick up prostitutes to use their serum for his daughter? This is beyond belief—let's do it!*

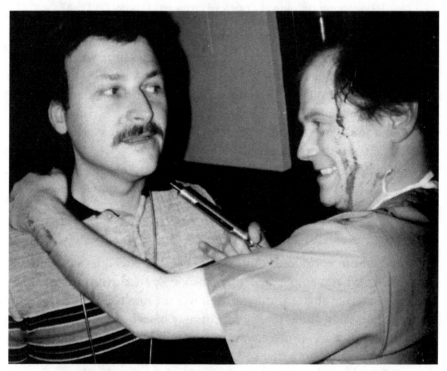

Neil Munro doesn't take direction well. Photo courtesy of Armand Mastroianni.

"I didn't care about censorship at that point. I figured we could always trim it. Well, we put it together and it was *really* good. I remember Frank Mancuso Jr. showed it to his family just before it aired, and his mother was totally grossed out by it. She couldn't stand watching it. They asked us to go in and make a very slight trim in the air master, to abbreviate the needle. That episode became the first show on television that came out with a disclaimer on it. I was the first person to get that! I don't know if it was a blessing or a curse. It certainly sensationalized the show. It brought so much more attention to it." Even before the episode aired, the producers asked Mastroianni to direct more episodes.

When it came to filming, like most directors on the series, Mastroianni has a story about the stupefying cold in Toronto. "We were filming in the wintertime, and in Toronto there were such extremes. You would go through incredible heat and humidity in the summer, but in the winter it was bone-chilling cold. I remember this poor woman escapes [Voss' home] at the beginning of the episode and gets hit by a car. I needed her to be absolutely still, because she was supposed to be dead. It was so cold, we were all wearing down jackets and had those things in your pockets to keep you warm. The poor girl goes over the car and falls into the road. The way I had the shot set up, you could see her body was shaking—she was trembling because she was so cold. I had to change it so that she wasn't 100% dead. We went in and did a shot where [her breathing is raspy] and we can assume she dies. You could see the vapor coming out of her mouth."

The details given about Thomas Neill Cream, though sparse, are not accurate. Known as the Lambeth Poisoner, with five confirmed murders, Cream was actually born in Scotland and raised in Quebec. He went to medical school in Canada and London, but set up his practice in Ontario. He didn't go to the States until he was accused of murder and blackmail, and once there he set up a practice in Chicago. He was suspected of two murders, and convicted of a third, but he was released from prison after his brother allegedly bribed the governor. Upon his release in 1891, Cream went back to London, moving into a poor area called Lambeth (which is where he got his nickname). It was here that he killed four prostitutes and attempted to kill a fifth woman. It was for these murders that he was hanged in 1892, less than a month after his conviction. The hangman, James Billington, claimed that Cream's last words were "I am Jack the… ." which he insisted was a confession to the Jack the Ripper murders. However, no one else at the execution could back up this statement and, in fact, Cream was in prison in Illinois during the 1888 Whitechapel murders.

"Scarlet Cinema"

Written by: Rob Hedden
Directed by: David Winning
Original airdate: February 20, 1989
Cursed antique: Film camera

Dorky film student Darius Pogue (Jonathan Wise) is obsessed with *The Wolf Man*. His dorm is a shrine to the creature feature; he always attends revival screenings; he has every line of the film memorized. More than anything, Darius wants to *be* the wolf man. After a screening of *The Wolf Man*, he goes into an alley, unbuttons his shirt, and scrapes his chest with a stuffed wolf's paw while chanting this little poem: "Even a man who's pure at heart and says his prayers by night; may become a wolf when the wolfsbane blooms and the autumn moon is bright." Nothing happens, but a trio of preppy kids, led by Blair Westlake (John Graham), are filming him, laughing, from around the corner.

The next day in film class, Blair is the obnoxious, pretentious "foreign films are better than American films" kid that draws eye rolls from everyone—including Professor Schwartz (Peter Messaline). Darius, on the other hand, inquires about the horror genre, or, as he calls it, "scarlet cinema." I was a critical studies film major, with a focus on horror and cult films, and I never heard it called "scarlet cinema." I like it, though. Anyways, Blair and his buddies hijack the class to screen their impromptu "film." The class giggles, and the professor doesn't make them stop until Darius' "ritual" is complete. Darius stands and shouts a line from *The Wolf Man*: "You're treating me like I was crazy!" before running from class.

Carissa (Julie A. Stewart), one of the girls from Darius' class, visits Curious Goods to rent some props for her short film. She needs masks, as her film is about the "facades people put up," instead of revealing who they really are (in other words, pretentious film class nonsense). Jack puts her in touch with an old friend, Taylor McDougall, who will rent/sell her a camera.

McDougall (John Swindells) is happy to give Carissa the "friend of Jack" discount. While she is shopping, Darius comes in to rent his own camera. Carissa attempts some awkward small talk with him, but Darius is too shy to engage, even after Carissa tells him he is a better filmmaker than Blair. She returns to her shopping, and Darius to his. He spies a camera, a big, vintage 1930s camera, and films a few scenes in the shop. He decides he must have it. When McDougall informs him it is not for sale and returns to helping Carissa, Darius snatches it and heads back to his dorm.

In his room, Darius examines the camera. It moved on its own, and he looks through the viewfinder to watch the clips he shot of McDougall earlier. Scenes from *The Wolf Man* are mixed in, then it changes to show a "live stream" of McDougall in his shop. McDougall hears a noise and thinks it is Jack, there for a drink. But it's not Jack; it's the wolf man, who leaps in through the door and rips McDougall to shreds.

Jack shows up at McDougall's store for after-work drinks, only to find a police cordon and a bloody body being wheeled out on a stretcher. A detective fills Jack in, describing it as a wild animal attack. "Twenty years in homicide, I've never seen anything like it." Darius hovers towards the back of the crowd, watching the scene unfold. Back at the dorm, Darius pulls the film out of his camera. Scratched into the film strip it reads, "Three deaths and you get your wish." As a sign of good will, a star magically appears on Darius' chest, mimicking the one from *The Wolf Man* exactly. Meanwhile, Jack goes back to the store and tells Micki to start pulling files on werewolves.

Darius films Blair in secret, then goes straight to the revival theater for the night's screening of *The Wolf Man*. The cinema is right across the street from McDougall's pawn shop, which Ryan was checking out. He decides to take in a movie instead. While in there, he notices Darius' obsessive attention to the screen, and sees him reciting every line of dialogue. When the movie ends, Ryan decides to follow Darius back to his dorm.

Darius sits to enjoy the footage he shot of Blair, and watch the camera spool out its own film. Through the camera lens, Darius has a live view of Blair as he gets into his car and places a call on his car phone. Suddenly the wolf man appears, pulls him from his car, and tears him to pieces.

At this point, Ryan is moving down the hall when he hears screams and growls. As he approaches Darius' room, all becomes quiet. He knocks, and when Darius answers suspiciously, Ryan claims he is looking for his friend, Jon Andersen. (Fun fact: Jon Andersen is the supervising producer of the series.) Darius tries to blow him off, but Ryan compliments him on his creature feature decor, then on the sound effects from the film Darius is working on. Darius slams the door on him.

On the set of "Scarlet Cinema." Photo courtesy of John LeMay.

Ryan leaves, and Darius watches him through the window, then he starts to film him. Through the lens, Darius watches the wolf man chase Ryan across campus. Ryan makes it to the car, but the wolf man breaks the window. Ryan screams, and Darius' neighbor yells at him to keep it down. When Darius returns to the camera, the wolf man is throwing a temper tantrum and Ryan is gone. The spell is broken.

Ryan returns to the safety of Curious Goods and relates his evening activity to Jack and Micki. Jack found something of interest in the manifest, a tri-lens movie camera. It doesn't say who Lewis sold it to, but Jack is pretty certain that is the camera McDougall reported stolen. Before they can go after a cursed camera that may have released a werewolf onto the world, Jack has to get protection: silver bullets.

In class the next day, the professor addresses Blair's death but "life goes on," and so will the critiques of their midterm projects. Darius is quite proud that his film is first—until it rolls. His film starts with footage of the wolf man creeping across foggy moors, and ends with the footage of Blair being torn to shreds. The professor rips the film apart, a classic example of irresponsible filmmaking. Not only has Darius stolen scenes from the original *The Wolf Man*, he has duplicated the death of a fellow student. "Simply giving it an F didn't seem adequate," the professor rails, "I was tempted to burn it." The professor rants on like this until Darius runs from class.

Jack returns to the shop with a half-dozen silver bullets, custom-made for him by a gunsmith who just made some for another customer, who sounds an awful lot like Darius. Carissa comes in to return the rented masks and asks about Darius. She shares with them his midterm critique, and Jack realizes that Darius' next victim will be the professor.

Darius paces in his dorm. The camera starts whirring, playing the few seconds of footage Darius shot in class before he left. The camera switches to the wolf man, sneaking across campus, until he finds the professor, in his office. He attacks.

Darius waits at his flatbed editor in his dorm until the wolf man appears. Wolfie bites Darius on the neck, then Darius pulls out a gun. "You are being replaced." He shoots, and the wolf man ignites like a negative, then seems to evaporate back into the camera. I've got to say, for a selfish madman, the fact that Darius prepared to kill the wolf man makes him smarter than the average antique owner. Darius' transformation begins, painfully, as Ryan and Micki come to the door, demanding he open up. We flash through scenes from *The Wolf Man* as Darius transforms. Ryan and Micki break down the door in time to see the wolf man escape out the window. At least they get the camera back.

After picking up Jack, the trio heads out to find Darius. He is currently stalking Carissa on campus, telling her not to be afraid—he's just going to make her like him, so they can be together forever. Nope, nothing to be afraid of here. Ryan shoots at Darius. He misses, but it scares Darius away. Ryan wants to follow, but Jack declares it a suicide mission. Instead, they take Carissa back to Curious Goods.

Ryan and the girls hide in the vault, leaving Jack alone in the dark store. Waiting. Watching. Darius breaks into the shop through the back door, knocking out Jack and heading directly to the basement. Using his werewolf strength, Darius yanks open the vault doors and carries Carissa out. Ryan remembers that old film is coated in silver nitrate, and removes the film from the camera. He garrotes the wolf man with the film, his flesh searing. They watch as the wolf man transforms back into human Darius.

Status: The camera is locked up.

* * *

The professor's rant against Darius' film was a classic moment for me. First, why would Darius think that any part of his short film was good? Even if we the audience didn't see the whole film, there was no narrative structure. We see footage from *The Wolf Man*, then footage of Blair being killed. Darius didn't even really film any of it. Second, on what planet is it a good idea to publicly display an actual snuff film? This episode was shot and aired in the late 1980s, which is around the time that legends about snuff films were making a resurgence with the *Guinea Pig* and *Faces of Death* series. But even if snuff wasn't in the public consciousness, why would it *ever* be a good idea to screen footage of a murder you caused? The professor's "critique" of the film was overblown and nasty—if true—and that is what makes the scene hilarious.

Writer Rob Hedden remembers his love of cameras being the jumping off point for the script. "*The Twilight Zone* had done an episode about a still camera that could reveal the future, so that exact notion was out, but I wasn't ready to give up on the idea. Wish fulfillment with a Faustian tradeoff plays a huge part in those who obtain an evil antique, so I went in that direction: how about a kid who dreams of being his favorite movie monster, and a cursed camera grants him that wish? Being a classic horror staple with carnal appeal, a werewolf seemed like a good choice."

Director David Winning studied the original 1941 *The Wolf Man* in an attempt to match the visual style in many of the flashbacks. He tried to maintain the old Noir-style of monster movies. "I was very proud of designing a cool cinema-esque shot following Jack and the gun as he searches for the wolf in the store. It was an incredible 180° panning dolly shot from one end of the store to the other. With film lighting, it's tricky and challenging to shoot two directions of a set in one shot."

Winning was only twenty-seven when he shot "Scarlet Cinema," his second of three episodes for the series. "I was homesick for Calgary," he admits. "Whenever I could, I'd hide home references in the show. Darius' dorm room number is 403, which is the Alberta telephone area code. A lot of the movie equipment and editing machines in Darius' room are exact models of stuff in my room growing up."

Matt Birman, a regular stuntman for the series, played the Wolf Man. "He had so much fun in the suit, although I recall it was a bit confining and hot," says Winning. "Such is the life of a wolf man." Indeed.

"The Mephisto Ring"

Story by: Peter Largo
Teleplay by: Marilyn Anderson & Billy Riback
Directed by: Bruce Pittman
Original airdate: April 10, 1989
Cursed antique: 1919 World Series ring

Donald Wren (Denis Forest) has a gambling problem, something he got from his father, who was killed six years ago over gambling debts. Donald is in to Anthony Macklin (James Purcell) for $40,000, and one of his goons, Angelo, comes by the junk shop Donald owns with his mother to collect. Angelo punches Mrs. Wren (Doris Petrie) before breaking Donald's thumbs, taking money out of the till, and pilfering some of mother's jewelry. He finds an old World Series ring and tries it on for size. A green light shoots out of the ring and throws Angelo around the room until he is dead. Donald watches in shock, then takes the ring from Angelo's dead hand. The stone of the ring shows Donald the winner of the eighth race at the horse track: Dandy Don. He knows what this means, and promises his mother that everything will be fine.

The ring was made for the 1919 World Series, declaring the White Sox as the winners. It was Chicago versus Cincinnati, and Chicago was considered a shoo-in to win. They were a much more established team with a long history of victories. But several White Sox players conspired to throw the Series, making the Reds the unexpected victors. Interestingly, the "Black Sox" scandal, as it became known, is never mentioned in the episode. Jack makes a vague reference to the game being thrown for a "gambling syndicate." But I suppose this is a horror show, not a history show, so you can't really blame them.

Mrs. Wren knew about the ring and the powers it possesses. She got a mailer from Curious Goods about it, but didn't contact them because she didn't know if they could be trusted. Now that her son has the ring, and she is fairly sure he plans on using it, she needs the help of Micki, Ryan, and Jack.

The World Series ring was the first item listed in the manifest, the first cursed object Lewis sold; therefore it has been out in the world the

Gag shot of director Bruce Pittman giving acting tips to a beaten-up Denis Forest on "The Mephisto Ring" Photo courtesy of Bruce Pittman.

longest. So, the team has already been researching the ring, trying to track it down. They suspect it has something to do with gambling, but can't tie it to anything. Mrs. Wren comes into the store and confirms their suspicions. Her husband used it to gamble and win, but it turned him into a murderer. Mr. Wren was shot to death, possibly by gangster Anthony Macklin, but there was no proof. Donald owes him money, and she is worried he might use the ring. And of course, he does.

Dandy Don earned Donald a lot of money, and one of Macklin's men, Johnny, goes to collect. Donald promises to have the money tomorrow—first he wants to buy something for his mom. Johnny drive Donald home, and Donald offers him the World Series ring as collateral. He heads into his shop while Johnny tries on the ring—with predictable results. Donald returns for the ring, and gets the winner for a hockey game. He dumps Johnny's body into the sewer. Mrs. Wren watches all of this from the window. Donald does buy his mom some gifts: a television and a necklace, but she refuses to take them. She knows that it is blood money and wants nothing to do with it. Donald blows her off and insists he is done losing.

Donald returns to the bar and pays off the bartender, insisting he is going to "own" Macklin. An acquaintance, Benny, follows Donald out of the bar and wants in on his tips. Donald refuses, naturally, but Benny threatens to tattle to Macklin, and Donald has a change of heart. He gives Benny the ring, which tosses him around the alley until he is dead. Donald gets the winner of a college basketball game.

He goes back into the bar to watch the game, and Micki and Mrs. Wren come in. Mrs. Wren tries desperately to convince her son that the ring is evil, that dad died because of that ring. Donald promises he won't use it again after tonight. She leaves sadly, and Ryan puts her in a taxi while Micki uses her feminine wiles to get Donald to take her home with him. While Micki makes eyes at Donald, the bartender calls Macklin and tells him he thinks Donald is responsible for his missing guys.

Micki wastes no time in getting Donald to leave the bar with her. In the car, she checks herself in her compact, but is really making sure Ryan is following them. He is. Donald becomes paranoid and accuses her of working for Macklin, setting him up. He changes course and takes her to an industrial area and forces the ring on her finger. Micki bites his broken thumb and runs from the car. She hides as another car pulls up, and watches as Angelo puts Donald into the car at gunpoint. Ryan collects Micki and they follow Angelo.

Donald is brought to Macklin, who wants to know about his sudden change of luck. He talks some smack about Donald's dad, and grabs him by his broken (and bitten) thumb, demanding to know about his system. He won't share, so Macklin cuts off his finger. "Don't worry, you've got nine more to go before I even think of killing you." Macklin keeps Donald around, trying to get info on whatever sporting event he is watching. By the end of the night, Donald is badly beaten.

Micki and Ryan check in with Mrs. Wren, who explains that Donald blames Macklin for his father's death. The pair head to Macklin's club down by the river. Mrs. Wren still maintains that everything is the ring's fault. Ryan and Micki stake out the club, until they see Mrs. Wren arrive by cab and decide to try the back door. That doesn't work, so Micki flirts with the bouncer while Ryan sneaks up and knocks him out.

Inside the club, Mrs. Wren is worried when she sees the sorry state Donald is in. Realizing that Donald isn't too worried about losing his fingers, Macklin tells him to give up his winning gambling system or he will kill his mother.

Angelo drags Donald into the back, where Donald gives him the ring, telling him that is the system: it gives him luck. The ring kills Angelo, and his screams draw Macklin and Mrs. Wren. Donald removes the ring and sees the winner of a bare-knuckle boxing match. He gives Macklin the details of the fight, and Mrs. Wren tells Macklin it is the ring. "Put it on, you'll see," she tells him. Macklin takes the ring, but does not put it on.

Micki and Ryan are still hiding out, and they follow Macklin and his crew next door to an underground fight club. Bare-knuckle boxing, no ref, no bell, just fighting until someone falls down. This is the fight Donald saw in the ring. Macklin puts money down on the guy Donald foresaw winning. He wins, twenty to one.

Macklin takes the Wrens into a back office and demands he show him how to "empty pockets" (basically, fleece the other bettors). Mrs. Wren tells him to put the ring on. He does, and gets beaten to death by the ring. Donald takes the ring but Mrs. Wren wants to get rid of it. He never will. On their way into the office, Ryan is attacked by a goon, and in a ridiculous, clichéd moment, Micki beats him away with her purse. The pair enters the office just in time to see Mrs. Wren shoot her son dead. She shot her husband, too.

Status: The ring is returned, and because Mrs. Wren shot her husband and son to stop them from killing more, the Curious Goods crew agrees not to tell the police.

*   *   *

Doris Petrie was not the first choice of actress for the role of Mrs. Wren. "We had another actress who was cast for the part," explains director Bruce Pittman. "She was a wonderful actress but she couldn't remember her lines. She was going through the initial stages of what turned out to be Alzheimer's. We were embarrassed for her but we didn't quite know what it was. There was obviously something going on that we didn't know about. I actually went to public school with Doris' son, so she was always Mrs. Petrie to me. She was a real trooper. I told her the situation and she either came down that night or the next day and it didn't affect the shoot at all.

"It wasn't until about eight years later that I found out our original actress had Alzheimer's. I was working with her husband—another good actor—and he told me. She had since died. I think at the time, not many people knew about Alzheimer's. There was obviously some sort of physical ailment there, and she felt terrible."

Pittman also tells me about another actor who has since died: Denis Forest, who played Donald Wren. "I loved working with him. I think he was a Method actor. He'd sit by himself then come out and do these wonderfully manic scenes. He was quite crazy in this episode. I thought

Even between takes, Denis Forest stays in character. With director Bruce Pittman on the set of "The Mephisto Ring." Photo courtesy of John LeMay.

it might be over the top, but it was just so damn interesting to let him go. I think a couple of times I may have come in and said, 'a little less,' but generally speaking, I was just delighted with what he was doing with it. He was just so crazed. That vein in his forehead.... .

"When we were finished shooting, it was right around Christmas. I asked him what he was doing for Christmas. He never looked up, he just said, 'I'm gonna go home and clean my gun.' [Laughs.] He was just in character the whole time! So, now I use that line all the time, but I say it much more cheerfully.

"I know that we did shoot a close-up of one of his fingers being cut off. James Purcell [Macklin] whipped out the knife. I loved that scene, and I loved what I did with him, dragging him into that club at night. We like to put in a little gore here and there. But I think that one was a little over the top. The FX guys were great. They had spurts of blood. I don't think that is in the finished version. I think the powers that be went in and said to tone it down a little. The footage was there if they needed it."

"A Friend to the End"

Story by: David Morse and Scott J. Schneid & Tony Michelman
Teleplay by: Scott J. Schneid & Tony Michelman
Directed by: David Morse
Original airdate: April 17, 1989
Cursed antique: Child's coffin; shard of Medusa

It is a dark and stormy night when Howard and Marjorie, an older couple, break into a crypt and steal the corpse of Ricky (Keram Malicki-Sanchez), a boy who has been dead for nearly a century. They take him home and set him up in a child's-sized coffin. A nanny arrives, new to the city (and the country, it seems) to care for Ricky. Ricky sits up, now alive in the coffin, and we hear panicked screams. "He's home now," Marjorie sighs. The door opens and out comes Ricky, dressed in all white, turn-of-the-century clothes.

Elsewhere, an artist, DeJager (Donna Goodhand), is sketching a model. The model is draped in a sheet and holding a chunk of rock in her hand, the shard of Medusa. The model complains: the rock is getting heavy; her muscles are starting to cramp; it's hurting; she can't breathe. Frozen in place, the model drops the rock and screams. DeJager finishes her sketch, takes the fallen shard of rock and plunges it deep into her back. The model instantly turns to stone. Ryan has been racing to get into the building; he ends up taking the fire escape to the roof. Through the window, he can see he is too late.

Back at the shop, Micki is vaguely annoyed. "I guess it's my turn." The plan is to go meet DeJager at her art show and entice her into using Micki as a model. But there is a kink in the plan: a child is waiting for them at the front door. This is Micki's nephew, J.B. (Zachary Bennett). Ever since Micki's sister's divorce, she has been a little... irresponsible. She is gone before Micki can catch her.

"Oh no, not now," Ryan groans. J.B.'s mom has run off with her boyfriend o' the week, but he offers to go stay at a hotel, like last time. Micki can't have that, so they bring him into the store. J.B. and Ryan eye each other uneasily as Micki retrieves a bike from the back of the store, one Ryan and Jack just finished rebuilding. Ryan isn't thrilled that she is loaning a kid his bike; J.B. isn't thrilled to be riding a "junky girl's bike," but he takes it to the park while Micki and Ryan head to the art show.

At the park, J.B. sees a group of kids doing bike tricks and wants to join their gang. He auditions with a couple of weak-sauce "tricks" that the kids like. But there is one more thing they need him to do, to prove he's got guts.

Nearby is the local "haunted house." The people who lived there were murdered, but their bodies were never found—just blood and gore. Legend has it that the place is haunted by their son, Ricky. People go in, but never come out. The kids want J.B. to steal a toy from Ricky's room. He marches in, but the moment he is gone, the kids run off with the bike. J.B. goes upstairs, to Ricky's room, and spies a top spinning alone on the floor. J.B. grabs it, and from the shadows, Ricky asks, "Will you be my friend?" More startled than scared, J.B. runs outside. The boys are gone and so is his bike, but there is a figure in white watching from one of the boarded up windows.

J.B. races into Curious Goods, screaming for Aunt Micki. "I saw him! I saw him!" Ryan is more concerned about his bike, and when J.B. admits it was stolen, Ryan's interest becomes focused on that, not J.B.'s tale of bike gangs and ghosts. J.B. is excited about the ghost, not scared, but Ryan doesn't believe him. J.B. stomps off to hide in Micki's room while Ryan fumes. "What would you like me to do, put him in a kennel?" Micki asks before checking in on J.B. She ignores the ghost story, doesn't broach the topic of the stolen bike, and instead wishes that she could make his mom act more like a mom. With a kiss on the cheek and dinner in the oven, Micki leaves J.B. playing with the stolen top while she and Ryan are out.

J.B. takes this opportunity to sneak out and go back to visit Ricky. He is armed with a flashlight, but finds the house filled with lit candles. He calls for Ricky, and he appears behind him. "I knew you'd come back." The two become instant friends and play foosball. When the ball jumps from the board, J.B. chases it to a closed room. Ricky grabs his wrist before he can enter, insisting he is not allowed in there. The tense moment is forgotten when Ricky hears horses and his head hurts. He hears his father scream at him, the sound of a whip, and he reacts as if he has just been struck. Ricky cries and J.B. is worried. He promises he will look after him.

While waiting for his headache to abate, Ricky and J.B. share stories about how grownups are a "bunch of jerks." J.B.'s mom's doctor says his nightmares stem from being dumped with people. But she didn't stop; "she just changed doctors." (One of my favorite lines.) J.B. thinks his mom blames him for his dad leaving; Ricky admits his dad used to beat him, but now both of his parents are dead. His nose starts to bleed, and Ricky asks J.B. to have the drugstore send over something for it. J.B. agrees and promises to see him tomorrow.

Meanwhile, Micki has gone to DeJager for her modeling appointment. DeJager positions her before instructing her to take off her clothes. She removes the shard of Medusa from its case, explaining it is the inspiration for her art and sharing the legend of Medusa: the Gorgon, the hair of snakes, turning men to stone, she herself being turned to stone when she saw her reflection in Persius' shield. This shard, DeJager explains, was a piece of that statue. She hands it to Micki, who promises it is the last time she will use it—and drops it out the window, to Ryan waiting below. The girls shove each other a bit, then Micki escapes.

While Ricky waits for the drugstore delivery, his hallucinations become more severe. Suddenly he is back in his old nineteenth century house, and his father comes raging in, warning him to take his punishment like a man, and whipping him mercilessly. The delivery guy arrives. When no one answers, but the door is ajar, the man lets himself in and follows the sound of crying upstairs. He sees the coffin and wonders if this is some kind of joke. Ricky sits up in the coffin, his face showing signs of decay, and attacks the delivery man, eventually throwing him off the second story landing. Ricky drags the corpse into his secret room.

Micki and Ryan return to Curious Goods with the shard of Medusa, and Ryan is annoyed to find J.B. still awake. He shuts the hell up when DeJager appears behind him. She is calm, and J.B. doesn't seem frightened—until DeJager takes him downstairs and holds a chisel to his throat. She demands Ryan give the shard to the boy, which he does, then J.B. walks her to the door. She thanks him for the shard and runs. Ryan chases after her while Micki checks on J.B. The kid is unfazed by his brief time as a hostage; he is more concerned with his sick friend Ricky. Ryan returns and starts yelling at him for telling ridiculous stories.

J.B. yells back, then stomps upstairs, screaming "I hate you!" Ryan feels bad, but Micki says she's not doing much better. (Yes, Micki, you are.) Ryan goes after DeJager again, while Micki stays to keep an eye on J.B.

The next morning, Micki is the picture of domesticity in her apron, making pancakes for J.B. He's not hungry, but agrees to sit for a glass of milk, and Micki asks him about Ricky. He relates the tale of murder to her, which doesn't shock Micki, but she does tell him she doesn't want him to go out because she doesn't know anything about this Ricky. "He's my friend, my best friend, the only friend I've got!" J.B. pleads. Micki stands firm, but does say Ricky can come over. By the time she turns back from the fridge, J.B. is gone.

Rather than looking for her nephew, Micki returns to the never-ending "work" of going through Lewis' letters, news clippings, and files. A clipping catches her eye, telling of the disappearance of Howard and Marjorie Harper and their twelve year old son, Richard. Micki then checks this against some of Lewis' letters and finds one from Marjorie, thanking Lewis for blessing them with a beautiful boy, Ricky, but complaining about the "hunger" that comes upon him more often than it used to. The letter is signed, "Your friends in his service." A quick flashback reveals, in case we hadn't figured it out by now, that Ricky killed his new parents to feed his hunger. Concern flashes across Micki's face.

When Ryan calls later, it is to warn Micki that DeJager is on her way to Europe with the shard. He thinks he can stop her, but Micki tells him to forget about that—J.B. is in trouble. Two years ago, an older couple desperately wanted a child, and Lewis found them a way to get one with a child's sized coffin. She found it in the manifest: when the body of a dead child is put in the coffin, it becomes a living child, and J.B. is playing with that "living" child right now.

J.B. and Ricky are having fun, chasing each other through the dusty house. As Ricky runs down the hall, he is "whipped" to the ground by the specter of his father. When J.B. promises he would do anything for him, Ricky tells him he needs to bring someone to the house, and make sure no one sees you.

J.B. runs, screaming for help, and finds a cop who comes back to the house with him. The cop follows the sound of crying upstairs, but finds only the closed coffin. He thinks he is being tricked, but Ricky jumps out and slashes at him.

It all becomes clear to J.B. He begs Ricky not to kill him, but Ricky insists it is what he has to do to stay alive, and he's "just a grown-up." "Someday I'll be grown up, too. What happens then, will you kill me?" J.B. challenges him. Ricky chases J.B. into the basement. The stairs give way, burying J.B. under a pile of wood and rubble. This is where Ricky has been hiding the bodies, all dry and desiccated. J.B. begs for help.

Micki arrives at the house and calls for J.B. She follows his voice to the basement and, seeing the scene before her, tells J.B. not to move (as if he had the option). Ricky appears and takes a swing at her. His skin is mottled and decayed. Micki dodges, and J.B. begs him not to hurt her. "You're supposed to be my friend! Friends don't hurt each other." Ricky takes this to heart and gives up. He falls to his knees and collapses into a pile of dry bones.

Status: The coffin is recovered, but the shard is somewhere in Europe. J.B. promises not to tell anyone about Ricky, his ghost friend who was killed by his father one hundred years ago. Ryan, perhaps taking pity on the kid, invites him to stay with them again. Most importantly, the police found Ryan's bike, and he is having them deliver it to J.B.'s house.

*   *   *

"A Friend to the End" is the only episode to focus on two different cursed antiques. I like that we didn't have to spend any time playing "detective" to figure out what antique caused a recent rash of murders/disappearances. It's logical, but it can become formulaic. With the shard of Medusa, we are already halfway through the investigation; with the child's coffin, there is no investigation. They more or less stumbled upon it.

Writer Scott Schneid went in to pitch to the *Friday the 13th: The Series* writing staff with his then-partner Tony Michelman. "We had some ideas that we pitched to them, then they had a couple ideas, and I think what happened was we decided to combine the two," explains Schneid. "One of our ideas with one of theirs, basically doing a double episode. I said that's cool, as long as the dovetail nicely. Even though they are separate stories, they had to somehow intertwine. Obviously that presented challenges because then you have to split your focus.

"When we handed our episode in to [story coordinator] Rick Schwartz, he called us and said, 'I just want to tell you what a great job you did. We think its one of the very best episodes of the season and we are submitting you for Emmy consideration.' That was before it was even shot. I think they also submitted Brian Helgeland's 'Crippled Inside' along with ours. It was not nominated for an Emmy, but it was very cool."

Schneid was disappointed to discover that producers in Toronto changed roughly "thirty or thirty-five percent" of their original script. "I thought it made it worse." Schneid was kind enough to send me his original script and let me check it out for myself. There were certainly major changes made in the details, though nothing that drastically changes the arc of the story.

The most notable change is that the shard DeJager uses is not stone, but a pulsing blue crystal shard that turns her victims into crystal sculptures. The shard also didn't have any back story—it was just a blue crystal shard. I prefer the shard of Medusa angle myself: I like having a back story to the shard; otherwise it is just a chunk of glass (or stone). Who just buys random chunks of minerals if it doesn't have a back story? Also, I have to imagine from a production stance, the technology to create the blue crystal effect was not as good as the technology to create grey stone, and probably considerably more expensive. Since DeJager gets away with the shard in the original script, Schneid told me he was expecting there to be another episode about DeJager and the shard, and figured the audience could find out the shard's history then. "We thought you didn't need to know everything, we thought it was enough to know about the coffin," says Schneid. The shard of Medusa doesn't get a second episode; it gets a brief mention during "Crippled Inside."

The other major difference is that, in the original script, there is no back story for Ricky. Towards the end of the script, Micki finds some mention of Ricky's "adoptive" parents getting help from Lewis, and that they eventually committed suicide (Micki assumes it is out of guilt). The original script does not open with a flashback showing Ricky killing his adoptive parents; nor do we see or get any insight into Ricky's original, non-resurrected life. I prefer the episode's version of what happened to the parents (that Ricky killed them) than the we-can't-handle-the-guilt version in the original script, but I agree with Schneid that the episode flows better without seeing the actual flashbacks.

"I think they probably added that to create more of a bond between Ricky's back story," suggests Schneid, "with parents that physically abused him, and J.B.'s back story, whose mother emotionally abused him."

In the original script it is blatant that Ricky survives by feeding off the hearts of his victims; in the episode, it is only suggested that Ricky must kill to survive.

It was Ryan who was DeJager's model originally, but the plan was identical. Instead of DeJager taking J.B. hostage, she brings the police around, who collect the shard without incident. I prefer the hostage version. It amps up the tension, and it is more believable that she would take a kid hostage rather than call the police. Ryan is also far more patient with J.B. in the script, an aspect I liked better. I never understood why

Ryan was such a dick to the kid. J.B.'s bike is stolen by the kids in the park, but Ricky materializes a new bike for his friend. (I prefer the episode version.)

The stars of "A Friend to the End" were children. Zachary Bennett, who played J.B., was nine years old and Keram Malicki-Sanchez, who played Ricky, was about fourteen at the time. From Bennett's point of view, Malicki-Sanchez was "super cool" and "kicked ass." Malicki-Sanchez saw Bennett as a "little brother."

As a nine-year-old, your priorities are very different than those of an adult. "You couldn't keep me away from the craft service table. That was my goal. I honestly didn't give a fuck where the money was going, as long as I was high on sugar or fake cheese," Bennett remembers. The other thing that sticks out to him was the birth of his little sister. "My sister was born while I was shooting that show. My agent had to call onto set, and they had to hold set. Before they started shooting again, they called me over to a phone where my agent told me, 'You've got a sister, congratulations!' I was nine, so I think I enjoyed the attention more than anything. I think my mom went into labor very close to my pick-up time. So, my dad sent me to set with the driver and he went to the hospital instead of coming with me. I knew that was happening, but it was wild to be told, on a sound stage, there is a phone call for you."

Malicki-Sanchez absolutely loved everything about the spooky sets. "I remember lying in the bed, covered in makeup and my little eighteenth century nightgown, alone, with a blazing hot light on me and thinking, *wow, my childhood is strange.* But I loved working there."

Interestingly, both men remember the smells of the set. For Bennett, it was the glue that was "everywhere," like a "rubber cement and talcum powder smell. That smell, to me, was so foreign." Malicki-Sanchez "will never forget the constant smell of the fog being pumped out of the machines. It was there all the time, and you looked at everything through that smoky haze."

"David Morse is probably my earliest memory that sticks of working with a director," says Bennett. "He was extremely accommodating. I think it's because he is an actor. He has this very accommodating face, like, 'Come here, tell me your life, I want to hear it.' As a director, he was wonderful. He was very quiet, he said, 'Hey man, so this is what's going to happen. How do you feel?' That actually stuck with me, that tiny little interaction he had with me as a kid. It stayed with me, the director's calm. A good director is calm, centered, knows exactly what he wants and can tell you." Bennett keeps this in the forefront of his mind as he readies his feature directorial debut.

"One of my favorite things to do was wander around the set when everyone was at lunch and just look at all the interesting curios the props department had aggregated over the run of the show," says Malicki-Sanchez. "It really was like walking through a curiosity shop mixed with a fun house. A curious kid's dream." He also remembers shooting *Friday the 13th* in the same warehouse complex as two other shows he was in, *War of the Worlds* and *Catwalk*. "I miss that dingy, awesome place."

"The Butcher"

Written by: Francis Delia and Ron Magid
Directed by: Francis Delia
Original airdate: April 24, 1989
Cursed antique: Nazi swastika amulet

A couple of Germans break into some kind of freezer and thaw out "der fuhrer's successor," Rausch (Nigel Bennett). Using a Nazi swastika amulet, Mueller (Colin Fox) brings Rausch back to life. The dead man's eyes fly open, he sits up, and garrotes Mueller's companion with the barbed wire clutched in his hands. Mueller kept his promise to Rausch, and now that he is "alive," their minds are linked. "When you have killed all my enemies, we will have the future our fuehrer promised: a Reich which lasts a thousand years."

During WWII, Rausch was known as the Butcher. A favorite of Hitler's, he was best known for killing P.O.W.s by garroting them with barbed wire. Jack fought in WWII, and through a series of grainy, black and white flashbacks, we see he was a P.O.W. who was nearly killed at the hands of the Butcher. His squad liberated him from Belberg, just as the Butcher was tightening his barbed wire around Jack's neck. Jack killed the Butcher, and Mueller, one of Hitler's lead scientists, was caught, eventually going to prison.

One of Jack's squad, Lefty, is playing solitaire when there is a knock at the door, claiming to be a war buddy of Jack's. "Any friend of Marshak's is welcome here," Lefty says as he opens the door. He doesn't recognize the Butcher, but does remark that he doesn't look old enough to have fought in WWII. Rausch doesn't waste time—he strangles Lefty dead. Through the amulet, Mueller tells him, "Very good."

Shaw and Simpson (John Gilbert and Julius Harris) come to town for Lefty's funeral. Jack doesn't want to go; he has been plagued by nightmares. "What good will it do?" His friends talk him into it. At the funeral, Jack hears that another from their squad, Caruthers, had also been murdered. At the coffin, Jack notices Lefty's poorly-concealed strangle wound. The men adjourn to the bar, where Jack places a call to the veteran's administration. He discovers that LaRoux is dead, as well, and wonders if he was murdered, too. Jack reminds his friends that barbed wire is how the Butcher killed; Shaw and Simpson remind Jack that the Butcher is dead—Jack killed him. Jack is not convinced. Shaw decides to stay with Jack a few days, while Micki and Ryan are out of town, to "buck him up."

A package arrives from the V.A. Sure enough, LaRoux and a couple others from their squad were killed, all strangled with barbed wire. Once again, Shaw tries to reassure Jack that it couldn't be Mueller or Rausch. Jack reminds him that Mueller was experimenting with reanimation and cryogenics. "No one comes back from the dead," insists Shaw.

Rausch is now hosting a right-wing radio call-in show under the name Karl Steiner. It would fit in frighteningly well on modern-day Fox News, advocating governmental sterilization, preaching racism, and decrying welfare. When interviewed for a news magazine, "Steiner" refuses to talk about his past; he is only interested in the future. The swastika starts whispering to him, so he wraps up the interview quickly: "We must restore this country to a position of power. Let the weak, the lazy, and the uneducated get out of the way." He is in pain and rushes to the bathroom, where he finds a man washing up. Rausch's first instinct is to grab his barbed wire, but Mueller hisses "Nein! You kill only those I instruct you to kill." He promises he has found his next victim, Simpson, and his death will "make you whole again." Sure enough, the Butcher waits in Simpson's car. When he gets in, he garrotes him from the back seat.

Jack opens his footlocker, which he hasn't done since the war. Together with Shaw, they pour over the contents: weapons, Nazi memorabilia, and a notebook. Mueller's diary. It is marked with a swastika in a circle, which is the symbol of the Thule Society, a group of alchemists and warlocks who believed they could grant "ten centuries of life." The Thule Society was feared through Europe, and was said to have learned their powers from the Norse gods. Thules infused power into silver amulets which could seek out their enemies, communicate over great distances, and even raise the dead. Jack believes Mueller used Thule's secrets to bring the Butcher back to life. The two are waiting anxiously for Simpson to arrive; instead they get a call. Simpson was strangled.

This is all the ammunition Jack needs. Regardless of Shaw's beliefs, Jack calls the West German prison which holds Mueller. (It is so weird to hear it referred to as "West" Germany.) The warden insists Mueller is still in custody, but he is forbidden from phone calls or mail. He can only speak to Mueller in person, after a security clearance, a policy that began after Mueller's escape one year ago. Apparently, he got over the Berlin Wall and East German police picked him up the next day, with no trouble. Shaw refuses to go with Jack and maintains that he will be safe. Jack doesn't believe him, but can't force him to come.

While Jack waits to see Mueller, he dozes and dreams of being held captive by the Butcher, then being liberated and killing the Butcher with his own barbed wire. But in this dream, the Butcher's eyes open after he is declared dead. Jack wakes, scared, and calls Shaw. The Butcher is at Curious Goods and when Shaw goes for the phone, the Butcher goes for his throat. Shaw never answers the phone.

Mueller laughs when Jack comes in. "Your friends are dying halfway across the world—what do I have to do with it?" he taunts. Jack accuses him point-blank of bringing the Butcher back to life, and Mueller stops pretending, insisting he did it so the Reich could be reborn. He taunts Jack, telling him his friend is dead and that Jack is now the only living person who put him there. "I saved you for last." Mueller gives Jack his piece of the amulet, and tells him to bring it to Rausch. He starts spouting master race nonsense as Jack leaves.

Upon returning home, Jack finds Shaw, dead. He cries. But he sees the magazine that Shaw was reading when he died, and recognizes the radio host "Steiner" as the Butcher. Jack calls into the show, speaking German and addressing him as Colonel Rausch. "I have what you want, come and get it." Steiner gets his head back in the game and announces this is his last radio show—he is getting involved in politics.

So, he waits. Jack tries to sip tea to calm his nerves, but he can't even hold onto the cup. Instead he loads his gun and readies his knife. Despite his best efforts, Jack dozes. He is woken around 1:00 a.m. by the sounds of a violent break-in. Jack responds with a huge spray of ammo, which succeeds in doing nothing but shutting off the power. The Butcher is there, and has been dreaming of this moment. "Give the amulet to me now, and I promise you a quick death." He tightens his barbed wire around Jack's wrist, causing him to drop his gun and his piece of the amulet.

The Butcher abandons Jack to retrieve it, claiming to be invincible now. Jack gets his gun back and fires, but like Rausch said, he's invincible now. A shot to the head knocks Rausch down, but just for a moment. There is no blood from the wound. Jack surprises him, strangling him with his own barbed wire and tying him to the banister. He has enough time to cut the amulet off Rausch. Once it is off, blood oozes from Rausch's wounds. He is dead.

Status: Jack puts the amulet in his footlocker, along with all his other memories from the war, then tucks the entire trunk into the vault.

*   *   *

"I had become one of their go-to directors at this point and I asked if they would let me write something I could direct," writer/director Francis Delia remembers. "I think they encouraged the idea of a two-part episode because I told them I wanted to approach it like a feature film." For whatever reason, whether it was because of schedule or budget, the episode ended up being shot as a single, stand-alone episode.

Delia's previous episode, "Read My Lips," with the Nazi boutonnière, sparked his idea for "The Butcher." "One thing that caught my attention was the Nazi thing. It seems to have come to symbolize man's inhumanity to man, and literally the embodiment of evil, the Nazi regime. You just don't get too many people who are trying to defend it—you do, they are out there—but it just seems to be one of the most unjustifiable examples of man's rabid inhumanity to man. That could really work in a piece." I have long contended that Nazis are the perfect movie villains because there are no redeeming qualities to Nazis. They are all hate-mongers and the only people who could possibly attempt to defend them are other Nazis.

Originally, Delia envisioned the episode revolving around Elvis Hitler. "I'd always heard that Hitler was considered a 'rock star' among his own Reich. I don't speak German, and he seems like a raving maniac, but people said he was seen as having a real charisma and having special skill as an orator. I was already thinking Hitler, or the 'great white hope' of Hitler had been cryogenically preserved and he comes back as a rock star.

"It seemed just a little farfetched," Delia continues. "I was always a bit of a talk radio fanatic, and when I met [Richard] Belzer he was a talk radio celebrity in New York. He pre-dated Howard Stern as a bit of a wise-cracking radio guy. So, I started thinking along the lines of making [the Nazi character] a sardonic talk radio guy. At that point, I really don't think I was thinking of Rush Limbaugh or Howard Stern, but they were the kind of people that had this wildly fanatical following. I thought, *Why not make him a politically-oriented talk radio guy?*"

Looking at this episode from the perspective of the year 2015, the Karl Steiner show is ominously modern. This episode aired in 1989. I was nine years old, and have no idea what the political rhetoric of the country was. But the Steiner show feels like it was modeled around Rush Limbaugh (or what I know of him today, as an adult), whose radio show went national in 1988. Delia doesn't remember if he based Steiner on Limbaugh specifically, but is sure that, because he is a "talk radio nut," Limbaugh was on his radar within weeks of his first syndicated broadcast.

"The first thing I wanted to do was streamline down to Jack, just let this be his story," says Delia. "Jack seems to have been of the right age to be a WWII vet. I'll bet Chris Wiggins was a WWII vet. I remember what a wonderful guy he was and I loved the idea of writing something just for him." By this time, Elvis Hitler had evolved into the Butcher. Delia loosely referenced the real life Butcher of Lyon, Klaus Barbie, for his Nazi psychopath. Barbie started as a Hitler Youth and eventually became the head of the local Gestapo in Lyon, France where he tortured men, women, and children with his own hands. Historians believe Barbie was personally responsible for the deaths of 4,000 people, and deported another 7,500 people to concentration camps. He was eventually found guilty on 341 separate charges of crimes against humanity—but not until 1987. Similarly, the Thule Society was a real cult that came to prominence in Germany in the 1910s. While there is no evidence that Hitler was a part of the society, many scholars believe that the Thule Society, whose chief focus seemed to be the occult and keeping the Aryan bloodlines pure, paved the way for the Third Reich.

When it came time to shoot the Butcher flashbacks, Delia said it was a "no-brainer" to shoot black and white, and he knew he wanted a format smaller than the series' usual 35mm. "We shot four or five variations on 16mm. When I say variations, I mean under-exposed one stop, over-developed. Over-exposed, under-developed. They all looked a little different. I think we were going for something that was, to a degree, stylized." Delia is quick to point out that he is sure the WWII prisons were far more horrifying than anything he could depict. "When you see the stills… it's just beyond belief.

"It was a cautionary tale, almost a fairy tale—a horror fairy tale," Delia summarizes. "[Steiner] is cryogenically frozen, thawed, and comes back as Rush Limbaugh on steroids. The point is that this could come back, in different forms."

I didn't watch this episode much as a kid. I didn't like that Micki and Ryan weren't in it. With just Jack and his war buddies, the show felt too "old." "I love hearing that," Delia enthuses. "You are giving me a perspective that I never would have really had otherwise."

"The Secret Agenda of Mesmer's Bauble"

Written by: Joe Gannon
Directed by: Armand Mastroianni
Original airdate: May 1, 1989
Cursed antique: Crystal pendant

Record store clerk Howard (Martin Neufeld) is, well, he's not an attractive man. A large hooked nose and pock-marked skin make him shy and awkward, and leads to giggles and whispers from strangers. The only time he really perks up is when he talks about Angelica (Vanity), a sultry pop star whom he is hoping will do an album signing while she is in town.

On his way home from work one night, Howard sees a smash-and-grab at a pawn shop. The thief drop a glittering pendant in his haste to escape, and Howard picks it up. A passerby grabs him and accuses him of the theft. The men argue, and Howard wishes the "good Samaritan" would drop dead. The pendant begins to glow. The Samaritan stumbles a few steps away, clutches his chest, and drops dead.

Once home, he studies the pendant, wondering what else it can do. "Fix my skin?" he asks hopefully. The pendant does so. Howard then asks for it to fix his face, "make it look good," but he used up his one wish. Nothing happens, but the next day at work, his manager notices how nice his skin looks.

At work, Howard meets with Anita (Laurie Paton), Angelica's manager, and they go into the storage room to check on the store's Angelica inventory. Howard asks obsessive questions about Angelica ("Does she sleep naked?" "What does she smell like?").

Anita is disturbed.

"What turns her on?" Howard begs.

"Guys who don't look like you!" she snaps.

Howard takes out the pendant, vowing that he will have Angelica. He steals Anita's backstage pass and suggests she go for a walk, go play in traffic. She wanders out of the store, as if hypnotized, and shuffles into the street. She is smashed by a big rig. That night, Howard uses his wish to become beautiful, someone Angelica will notice. His face wrinkles, and he doubles over in pain, but it works: his hooked nose is gone, and his features attractively angular.

Howard uses Anita's all-access pass to get into the rehearsal for Angelica's intimate club show (for which Ryan has tickets). He tries to introduce himself to Angelica, but her manager/boyfriend Roger (Tony De Santis) is having none of it. Roger follows Angelica outside to sign autographs, then grouses that she drops everything for her fans. Howard hides in Angelica's dressing room. She returns and he watches her undress. Roger gets close to Angelica, and Howard is frozen with jealousy.

This leads to Roger's death, of course. Roger is at his hotel, shaving, when Howard comes to the door. He waggles the pendant in his face. Easing Roger back into the room, he coaches him to continue his shave... a real close shave. The sink fills with blood as he slits his own throat and drops dead. Howard doesn't waste a second on his next wish: "I want her. I want to be her lover."

Jack goes over the police report from the pawn shop theft and recognizes the crystal pendant. He matches it up to Mesmer's Bauble in the manifest. It is an eighteenth century crystalline pendant with a gold lattice frame, owned by Franz Mesmer, a German who invented the "science" of hypnotism. Micki and Ryan follow a standard procedural path in their investigation: the police show it wasn't in their inventory; the pawn shop owner ID'd an "ugly kid" who worked at the music store; the music store manager informs them the "ugly kid" quit this morning.

They visit Howard at his apartment, who claims he saw nothing of the robbery. Micki is concerned because Howard is "not an ugly man," but his wall is plastered with Angelica posters. Worried about the singer's safety, they visit her hotel, and that is when they see Roger's corpse being wheeled out. "You know what these rock and roll types are like. They're always killing themselves," a jaded onlooker tells Micki.

Later, in a newspaper article on Roger's death, Jack finds a quote from Howard, stating that Roger had been depressed. This, combined with what Jack found out about the curse, seals it: Howard must have the pendant.

Angelica is still mourning Roger when Howard pays her a visit backstage. She cries on his shoulder, saying she cannot do the show without him. Howard gives her a pep talk that only he could understand: "You make people's lives worth living. They need you, like you needed Roger. Like you need me." She agrees to do the show tonight, but first Howard has something to show her.

Howard takes Angelica back to his apartment and proudly shows off his altar to her, with a larger-than-life-sized poster as the centerpiece. Rather than being terrified and running for her life, she teases him. "Do you like her? Do you want her?" Stupid question. As the two start to fool around, it quickly becomes apparent that Howard is not so much making love to Angelica, but worshipping her. He looks back at the dozens of two-dimensional Angelicas watching over them, then looks back at Angelica, touching the pendant still draped around his neck. She kisses him, fondles him, but Howard stops. "I can't do this. This isn't what I want."

Angelica's ego is deflated. "Don't you want me?"

"No," Howard answers. "I want to *be* you."

I would hope that this would have been a big "RUN!" signal had Angelica not been hypnotized by the bauble. Touching her hand, like he did so many times with her posters, Howard and Angelica roll around on the floor. In the process of their lovemaking, their skin becomes melted and gooey. There is a very 1980s effect here, with the silhouette of them making love superimposed inside the bauble. Howard literally crawls into Angelica's skin.

After the sex, Howard-as-Angelica admires her new visage in the mirror, laughing. She returns to the club, and Micki and Ryan come by the apartment. All they find is the puddle of goo on the floor. They have no idea what that may be, so they head back to the club.

As we countdown to show time, Micki and Ryan push their way to the front of the stage, looking for Howard. With all these stagehands

With Vanity on the set of "Mesmer's Bauble." Photo courtesy of John LeMay.

and adoring fans, they figure he wouldn't try anything; Angelica is safe. Indeed, she starts the show right on time, and Micki notices that she is wearing the bauble around her neck. It takes two tries, but Micki finally snatches it off Angelica's neck when she bends to flirt with the audience. Angelica is so into her show, she doesn't notice. Not until her voice becomes an atonal male voice. Angelica's breasts deflate, and she morphs back into Howard, with a brief stop as a monster in between.

The crowd screams as sexy Angelica becomes ugly old Howard in Angelica's clothes. He is horrified by his own appearance, and stumbles into a pit of lights, electrocuting himself.

Status: The bauble is vaulted, and the trio discusses how bizarre this case is. "Bizarre doesn't even begin to scratch the surface," Micki bemoans. Always the sage one, Jack suggests Howard's mind was "so twisted by fantasy I don't think even he realized what he wanted until it was too late."

* * *

The 1980s gave birth to the insult, "That's so gay," and perpetuated the stereotype of "you throw like a girl." So, "Mesmer's Bauble" was a refreshing look at gender identity. Because I don't think that was meant to be the focus of the story, it made it all the more subtle. Howard doesn't really suffer from gender confusion; he suffers from self-doubt and low self-esteem. Unfortunately, lurking beneath the gentle (if unattractive) exterior lays a troubled psyche that has been badly damaged by years of abuse and ridicule.

What is refreshing about Howard becoming Angelica is that he is not worried about becoming a woman; he just wants to be someone with fame, power, and worshippers. Man, woman, or cow; it doesn't matter to him. He just wants to be someone else. In fact, it may be less a look at gender identity and more a look at mental illness and bullying.

I will let episode director Armand Mastroianni tell of his experience on the episode:

"It was a concept that Jim [Henshaw] threw out to me, about an obsessed fan. Vanity was big at the time, she was Prince's protégé. I was really getting comfortable [with the crew] and wanted to push the envelope. I suggested that he doesn't just obsess over her; what if he wants to *become* her? Literally. We discussed how we would do that, and I suggested it come out of this sexual scene. They are making love and he starts entering her—then he enters her for real.

Vanity looks ready to attack! Photo courtesy Armand Mastroianni.

"We didn't have CGI in those days, so we had to do special effects. [The special effects crew] said they could create prosthetic pieces and latex, and we would see the hands crawling under the flesh. The concept of *Friday the 13th* was always that there was this duality where almost anything can happen. I wanted to explore this guy's true desire for her, which becomes more and more perverse as it goes. We juxtapose that with the early stages, when he was this ugly guy with this hook nose prosthetic, and he would stand in front of her posters and masturbate to her. They asked if I was really going to show that. I said we'd shoot it in a way... I just wanted to show that this guy is really off the deep end for this woman, and that really sets us up for how crazy he is.

"The shooting of him actually entering her almost turned into an X-rated film! It required the actors to be naked, and required hours and hours of prosthetics and shooting angles and lighting and stuff like that. I remember it was so hot and humid, the actors were sweating, and the [prosthetics] would peel off. At one point, Vanity said, 'Fuck it! I'm just gonna walk around like this!' and she walked around naked all day! Martin Neufeld was eating at the craft service table with pieces of flesh falling off. It was very funny.

"It was tense, too. There was a lot of pressure on the actors to perform and 'be on' for those moments, while it was so complicated and technical. The camera was moving. 'Sorry we see too much, let's try it over here, put your elbow down when you're doing that.' It's all very technical and they were both getting frustrated because it was an incredibly long process. Naturally, when the film got cut together, it was too intense and too sexual to be shown on television. The outtakes circulated all through Paramount, I heard. Frank said we would have to make some concessions—the network would *not* air it this way. It was just beyond what they would allow. I was so disappointed. A day and a half of shooting for less than a minute of air! He had an idea, and we took some of the lovemaking scene and reduced it and put it inside Mesmer's bauble. You weren't quite sure what you saw, but you saw figures, writhing around on the floor. I had the actual footage, which was far more intense and informed as to what was going on.

"Vanity was lovely, but to keep her energy up she kept drinking espresso, so by the end of the day, she was jittery. But she was a lot of fun to work with. She listened to me but I'm telling you, by the end of the day she had so much caffeine that she wasn't focused. I was begging her, 'Just look in his eyes… just look in his eyes.'" It is very nice of Mastroianni to blame Vanity's jitters on caffeine, but Vanity had a severe addiction to crack-cocaine around this time. So severe that, in the early 1990s, she went into renal failure and was given three days to live[1]. "The one with Vanity was crazy. She was crazy. There are some stories best left untold about Vanity," says line producer J. Miles Dale. Vanity now goes by her birth name, Denise Matthews, and is an evangelical preacher. She declined to comment for this book.

The benefit of having an experienced singer in the role of Angelica is, of course, that she knew how to handle herself on stage and in a recording studio. Mastroianni was the one who requested she perform Nat King Cole's "Nature Boy," as well as her own single, "Undress Me." Composer Fred Mollin recorded both songs, as well as musically supervised her live stage performance with the band. "I was involved in that stuff to help the director," Mollin explains.

---

1. *Jet Magazine*, Nov 26 2007

"Wedding in Black"

Written by: Peter Lauterman and Angelo Stea
Directed by: Rodney Charters
Original airdate: May 8, 1989
Cursed antique: Snow globe

In Buenos Aires, an American man named Calvin (Stephen Meadows) strangles a prostitute to death. He is imprisoned and put to death within weeks of his capture. He begs not to let them do this to him, that he has been "your servant," and "we had a deal." An echoing, demonic voice (presumably only audible to this man) tells him he is needed somewhere else.

In Nigeria, a White priest named Antonio (Guy Bannerman) prays fervently. A local woman enters the hut and he forces himself on her, claiming he "deserves something for all I do for you people." The villagers respond to her screams and remove the woman before strapping the priest to the bed and setting him alight. The same demon voice assures Brother Antonio that he needs him.

In Miami, Maya Zedler (Carolyn Dunn) watches herself on the nightly news. In the report, she is being taken away in handcuffs, having allegedly murdered seventeen people in her capacity as a nurse, believing herself to be an angel of death. Maya, who I assume is out on bail, goes to the bathroom and slits her wrists. The demon voice urges her to come to him.

The three of them arrive in your typical vision of hell: fiery caves, brimstone, etc. The demon, still a disembodied voice, welcomes them home and offers them another chance at life. "There are three who resist me, gathering my objects," he explains. "Each has a past with you, and you will end them."

Micki receives a package from Argentina. Inside, she finds a large snow globe, the same one Calvin used as a conversation piece while flirting with hookers. Micki immediately recognizes the castle inside as the Magic Castle, a tourist trap near her childhood home that she was obsessed with.

Calvin walks into the shop, and she puts the globe down in favor of greeting her old friend with a hug. They haven't seen each other since Micki and Lloyd got serious, insinuating there was an intimate relationship between the two. He was just "passing through town" and thought he'd look Micki up. After some time catching up, Calvin invites Micki with him to Quiet Springs Lodge for a weekend escape. Micki is hesitant, as I think any woman would be in that situation, but both Ryan and Jack encourage her to go. "What is this, a male conspiracy?" She agrees to join him.

And then there were two. Jack examines the snow globe, and Brother Antonio, an old friend of Jack's enters. Ryan is immediately suspicious. Jack's decision to join Antonio at a monastery for the weekend sets off warning bells for Ryan, who tries to dissuade Jack from going. "Two old friends just popping up, one after the other?" Jack brushes him off and heads out with the "man of god."

Calvin and Micki, and Antonio and Jack have a similar voyage to their respective getaways. Both couples must cross through a terrifying blizzard before the weather clears into a snowy wonderland. Both are at the same place: the Magic Castle. But they are each in their own "timeline," so they don't cross paths (at least, not yet). Micki is excited to see the place, an exact copy of her childhood Magic Castle. "I've always wanted to bring you here," Calvin admits. Jack has seen this place before, but Antonio claims it is a copy of a monastery in Italy. In case it isn't clear to everyone, the getaway actual takes them *into* the snow globe, sitting on the desk at Curious Goods.

Back at the shop, Ryan scours the manifest, but finds no snow globe. He examines the globe, turning it over, looking for some trick. Maya walks in with a warm smile, claiming to have just moved to town and thought she would look him up. Ryan is not as happy to see her. "You walked out of my life five years ago. You think you can just walk back in?" She tries to soothe him, explaining there are reasons why she left. She wanted to be a doctor, but never got past pre-med, so now she is a nurse. She just wants to be friends, but Ryan rebuffs her, saying that right now is a bad time. She is persistent, and offers to help him. He relents—or rather, he stops arguing. He is concerned about Micki and Jack and doesn't want to waste time arguing with Maya.

At the castle/in the globe, Micki and Calvin have a drink before heading off to a black tie dinner. (I wonder if the devil arranged for phony diners to join them.) Jack and Antonio are just walking the halls. The two couples are walking directly towards each other, but neither sees the other; in fact, Jack and Micki walk right *through* each other.

Ryan has a few calls to make. The first is to the Quiet Springs Lodge, which he soon finds out doesn't exist. Maya tries to calm him down, but Ryan doesn't want to be calmed. His next call is one he clearly doesn't want to make: to Lloyd. As we pick up Ryan's end of the call, it seems like Lloyd is trying to win Micki back. Ryan fills in Maya on what he learned: Calvin was arrested two years ago for the murders of several women. He was let go for lack of evidence, and quickly left the country. Three weeks ago he was sentenced to death in Argentina.

Calvin walks Micki back to her room and insists on a nightcap. She turns him down, but clearly doesn't want to. Calvin picks up on this and presses the point. Micki relents. Jack, meanwhile, is asleep (not much to do in a monastery) when he hears a voice. Micki's voice. Apparently the devil couldn't invest in soundproofing. Jack follows the voice to the library, and hears Micki telling Calvin that she went to business school, then took over the store after she inherited it. Jack finds an old television set, which is playing Micki and Calvin's conversation. Calvin looks directly into the "camera," seemingly staring right at Jack. Jack is spooked and runs into Antonio. He can't explain it, so he takes Antonio back to the library to show him.

The library is now Micki's room. Jack can see her, but she can't see him. He tries to hug her, but he just falls through. "Micki is too busy falling in love with that young man," Antonio informs Jack. He then fills in Jack on the whole, rotten plan: "Our master has watched you undo his handiwork for the last time. You brought this on her, Jack. You inspired her sense of mission—and Ryan's. You have been successful beyond the master's belief."

The other shoe drops: Micki is to bear the devil's child. Calvin is just there to "break the ice" for him. Antonio reveals his true, burnt face, and offers a trade: her virtue for Jack's soul. Jack reminds him that she must submit willingly, and Micki would never do that. "Accepting one evil is the same as accepting another." I'm not sure if Antonio is referring to "the evil" as Calvin (since he is a murderer) or the act of sex itself; either one seems to work in the strangely old-fashioned gender roles of this episode. I am leaning towards Calvin as the evil because *F13* has always been sex-positive.

Ryan has found a newspaper clipping about Calvin's case, and confirms that it is the same Calvin who whisked Micki away. He needs to go find Jack. Now. Maya starts whining, "What about me? I came back

Let it snow! Filming the finale of "Wedding in Black." Photo courtesy of John LeMay.

to you!" She tries to kiss him, but Ryan is having none of that. He leaves Maya behind. She puts her hand on the snow globe and is transported to the devil's chamber. He is *mad*, and Maya is starting to have second thoughts. She remembered how good Ryan is, and wants to know why the devil wants to hurt him. The devil informs her that Micki will be the mother of his child, and makes the slits in Maya's wrists open up. "Imagine your pain going on forever." She begs, will do anything to keep that from happening. Her master sends her back to Ryan, with the warning to keep him away until their "child" is conceived.

Jack tries to leave the "monastery" but Antonio stops him. There is no way out. "Your soul, or her body." Jack ignores him and sneaks through the woods, until he comes to a glass barrier. Looking through the snow, he sees the shop and tries to flag Ryan down. Meanwhile, Micki is blissfully unaware as she takes a midnight stroll with Calvin. She rebuffs his attempt to kiss her, and the devil hisses "Take her!" in Calvin's head, causing him immense pain.

Ryan has now found out that Brother Antonio died in Africa two years ago and the monastery he took Jack to doesn't exist. Then he confronts Maya with the news of her own suicide.

"I had no choice!" she bursts out. "The one whose curses you seek to destroy, he said you'd go crazy from the guilt." She confirms that Jack and Micki are alive—in the snow globe.

Apparently, Maya has a change of heart, and takes Ryan into the snow globe. She insists he not let the bad weather deter him. She drops, wrists bleeding, and the devil tells her she is finished—and so is he. Maya encourages Ryan to go on without her; she has resigned herself to an eternity of pain. She disappears and Ryan hurries on. Inside the castle, Ryan calls for Micki. Calvin and Antonio laugh as they walk through him, and plan to give him the same choice they gave Jack. Ryan finds Micki, but the only one who can see him is Calvin, with his ghoulish, dead skin and evil laugh. "She is almost mine!" he promises. Micki starts fading and Jack, who heard Ryan's calls, takes him out into the hallway to explain what is going on. Antonio interrupts, offering Micki's body in exchange for Ryan's soul; Jack ignores him and pulls Ryan away. He has an idea.

Calvin goes back to plying Micki with booze. She is worried, but promises it has nothing to do with Calvin. She doesn't specify what she is worried about, but he says all the right words: "I have wanted you my whole life, and whatever happens tonight, it has to last me a lifetime."

This is the panty-dropper, and Micki starts kissing him. Calvin carries her to the bed, then checks with her one more time. "I'm not the man you thought I was, are you sure you want to keep doing this?" She is. "If I wasn't the man you thought I was, would it make any difference?" No, never. Calvin's deathly visage returns. The room turns black, lit with devilish red light and decorated with pentagrams and inverted crucifixes. The devil's bedroom. Someone get him an interior decorator. Micki screams and runs for the door, but Calvin calls Lucifer to come "look upon his bride, she has submitted." Calvin smacks Micki, knocks her out, and dumps her on the bed. The devil appears, but we don't see him. Instead, we see Micki from the devil's point of view. "I am here. Our child awaits," he growls. Micki tries to crawl away, but somehow she just looks more becoming. Her eyes are vacant with fear.

Jack's plan is to knock the snow globe off the desk, where Ryan left it. The storm marks the edge of the illusion, and they drive (in Calvin's car—can't ruin the beautiful Mercedes) until they find it. Ryan steps on the gas, and the car hits the glass wall. The car doesn't go through; instead it crumples.

But the snow globe does wobble, and tumbles off the desk in the shop. The whole world trembles and turns upside down, allowing Micki the chance to escape. Antonio chases after her, but as she escapes into the woods, he lights on fire.

The snow globe shatters on the ground, and Micki, Ryan and Jack wake on the floor of Curious Goods. They are wet and covered with flecks of snow globe snow, but they are safe.

Status: Micki's "virtue" is still intact, but Micki remembers the devil's eyes. "They were so cold, so empty." Jack suggests that maybe that is what pure evil is: "not something, but the absence of something."

*   *   *

This one felt very emotional to me. I remember loving it as a kid, but not watching it since then, so a lot of the scope was forgotten to me until now. Some of the finer points escaped me back then. I don't know how much I followed the idea that the devil wanted to impregnate Micki. I know that it wasn't until I was an adult that I realized Calvin, Antonio, and Maya didn't show up at Curious Goods until their respective friends shook the snow globe. My initial thoughts after re-watching this episode include: How is Micki not more traumatized? Why is it that the offer is Micki's body or the guys' souls? I'm hardly one to give in to feminist propaganda, but that seems a very uneven trade. Would Micki lose her soul automatically if she carried the devil's baby? What do you buy for that baby shower?

The Magic Castle is an actual castle in Toronto called Casa Loma. Originally built in 1914 for Canadian financier and soldier Henry Pallatt, Casa Loma was the largest private residence in Canada, boasting ninety-eight rooms spread over seven stories. The grounds include a hunting club, stables, gardens, and secret tunnels. Construction was halted during WWI, and by the time the war was over, Pallatt fell on hard times, which means things like the swimming pool, bowling alley, and shooting range were never completed. He eventually left the castle in 1923. Over the years it was used as a luxury hotel, a popular nightspot for American tourists during Prohibition, and was nearly demolished in the 1930s because it fell into such disrepair. It became a tourist destination in the late 1930s when the Kiwanis Club took over operations (although they did use it as a cover for sonar research during WWII).

Director Rodney Charters loved this episode, figuring out all the technical stuff, trying to "create an invisible wall," and doing things in those days they would never let them do now. "The biggest light we had was a 12k HMI, and that was our go-to light for strong, moonlight backlight. Everywhere we went, we put this up. We had to get up on a really tall crane and photograph [the castle] as though we were looking down at it from a snow globe, so we got an industrial crane that went to 125 feet, which was pretty high for us. [The average height for production cranes, at least back then, was eighty feet.] Nowadays you have to be strapped down and there are all kinds of special safety things. In those days, it was wide open. [The crane owner's] solution was to weld a special platform that was open, that had three spigots in it, so we could mount our lamp—or mount three lamps if we wanted. We generally didn't have enough money for three! You stood on this platform, hooked yourself into a belt and you looped it to this thing, but the platform was open—no rails or bars at all. I remember fondly going up one time to photograph from there, at 125 feet, with nothing around you… it's a fun experience. You just can't do that now. I'm not saying that bars and rails around a platform like that aren't a good idea, but I do love the fact that, at that time in Toronto, we could blow through all those rules.

"I do remember the smashing of the snow globe, because it was the first time I had ever used a camera that was 360 frames per second," Charters continues. "Nowadays we have a Phantom that goes over 2000 frames per second, but back then, it was a very, very special image. The beauty and the exquisiteness of the way the water and the glass shattered. It was special to see those dailies. You can't see it on the set; we didn't have any of those devices that would play it back in the speed you would shoot at. That was a special moment."

Guy Bannerman played Brother Antonio in this episode, and he believed his character to be evil. "I think part of the reason for casting me in the role was that, as one director said to me, I have a 'willing face,' an appearance of being open and friendly. This, of course, was important for Chris Wiggins' character to be able to trust me." Bannerman had a small role in a play with Wiggins in the 1960s, so he was pleased to be reunited with him. "It made me feel much less intimidated by the excitement of the shoot.

"I was very concerned about the rape scene," Bannerman continues, referencing the scene in which Antonio is killed. "I was relieved when I arrived on set to find that my scene partner was Michelyn Emelle, a theatre friend. She too was relieved, and when we expressed concerns about how the scene would be shot, we were both impressed by the complete professionalism of the wardrobe staff. Michelyn was covered demurely and thoroughly, and the scene, as I remember, was shot to emphasize the violence of the assault rather than the sexual aspect."

Before *F13*, Bannerman was a regular on a series done for CBC, Canada's public broadcaster. It was pretty much a nine-to-five job. No overtime allowed. So, it was quite a surprise when, on Bannerman's first day on "Wedding in Black," they kept shooting into the evening. "When I inquired as to when we'd finish, the A.D. replied, 'When we're done.' Basically when we completed the shot list. This practice often results in a substantially higher paycheck for guest players like myself. Another actor told me how, in the previous season, this method of work had had an interesting result. Because crews were required to have a ten-hour break between shooting days, night shoots gradually shifted the work day into the evening hours, so that by season's end, the cast had days off, and shot all night. This, of course, played havoc with family life, and I was told that the new season's contracts for some leading actors contained a clause to ensure it wouldn't happen again. However, somehow it seemed appropriate for the show!"

For Stephen Meadows, who played Calvin, the highlight of his time on *Friday the 13th* was meeting Jill Hennessey. She had tiny roles in several episodes before eventually finding mainstream success in *Law & Order* and *Crossing Jordan*. "She was cast in a small role as a Hispanic prostitute that my character passionately strangles in the opening scene," recalls Meadows. "What can I say? You know when there is an attraction under these circumstances." Their relationship didn't last long, but it was clearly important to Meadows.

The Maya aspect of the story felt off to me from the start. Surely, if Maya killed seventeen people, her story would make the national news. I feel as though Lucifer had really low expectations of Ryan; that he would not only forgive Maya because she has a pretty face, but also that he would listen to his penis over his head. If you want to get real femi-nazi about that, the argument could be made that the men in this episode have great control over their baser instincts, while the women do not.

But I don't want to get femi-nazi about it. Because frankly, I do not think—and have never thought—that this show talked down to women.

Micki was my role model as a child, and I think that served me very well as an adult. The sad fact is that there is only one thing women can do that men cannot: have children. So, if someone is going to carry Lucifer's baby, it has to be Micki.

"I remember people driving by and yelling, 'Hey Micki! We love you!' That was great! Except that I was in stocking feet in the freezing cold, with just a dress on," Louise Robey recalls of shooting the final scenes of the episode. "We had a little fire going, and they issued us great big parkas. Mine caught on fire." Turning to the actual shoot, "I was being chased down the hill, and someone had to blow up on fire. Our stunt person was wrapped up like a mummy. He had this little thing on his thumb which he could press and he would go up in flames. It was him and me. I was in stocking feet—that alone would have been dangerous, there was ice all over the place. There we were with the walkie talkie, waiting for the 'action' command and this guy fell over. Just fell over. He could have gone up in flames if he [fell] on the button. I thought, *What the hell am I supposed to do?* I actually managed to [help] him back up. That was something. It could have been potentially fatal to both of us. So, there we were in this little hut, and they yell action, and I come running out the door, and I swear I really was running! I was running for real! He pushed the button, and it was all good."

That stunt man was portraying Bannerman's Brother Antonio, but Bannerman had his own experience with makeup effects. "A fun aspect for me was the necessity of creating a 'death mask' of my face, in order to fit latex pieces of 'burned skin' and 'scar tissue' accurately to my face. This involved having my head covered in plaster and breathing through two straws for twenty minutes or so while the plaster dried, creating a negative mold which was then used to create a positive cast. I was given a series of Polaroids of the process, which are probably still among my photos somewhere. My final scene (played by a stunt man) in which I burst into flames as I ran from the 'retreat' is certainly the most dramatic death scene of my career to date."

"Wedding Bell Blues"

Written by: Nancy Ann Miller
Directed by: Jorge Montesi
Original airdate: May 15, 1989
Cursed antique: Pool cue

Danny and Jennifer (Justin Louis and Elizabeth MacLellan) are far from the perfect couple. He is a terrible pool player who can't work due to a "back injury;" she is a bar waitress who lives in a fantasy world about their relationship. Co-workers and family members have tried to tell Jennifer that Danny isn't good enough for her, that he will never marry her, but Jennifer tunes them all out. Love is blind.

Danny is practicing for a pool tournament. He has been playing another barfly and keeps losing. Frustrated, he demands Jennifer's tip money so he can play another game. Before the game begins, Jennifer follows a fellow waitress downstairs and impales her on Danny's pool cue. I think we are supposed to think it is Danny who does the killing, but it is a woman's hand gripping the cue. Regardless, Danny wins his next game, and Jennifer is relieved.

Jennifer's sister, Christy (Lolita Davidovich), comes over to her apartment to tailor her wedding dress. She approaches her upcoming nuptials like a little girl, imagining the perfect wedding, to the perfect man. What starts as cutesy, girly gabbing about boys turns into a harsh reminder about the realities of their relationship. Christy reminds Jennifer that Danny has been stringing her along for a year, and he is not the marrying kind. Jennifer makes excuses, and isn't bothered when Christy tells her to stop eating so much—she has to let out the dress again. That night, Jennifer is pasting together collages of her dream wedding while Danny sleeps. Suddenly Jennifer gets sick and runs to the bathroom to vomit. She assures him she is okay; but he doesn't care. After being woken momentarily, he goes back to sleep. Clearly, Jennifer is pregnant.

Jack and Ryan are on their way out of town, hunting cursed snowshoes. He mentions to Micki that "a kid he met" named Johnny (Steven Monarque) might call if he finds anything on a pool cue he had been tracking. And call he does. The Johnny that we meet in his first episode is much "harder" and "slicker" than the Johnny who eventually becomes the third antique-hunter. He is watching Danny play pool, and he hasn't missed a shot all night. He calls Curious Goods and is wary when he reaches Micki. She promises she is coming right down there, wearing a red sweater. "I hate red," Johnny grumbles before telling her to "look for the best looking guy in the place."

Micki enters the bar just as Danny wins his round, sending him into the semi-finals. Johnny approaches Micki. "I take it back. Red is my favorite color." Micki looks flattered, but not swayed. He points out Danny, and Micki thanks him, ready to take on the "case" by herself. Johnny has already moved on from the cue and asks if she and Ryan are married. They are not, and Johnny decides to impress her by challenging Danny to a game. Danny misses his second shot, an easy one. He puts his cue down, and Johnny grabs it and makes a run for the door. The bouncer catches him, Danny and a few other regulars land a few punches, and Johnny is kicked out.

"I've got six sisters," Johnny tells Micki outside, "this is nothing." She appreciates what he tried to do, but she will take it from here. "Maybe we can do it together, start off with a little dinner, a little cha cha cha?" he suggests. What a charmer. Micki is flattered, but no. Johnny asks, "You don't date younger men?"

"You're not that much younger," she replies and leaves.

As a ten year old kid, this line and Micki's delivery made a lasting impression on me.

Back at the bar, Jennifer is cleaning up and we find out that the man Danny beat is Gil, his "best friend." He is amazed at Jennifer's stupidity and suggests she walk away. "I can't," Jennifer says before impaling Gil on the pool cue. And the reason she can't? She's pregnant. A visit to the clinic tells her as much. It is the first time in my life I heard the phrase "Your rabbit died" in reference to being pregnant, and this horrified me. Without the easy access to information that we have today, it was years before I understood the phrase. As someone who had pet rabbits throughout my life, this may be yet another reason I never want to have kids.

But I digress. The next night, Micki goes to the bar looking for a job. Since Jennifer had killed the other waitress a few nights prior, there happens to be an opening. She follows Jennifer downstairs and introduces herself. Jennifer is friendly enough, and they chit-chat about Danny, their wedding, and the tournament. Micki asks if Danny uses the same cue every game as she opens the ice chest. Jennifer closes it quickly when she sees a hand sticking out. She promises to take care of the ice while Micki takes care of the customers. Alone, Jennifer rearranges the ice around Gil and talks to her baby, promising it will have a daddy. Unsurprisingly, Jennifer did not have a father. Jennifer returns upstairs to watch Danny win his game and get a trophy. He is going on to the finals. Danny puts his cue down on the table, but Micki's path to it is blocked by the crowds. Jennifer wants Danny to spend the night at her place, but he can't—he is too busy making eyes at a slutty blonde at the bar.

The next day, Johnny comes by the store, claiming he was "just in the neighborhood." Micki is in no mood to deal with him, especially when he starts poking around among the antiques. "Ryan will be back in a couple of days, and he'll settle up with you then, okay?" she says, in hopes he will take the hint. He doesn't, and again wants to take her to dinner. She declines and tries to walk away, but he stops her. "I'm a nice guy, is there some reason you don't want me around?" (It might be because you are being creepy and physically restraining her.) "I've got a lot to do and I have to do it alone," she insists through gritted teeth.

Another dress fitting, and another opportunity for Christy to tell her sister she is too good for Danny. Danny comes home with flowers, and any anger or frustration she may have had with him disappears. Christy leaves, and Danny starts smooching on Jennifer. Jennifer isn't interested; she wants him to look at wedding stuff. They argue, but Jennifer backs down first and promises to take care of him. He relaxes and decides to "start the honeymoon early."

Closing time at the bar. Micki and Jennifer are cleaning up as Danny practices. His luck is running out and he throws the pool cue angrily. Jennifer reminds him that was his engagement present and, once again, asks him to come home with her. Again, he declines—probably because that blonde is at the bar, and she leaves shortly after he does. Jennifer puts his cue on the rack on the wall. The evening wears on, and Micki and Jennifer turn to small talk. Micki tries to steer the conversation gently towards pool, which doesn't seem to bother Jennifer, but when Danny's confidence is mentioned, Jennifer suddenly turns defensive. "Getting married makes you more stable!" Micki decides to try the direct approach and asks where Danny got his pool stick. Jennifer doesn't know, but now she is suspicious. With Micki's back to her, Jennifer retrieves the cue from the wall and takes aim. A knock at the door startles the cue down to Jennifer's side.

Johnny is at the door. Micki rolls her eyes, and Jennifer recognizes him as the guy who tried to steal Danny's cue. "I told you I wasn't interested. I've got a boyfriend. Now, get out of here!" Micki demands.

"You can't get rid of me that easy, sweetheart."

"Watch." Micki holds the door open and waits for him to leave.

Johnny wants to walk her to the car, and Jennifer tells her to go ahead. Micki smiles, but once in the parking lot, she says furiously, "I don't want to see you again ever! I would have had it if it weren't for you; now it's locked up in there." Johnny sees this as meaning Micki is free for the rest of the night. "Listen to me!" Micki insists. "You don't know what's going on, so stay out of it."

"I think this is the part where I say I'm already in it. Why don't you tell me what's going on?" Johnny begs.

"You're driving me crazy," she says and drives away.

Johnny goes back to the empty bar and breaks in. He rips all the cues from the wall and wraps his bloody hand in a towel. He heads downstairs to get some ice for his injured hand and finds Gil in the freezer, still dead. Johnny goes straight to Curious Goods, waking Micki up. "I couldn't tell one from another, so I brought them all," he says, marching in and dumping the cues in an umbrella stand. "And I found a dead guy in the ice machine. Are you going to tell me what's going on?"

Micki says nothing, just turns on the light and starts cracking cues in the banister.

Johnny continues with his rant. "This isn't funny anymore. Ryan never told me about people getting killed over this."

Micki remains silent, and breaks another cue.

Johnny is enraged by this point and starts snapping cues over his knee. "You wanted these so you could break them?"

Micki finally speaks: "The one I want can't be broken. Never mind, it's over your head."

Johnny won't let that stand. "I knock myself out for you and this is the thanks I get? Stop treating me like I'm some dumb kid!" (Oh, but Johnny, you are.)

Micki stops, takes a deep breath, then: "That cue stick is cursed."

"What, like by the devil?" She finally lets him into her world.

The two start going through the files, and Johnny finds a clipping about a waitress, Sherri McGrath, held for questioning over the murder of an intruder—she killed him with a cue stick. There is a picture with the article. Sherri is Jennifer. Micki slips into Jack mode here, telling Johnny about the curse, how killing people powers it, and gives you something special in return. It's so cute. She acts just like Jack here. The pieces all fall into place, and Micki realizes it is Jennifer who is doing the killing.

Morning comes and Micki and Johnny go to Jennifer's apartment. There is no answer and Micki bemoans forgetting to bring the lock picks. Johnny laughs and kicks the door in. They find some obsessive wedding stuff and more stuffed animals than any adult should own, but no pool cue. The police knock at the door, and Johnny instructs Micki to climb out the window. "They'll see me," he says and answers the door, the first gallant thing he has done.

Before the tournament finals, Jennifer stops by Danny's apartment, and walks in on him fucking another woman. Not just any woman— Christy. Danny takes an interesting approach to this situation: he gets mad at Jennifer for coming over without calling first. Christy sends Danny to make a drink; she'll handle this. "He's fun," Christy says by way of explanation. "It's not the first time, and I'm not the only one. He'd never marry you, and even if he did, he wouldn't change." Jennifer begins assembling the pool cue and assures her sister that no one is going to stop this wedding.

As Danny comes into the room, he sees Jennifer impale Christy on the cue. He is horrified and scared. "I've been doing this for you, sweetheart. This is how I've been making you win."

She puts the bloody cue to his throat and informs him that "you're going to marry me, you bastard. I've been waiting long enough."

The city-wide eight ball championships are a much classier affair than previous rounds, and Micki dresses accordingly. Danny plays nervously, but wins his round and heads into the finals. Johnny shows up, explaining that he called his bail guy to get him out of jail. Of course Johnny has a bail guy. Judging by the way he is playing, Micki assumes Jennifer used the cue again. But as he makes some practice shots, he starts to miss. Jennifer is going to have to power it up. Micki and Johnny split up, trying to find her in the crowded bar.

Jennifer is waiting in an adjoining room. She is in her wedding dress, and the entire room is decorated: flowers, chairs, a huge wedding cake. Danny bursts in, saying the cue isn't working. He wants to bail, but Jennifer is pissed. "We're not leaving until you win this tournament!" She has to get someone else, and Danny tries to stop her. Johnny bursts in, surprising everyone, and Jennifer knocks him out with the cue. Before she can take it further, Danny starts fighting her for the cue. Danny wins, beats her away, and rushes back into the pool hall for the final round.

Danny sinks his first ball. His second is interrupted by a sing-song voice. "You're not gonna win," taunts Jennifer, covered in blood. "You didn't kill me. I should have listened to everyone. They said you were a loser." She stabs him violently with the cake cutter as the crowd looks on, horrified. Jennifer's boss pulls her away and she collapses in his arms. In the commotion, Micki slips away with the cue.

Status: The cue is returned, and much to the surprise of Micki, Ryan, and Jack, Johnny wants to help them get "other weird things back."

Mentioned but not explored: Snowshoes. Their status is unknown.

*　*　*

I have probably watched "Wedding Bell Blues" more than any other single episode of *Friday the 13th: The Series* because I loved watching Micki out-fox Johnny at every turn. "It was hard for Steven because he was coming into a successful show and he was filling very big shoes," reasons Louise Robey. "John and I were an established team. I think he did alright. Chris used to say, 'He doesn't have an acting brain. Bless.'"

When Jennifer comes out in her bloody wedding dress, she reminds me of the bride in the Disneyland Haunted Mansion. It's not just the homicidal way she waves around a sharp implement, but the lighting on her face makes her look ghoulish, with her eyes glowing eerily, just like the attic bride. I'm talking about the "original" bride, from the 1980s and 1990s, that was an expressionless (and virtually featureless) face with glowing eyes. Now, they have some ridiculous animation projected onto a blank dummy that reminds me of a soap opera actress.

"The Maestro"

Written by: Karen Janigan
Directed by: Timothy Bond
Original airdate: May 22, 1989
Cursed antique: Symphonia (music box)

"I dedicate my body and soul to the dance." This is the oath Anton Pascola (Colm Feore) makes his dancers recite when they join his dance troupe. Of course, this oath is said over a symphonia (a type of rare music box) that comes from Lewis Vendredi, so no good will come of it.

Pascola was a dancer, but an injury ended his career and left him needing a cane to walk. He ended up forming his own troupe, and has found great success with his modern-dance take on *Romeo and Juliet*. His current project, *The Legend of Shiva* is leaving him flummoxed. The show opens in a week and he still hasn't choreographed the finale. He brings in his Romeo and Juliet to rehearse *Shiva*, and wants them to let the music take them. He works them both to the point of literal exhaustion, but won't let them take a break. They continue dancing—and end up jumping out a window.

Grace Colwell (Cyndy Preston), whose father is good friends with Jack (enough so that she calls him Uncle Jack), has been invited to join Pascola's troupe. At eighteen, she is nervous and excited to join the world-famous group, and takes Jack, Micki, and Ryan with her to watch Pascola's show. At an after show cocktail party, she drags Jack with her to meet Pascola. She is obviously star struck, and agrees without question to "eat, sleep, and live nothing but dance." He hands her a video of some basic dance steps he wants her to learn, and Jack notices he has a symphonia in his cupboard. He is impressed and asks to see it, but Pascola shuts that down quickly.

Later that night, one of Pascola's dancers, Anna (Sonya Delwaide), comes to the studio. During the show, she had accosted Pascola for not giving her a chance. She begged and harassed him until he agreed to see if she has what it takes to dance Shiva. When she arrives, he makes her take the oath over the symphonia, then instructs her to follow the music, let it lead her. He still needs five minutes of choreography to finish this piece. The idea is that she is Shiva's life force. She is about to embrace death, and lose, but her death will bring rebirth. Anna spins and spins, and can't stop. She begs Pascola to turn off the music. "We must embrace pain to create art," Pascola reminds her as she spins, faster and faster, until blood flies from her mouth and she collapses, dead. Anton only got one new sequence. "I knew you didn't have the heart of a dancer."

Jack is already suspicious of Pascola. He noticed that in the rehearsal tapes Grace is watching, the symphonia plays instead of a full musical recording. He pulls out the manifest; not sure why, he just felt he needed to check. Jack naturally finds the symphonia, but it was sold to Jeffrey Lear. He and Micki visit Jeff's mother who tells them her son died. He was barely twenty-five. Jeff and Anton danced in the same company for a year, the "happiest time of Jeff's life." He worshipped Anton, and gave him the symphonia as a token of his respect. Anton practically begged him to join his new company, and worked Jeff to the bone. The coroner said that Jeff died from a heart attack, but his mother believes he danced himself to death.

In the span of one rehearsal, Grace has become Pascola's favorite, irking the more experienced dancers. He yells at them for not dancing fast enough, for not "diving for the floor." But with Grace, he simply states her "idols" could take a lesson from her. After dismissing the other dancers, Anton works with Grace, having her dance through the portions that she has been studying. He makes her hold a particularly difficult position, instructing her to breathe through the pain. She does, and Pascola is impressed. He wants her to be the best, make her immortal, and live dance every moment. To that end, he asks her to move in with him. He makes her take the oath over the symphonia.

Grace rushes back to Curious Goods, eager to tell Uncle Jack about Pascola's interest in her. "He only does this with his most promising students," she gushes. "He will work with me personally every day." She goes straight upstairs to memorize the *Shiva* choreography tape he gave her, not-so-cleverly edited to remove the deaths. Jack doesn't like the idea and worries that he may have other reasons for this. Grace is embarrassed; she clearly thinks Jack is worried he will take advantage of her. She doesn't think that he might be selling her soul to the devil. No one ever thinks that.

Jack works out the curse with Micki and Ryan. Every time he choreographs a new section, someone dies or disappears. Since he started working on *The Legend of Shiva*, there have been three suicides, two dancers who went missing, and a "fired" dancer who no one can seem to find.

The dancers who die are always among the best. Jack supposes that the symphonia only gives Pascola as much choreography as they can survive.

At rehearsal the next day, Pascola announces to the company that he has given Grace the lead as Shiva. Susan, the most senior dancer in the troupe (though I doubt any ballerina would want to be considered a "senior dancer") takes issue with this. Anton will not be swayed. She follows Anton through the halls, accusing him of giving the role to Grace because she is eighteen and has a pretty face. Pascola slaps her. His second slap sends her to the floor. "She is my image of Shiva. If you can't accept that, get out." Susan believes that she can create those last five minutes for Anton, and he invites her to the studio tonight.

Ryan and Micki go looking for Anna. They find her door unlocked, her clothes still there and her suitcase empty. But they also find her bloated corpse hanging in the closet. Reporting back to Jack, he realizes it is the perfect cover: Pascola demoralizes dancers, driving them to "suicide." With heavy heart, Jack goes upstairs to convince Grace not to move in with Pascola. "I'll be safe," she insists. "He's only interested in me for my dancing."

"That's what I'm afraid of," Jack murmurs. He is wound up, and begs her to wait a few more days before moving in with him. Grace finally agrees—but as any eighteen year old would do, she sneaks out after everyone has gone to sleep.

Susan arrives at the studio, and after taking the oath, begins to dance. She screams in pain, begging Pascola to make it stop, to turn off the music. Pascola only needs a couple minutes more, but Susan cartwheels through a mirror. "Not yet!" he screams. "It's not finished!" But it is too late. She is covered in blood, lying on a bed of shattered glass, with an enormous shard jutting from her chest, *Suspiria*-style. "You call yourself a dancer?" Pascola shouts at the corpse. "Why didn't you finish it? You are nothing!" Grace spies all this from the doorway.

It is show night. Rehearsals have begun in the theater, but Grace is late. Pascola encourages the troupe to use the news of Susan's death as motivation to keep dancing. Grace finally arrives, a strange determination in her eyes. Rehearsal goes on, with Thomas dancing as Death. But they still don't have a finale. Pascola loses it and clears everyone from the stage. He is running out of time—and running out of dancers. He goes to his office to retrieve the symphonia and discovers Ryan trying to break into his locked cabinet. He screams and kicks him out. The symphonia is safe—he hid it in a drawer.

The show is set to begin. Pascola summons Grace to his office and informs her that the final duet will have to be improvised. He tells her to let the music do the work. "I was hoping to save you for awhile, not put you in this position. But it has to be." Grace would "do anything for him," and he kisses her.

Showtime.

Jack, Ryan, and Micki are still at Curious Goods. Jack thinks Grace will be safe on stage because Pascola only uses the music box for choreography. Micki informs Jack that Pascola doesn't have a finale, and they watch one of Grace's rehearsal tapes. She takes the oath. Off to the theater they go, but traffic is a nightmare. Micki and Ryan proceed on foot, with Jack begging them to just get Grace out of the theater.

They enter through the stage door and see Pascola in the wings, too absorbed by his show to notice them. Grace leaps into the wings for a moment, giving Ryan enough time to grab her. Pascola sees this and beats Micki and Ryan soundly, getting Grace back on stage.

Thomas lands in the wings next, and Pascola tries to get him to take the oath. This is the last straw for the dancer, and he storms off. Pascola shuts off the music, which causes Grace to freeze, confused. He limps onto the stage and sets the symphonia down. He cranks it up, then takes the oath and put on Thomas' mask. Tossing his cane away, he takes Grace's hand and the two begin their dance. Grace screams, and blood flows from both dancers. The scene gets intense, cutting together with earlier scenes of Pascola pushing his dancers, with his dancers dying, with his frustration. The gears in the music box get gummy with blood. Jack makes it into the theater just as Anton drops, taking Grace with him. They are both bloody and the audience sits in stunned silence. Once Jack shuts off the symphonia, the audience realizes it is over and gives a tremendous standing ovation.

Status: The symphonia is recovered.

Mentioned but not explored: Listed in the manifest, we can see three different antiques, none of which ever make it into the show: a mahogany octagonal spice box (basketwork mouldings); blue Irish runner, cutting on a conical stem; and Lalique serpent glass.

* * *

Actress Cyndy Preston did not do any of her own dancing in the role of Grace. "There was a terrific dance double," she admits. "They highlighted her hair to match mine." The dance double was so convincing, her friends insisted that she was doing her own dancing. "They would freeze-frame it and they were sure it was me. They would say, 'We looked really, really close! It was you.' I told them, 'Think about what you are saying. You are telling me what happened and I was there.' It was funny."

Director Tim Bond remembers having fun directing the ballet scenes. "You have music, so that brightens up [the shoot]. The show shot nights, always. Our standard call time was six or seven at night, depending on the scene, and we would just go until the sun came up. So, it was nice to have music to keep us awake!"

Bond went through a lot to get those brief, extreme close-up shots of the symphonia disc playing. "The prop guys found this amazing music box, and I just had to make it a character." He did so by finding a lens that was actually used in medical operations. "It was this strange-looking thing, a metal rod a couple feet long, with a light at the tip of the rod, and a lens there. We were able to use that, take a picture of the music box from above, then push the camera dolly in. The camera guys had to be really clever about poking that rod under the disc while it was turning. At the same time, we would twist the rod so it was looking at the underside of the disc. The first time I saw it, you could see all the gears, all the oil on the gears. We did tons of shots of that.

"I think 'The Maestro' was my favorite episode," Bond continues, "because the story was so strong, and the performances are the best. The whole thing just works."

"The Shaman's Apprentice"

Written by: Michael Michaelian
Directed by: William Fruet
Original airdate: May 29, 1989
Cursed antique: Shaman's rattle

John White Cloud (Paul Miceli-Sanchez) is an Iroquois who left the reservation to become a doctor. His grandfather, Spotted Owl (Gordon Tootoosis), is the tribe's shaman, and he is hurt that his son wanted to be a "White man's doctor." John's younger sister, Sasheena (Heather Hess), is her grandfather's apprentice and tries to facilitate understanding between the two.

John doesn't have an easier time off the reservation. He works out of Riverview hospital, and the chief of surgery, Dr. Lamar (James B. Douglas), hates John because he is an "Indian;" John hates Lamar because he believes that Lamar will only help the wealthy and has no respect for John's "charity cases." An altercation in an operating room leads Lamar to threaten John with both physical violence and medical board censure.

Frustrated, John heads home to the reservation. He needs help with his patient, whom he worries will have a stroke due to Lamar's operating method. But Spotted Owl won't speak to him. Instead, Sasheena, takes John to the burial cave of the shaman. She lays a slightly lighter guilt trip on her brother. She begins chanting and John pokes around the cave and finds an old shaman's rattle, the symbol of his power over life and death. It shakes with power, and gives John a vision of an ancient ritual, taking place in this cavern, in which a healthy man dies so another can be healed. John pockets the rattle.

That night, John checks on his patient and finds Walker (Peter James Haworth), one of Lamar's protégés in the room. Walker threatens to call security after Lamar stripped John of surgical privileges. (Of course, Walker uses a far more colorfully racist phrase: "Dr. Lamar is going to nail your red-skinned butt to the wall for this." I guess the world was less politically correct back in 1989.) John takes out the rattle, and it flies from his hand, floating and twirling above Walker. Walker screams and claws at his face. A blood vessel in his head explodes, killing him. John's patient wakes, seemingly fine. The next day, Dr. Jeffries (Paul Miller) apologizes to John for yesterday's surgery, saying they were all doing their best. "Your best gave my patient a stroke," John seethes. This puts Jeffries on the defensive.

Micki goes to the hospital to visit Blair (Isabelle Mejias), a friend who has been hospitalized for serious chest pains. The diagnosis has come in: a very rare sarcoma that will likely kill her within a year. John comes in to check on Blair's roommate, Vera, a woman with a similar condition who is in such pain she is begging to die. Lamar comes in to tell John to focus his attention on the people they have a chance of saving.

That night, as Nurse Meredith is doing her rounds, John releases the rattle. It chokes Meredith and she coughs up a bit of lung. John then returns to Vera, chanting and waving the rattle over her. Blair sees this from her bed.

The next morning, Vera wakes up, perfectly healthy. The pain is gone, and she doesn't want any more tests. She wants to go out and enjoy her new lease on life. Before she leaves, she advises Blair to see Dr. White Cloud. When Micki comes to visit, Blair excitedly tells her about what happened last night. She doesn't draw a correlation between that and the nurse that dropped dead last night. But Micki does.

She returns to the shop and fills in the guys on what happened. Jack finds an Indian ceremonial rattle in the manifest, sold four years ago to Spotted Owl on the Iroquois reservation.

Jack goes to visit Spotted Owl on his own, worried about the sensitive nature of this curse. Spotted Owl appreciates Jack's directness and understands that this is important to him, but the curse is a "White man's curse, by the White man's devil."

"The rattle belongs to my tribe," he tells Jack. "I've held it. It does no harm."

Spotted Owl has spent years trying to buy back the tribal relics the White man stole from them. He won't let Jack take the rattle, but promises it is in a safe place, guarded by shaman spirits. Jack is frustrated, but there is nothing more he can say.

Spotted Owl and Sasheena go back to the cave for the rattle. It is gone, and Sasheena admits she brought White Cloud here a few days ago. Spotted Owl calls to the spirit of his ancestors, asking for a vision to know the truth. He gets one: a vision of the hospital, John following Lamar, rattle at the ready. Lamar is discussing a new surgical procedure with a nurse, and snaps at her when she questions its safety. John goes to this patient, releases the rattle, and watches as the patient rips his own chest wound open in a violent, bloody affair.

Mr. Harrison is an older gentleman dying of a rare disease. He has immeasurable wealth, and as such has spent it all searching for a cure. He visited Spotted Owl, who couldn't cure him. When Harrison visits John at his free clinic, John promises he can cure the man, but he wants a fully staffed, state-of-the-art clinic in exchange. Harrison wants proof, and John tells him to bring him a patient for him to cure. Harrison does, a young boy with the same disease. (No one mentions where this stray child, with no parents, came from.) Using the death that Spotted Owl saw in his vision, John cures the kid immediately. Harrison is sold, and makes plans to come back tomorrow morning for his own cure. As the boy is leaving, Ryan arrives to talk to John about what Blair had seen. He blows it off. "There is no magic to what I do. I simply cure people."

Jack goes back to Spotted Owl, who now knows that the curse is true. He will take responsibility for getting the rattle back—or die trying. He won't let Jack help ("A good White man is hard to find") and tells him to return to the reservation tomorrow. He will either bring back the rattle, or Sasheena will tell him how to defeat White Cloud.

Spotted Owl and Sasheena lead John into the cavern. Spotted Owl tells his grandson that he knows what he is doing, and warns him he has called on the spirits to take away the power of the rattle. Spotted Owl chants, and John warns him not to make him do this. Orange lightening sparks up and Spotted Owl tries to use it as a fireball against the floating rattle, but it has no effect. Spotted Owl has a heart attack and dies.

The next morning, Harrison walks out of John's clinic a well man. Lamar approaches, gleefully delivering a dictate from the medical board: they are shutting John's clinic down, and his medical license will be under review. John threatens to hit Lamar, but backs off—he doesn't want to add an assault charge.

Jack believes Lamar is an excellent candidate for John's next victim. But Blair is next in line to be cured. Micki tries to reason that it is okay if Lamar dies so she can live. Lamar is an asshole, and has already lived a long life. Ryan comforts her, and Micki knows it is a no-go.

John decides to make Lamar's death really special. He ethers him at the hospital and brings him to the shaman's cavern on the reservation, telling him he will be part of a special ritual his ancestors would use. Sasheena takes Micki, Ryan, and Jack to the cavern with the intention of doing the spell Spotted Owl left for them, and find White Cloud doing his own ritual. Sasheena sneaks in, tosses herbs in the fire, and calls upon the spirits. John comes at her with the rattle, but ghostly mask-like spirits appear to "fight" the rattle. A blinding flash of light, and White Cloud is gone.

Status: Deciding it is "not theirs to keep," Jack lets Sasheena keep the rattle in the burial cave. "I think Sasheena and the ancestors will guard it as well as we can." Except that they can't—otherwise John wouldn't have gotten hold of it in the first place.

*   *   *

Paul Sanchez played John White Cloud in this episode, and no, he is not a Native American. "I have portrayed Native American characters several times and consider it an honor," he tells me. "One thing about the show that really has stayed with me is the professionalism and warmth given to me the moment I arrived in Toronto," Sanchez enthuses. "That artistic support was especially comforting coming from producer Jon Andersen. He created such a safe and inclusive environment for the actor that the work could flow rather than having to force it."

John LeMay considers William Fruet, who directed this episode, one of his favorite directors to work with. "He was like a mad scientist director, real passionate, very emotional and a little bit hyperbolic. He was fun to work with. A real creative energy about him."

"William Fruet was a real firecracker," says line producer J. Miles Dale. "His classic line was: 'Bill, what's the shot?' 'How can I tell you what the shot is until I've seen it lit?' We had some pretty colossal battles with him. He worked a lot of overtime. I think he ended up getting slowed down in the rotation. Good director." He couldn't have been slowed down *that* much; Fruet directed ten episodes for the series, more than any other director.

I never cared much for this episode. It is basically "Doctor Jack" with a rattle instead of a scalpel. A doctor can heal, but only after he kills. I wasn't crazy about "Doctor Jack" either. It's an old trope. The ending was anti-climactic. A poof of herbs and a flash of light, and everything is wrapped up. Boring.

"The Prisoner"

Written by: Jim Henshaw
Directed by: Armand Mastroianni
Original airdate: June 5, 1989
Cursed antique: Leather bomber jacket

April 5, 1979. A heist by a four-person crew ends in a shoot-out with the cops. Three of the gang gets away, leaving Dayton Railsback (Larry Joshua) to be arrested and sentenced to twenty years in prison. Jane Chalfont (Belinda Metz), the lone female in the gang, promises Railsback that they will save his cut of the heist for him until he gets out of prison. "There is honor among thieves," she promises. Besides, he has the claim slip for the storage unit where they hid the cash; he is the only one who can access it.

Ten years later, and Railsback is keeping his nose clean in prison, hoping for an early release. He has spent his time studying the law and helps inmates with motions that their court-appointed lawyers drag their feet on. One such inmate, Woody Reese, pays for Railsback's help with a leather bomber jacket worn by Japanese Kamikaze pilots in WWII. When a prisoner is shivved and collapses into Railsback, he is surprised to discover that the man's blood on the jacket causes him to disappear. He wastes no time slipping out of the prison when the ambulance arrives. Though he is invisible, he is corporeal, and several guards are surprised when doors push open or when they feel someone bump into them.

Railsback heads straight for Riverside Storage, where the heist money is being kept. This also happens to be where Johnny's dad, Vince (Sean McCann), works as the night guard, and it happens that Johnny is bringing his father a sandwich at this time. They hear a clanging and Johnny calls the police while his dad checks on things. What he finds are boxes moving and paper being strewn about, and he hears cursing—but sees no human doing very human actions. Vince tries to attack whatever it is, and Johnny jumps into the fray, trying to wrestle a huge invisible form off his dad. Johnny is thrown off and knocked unconscious briefly. Railsback shoots Vince with his own gun, then plants the gun in Johnny's hand

"The Prisoner" is out on parole. Photo courtesy of Armand Mastroianni.

before heading back to prison. When Johnny wakes, he finds himself covered in blood and his father is dead. And the police are coming.

Johnny is arrested and held without bail. He tells his story to Micki, who promises she believes him and will get him out. The only thing Johnny remembers is the smell of cigars. Jack points out that a jury won't accept an occult angle, so he, Micki, and Ryan are more focused on figuring out what kind of cursed object is involved (because it *has* to be a cursed object) and getting it back. Frankly, it seems like our heroes are more concerned with the antique than with Johnny. As it should be!

Johnny gets a lot of hoots and catcalls in prison. With his slick hair and cautious ignorance, he will be popular. But this isn't *Oz*, so no one messes with him. He spots Railsback right away, smells the same cigar smoke but can't quite make the connection, other than something is off. Railsback casually shivs Reese when he tries to buy back his jacket. He rushes down the hall to a quiet corner, wipes the blood on his jacket and disappears. Johnny follows but finds nothing but a dead end.

Railsback's attorney has been tracking down the gang for him, in exchange for a cut of the heist money. Apparently the gang didn't need the claim ticket to remove the money from the storage unit and place it in a safe deposit box. Bittner, Chalfont, and Kingston each have a safe deposit key, and all three keys are necessary to open the box. Railsback is using his new Invisible Man shtick to hunt them down, kill them, and take their keys. Bittner is first on the list. Railsback calls him, more of a taunt than a warning, and Bittner in turn calls Chalfont in a panic. She tells him it is time to move and change his identity again. We learn that they still have not spent the money, out of fear of being caught. Apparently ten years is not a big enough cushion. Railsback makes himself known to Bittner, but he is confused and spins around, looking for the voice. Railsback sucker punches him, ties him to a chair, and snatches the key from around his neck. Bittner won't—or can't—give up the location of the other two, so Railsback strangles him.

Railsback makes it back to his prison cell as guards are searching the inmates for weapons. Johnny is confused: one minute Railsback's cell is empty; the next, Railsback is back. While he is being searched, Johnny sneaks into Railsback's cell and finds the storage ticket with an address written on the back. He copies it down, and Railsback catches him. A fight ensues, which is broken up by Johnny's cellmate, Arkwright.

Micki and Ryan visit Johnny and tell him about a WWII kamikaze bomber jacket in the manifest, sold to a Woody Reese. Kamikaze pilots believed they were invisible until impact, and the curse made it a reality. Ryan was going to buy it back from Reese when he was released next week, but clearly, that isn't going to work out. Johnny gives them the names Bittner and Kingston, and they go investigate. First up is Bittner, but he is already dead. Chalfont shows up, sees the scene before her, and claims she is just there for a cleaning job. But then she pistol whips Ryan and runs.

Another jailhouse murder, and this time Johnny sees Railsback disappear. He has gone to Chalfont's house and watches as she draws a bath. She hears a splash and goes to check on it. Seeing nothing unusual, she checks the water and an invisible hand reaches from the water and tries to drown her. She runs to the front door, but Railsback blocks her escape, so she hides in a closet. He shoots his way in, demanding to know where the money is; strangles her and snatches away the key, also hanging on a chain around her neck. Micki and Ryan arrive in time to see the dead body and the door move as invisible Railsback leaves.

Johnny actually sees Railsback reappear in his cell. In the prison showers, Johnny punches Railsback, accusing him of killing his father. Railsback takes a razor to his throat, and the guards break it up. Back in his cell, Arkwright admits he found an escape route through an air vent. He was going to use it once but decided he wouldn't fit in the outside world. But Johnny needs to leave. Another night in here, and Railsback will kill him. After lights out, Johnny sneaks out of his cell, into Rails-back's cell, and tries to steal the jacket off him. Railsback wakes and stabs Johnny. He drags him back to his own cell and tells Arkwright to put him to bed and think of a reason he is dead.

Railsback tries to use Johnny's blood on the jacket, but Johnny appears. "You've gotta kill someone to make that work." He reveals a poor man's flak jacket, beneath his prison clothes, and the men fight. With Arkwright's help, they lock Railsback out of his cell, with the vent left wide open, setting up a plausible way for Railsback to keep escaping. When Johnny calls for a guard, Railsback moves to stab him again, but Arkwright gets in his way.

Director Armand Mastroianni takes Johnny to jail in "The Prisoner."
Photo courtesy of Armand Mastroianni.

He takes the shank and Railsback disappears before the guards can arrive. He fights his way out of the prison, with Johnny quick on his invisible tail. They end up in some basement room of the prison, Johnny fighting a losing battle against an invisible opponent. Johnny finally tosses something flammable in Railsback's direction and lights him up. His outline appears as the flames engulf him. He eventually becomes visible, just in time for the guards to arrive and see him burn to a crisp. The jacket remains unharmed.

Status: The jacket is retrieved, and Johnny is set free after the warden reviews the evidence and decides that it was Railsback who killed Vince, not Johnny. He is not charged with Railsback's murder.

* * *

While Johnny first appeared in "Wedding Bell Blues," it was "The Prisoner" that cemented his place as part of the team. "I remember getting called into the office and they told me they were going to write a new show and bring Johnny in," says director Armand Mastroianni. "He had only appeared as a friend. They said he was going to come in and become part of the team. I think they called John LeMay's bluff, which was sad because John was good. Steve Monarque was great, I liked him a lot. But you know… politics. Essentially, what we needed to do in this show was introduce Johnny as a lead, not as just a supporting character.

"So, the show was specifically about him and the death of his father. The shift of the group changed, and from then on, he was part of our team. It was essentially a show that had to work to create a new character, and make that character one the audience would like and want to be watching every week; not a peripheral character." Clearly, that didn't happen—at least, not with me.

"We were shooting in a place called the Don Jail in Toronto," continues Mastroianni. "It was a real jail. It wasn't the best of situations to shoot up there. I don't think it was active [at the time] but I think it was recently active, and they closed it down because a few companies had come and shot there." Don Jail was built in 1864 and the main prison facility remained open until 1977, at which point it was closed due to overcrowding and its reputation as a "hellhole." [1] An east wing, built in the 1950s, was still active at the time this episode was filmed; the east wing wasn't shuttered until 2013.

---

1. http://www.theglobeandmail.com/report-on-business/industry-news/ property-report/historic-don-jail-buffed-up-refitted-for-a-new-purpose/ article5422710/#dashboard/follows/

"The Prisoner" included a number of effects that were far more involved back in the 1980s. "I had this idea about the woman he screws over, she is having a bubble bath and since he is invisible, he is sitting in the bathtub waiting for her," Mastroianni explains. "She comes in and is doing all her stuff, and we are expecting at any moment this guy is just going to pounce, but nothing. She goes to shut off the water and notices an odd shape in the water, as if someone were sitting there. She looks at it, goes to touch it—then suddenly she is pulled in to it! I didn't know how we were going to do that, I just had this visual in my head. So, we filled the tub with certain kinds of suds, we shaped it, some of it was fake... with CGI today you can do anything you want, but back then it was different. There was a lot of second-unit on that episode. We had to do footprints, and that takes forever because it is stop-motion photography."

"Coven of Darkness"

Written by: Wendy Rodriguez
Directed by: George Bloomfield
Original airdate: June 12, 1989
Cursed antique: Witch's ladder; sculpting tool

We open with a black mass. Lysa (Maria Ricossa), the coven's leader, is calling on the spirits to lead them to the "keeper of the knot." She plunges a sculpting tool into a lump of clay, and it molds itself into a figure. "Follow the right-hand path," a voice says.

Jack and Micki attend a coven meeting of white witches (white as in "good magic," not race—although the coven is made up of all-White folks). Gareth (Maurice E. Evans), the coven's leader, reveals the witch's ladder, bound with nine knots containing the power of the warlock that created it. It can be used to amplify powers, aid in healing, and spread good will, but this one was created by Lewis Vendredi. He is returning it to Micki and Jack so it will never fall into the wrong hands.

After the meeting, Gareth chats up Micki and Jack as the rest of the coven leaves. Lewis' coven was bent on wiping out Gareth's coven, and if they had the witch's ladder, it would have happened—it can amplify a witch's power a thousand times over. There is no sign of Lewis' coven, but Jack isn't too sure that they are all gone. Gareth shakes Micki's hand before she leaves, and he asks if she has ever practiced witchcraft. He senses occult powers within her that he could nurture. (Nope, not a creepy come-on; a genuine inquiry.) Micki says they will discuss it, but she seems like she is humoring him. They leave, and Gareth says goodbye to Brother Shannon. (Fun fact: Gareth tells Shannon he will "see you next Tuesday.") As Shannon is leaving, one of Lysa's cloaked cultists leaps out of a tree and attacks him. It is rather ridiculous, and it seems that no one notices.

Brother Shannon is brought to the black coven and tied to an altar. He had been the keeper of the knot, but it is not among his belongings, and Lysa wants to know where it is. Shannon is carved up torturously, and Lysa promises it will end when he tells her where it is. It doesn't take long for him to break, and he names "Vendredi's old store, Curious Goods." Lysa puts an end to the torture by stabbing him to death.

While Micki and Jack are downstairs discussing witchcraft, Ryan is on the shop floor, dusting. Lysa comes in, dressed as a normal human being (no robes, no inverted cross on her forehead). She introduces herself and tells him Gareth gave her his name. They shake hands, and Ryan pulls away, pricked by Lysa's ring, which "accidentally" turned around. She dabs the blood from his hand with her handkerchief while she inquires about the ladder. She claims to be a psychic researcher who is tracking Lewis Vendredi after he killed her sister with the ladder. Ryan assures her it is somewhere safe, but Lysa made a promise to her sister to destroy everything Lewis ever created. "As long as it is near you, its evil will work on you," she insists. Ryan wants his partners to meet her and goes to get Jack and Micki. By the time they get upstairs, Lysa is rushing away.

That night, at another coven meeting, Lysa has a wax sculpture of Ryan. "This figure encloses his spirit," she chants. "May he writhe in torment until the ladder is returned." She wraps it in the bloody hankie and stabs it with needles. At the store, Ryan wakes with stabbing pains in his head. "May you sear in hell until the ladder is ours," Lysa continues. Ryan stumbles downstairs, making enough noise to wake Micki. She follows him to the vault, which Ryan opens and starts digging around in for the ladder. It is right next to Veda. Micki is concerned and grabs him. He collapses into her arms and she holds him, promising they won't let anything happen to him. At her altar, Lysa doubles over in pain. "Someone who cares for him interfered," she murmurs. "Someone with a great amount of power." She sends Crystal (Catherine Disher), her right-hand, to take some of the coven members to run interference while she takes care of Ryan.

Ryan has snapped out of his spell, but he is angry and frustrated with the situation. He believes that the ladder will corrupt them just by being around it, like Lysa said. Ryan seems to feel like there are no good options here. He stomps up to bed, and Jack decides to stay downstairs for a bit and do some research. Micki didn't get a good look at Lysa, but Ryan told her she was wearing a pendant, a lizard with wings. (Which, apparently, is very different from a dragon.)

Jack puts a lock around the vault, just in case, then calls Gareth, who is offended that Jack is calling at 3:00 a.m.—even though Gareth is fully dressed, reading by a fire, so I'm not sure why he is so annoyed. Jack asks him about the pendant, which Gareth identifies as the mark of a black witch and leader of a black coven. Jack mentions Lysa's name and Gareth is frightened. She was Lewis' second-in-command. A knock sends Gareth to the door. There is no one there, but a bloody pentacle is drawn on the door, punctuated with knives at the points. There is no one outside, but Gareth steps to the edge of porch and looks around. Brother Shannon's body swings down from the roof, crucified on an inverted cross. Suddenly inverted crosses light up on his lawn.

Ryan wakes suddenly, to more pain, and Lysa's voice in his head, telling him to feel the power. The phone rings. Lysa is on the other line, telling him to get out of there. She can feel the ladder's power calling to him. He worries about his friends, but Lysa insists that he is the only threat to Micki and Jack. "I will meet you at the corner. Don't question me!" Ryan sneaks out and finds Lysa. She is scared and claims she isn't the only one who wants the ladder, believing someone from Lewis' coven was following her the other day. She pours him some tea from a thermos, to warm his up and calm him down. He admits he thinks the ladder drew him to the vault tonight, and Lysa insists on taking him someplace safe, far from it. Ryan sips his tea and Lysa takes him to his friend Danny's garage.

Morning dawns, and Micki finds Jack still researching downstairs. Ryan, he informs her, left some time in the middle of the night—yet he doesn't seem as concerned as he probably should be. Jack fills her in on the call with Gareth and suggests she start calling Ryan's friends, when Gareth comes into the store. The line is dead, and Lysa has definitely re-formed the coven. The three start on the research, and Micki finds out that Lysa was in jail for grave robbing, which explains why she waited until now to get the ladder. Gareth wants the ladder, insisting only white magic can stop her, but Jack flat-out refuses. Seeking other options, Gareth surmises that Micki's concern for Ryan was stronger than Lysa's evil. Gareth doesn't have the strength to fight Lysa on his own, but if Micki overcame her before, maybe she can do it again.

Crystal takes her car into Danny's garage, but Ryan doesn't notice her (Danny can't help but notice her) because he is trying to call the store. After being blown off by Crystal, Danny realizes that Ryan looks feverish and clammy, and suggests he lie down. Danny wakes him a few hours later, after he closes the shop. He doesn't notice the black robed figures climbing out of Crystal's trunk because he is worried about Ryan. Before he knows it, two hooded figures grab Danny and stab him mercilessly. To Ryan, it looks like a blurry nightmare he can't escape. He passes out again.

When he wakes, he is far more lucid. Danny is dead, Ryan is covered in his blood, and the knife is in his hand. Lysa arrives and holds Ryan as he cries onto her shoulder. "You didn't kill him," she assures Ryan, "the ladder did." She will take care of Danny, but he has to get her the ladder. "It won't let go of you until it is destroyed."

Jack has found Lysa's name in the manifest. She bought a sculpting tool that Gareth identifies as a tool to model her victims in wax. With that and the ladder, she can destroy all of them. Gareth is helping Micki channel her power. They have set up an altar at the shop, and Micki first must will all the evil away from the altar. Next, as she lights some candles, she imagines Ryan bathed in white light. While focusing all her feelings on him, she is to repeat this spell: "Here I place a circle of protection around the spirit of Ryan Dallion. Within this circle is a circle of strength. May he be protected from evil." She is to repeat this seven times, and Ryan will be protected as long as the candles are lit.

Lysa takes Ryan back to the shop and he enters through the back. He watches Micki and Gareth at the altar, then goes down to the vault. Finding it bolted shut, he takes an axe to it. Micki's next spell, "Here is found the strength required to overcome all evil. As burn these candles, so burn the truth within the heart of Ryan Dallion" is interrupted by the commotion in the basement. Jack finds Ryan there and calls Micki and Gareth to help. "It has got to be destroyed," Ryan insists. He makes it into the vault and swings his axe at anyone who tries to get in his way. Jack is knocked out and Micki is tossed to the side.

Gareth follows Ryan upstairs. He now has the ladder and delivers it to Lysa. She faces off against Gareth and the ladder shoots blue lightening at him, burning a pentacle into his chest. Scared, Ryan gets in the car with Lysa and they drive off just as Micki makes it to the street. She is too late to stop Ryan, and too late to save Gareth.

Ryan waits in the car while Lysa takes the ladder to her altar. "Since Lewis' death, we have languished. But tonight, our power is returned. Tonight, white magicians are going to die. Tonight, darkness returns!" Lysa wraps the ladder around the sculpting tool and dips it into a chalice of blood before plunging it into wax, creating dozens of wax figurines.

Micki helps Jack up and fills him in. There is no time to mourn Gareth; the candles have melted down and they must finish the ritual. Micki is doubtful. Lysa has the ladder and Micki doesn't understand her powers. Jack reminds her to simply concentrate on Ryan, make him see the truth. "He's our only way." Micki returns to her chanting. As she begins on her seventh recitation, it seems to strike Ryan. Still in the car, he hears her—and he hears Lysa telling him to burn with fever until the ladder is returned to her. He remembers Danny's death differently, and it becomes clear: Lysa is responsible for everything. Micki is encouraged—she knows Ryan heard her. But now an even more daunting task is before her: she has to go after Lysa. "Even the smallest distraction may give Ryan a chance," Jack encourages. She begins on her next spell: "Arch sorceress, who attacks the right-hand path, your spell shall be reversed, your curse returned to you a thousand fold." Lysa doubles over in pain, but insists she is fine.

Ryan has left the car and silently knocks out a follower and puts on his robe. No one notices. Lysa waves the ladder over each figure before handing it over to a follower. Micki's chants again knock her over, and Lysa redoubles her efforts, chanting and passing out figures more fervently. Ryan is last in line. Instead of taking a figure, he rips the ladder out of her hands. The ladder is literally leaking power. It zaps a follower, and another. A knife flies out of one follower's hand and stabs Crystal in the back. Lysa is deeply upset by this (perhaps Crystal was her lover?) and tries to chant. The ladder is too strong and blasts her out of the coven.

Micki faints into Jack's arms.

Status: Ryan returns to Curious Goods with the ladder and the sculpting tool. Micki wakes and Jack tells her she may have been the first to use up her entire reservoir of psychic energy in one night. "All my magic is gone?" she asks. "Let's just leave it awhile before you try to use it again," he suggests.

* * *

Catherine Disher, after guest-starring in "Double Exposure," was surprised the producers wanted her back for a second episode. "I knew one of the other witches, Maria Ricossa, and when we came out of our trailers in our costumes and make up, I realized that that all the other witches were in full length, plain black costumes, with very little makeup, and I was in a short black dress, high heels, with a see-through black lace cowl, lots of eye makeup and bright red lipstick. I remember Maria saying to me, 'Why do you get to be dressed like that and the rest of us look so plain?' and I had a horrible realization—I was the blonde bimbo!"

Regardless of whether or not she was meant to be a bimbo in the episode, Disher did have a fun death scene. "I was wearing some kind of elaborate harness. The idea was that I would die by having a knife thrown at me but in reality, the knife was attached to the harness and would spring out of my chest to make it look like the thrown knife hit its target." Movie magic!

Despite my early fascination with Micki's witchcraft, it never felt like it was a real "fit" for the character. Executive story consultant Jim Henshaw talks about the decision to try it, and ultimately let it go: "I know that a lot of times we would try stuff and we just weren't happy with the way it worked out. Or we thought it would take us into places that it didn't take us. With Micki's witchcraft, I think we tried it and the audience reaction wasn't great."

Season 3

JOHN LeMAY (Ryan Dallion) – I don't feel like I was challenged enough, ultimately. I wish I would have found a mentor, who would have taught me how to dig deeper into the job of being an actor in a television series. I would have found somebody who would have helped me find ways to make that experience continually artistically enriching. I think I was immature and didn't find that on my own. As thankful as I was to be a working actor, I constantly want more out of life. I want to continue to grow. At a certain point it felt like it just had to be me in front of the camera. That's my fault, for not finding a way to be me in front of the camera, but also find a way to make that experience a continually growing one, and I didn't.

LOUISE ROBEY (Micki Foster) – He had had enough and he just left. I heard him in his trailer, just trashing it, around three in the morning, and I can fully understand. You are in full hair and makeup, and nothing happens for six hours. And it was often freezing cold. We shot in temperatures that were unbelievable. The extras were being picked off the fields like flies because they were just frozen.

FRANK MANCUSO JR. (creator, executive producer) – Syndication television is tough. It takes a lot of time and any television series you are going to do, whilst providing you work, opportunity, and some money, it does limit what else you can do, just by virtue of the time it takes. This isn't uncommon, but some people think, "Well, I've made my mark here, now it's time for me to go and exploit that and jump into this other thing." More often than not, it doesn't work out like that. More often than not, people look at you in a certain way, they like you doing what it is you are doing, then all of a sudden you are doing this other thing and they don't necessarily follow. Sometimes they do, and I don't really know what happened to John after that, but I don't think he found himself in the center of something like that.

Tom McLoughlin (director, story editor) – Frank came to me at one point and said John LeMay was going to be leaving the show. I said, "You're kidding me."

He said no, and made some classic Frank joke, like, "The next thing that is going to come out of his mouth is 'Do you want fries with that?'"

I said it wouldn't be like that.

He said, "I know, it just pisses me off."

Tim Bond (director)- John LeMay's agent kind of made a little bit of trouble. She kept telling him he got the best out of the series, that he was a household name, that she could get him movies… all that stuff that agents do. He kind of fell for it and started being a bit difficult on the set and showing up late. When you show up late to a *Friday the 13th* call, that means showing up at 9:00 p.m., and shooting until the sun comes up. So, he made himself a bit unpopular on set. I took him aside and said, "John, I know what's happening. Paramount knows you are coming late, they know you are trying to break your contract. You don't want Paramount to know that. When Paramount knows that, everyone knows that. They all call each other. It becomes common knowledge. You are a nice guy, you are not a bad actor, but it's going to be a tough road to hoe to be a movie star. I hope it happens for you, but see this series through so you're not branded as a quitter." Of course, he was young and didn't listen. At his agent's instruction, he did enough things to cause Paramount to terminate his contract. They made a deal with him that they would let him out of his contract if he did the first double episode of season three. Then they replaced him with Steve Monarque.

I worked with John LeMay about four or five years later, on some series at Universal. He told me it was the first job he had since he quit *Friday the 13th*.

J. Miles Dale (line producer) – John LeMay left, which no one was happy about because John was a very good actor and a very charismatic guy, a nice guy. He found some loophole in the actor agreement to get out. Steve Monarque was a nice guy, but comparatively, acting-wise, he was kind of a lightweight. He didn't have the same chemistry with Robey or with Chris.

Jim Henshaw (executive story consultant) – The cast change that went on between season two and three, when John LeMay left, we didn't just want to kill the character off. There were a lot of discussions about that. Between seasons two and three I spent a lot of time down in L.A., just mapping out the show and making sure we knew what we were producing and when. We had a few pretty big shows in the final season, so there was a lot of pre-planning that went on for that.

J. MILES DALE – It's too bad that John left because some of the shows we did in season three, he really would have elevated those.

TOM McLOUGHLIN – I was part of the casting of Johnny. He was picked partly because he had a completely different vibe from Ryan. It looked like there could be much more of a romantic aspect. Something went amiss and I don't know exactly what. I remember fans saying it wasn't quite the same. It didn't appear to me that the chemistry [between Micki and Johnny] was there for that first episode I was involved with. You can usually see people spark to one another. Sometimes it does happen over a period of time.

STEVE MONARQUE (Johnny Ventura) – I think they knew John was leaving the show, so they basically cast me to come up there and replace him. It was the pool cue episode that was my first one, but they knew, and I knew. I had a contract already. It wasn't like I was a guest star and they decided to use me. I had to go to Paramount and audition, meet with Frank Mancuso Jr., the whole thing. They called me the next day and asked if I wanted to go live in Toronto. I said okay.

JIM HENSHAW – When Steve came in, he was very much like Robey. Very instinctive. With him, you didn't want to rehearse too much because it would be really good on the first few takes. You just figured out how he talked, how he moved, and wrote to fit that.

FRANK MANCUSO JR. – What became obvious was that it wasn't the same. They weren't the same. It had nothing to do with Steve—he was just a guy trying to do a gig. I thought he was absolutely fine. Had there not been a show with John LeMay before it, nobody would be complaining. You can like it less, or you can like it more, but use the context you are supposed to in order to come up with a view on what it is. I got a little frustrated that people were taking shots at him, like "John LeMay wouldn't do it that way." Right. So what? It's like, the guy didn't wanna do it anymore, whaddya want me to do? I can't change his mind. That's not my gig.

LOUISE ROBEY – I said to Frank, jokingly, "Is this a cousin of yours? How did he get the job?" Sometimes the camera would be rolling and he'd do silly things like pick up fake fruit when there was real fruit. Our DP would call cut even before the director did and say, "Mate, there's fruit on the floor, just pick it up, because you're on camera."

STEVE MONARQUE – It was like Robey's show. I came in and basically just respected what she was doing and was part of the structure. She was very supportive, and we had some laughs and some fun together. When things got tough, we leaned on each other. She was always very sweet to me.

Chris Wiggins is a wonderful actor. I learned a lot from him. He was like a mentor. He was awesome. He had the whole package. Very calm, debonair, very articulate. Quite smart. He had a great humor—a very funny man.

ANGELO RIZACOS (guest actor) – I remember that Steve was calm in physical scenes. Having been injured on another series by a lead who let his adrenaline get the better of him when the cameras rolled, I was thereafter appreciative of actors who didn't.

STEVE MONARQUE – I did have an awesome car. That T-Bird. I got to drive it a little bit, then in the studio, fake-driving.

LOUISE ROBEY – Chris once took me into his trailer and said, "Louise, I hope they are paying you well, because this show will age you."

TIM BOND – It was so much fun to do because it was so creative, and we weren't being censored. It really came down to Frank Jr. He was pretty liberal, and never told us we couldn't do something or couldn't say something. We were very imaginative and gory. The gore was always fun. We went through a lot of gore. They kept it in gallon bottles.

In one shot once, there was a close-up of a guy being dragged off the windshield of a car after he had fallen off a roof or something. I told them to put some blood on the windshield. They put some on, and I kept saying, "More blood, more blood." They were using like an eyedropper. I grabbed the bottle and just poured the whole thing on the windshield and yelled, "Roll the camera! Drag him off!"

ALLAN EASTMAN (director) – We used to order our movie blood by the barrelful and just poured it on the actors. Nothing subtle about it.

STEPHEN ROLOFF (production designer) – The high body count lead to a couple of defining moments, one when we discovered that we had "drained" Toronto's entire supply of stage blood, and the other when a group of us sat around a table during prep trying to think of something new that someone could find in a tool shed to kill someone – and realized that we had already covered all the standard tools.

"The Prophecies"

Written by: Tom McLoughlin
Directed by: Tom McLoughlin
Original airdate: October 7, 1989
Cursed antique: Book of Lucifer

Jack arrives in France, in a small town called Marie-Mere. He is there a few days ahead of the Feast of Marie-Mere because he wants to speak with Sister Adele (Marie-France Lambert) before the crowds come in. Sister Adele is a young nun in the local convent, who has become a reluctant celebrity. Orphaned as a child and raised by the sisters, she was visited by the Blessed Mother, who restored her eyesight and dedicated the waters of their shrine to God's work.

At precisely 3:33 a.m., all hell breaks loose. The church bells clang, the townspeople rush from their houses, and Jack wakes up. In the convent, many of the nuns are frightened. Sister Adele prays, and another nun is tormented by violent nightmares. Asteroth (Fritz Weaver), a minion of Satan, reads the first prophecy: "It was written that three messengers should herald his arrival, and the most blessed among them would be the first to feel his power. One shall speak of his coming, another shall prepare his path, and the last shall make way for his return." The nightmare nun wakes with yellow devil eyes and rushes to Sister Adele's room, speaking in tongues. She tries to strangle Adele, but a number of other nuns, along with the priest (Jean Brousseau), separate the two, throw holy water, and the devil nun is thrown against the wall. Asteroth stops chanting, proclaiming "The first prophecy came to pass." The devil nun returns to normal before dying. As the clock flips to 3:34 a.m., everything becomes quiet.

Back in the States, Ryan is depressed. It is the anniversary of his kid brother's death fourteen years ago. He spends some time at the cemetery. James Peter Dallion, 1968-1975. He flashes back to that day, when he and Jimmy were playing catch and Jimmy chases a rogue throw into the road, where he is promptly hit by a car. Ryan is shaken from his reverie by a female voice. His mom. "My god, I thought you were... ." He can't bring himself to say the word; she couldn't face being around Ryan or his father after it happened. "So, you disappeared," Ryan concludes. "I thought you blamed me." Mrs. Dallion (Jill Frappier) admits it has taken her years to realize it is no one's fault, and horrible dreams brought her to reconnect with her living son. Ryan is remarkably mature about this whole situation: he suggests they go someplace to talk.

The priest greets Jack at the church and promises that the ruckus last night was due to a mechanical error with the bells. Sister Adele isn't receiving guests until after the feast and bids Jack farewell. Sister Theresa warns Jack that three nuns have died trying to kill Adele and they must hide her from the demons. The priest sternly warns Theresa away. Jack keeps watch over the convent from a cafe across the street, and sure enough, under cover of dark, the priest and Adele rush through the streets with a suitcase. Jack follows them to a small flat off an alley, and waits on a stoop across the street. Inside the small apartment, the priest blesses the place, and gets into a disagreement with Adele about God's will.

The bells start clanging roughly again, and Jack checks his watch. 3:33 a.m. Asteroth, in an abandoned building, recites the next prophecy: "And on the fourth night the beasts were filled with his unholy presence. For he shall rule them and dominion on earth shall return to the beasts." A wolf appears in the alley and rushes through the streets as the priest and the nun pray together. The wolf jumps through the apartment window and starts "attacking" (as a life-long dog owner, that pup was totally playing). The priest takes the brunt of the damage, which is a few scratches to the face and a bite on the arm. Jack comes in and stabs the beast dead. With its dying breath, the wolf speaks a single, human word: nema. The Satanist's version of "amen."

And the second prophecy came to pass.

Jack has finally been granted an audience with Adele, who insists there is nothing they can do about the evil power that seems to be manifesting in Marie-Mere. The Blessed Mother told her that ten years after her visit, they would be visited by God's fallen angel, Asteroth. He has walked the earth for centuries, doing Lucifer's work, and is now ready to fulfill the prophecies of Satan. He possesses the Book of Lucifer, the devil's Bible. If he can complete the six prophecies therein, Satan will ascend onto the earth. Last night was the second prophecy. "If he can corrupt this sacred place, what chance is there for the rest of the world?"

Sister Adele returns to the Marie-Mere hospital, to visit with patients in the psych ward—her special calling. Jack worries that it isn't safe,

On "The Prophecies," you can never have too many Ryans. Photo courtesy of John LeMay.

but Adele cannot be swayed. He goes into the streets, to try to ask some townspeople why they are leaving so hurriedly and if they have seen anything weird. They all blow him off, except for a blind beggar who laughs creepily. "Lucifer is coming! Prepare his way!" the old man cackles. "I saw his prophet—he took my eyes so I will have eternal sight." Jack tries to get more info out of the man, but he just dissolves into deranged laughter. The blind beggar really has no point in the show, other than he is fantastic local color.

Micki and Ryan are on their way to France, at Jack's request. Ryan is uneasy about leaving his mother, especially since they have been apart for so long, but he knows Satanic hoo-hah takes precedence. Mrs. Dallion takes Ryan and Micki to the airport, and mother and son watch a church group give wheelchair-bound Christina (Tara Meyer) and her father, Burt (Lee J. Campbell), a fond farewell. They are traveling to Marie-Mere in the hopes of being healed by the Blessed Mother. "If there is a god, I'm sure he will take care of that child," Mrs. Dallion sighs, "and he will bring you back safely." Micki and Ryan get ready to board the plane. Chris asks if they are going to Marie-Mere, and introduces herself. She shakes Micki's hand, but when she takes Ryan's, Chris starts hyperventilating and seizing. Her eyes roll back in her head, and she rasps, "Don't go!" Burt wheels her out of line and assures them she is alright—this happens sometimes. He gives her some medicine and she calms down, but she still begs Ryan, "Please, don't go."

Back in France, Jack and the priest take Sister Adele to a prayer room directly beneath the altar. She feels it is unnecessary, but Jack insists that keeping her alive will stop the chain of prophecies. "We can't stop evil but we can remove the tools by which it is committed." They leave her to pray, but at some unknown location, Asteroth begins the third prophecy. "And it is written on the fifth night that those with tortured minds and souls were filled with his presence, and the works of the holy were undone." The psych ward goes, well, crazy. The patients are clawing at themselves, at each other, turning feral, killing each other. A nurse goes into the ward to quell them and is attacked. A pair of orderlies come in to help. One is attacked; the other is smart enough to leave when he can. The patients crucify the nurse to the wall with oversized syringes, then they throw the orderly out the window. The patients lean out the window, screaming into the night for Lucifer. A huge crowd, including Jack, has gathered outside to watch the spectacle. Jack notices a boarded-up building next to the hospital, and breaks in.

This is where Asteroth has been performing his rituals. He hears Jack enter, and wraps up the prophecy hastily. The commotion outside settles down. Jack races upstairs and comes face to face with Asteroth. "Did you come to praise Lucifer as your lord and master?" he asks Jack. "I think not. I sense your good work. This place of God now witnesses the powers of Satan." He throws Jack over the railing, sending him down several stories. Jack is motionless on the floor, eyes wide open. Could he be dead? After a commercial break, we open on a bloodied body covered with a sheet being wheeled through the hospital. Micki and Ryan show up a few moments later, asking for Jack's room. He is alive but comatose. Sister Adele prays at his bedside, and warns them that Jack's fate awaits them all. "Our village has become a battleground. Asteroth is weakening our faith. If he does, Lucifer will walk the earth." Micki wants to put Jack in an American hospital, but Ryan assures her they are taking good care of him here. Frustrated, Micki suggests they check the files they brought with them—that's all they have to go on.

The Feast of Marie-Mere begins, and a crowd of devotees flock to the blessed fountain. The priest stands at the altar, sprinkling water and blessings on the believers. Ironically, for a destination for the handicapped, there is no wheelchair access, so Burt has to carry Chris to the altar. She believes deeply that a miracle will happen today. Asteroth walks among the believers, to a spot at the back of the fountain, and prepares for his fourth prophecy. "And on his ascension, the holy places were turned against the holy, the miracles of healing became the miracles of pain, and all faith and hope departed from the world." With a wave of his hand, Asteroth stops the waters from flowing in the fountain, and a cold wind picks up. Chris, near the head of the line, encourages the priest to keep his faith. He continues on, and reaches into the water. At the same time, Asteroth also plunges his hand in, causing the water to bubble and boil. The priest's hand is badly burned. Chris screams; Asteroth laughs.

As Micki and Ryan arrive, Asteroth speaks to the entire assembled group: "These are the works of Satan... a new age of darkness begins. One among you will be his disciple." He seems to point at Ryan as he says this. Ryan and Micki take off after Asteroth and chase him through the streets of Marie-Mere. They get separated, and Ryan follows him into an alley. There is no sign of Asteroth, but the book of Lucifer is just lying there. Ryan grabs it and yells for Micki, but Asteroth jumps out of hiding and knocks him out behind a stack of crates. Micki arrives at the alley but see nothing and runs the other way.

Asteroth speaks. "And then it came to pass that a new disciple came forth. And by his deeds Lucifer gained entrance into the flesh and spirit. This disciple was marked by the sign of the beast." Asteroth opens Ryan's shirt and scratches 666 into his skin with his talon-like nails.

And so ends part one. On the DVD set, "The Prophecies" is set up as one episode, with no "To be continued" cards or separate menu listing for the second episode. The other two-part episode in the series, "Quilt of Hathor," was set up in two different episodes on the DVD set, which is ironic since "Quilt" also aired on local television stations as a matinee movie.

Part two picks up seamlessly, with Micki in the center of town, and Ryan heading stiffly towards her. He tried to get the book, but Asteroth got away. Micki wants him to see a doctor; Ryan promises he is fine, he "just got knocked out for a moment." That moment, according to Micki, was over an hour. Micki wants to go check on Jack, but Ryan wants to see Sister Adele. Micki wins.

With a wave of his hand, Asteroth lets himself into a deceptively large crypt. He blows open burial tombs until he finds one with skeletal remains, then giggles as he plots for Lucifer's return. On the other end of the spectrum, Chris is praying fervently at the church. Burt wants her to eat something, but she is too scared. "Something horrible is happening."

Back at the hotel, Micki is poring over the research files she brought for Jack. According to the files, there are three books of Lucifer. One is safely stored at the Vatican; the other two are lost. It says the final prophecies need to be directed from a place of the dead. She is frustrated that Ryan has no interest in helping her; he just stares out the window. "Going through that junk is a waste of time," he deadpans, then reiterates his desire to see Sister Adele. Micki reminds him that she is not seeing anyone right now. "I'm not just anyone," he responds, then marches out of the room. "Fine, do it your way," Micki grumbles as she returns to her research.

Ryan is outside the convent, breathing heavily, and Asteroth, from his crypt, chants his new orders: "And the disciple went forth and slew the most holy so darkness could rise to envelop the earth." Ryan demands of the sisters that he sees Sister Adele, and throws a fit when he is refused. Adele hears this and says it is okay. Her fellow nuns are concerned that Ryan must speak to her in private. She leads him to her room, and he shuts the door. "I met him today," Ryan says ominously. "You are not his, no matter what he claims," she insists. "You were born in God's love." Ryan looks up at her, his eyes like a demon, and in a possessed voice says, "And you will die in Satan's hate." Adele clutches her crucifix and prays as Ryan chokes her. Nuns and priests are banging at the door, which is bolted shut. Asteroth, in his crypt, laughs. Ryan opens the door and announces Adele is dying for her faith. The priest and the nuns pray, but Adele is dead, crucifix still clutched in her hand.

Ryan, wholly Ryan for the moment, is back in the alley where Asteroth first cursed him. He cries over and over, "Why? Why?" then unbuttons his shirt and sees the etchings in his skin. He screams into the night.

Micki is so desperate that she decides to call in the last line of defense: Johnny. Johnny thinks she is overreacting to Ryan's little head injury, but Micki doesn't even know where Ryan is, and she certainly can't depend on him—too many weird things are happening. Johnny agrees to find his way out there. Micki has scarcely hung up with Johnny when there is a knock at her hotel door. But it's not Ryan, as Micki had hoped; it is the police, looking for Ryan. They take Micki in for questioning.

While Micki is with the police, answering for (or not) Ryan's crimes, Ryan is seeking forgiveness from a comatose Jack. "I killed Sister Adele, and I don't understand why," he cries into Jack's chest. "I need you, Jack." Asteroth begins his chanting, and Ryan is overcome by Satan. He tries to fight it, begs Jack to help him, but it is no use. His eyes turn demonic and nurses come running. Ryan jumps out the window and runs off into the night. He meets Asteroth at the crypt, where he "baptizes" Ryan in the name of Satan and sends him out to find a child to lead them.

Johnny's taxi delivers him to town in the middle of a candlelight processional for Sister Adele. The hotel manager informs Johnny that Micki was arrested, and he rushes to the station to bail her out. Since they didn't arrest her, there is no reason to keep her. But, the chief warns, if she doesn't convince Ryan to surrender, they will arrest her as an accomplice. The two race to the fountain, where a huge crowd of mourners have amassed.

Ryan is among the mourners, too, but only for a moment. He sees Chris and insists he knows where she can be healed, then takes the wheelchair from her father and rushes her away. Chris is scared, and downright terrified when Ryan informs her he is taking her to "fulfill Satan's promise." When Burt tries to stop him, Ryan throws him aside. "Don't be afraid," he reassures Chris—in his demon voice, "soon you shall be the one others fear." They arrive at the crypt, and Ryan carries Chris down the stairs and lays her on the makeshift altar. "Welcome this most unholy child."

The priest leads the mourners in prayer. As they pray, Jack wakes from his coma. "The child," he croaks. The nurses come in, but find Jack gone. Micki and Johnny rush in, and the nurses have no answer to where he is. Jack is in the alley, moving surprisingly well for a man who just spent the last few days in a coma. He finds Burt, barely conscious himself, only able to say Ryan took his daughter. He begs for Chris, then stops. He is dead. Micki and Johnny find Jack, but the happy reunion is short-lived. They must find Ryan and Chris. Micki recalls something about going to the place of the dead, and they rush off to the cemetery.

Asteroth has Ryan stand Chris up on the altar. She takes a few hesitant steps. Asteroth instructs her to praise Lucifer, and she refuses, so down she goes, her legs once again useless. "The deed will be done," Asteroth insists. "These scriptures prophecy a child. It will be fulfilled." He takes a discarded bone, fractures it into a stake, and asserts that since Chris

Fritz Weaver is all smiles on the set of "The Prophecies." Photo courtesy of John LeMay.

will not accept Lucifer willingly, she will die so that he will resurrect in her body. As Asteroth starts his chants, Chris pleads with Ryan, trying to reach him. These pleas trigger flashbacks to him and his brother playing ball, and he breaks through, throwing himself in front of the makeshift dagger. Jack, Micki, and Johnny burst in, and Ryan begs Chris to pray for him. He collapses, and a blue light engulfs his body. When it clears, Ryan has reverted to his ten year old self. Asteroth thinks this means the prophecy has been fulfilled and begs Lucifer to ascend into the child.

A blinding yellow light spreads across the sky at the fountain, and many mourners pray; others turn away. The light reaches down into the crypt, making Asteroth cower. "This child is Satan's!" he insists. Chris stands and looks directly into the light. Jack helps her down, then brings both children to Micki. Asteroth tries to grab the book of Lucifer, but the mythic light sets him on fire. He begs Lucifer to save him, but it is too late. Asteroth is fully engulfed in flames, his face red and bulging, eyes melting, and horns exposed. He then explodes.

The group heads to the shrine, Chris leading the way. They go straight to the priest, who immediately tries to exorcise the demons out of the writhing, spitting young Ryan. It doesn't seem to work, so Chris kneels and prays to the Blessed Mother, asking she return him to what is God's will, not Lucifer's. The silhouette of the Blessed Mother appears, the light grows brighter, and Ryan screams. The light disappears, returning the world to middle-of-the-night darkness, and Ryan is quiet. He wakes, and doesn't know where he is or who he is with. Jack introduces himself, and Ryan remembers him, a friend of his uncle's. Chris introduces herself, but he doesn't remember her. He asks "Uncle Jack" to take him back to his mom. Then he notices Micki crying. "Are you okay lady?" "It's me, Micki." Ryan has no knowledge of Micki as an adult, but he does have a cousin named Micki: "She's got red hair, too." Micki hugs him close.

Status: Chris, now an orphan, informs the priest that the Blessed Mother wants her to stay. He welcomes her. Micki, Jack, and Johnny return to the states with young Ryan. Jack couldn't figure out how to tell Mrs. Dallion about Ryan, so he lets it be a surprise. At first she doesn't recognize him, but Jack assures her this is Ryan. She decides not to ask questions; she just accepts a second chance at raising her son.

As for the book of Lucifer... I assume it burned up with the same fire that killed Asteroth. It wasn't technically a cursed object from Lewis' store, so I guess it can be destroyed.

* * *

"Frank said we hadn't tackled a religious exorcist thing. I said, 'Well, you're talking to a guy who was supposed to be a priest,'" says Tom McLoughlin, writer/director of the epic farewell to Ryan, "The Prophecies." "I had every intention of being a priest. When I saw *The Exorcist* in the theaters, it changed my life. I went back so many times to see it and probably studied it more than any other movie. Every aspect of it: the sound design, the photography, the voices, the sounds of the beast... there are so many little tricks and things they did with that movie. The bottom line is that it sent people to church, even people who weren't religious! So, when Frank asked if I wanted to do something with an *Exorcist* theme, I said yes.

"But then it was like, 'What can I feed off?' There are so many stories of these little girls who saw the Virgin Mary. I thought that could be interesting, if she [Sister Adele] became a nun—which many of them did—and if there was a way that somehow she is the religious aspect of this thing. I had this fascination with the archangels that were banished from heaven with Lucifer. There was one called Asteroth. What if the quickest way to 'win' was to destroy the faith of whatever he is battling? If you look at Catholicism versus devils and demons, if you can destroy the faith of the faithful, you have a much better chance of bringing them over to the other side.

"So, the whole idea was to have this Asteroth character create a scenario where this nun is going to be killed and he needed someone to do it. So, there is another girl who is going to be the next 'religious figure' and she gets involved with Ryan. Instead of killing Ryan, we brought him back to some traumatic event in his childhood that changed everything: the death of his brother. My mother was a twin. Her twin died, and she didn't, so there was always this sense of a missing element. So, in this episode, Ryan felt like he was never complete."

I am not a religious person. I never really understood the idea of Ryan reverting to his childhood self. I asked McLoughlin if this was related to some sort of religious story or iconography. He said it wasn't; it was just from his "fevered imagination."

"Somehow, in saving him," he said, "we brought him back to a place where he was the most innocent. To be able to deliver him back to his mother, that was important to me. I thought about the death of his brother and how that wove in with his relationship with his mother... what could change that? Nothing short of a miracle! So, this dark situation would have some kind of positive spin. What if something really horrible solved something? Was it bad that he went back? If a helpless priest and a nun are actually killed by our lead, how the hell is he going to get out of that? So, it needed to be very supernatural. It had *The Exorcist* aspect to it, but not the way [an exorcism] could have been interpreted. Frank was absolutely fine with it."

"I didn't get that one," admits Steve Monarque. "What's going on here? Is he actually metamorphosing into a boy again? We all joked about that kind of stuff. While we are doing it, it's all bizarre to us. As actors, you have to act like it is happening—that's the challenge, right?"

Production used Quebec City as a stand-in for France in this episode, which meant many of the guest stars were French-Canadian. "I hope they were speaking more Parisian-French than Canadian-French. Still, to this day, I don't know! I was told yes, but I don't know; to me they sound the same," worries McLoughlin.

Friday the 13th was the first film crew to shoot at the Ursuline Convent of Quebec City. Built in 1639, it is the oldest convent in North America. Production designer Stephen Roloff remembers touring the buildings with his location manager and the convent's Mother Superior. "She asked me about the story line. She was a sweet, tiny elder, and when I gently told her that one of our characters becomes possessed by a demon and kills a nun, she got very concerned. Then I said that the Virgin Mary shows up and performs a miracle, cleansing the demon and turning the possessed man back into an innocent child. All was well with the world, and we where welcome to film there."

"'The Prophecies' was a really good double-episode, but in a lot of ways, I think we swung away from what we were doing," laments Jim Henshaw. "We just got tied up with making sure Ryan got a great exit. Some of the thematic stuff in there I just don't think worked. I think we overdid it. I don't think we got any negative reactions from it, in terms of church people, but it was just that kind of thing where we were trying so hard to make a special show for Ryan that we kind of got away from what we did best."

"Demon Hunter"

Written by: Jim Henshaw
Directed by: Armand Mastroianni
Original airdate: October 2, 1989
Cursed antique: Ceremonial dagger

11:00 p.m. It's a full moon and the Cassidy family is on the hunt in a tricked-out (for 1989) Mystery Machine. Father Faron (Dale Wilson) is at the wheel; daughter Bonnie (Allison Mang) is tracking their subject on a green and black computer screen. Sons Travis and Vance (David Stratton and David Orth) are on opposite ends of a field, following Bonnie's directions. She insists that the beast is heading right for Travis, is right on top of him. Travis sees nothing, but his tracking device is going haywire. He starts to run, and suddenly, the beast is upon him, a hideous thing that looks like the Predator with chicken feet. The creature impales Travis on the handle of farming equipment, leaving him for Bonnie, Faron, and Vance to find.

11:06 p.m. Jack acts like he is nervous because the power keeps browning out, but really, he is nervous about the papers Micki is making him sign, giving him Ryan's share of Curious Goods. "Ryan will always be a part of my life, no matter what happens," she assures him. "But should anything happen to me, I'd like the store to be in good hands." They toast to their new, legal partnership, then Jack remembers a package that arrived earlier. It is from a museum, in response to one of the mailers. No one at the museum purchased anything from Lewis, but the enclosed dagger was donated anonymously in Lewis' name about a month ago, with no return address. Jack recognizes it as an Enochian dagger, a demonolater's sacrificial knife.

Jack explains. Demonolaters worship demons. They perform a human sacrifice in a chamber that has been specially created for necromancy and can raise up any demon straight from hell. Whoever performs the sacrifice becomes the caller, and can summon any demon he needs. They sign a pact, setting up the demon's tasks (who the demon is to kill). The demon is paid in souls. Jack calls demonolaters the most "dangerous people alive." The pair take the dagger into the vault, but while in there, the power goes out again. Jack accidentally cuts himself on the dagger. Micki examines his palm with a flashlight and notices that the blood spilled on the vault floor has been absorbed into the floor and disappears without so much as a stain.

The Cassidy family takes Travis back to the van. Faron is more determined than ever to find the beast and kill it. Bonnie is tracking some negative energy coming from town, but Faron won't go in blind. While she works on getting a fix on the spot, he and Vance explore a nearby barn.

Through a series of flashbacks, we learn Faron's true motives behind the hunt. Bonnie was kidnapped by a demon-conjuring cult and the boys go in, guns blazing, to rescue her. Bonnie tries to stab her father with the dagger, but when she realizes who it is she is attacking, she stops and sobs into his arms. While Travis protects Bonnie, Faron and Vance go Rambo on the cult and open fire. Later, with Bonnie safe, she apologizes to her father because she couldn't do anything to stop the cult, and it's not over. She saw the cult remove the heart from their sacrifice and feed it to the beast that climbed directly out of hell. "He is worse than any of them," she sobs. "You have to stop him! The devil is alive!"

11:18 p.m. Johnny is putting together a model ship! He gets a call from Micki. Something weird is going on, but before she can give any specifics, the power goes out again. Johnny rushes to the store and is rather annoyed when he is greeted with a minor inconvenience, rather than the emergency he expected. They explain what is happening and Jack reads from a grimoire that says blood will be drawn to stone in a place built to accept blood. Jack wipes more blood on the ground, and Johnny's annoyance fades with the blood. Jack uses a hammer to knock on the vault floor until he finds a hollow spot. With Johnny's help, they crowbar up an enormous stone plate of flooring. Beneath is a staircase and a hideous stench. (Curious Goods: the gift that keeps on giving.)

They descend and we see this was the same place Bonnie was being kept when Faron rescued her. Jack recognizes it only as a church of necromancy, a place where demons are raised from hell. A human skeleton hangs on the wall, runes and sigils are carved into the walls, and a tunnel joins with a bunch of other tunnels that smells like it connects with the sewers, meaning people could have been in here while they lived upstairs.

In the center of the "church" is a huge hole in the floor, filled with blood. This is where demons are raised. Johnny doesn't believe it, but Jack finds one of the demon contracts: reverse Latin text, runic symbols, and a sigil—the signature of the demon itself. It fits with everything Jack has read about demon lore; it fits with every horror movie Johnny has ever seen.

Jack comes to a very interesting conclusion at this point. He never understood why Lewis would build the vault in the store, which I never thought about before—he doesn't need a "safe" place to store the cursed objects. But knowing about the temple below, Jack figures it out: the vault could keep any unwanted or uncontrolled hellspawn there until they could be sent back. A beast could never get out of vault unless it was led out. Jack says the only way to break a contract is if the caller is killed with the knife used in the sacrifice. Johnny still doesn't buy it, but he is getting closer when Micki finds blood dripping down the walls. Turns out there is blood all over the place, seemingly fresh blood. Jack leaves Johnny in the chamber while he and Micki go upstairs to pour over the contracts he found. Johnny is not happy about this.

Meanwhile, the Cassidy boys are tracking the beast through a huge barn. The tracker starts going nuts, and the demon comes up through the floor and grabs Vance. Faron shoots at it, but only succeeds in causing Vance to drop through to the bottom floor. The demon tears him. Faron tries stabbing the beast with a little, ineffectual tool, and the demon tosses the father outside. Bonnie hears all this from the van and drives up. She sees the beast, but rather than going after it, she goes to help her family.

11:32 p.m. Bonnie has figured out that the demon's time is running out, and he's going back to where he came from. She feels bad and is convinced her father would have been better off leaving her with the cult—at least he would still have Vance and Travis. She wants to end this hunt, but dad refuses.

Micki finds a contract with today's date, but the contracts were written years ago. Jack explains that demonic contracts are dated when it becomes due. And tonight is the full moon, which is the only time a demon can rise or return. "The demon is coming here," Jack asserts, "before the contract expires at midnight." Jack starts researching the demon's sigil, hoping to find something to render it powerless.

Down in the chamber, Johnny is creeped out by the bloody walls. He hears pained wails and looks in the hole in the floor. It is filled with churning blood, and he sees faces in the blood. Jack and Micki return, and Jack explains that those are the souls that the demon Ahriman collected. According to the contract, the cult members were being killed, and Ahriman was called to avenge them. If he kills the attackers—those listed in the contract—by midnight, the cult will come back to life. Johnny

An aerial view of Curious Goods. Photo courtesy of Armand Mastroianni.

suggests something in the vault might kill it, but Micki suggests it might be the vault itself. "If it kept demons from getting out, maybe it can keep demons from getting in." The other way around this is that the caller must be coming back, too, and the caller is human—they know how to stop a human. The caller's symbol is on the contract, and that same symbol will appear on the caller's body.

A gun cocks, and the trio turns around. Faron is there. Bonnie joins her father after setting TNT charges throughout the tunnel system. Faron thinks that Micki, Jack, and Johnny are the ones who called the demon, and Bonnie wants to kill them immediately. Faron doesn't want the beast to know they are here—there will be plenty of time to kill them after they kill the beast. Jack identifies Faron as the one who was killing off the cult members and tries to convince him that they are on the same side. Faron doesn't want to hear it and he and Bonnie seal them into the chamber. Johnny gets Jack to help him pry up the plate so they can get into the vault. Johnny still wants to use something in the vault to take care of the Cassidys, and Jack still refuses.

Bonnie does a sweep upstairs while her dad patrols the front of the store. She goes into Micki's bedroom and opens the window for a little fresh air.

11:48 p.m. Johnny and Jack finally get the plate up and they make it into the vault. Johnny finds the demonolater knife and holds onto it against Jack's wishes. "No caller is going to get by those two—unless he is one of them," Johnny says, referring to the Cassidys. Of course, they don't know which one it is. "Let's hope we get lucky the first time."

The demon comes into Micki's room through the open window. Bonnie reveals a sigil scarred into her chest and smiles at the beast. She is the caller. Bonnie goes downstairs while her father goes up, instructing her to check on their captives. Faron's tracker is going bug-nutty, and the demon jumps out of Micki's room. Faron fills him with bullets. It doesn't kill it, but it does knock the beast out the window. The beast survives the fall, of course. The tunnels blow and the explosion knocks Faron back.

Johnny leaves the vault, but Jack refuses to let him take the knife with him. He jumps on Bonnie, waiting just outside. She shoots but misses, and Micki grabs a spare gun on the floor. "Freeze!" she yells, and Bonnie does. Johnny holds her back, and Micki sees the sigil on Bonnie's chest. Faron joins them downstairs, and they hear the demon following. Jack herds everyone into the vault, including Bonnie. The beast tries to get in, but it can't. Jack hints to Faron that Bonnie can stop all of this, and Micki turns over the gun as a sign of solidarity. Bonnie is still trying to convince her father to kill them. But finally, she drops the act and admits she wasn't kidnapped. She unleashed the beast when her father started wiping out cult cells and kept it one step behind him until the time was right. "She used that thing to keep you busy until she could turn it on you," Jack explains. Johnny tries to stab her, but Faron stops him. Bonnie opens the vault and tells the demon the path is clear for it. Faron throws a grenade at the beast and it drops through the floor, back into the cavern. Johnny is down there, and is stuck trying to fend off the slimy beast. Bonnie tries to get down there, but is stopped by her father, who fights her. Suddenly the beast lets out a dying cry and Bonnie collapses against her father. He stabbed her with the knife. In the cavern, the demon drops Johnny and is pulled back to the depths of hell.

Status: Jack seals up the hole to hell with a chunk of cement and protection runes. Micki is glad they found this place; they were running out of room in the vault (a complaint we have heard since, like, day three). Johnny finds it fitting that the dagger would be the first item placed in this new vault annex.

* * *

I have absolutely no memories of "Demon Hunter." I didn't even remember the episode. While preparing for my interview with director Armand Mastroianni, I saw this episode on the list and could not place it. Reading the blurb did not help. It drove me crazy. Was it possible that I had never seen this episode? No. Not possible. It was more likely that I suffered a severe injury and lost a chunk of memories. So, I finally sat down to watch the episode. Once it was on, I remembered it—and I figured out why I couldn't remember it.

It wasn't memorable. This episode feels like two very different episodes that don't merge until the end. It is half *Predator*, half *Night of the Demons*. Ironically, after watching the episode, I had one very specific memory of the episode: Jack's closing quote. "If of the many truths you select one and follow it blindly, it will become a falsehood and you a fanatic." I always liked that quote.

Director Armand Mastroianni agrees that it wasn't particularly memorable. "'Demon Hunter' was more of a comic book, popcorn-type movie. It was an action, monster-type film. It was fun to make, but it wasn't particularly memorable. We had that one note: let's make a monster film. There was no subtext going on there. It reminded me a lot of those 1950s and 1960s monster movies. But it was fun. It was an experience for me."

Actress Alli Mang, who played Bonnie, had fun, as well. "Armand made sure that everyone had a great time. He gave us room to do our work and his utter passion for the project was palpable! Talk about a great leader and director." Mang shares a favorite memory from one of the long nights on set. "We were shooting in the van and I was inputting stats into the computer. We had been shooting all night and everyone was exhausted. The van was *so* hot and it was the last shot of the day. When Armand yelled 'Action,' I was busy inputting data, thinking I was really making it look real. We did the scene and then Armand yelled 'Cut. Great take everyone—Allison, what are you writing? A term paper for University?'"

"Alli was the star of this show," enthuses Dale Wilson, who played Faron. "My job was to keep the tension up and move it to its surprising end without taking any of the focus away from our lovely and seemingly innocent star."

"Demon Hunter" was a special effects-heavy episode. "Special effects we didn't have," Mastroianni says. "We had different prosthetic pieces for it, feet and hands. There was a guy with sticks doing that. It was all about cleverly positioning the camera so it looked like the real thing." Though Mang didn't have any big stunts, she does remember working with the prop guns. "The gun was much heavier than I expected. Walking up and down the stairs and running with that weighty item in my arms was quite the workout."

"Crippled Inside"

Written by: Brian Helgeland
Directed by: Timothy Bond
Original airdate: October 9, 1989
Cursed antique: Wheelchair

High schoolers Rachel and Marcus (Stephanie Morgenstern and Greg Spottiswood) are on a first date, taking a walk through the park before a concert. They race to a secret spot in the woods, where she says she wants to be a figure skater; he just wants to be loved. They kiss, and Rachel pulls away, nervous because he is so popular, he could have any girl he wants. To prove he wants her, he pulls her close and starts kissing her neck, then starts pulling down her shirt. Rachel pulls away and things go real bad, real quick. He grabs her forcefully and starts to fondle her while three other schoolmates show up. Marcus passes her around to Peter, Ed, and Scott (Dean McDermott, Andrew Simms, and Richard Chevolleau), who each kiss and fondle her before tossing her to the next boy. When she gets to Scott, he decides he doesn't want to participate—but he doesn't save Rachel, either. The other three boys take her back, and Ed and Peter hold her down while Marcus unzips and takes out a knife. Scott protests: "This isn't how you said it would be. She doesn't want to!" "Then we make her want to," Marcus said, moving the knife close to Rachel's face. He tries to mount her, but she kicks him with those strong skater legs and breaks free.

Rachel runs, screaming through the park, the boys chasing after her. She gets to the road and desperately waves down a car, but the car doesn't see her in time and hits her. The boys see this happen from a short distance and scatter.

Now a quadriplegic, Rachel is confined to a motorized wheelchair she controls with her chin. She is horribly depressed and hardly leaves the house. Her mom, Judith (Diana Leblanc), convinces her to take a walk, and they come upon a yard sale. Rachel is self conscious, but an old man wheels over an antique wheelchair to her. "Pretty, isn't it?" he asks. He tells her he was once like her, trapped in his own body, but it is a special chair. It healed him; it can likely heal her. This piques Rachel's interest and she asks her mom if she can have it. Judith thinks it looks rickety, and worries that Rachel will hurt herself (how much more hurt could she really get?) but the smile on Rachel's face makes it easy to give in. The old man insists on gifting it to the young woman.

Johnny is annoyed that they are working on a Sunday. They got two good leads, for an umbrella and a wheelchair. He doesn't understand why they don't just go pick up the items on Monday. "Johnny, you've got to start taking this seriously," Micki tells him. "The objects are extremely dangerous. This isn't a game."

They head out, and return with the umbrella and a new address to follow up on for the wheelchair. There is a telegram waiting for Micki at Curious Goods: Jack is in England and has tracked down the shard of Medusa, but needs Micki's help. She is excited and rushes to pack. Johnny is nervous that he is left to track down the wheelchair on his own, but it is really Micki who should be nervous.

Johnny goes to check up on the new address for the wheelchair, the yard sale house. The woman he speaks to says they got rid of it after her father recovered from his stroke. The girl must live nearby, because her mother walked over to pick it up.

Judith brings the wheelchair into Rachel's room, setting it by the window. She helps her daughter into it, and is glad to see her smile. At her daughter's request, Judith leaves her alone, but mentions she is working late. It doesn't matter; Rachel is already in her own world, a million miles away. Rachel flashes back to that horrible night, and to the old man's words to her. Suddenly her fingers and toes twitch, and she "separates" from her body, leaving a paralyzed shell staring out the window. Excited, she runs out of the room.

It is night when Marcus drives his crew to school and sends Peter in to steal the answers to the chemistry test. The school is creepy when it is dark and empty, so every little sound makes him jump. But one noise justifies the reaction: Rachel. Walking Rachel. She just wants a confession, wants him to tell the police what he and his friends did to her. Peter, scared, backs into a shelf of chemicals, which tips over on him. His skin bubbles and burns as acid eats away at him gruesomely. Rachel runs, scared. The guys, still outside, hear Peter's tortured cries and rush in to find him a gooey, melted puddle on the floor, more sludge than human. Marcus urges the guys to get out of there—clearly there is nothing they can do for him.

The old man stops Rachel as she is running from the school. "You did the right thing," he assures her. "The chair will start to heal you now." She smiles and runs down the street, disappearing. She reappears in her room and rejoins her paralyzed self. Her fingers start to twitch. Judith is at the door with dinner, and she drops the tray when she sees her daughter's fingers twitch. "I can feel my fingers!" Rachel cries excitedly as the women weep with joy.

Mom wants Rachel to go back to the doctor, but Rachel flat-out refuses. All the doctors want to do is poke and prod her, and she is sick of it. Doctors told her she would never regain feeling below her neck, to get used to a wheelchair, but now all that has changed. "I have devoted every waking moment to you, without a dime from your father. If there is a chance of recovery—"

The argument is interrupted by a knock at the door. Johnny is there, having driven around the neighborhood and seeing the wheelchair ramp out front. He makes his spiel about buying it back, but Judith politely declines. Rachel hears all this from upstairs, and watches Johnny get back into the car. When her mom comes back in, she apologizes for bringing her dad into this and requests to be transferred into her new old chair. "It's nice to feel the sun on my hands."

After striking out at the Horn residence, Johnny heads to the local high school. He stops a couple to ask about Rachel, and Scott overhears. He claims he doesn't know her. The other students are all under the impression that Rachel was just in some kind of accident, and suggests they talk to the guys in 4B, they had class with her. Of course, one of those guys dissolved himself in the chem lab last night, so there is one less guy to talk to.

Johnny returns to the car and is surprised when Scott jumps into the passenger seat. He admits that a year ago, some guys from his class tried to rape Rachel. He swears he didn't hurt her—he liked her. "I never should have listened to Marcus when he said she'd party with all of us," he laments. (Here's a tip: if a male friend says a girl is going to "party with all of us," it is a trap. Bad shit will go down, guaranteed.) Scott knows it is Rachel, somehow getting her revenge on them—Peter said her name as he died. Johnny has no sympathy for him: "Maybe you are getting what you deserve." Scott freaks out, swearing he didn't touch her, and Johnny calms him down. He gives him his card and asks where he can find the other guys.

Scott is walking home when Marcus drives by, inviting him to come watch him on his "date" tonight. Scott says no, and Marcus wonders what is wrong with him. Scott is upset about Peter's death, and shocked that he isn't. (Sociopaths are generally not upset by petty things like a friend's gruesome death.) Scott thinks that Rachel finally talked, and he thinks they should turn themselves in. Marcus threatens to kill him if he tells anyone—then invites him to a party. You know, to show there are no hard feelings.

That night, Ed is with a cute girl on an apartment building roof, looking at the stars and smooching while they are supposed to be studying.

The door opens, and Ed thinks it is Marcus, which freaks the girl out. "I'm not hanging around if that creep is here," she says and runs inside, locking the door behind her. The intruder reveals herself—of course it is Rachel. She taunts him, asks if he still wants to party. "Or can't you do it without your friends?" she mocks. "Peter couldn't." It finally clicks with Ed. She killed Peter. Rachel moves towards Ed, who is blathering the typical stuff one says in the face of a revenge killing: we never meant for you to get hurt. "You should have thought of that before you tried to rape me," she spits. Ed stumbles backwards, trips, and falls off the building.

Johnny happens to be in the neighborhood and races up to the roof, just in time to see Rachel fade away. When she returns to her body, she can now lift her hands and move her arms. She cries joyously for her mother. Outside, the old man hears her excitement and smiles.

It has been a good day, and Rachel reads in bed a bit before going to sleep. Downstairs, someone jimmies open a window and creeps into the house. She calls for her mom, who evidently isn't home, and throws herself out of bed in a desperate attempt to get into her wheelchair. Before she can make it, she is confronted by Marcus. "I'm still waiting for my goodnight kiss." Johnny is arriving at the house at this time, and when he hears Rachel scream, he breaks in.

Marcus gets Rachel back on the bed, and Johnny bursts in, throwing him against a wall. He takes Marcus' own knife to his throat, and asks "how bad do you want it?" Marcus is clearly scared shitless, and Johnny lets him go. He makes sure Rachel is okay before watching Marcus leave the property. I understand why you can't tell the cops about a wheelchair that heals supernaturally, but why didn't Johnny call the cops on Marcus? Breaking and entering, attempted rape, assault with a deadly weapon… all non-supernatural crimes, all witnessed by Johnny, and all felonies.

Johnny returns to Rachel's room and takes the wheelchair. She screams, begs him not to take it. "Animals like that don't stop until they are dead," she reasons. But Johnny insists that killing is wrong. She may get her body back, but she will lose her soul, even if she is killing people who deserve it. Johnny takes the wheelchair anyway—until he gets outside and sees the mysterious old man. The man reasons with him, pointing out that the boy will return, she won't be able to run, and he doesn't think Johnny will agree to be her bodyguard. "You can't protect people's souls for them. The boys made their choice; she made hers." Johnny actually relents and takes the chair back to Rachel. I have to say, I kind of can't blame Johnny for this one. He has done a lot of stupid things, but this time, the boys deserve what they get. The old man helps get Rachel in the chair and watches her step out of herself. Then he disappears. Actually, literally, disappears.

Scott goes to Curious Goods. No one is there, so he just lets himself in. Rachel comes in, and she takes a different approach with him: she seduces him. With sweet words and an understanding that he did nothing wrong, she tells him she wants her first time to be with him, right then and there. She lays him down on the floor of Curious Goods and loops his belt around a display case, holding him in place. With him out of commission, Rachel's attitude changes. She puts a foot on his chest, takes out Marcus' knife, and asks how it feels to be flat on his back, helpless. "You just watched, you are worse than the others." She cuts down a chandelier, which lands on Scott's face, crushing and electrocuting him. Johnny comes in, again just in time to see Rachel disappear.

When Rachel returns to her body, her mother is sitting on her bed. Neither notices the other, until Judith sees her daughter has full use of her arms. Rachel asks about the old man, then admits it is the chair that is making her better, by helping her "go after the boys who put me here." This rolls off Judith's back when Rachel announces she can feel her legs and manages to stand up. It is only a few seconds before she collapses, and Judith finally understands what is going on. She drags her daughter away from the chair, but Rachel anchors herself and pulls out her knife. Judith bites her daughter's hand, causing her to drop the weapon.

The mother-daughter fight is interrupted by Marcus, who has returned to finish ruining Rachel's life. He comes out of hiding and knocks Judith out before following Rachel, who crawls away and desperately tries to pull herself into the chair. He throws her across the room and grabs her by the hair, and she sprays hairspray in his face. This is the break she needs to get back into the chair. He wheels her to the top of the stairs, but she comes out of her body and strangles him with the phone cord. She returns to her body, in the chair as Johnny rushes into the house. Rachel is confused: she can't move her legs, and Marcus was the last one. But Marcus isn't dead; he was just briefly knocked unconscious. (Something tells me he has had a lot of experience with breath play and erotic asphyxiation.)

Marcus jumps up and pushes Rachel down the stairs. She grabs him and takes him down with her. Both end up in a crumpled heap of corpses at the bottom of the stairs. Judith doesn't question why Johnny is standing there, just takes comfort in his arms as she weeps over her dead daughter.

Status: The wheelchair is returned to Curious Goods. The old man pays Johnny one last visit at the store, begging him to let him buy it back, to use it to help cure handicapped people. Johnny chases him out with an axe, then has one of my favorite "idiot Johnny" moments: he turns the axe on the wheelchair, and pounds and pounds on the wicker chair. The axe doesn't even make a dent.

Mentioned but not explored: The umbrella.

*   *   *

I've always had a fascination with rape/revenge films: *I Spit on Your Grave* (1978), *They Call her One-Eye* (1973), *The Last House on the Left* (1972), *Irreversible* (2002). I can't help but wonder if it stems from "Crippled Inside." I saw this episode of *Friday the 13th* well before I saw any of those films. Like with those aforementioned movies, it is hard to view Rachel as a villain. The boys deserve what they get. At worst, you could call Rachel a vigilante.

I was never really sure what was going on with the mysterious old man. He is around long enough to help Rachel harness the curse, then he just disappears. Is he the ghost of the former owner? Does he "come with" the chair? I sense that the original script probably had a little more detail as to what is going on with the old man, but they never made it into the episode. Yes, I expect more from an Oscar-winning screenwriter (Helgeland won for his script for *L.A. Confidential*), even if this was one of his first scripts. Requests for an interview with Helgeland went unanswered.

"I enjoyed 'Crippled Inside' because of the wonderful actress Stephanie Morgenstern," says director Tim Bond. "She was impressively courageous. I enjoyed working out the technique where she would leave her body in the wheelchair and depart to wreak havoc. It was all done in-camera and with film-based opticals. With the camera locked off, I rolled a minute or so on Stephanie in the wheelchair and then had her get out of the chair and walk out of frame with menace. Optically, from the moment she got out of the chair we matched that frame and printed the shot both forwards and backwards, one superimposed on the other. So, when she got up out of the chair she appeared to leave herself behind."

Upon viewing this episode as an adult, there is too much in this episode that doesn't make sense. Who is that old man? Why wouldn't Rachel turn in her attackers? Why is Marcus such a foolish, stupid douche bag? I will say that, for all its faults, "Crippled Inside" taught me a lesson early on about going off alone with men. As a competitive figure skater myself, I identified with Rachel and could imagine the hell that would come with losing the use of my legs.

"Stick it in Your Ear"

Written by: Jon Ezrine
Directed by: Douglas Jackson
Original airdate: October 16, 1989
Cursed antique: Hearing aide

Phil and Adam (Chas Lawther and Wayne Best) have a low-rent mentalist act that they take to bars and lounges. It is basic stuff: Adam is the "face," sitting up on stage, blindfolded, while Phil goes into the audience, feeding him cues. Their act hits a snag when Adam can't hear the cues, and Phil insists he go to the doctor. He goes, begrudgingly, but refuses a hearing aid: "I'll look like a dork!" The doc leaves him to peruse the selection while he takes a call. Adam is drawn to a soft throbbing sound coming from a drawer, and he discovers an antique hearing aid, one of the first cordless models ever made. The doctor discourages him from taking it; naturally Adam slips it into his pocket.

The next show is a big one: Randi (Elizabeth Edwards), the talent coordinator from *The Stan Elliott Show* is in the audience. Adam wears the hearing aid, but is soon overwhelmed when he hears the thoughts of everyone in the room. His head aching and his mind reeling, Adam stands and rips off the blindfold. A man in the crowd heckles him, and suddenly everything becomes clear. Adam accuses the heckler of murdering his cousin over a business deal gone wrong, and the heckler pulls a gun—the same gun he shot his cousin with. Security tackles the heckler and Adam reads Randi's mind: she is impressed with him and wants to grab drinks. The pain in Adam's head is too much for him and he runs out of the club. His neck and ear are covered with pulsating, oozing pustules that are slowly growing. He rushes straight back to the doctor—who is on the phone at the time.

The doctor is on with Jack. He and Micki had gone to an estate sale and bought back five of six items purchased from Lewis. The sixth, the hearing aid, Jack assumes is buried with the deceased. The story rings familiar with Johnny, who read a tabloid article about that same man whose head exploded while in the doctor's office. So, Jack gives the doctor a call.

The call is interrupted when Adam races in, begging for help. He grabs the doctor and all those thoughts from the audience are transferred into the doctor's head—along with the gross skin condition.

Now that he knows how it works, a newly cocksure Adam heads over to Randi's house with some champagne, and they end up in bed together. Come morning, Randi offers two important bits of information to Adam: Stan Elliott (Christopher Bondy) wants him for the show tonight; and her dream is to run the show. Adam wastes no time in calling Phil and breaking up with him.

Since their phone call was so rudely interrupted, Jack, Micki, and Johnny head over to the doctor's office, and find him dead. They divvy up his patient list. Jack gets Adam, who crashes with Phil, but by the time he visits the apartment, the act has been dissolved. Phil is bitter and tells Jack where he can find his former partner.

Micki and Johnny show up to *The Stan Elliott Show* that night. Adam outs an audience member as wanting to propose to his girlfriend. It's TV gold. After the show, Randi is excited to inform Adam that Stan wants him back the next night. Adam will come back as often as Stan wants, provided Randi is running the show. Less excited is Phil, who is waiting for Adam in his dressing room with drunken accusations of Adam's fraud. Micki also stops by to congratulate Adam on a terrific show. While she is there, she thinks about the hearing aid. It is a ruse to lure Adam after her, and he takes it.

On the street, Adam follows Micki on foot while Johnny keeps tabs on them from the car. Bad idea, Johnny: pedestrians get in the way and he loses track of Micki. Micki isn't making the best choices, either: she turns off the main street and heads down an alley. This is the chance Adam was waiting for and he attacks, wrestling her into a pile of garbage and attempting to overload her head with the thoughts he picked up. Johnny finally gets his shit together and shows up, scaring Adam away. Adam still needs a release, so he goes straight to the apartment he shared with Phil and kills him. Randi catches him, but she proves to be somewhat morally ambiguous. After all, she did get the producing gig because of Adam. He promises her anything she ever wanted, and she relaxes. This could work.... .

Adam returns to *The Stan Elliott Show*. He is being considered for his own show, and tells Randi to cancel the other guests, a move that pisses off Stan. Spurred on by the idea of running her own show from the ground up, Randi is eager to prove her usefulness to Adam. When Jack, Micki, and Johnny show up at the show (their game plan: to overwhelm

Adam with thoughts), she locks them in Adam's dressing room. When the show breaks for commercials, Adam is ready for his next victim. Randi assures him she has "people" for him in his dressing room, but Adam is enraged—he specifically requested just one person. He has no time to be picky, and kills Randi.

Jack picks the lock on the door and they discover Randi, dead on the hallway floor. They rush into the audience, where Adam is requesting a new challenge. No one volunteers, so Jack steps up and challenges Adam to remove his hearing aid. Adam protests: "I need it to hear."

"I won't be saying anything," Jack assures him.

But Adam continues to protest, and Jack accuses him of using the hearing aid to take prompts from a plant in the audience. The audience becomes wary, and their minds race with suspicions. Adam is overwhelmed, his face and neck swollen with oozing boils and the pain overpowers him. With blood pouring from his ears, Adam rips out the hearing aid, but no one messes with the devil like that. He still dies, right there on stage, in a pool of blood.

Status: Antique acquired and vaulted.

* * *

"Stick it in Your Ear" holds a special significance to me: it was the first episode of *Friday the 13th: The Series* I ever saw. I was about ten years old and flipping through the TV channels Saturday morning. This was 1990, so there were no on-screen guides and less than a hundred channels to surf through. I came across a program that featured a man screaming in pain with oozing pustules throbbing over his neck, getting worse by the second. I was immediately entranced and remained glued to the TV for the remaining twenty minutes. After that, *Friday the 13th* became obsessive viewing for me—although the thought of wearing a used hearing aid disgusts me far more than the actual pustules.

Wayne Best, who starred as Adam Cole, had a similarly formative experience with his own young daughter and this particular episode. "Her grandmother taped the episode, and my daughter accidentally watched it. It scared her!" The makeup crew made a life-sized cast of his head for some of the more intense pustule scenes, and he was given the dummy head as a sort of parting gift. Wayne was able to use the dummy, something that his daughter used as a plaything, putting makeup and eyelashes on, to explain that it wasn't really Daddy's head that blew up. Though it may have been of comfort to his daughter, it nearly gave Wayne a heart attack. "I threw it in the car and had to go straight to the airport. When I came back a few days later, I had forgotten about it and initially thought someone had crawled into my car!"

The extensive prosthetic work for this episode wasn't too bad. "It added a couple extra hours in the morning, but most of the prosthetic shots were all insert shots," Wayne explains. "It was irritating having the hearing aid in my ear," he says, noting that it occasionally fell out during filming.

A point of honor with Wayne is that he does all his own stunts, or at least the ones the studio would let him do. That includes his attack on Robey in the alley. "I got to know her well on this episode. It was a late summer night [when we shot that scene] and was quite cool. We talked about Shakespeare that night." He didn't really get to work with the gentlemen much. "Working on a TV show can be a real grind, so if you don't have a scene directly with someone, you don't often see them."

"Bad Penny"

Written by: Marilyn Anderson & Billy Riback
Directed by: William Fruet
Original airdate: October 30, 1989
Cursed antique: The coin of Ziocles

We open on the last few scenes of "Tales I Live, Heads You Die," just in case you forgot what happened: the cult building crashing down and Ryan dropping the coin of Ziocles as they rush to safety; then the cult member's hand reaching weakly for the coin before it drops dead.

Now, a bulldozer is cleaning out that very same wreckage, and scoops up a skeleton and the coin. The construction workers decide not to report the body, as it would cause the project to be shut down. They dump the skeleton with the rest of the debris, but the coin slips to the ground.

That night, a pair of cops, Briggs and Goreman (John Bourgeois and Ed Setrakian), arrive at the construction site to wait for a gangster named Koslow (John Tench). Goreman and Briggs are dirty cops and are expecting a briefcase full of cash in exchange for one filled with drugs (presumably stolen from police raids). However, Koslow takes the drugs and leaves them with an empty case.

A shootout ensues, and Koslow kills Briggs. Goreman shoots Koslow in the leg, then approaches, ready to kill him execution-style. Koslow doesn't believe he would shoot in cold blood; he's a cop. Goreman picks up a discarded coin—one with a ram's head on it—and tells Koslow he will flip for it. The coin does what it does: flips, lands, glows, zaps. Koslow is dead, a ram branded into his forehead. Goreman is intrigued and pockets the coin.

Back at the station, Goreman gives his statement, calling it a stakeout gone bad. The desk sergeant accepts the story as truth but warns him that homicide will probably want to talk to Goreman about the brand on Koslow's forehead. They have a few unsolved cases with the same M.O., including the journalist Hewitt, who wrote about the symbol having to do with witchcraft.

Goreman sneaks into the file room and pulls Hewitt's case, reading up on the coin, which alludes to the coin killing and raising the dead. Intrigued, Goreman finds Briggs' corpse in the morgue and gives it a try. It works: Briggs comes back to life. They work out a plan to bring Koslow back to life so they can make him tell them where the money is hidden. First, they have to kill someone else, and Goreman settles on Rita, the hooker who tipped them off to Koslow.

Johnny is missing his dad. They always used to go fishing this time of year, and he is having a hard time without him. Micki and Jack offer him words of advice and promises that they will always be there for him. They leave Johnny to watch the store while they go to an estate sale.

When they return, Johnny is watching a news report on the Briggs shooting. The reporter mentions the ram's brand on Koslow's forehead and Micki freezes, dropping a figurine they picked up at the sale. Jack rushes to her side, insisting that they don't know if that is *the* coin, but Micki isn't listening. She runs upstairs, leaving Jack to fill Johnny in on this coin: the Satanic cult, people coming back from the dead, Micki actually dying, how he and Ryan tricked the cult into bringing Micki back to life, and the coin being buried beneath a thousand tons of rubble. Jack checks on Micki, who is curled up in bed, rocking like a child. Jack assures her that he is scared too, but they've got to go after it. "It killed me once, what is to stop it from killing me again?"

In the morning, Jack, Micki, and Johnny arrive at the construction site. Micki is filled with trepidation and waits with Johnny while Jack looks around. Micki has flashbacks to her death and Johnny finally asks what he has been dying to ask this whole time: what was it like to be dead? "It was cold and empty and he was waiting there for me. I could feel him." That "he?" Satan. "Aw, Micki, don't talk like that. Chances are that coin is still buried." Micki knows it's not, and decides she can't wait around any more. She will meet them back at the store, and literally runs from the construction site. Jack returns with no news: he couldn't get past the police barricades, but he is afraid that it is their coin. He vows to keep Micki out of this one as much as possible, and Johnny offers to see what he can find out at the police station—his dad had a lot of friends on the force.

Johnny returns from the police station excited. Jack finally got Micki down for a nap. She is convinced that whoever has the coin has her targeted. Johnny hopes his news will make her feel better. Goreman was the only witness, and he found out that Briggs went missing from the morgue. I have no idea how that would make Micki feel better, or why Johnny would think that it would, but she overhears this and comes downstairs. "So, it is the coin. It has given life; now it's ready to kill again." Johnny finally gets to the "feel good" part of the story: that Goreman just wanted his partner back. "Micki was dead, and she turned out okay. It didn't turn her into some zombie, so what's the difference? Briggs will be the same as before, a good cop." His reasoning is ridiculous, and Micki returns to her room, Jack right behind.

Johnny decides to be proactive, so he follows Briggs and Goreman to the hooker crawl, where they pick up Rita, then take her to an abandoned warehouse. She thinks they expect a freebie from her, and she swears she won't keep quiet about it. Goreman calms her by swearing that no one will lay a finger on her. He flips the coin and it kills her—but no one laid a finger on her. Goreman instructs Briggs to dump the body while he collects the coin, but Johnny jumps Goreman, grabs the coin, and runs.

At Curious Goods, Micki is curled up in bed, writing a letter to Ryan. (Fun fact: the photo of "Ryan" that Micki has on her dresser is John Le-May's actual headshot.) Jack comes in, and she tells him that the letter is so Ryan will "understand what happened after she's dead." Jack wishes she wouldn't talk so fatalistically. "If you give up your will to live, you are letting this thing destroy you."

She admits she is scared, and Jack hugs her. Over Micki's shoulder, he sees Johnny come up the stairs and shakes his head slightly, a "now is not a good time" motion. So, Johnny doesn't bother them. He also doesn't put the coin in the vault. He leaves the shop and goes straight to the cemetery.

Johnny cries at his father's grave, then starts digging. He manages to (somehow) get the coffin out of the grave and pries the lid off. His dad looks good for having been in the grave for a year (or two, if his tombstone is to be believed). Johnny places the coin, and Vince wakes. He is a little confused as to what is going on, but Johnny is overjoyed. He takes the coin and his dad on their annual Indian Lake camping trip. But something is definitely different about Vince. He is more sensitive, even a touch effeminate. Probably because he now has the soul (life force? chi?) of a woman.

Jack is annoyed because he doesn't know where Johnny is. His outgoing voice mail message says he has gone fishin' but Jack knows he wouldn't bail on them now. Just then, Johnny calls. The story he gives Jack is that he is following Goreman and Briggs. He is sure he can get the coin back, it just might take a couple days. Jack warns it is too dangerous, but Johnny is adamant and hangs up. Micki overhears this and her world comes crashing in. "First Ryan, now Johnny... ." Between her and Johnny, Jack is dealing with two spoiled brats, and he loses it. "If you are going to let your fear get the better of you, you are no good to either of us." She plays the "you don't know what it's like to be dead" card, and Jack reminds her—forcefully—that she is not dead now; she is alive, so start acting like it. It is the verbal equivalent of a slap across the face, which Micki desperately needs.

Briggs is furious with Goreman that he didn't kill Johnny outright. Goreman heard Johnny at the police station earlier, talking about his dad, so they head to the cemetery. They don't find him, but they find the empty grave, and with it the name that eluded them: Johnny Ventura. They head to his apartment and tear the place up, looking for the coin, or a clue that might lead them to it. They hear the outgoing message and Briggs finds a photo of Johnny and Vince at Indian Lake. "Looks like we're going camping."

The cops break up a peaceful, introspective father-son campfire with demands for the coin. Johnny claims he doesn't have it, so Briggs threatens to shoot Vince. Johnny reveals he has the coin, and offers to flip for it. Goreman gets nervous and makes a different offer: hand over the coin, and both Johnny and his dad can walk away. Johnny sends his dad to the car and the cops start firing. Johnny jumps in and drives away, losing the coin in the process. Goreman retrieves it and tells Briggs to let him go, "we got what we want" (well, what Goreman wants). Briggs wants the coin and shoots Goreman dead for it.

Micki and Jack show up at Johnny's apartment and find it trashed. Johnny shows up with his dad in tow. Johnny defends his decision by pointing out again that Jack used it on Micki, but Jack becomes furious and grabs him. Johnny insists his dad is fine, just the way he remembers, but Jack is mad that he lied to them. Johnny tries to throw them out, but first Jack demands the coin back. Johnny doesn't have it, and Jack gives Johnny a very strong warning: "Stay out of this. And stay out of everything we do from now on!"

Figuring if Briggs has the coin, he would go to the cemetery with it, that is where Jack and Micki go. Briggs sneaks up on Jack and knocks him into Vince's freshly dug grave. He then turns to Micki, holding up the coin menacingly. Micki has a panic attack and starts screaming. Suddenly headlights appear and Johnny shows up, running Briggs over with his car. The car dies and Johnny tells his dad to get out of there. He then grabs Micki and runs. Briggs chases them, and Micki falls into an open grave. She stays there while Johnny lures Briggs away, but he ends up losing track of Johnny, so he returns to the sure thing: Micki. Before he can flip the coin, Johnny shows up and pushes Briggs into the grave. Micki goes for the coin, but Briggs tosses her aside and again readies to flip it.

Micki finally pulls it together and using a shovel that fell in the grave, starts beating Briggs. Four hits knocks him out, and she grabs the coin, crying in relief. Johnny hoists her out of the grave and she hugs him until Jack appears. Micki rushes to him, excitedly showing that she got the coin back. "It's all over!"

Status: There is one loose end: Vince. At Jack's behest, Johnny kills him with one, final flip of the coin. He also thinks that Johnny shouldn't be here. "I don't know how to deal with this stuff." While Jack has no words of comfort, Micki learned that she cares more about him and Jack than anything else, even her own life. They group-hug, signaling Johnny has been re-accepted to the clan. The coin, finally, is put in the vault.

* * *

What was Johnny's long-term plan with his dad? Was he going to be roommates with him? Maybe hide him in the closet if he has guests? He certainly can't reintroduce him to society. Did he think that Micki and Jack would never find out?

Though writer Billy Riback remembers initially conceiving the coin as a "kinda-sorta two-parter," his writing partner Marilyn Anderson remembers it differently: "To my knowledge, it wasn't always the plan to bring the coin back. As I remember it, they just liked the episode so much that they wanted to bring it back." Regardless of how it happened, Riback was relieved: "We both needed the money back then, and that meant we were getting double the money!"

Anderson always referred to it as "Tails I Live, Heads You Die 2," though the draft they turned in came with the title "The Flip Side of Death." Frankly, I love that title, much more than "Bad Penny." Maybe it was a bit too much of a joke for the producers?

The nitpicker in me feels the need to point out that Vince Ventura's gravestone is wrong. He would have died in 1988 at the earliest, not 1987 like it says. The episode in which Vince dies, "The Prisoner," aired in June of 1989. The episode was probably shot in 1989, but let's say, for argument's sake, that the episode was written before New Year began. That would still make his death 1988. 1987 was the first season of the show, before Johnny was even a consideration, and nothing about *F13* leads me to believe that the show took place outside of the years in which it aired (except, of course, for time travel episodes). Therefore, Vince Ventura could not have died earlier than 1988.

"Hate on Your Dial"

Written by: Nancy Ann Miller
Directed by: Allan Eastman
Original airdate: November 6, 1989
Cursed antique: Car radio

May 17, 1954 is known as Black Monday to Ray Pierce (Michael Rhoades). It is not because that was the day the Supreme Court desegregated schools (although that didn't help). It was on that day that his daddy "got in trouble." His father, Steve Pierce (Martin Doyle), was an active member of the Ku Klux Klan in his hometown of Larksburg, Mississippi. He and his Klan lynched a black sharecropper, but Steve was the only one who was arrested. He was hanged for his crime. This was the ultimate injustice to Ray, who wasn't yet born and therefore never met his father. Yet somehow, he inherited his father's virulent racism.

Ray is working on his father's '54 Chevy with his "slow" older brother, Archie (Robert Silverman) when Archie's friend Elliott comes in, selling candy for his school. Elliott is a black kid who can't be more than fourteen years old. Archie welcomes his friend, who is marveling at the car. Ray eyes the boy warily. "Whatcha doing here, boy?" he asks gruffly before knocking the candy out of his hands and telling him to get the hell out of the garage. Ray knocks the kid backwards, and he falls into the car, knocking over a radio Ray was working on. Ray grabs a shotgun and aims it at Elliott, and the kid runs. "I'll get you another time, boy," he grumbles under his breath. The entire time, Archie hides in a corner, hands over his ears, trying to make the whole situation go away.

Johnny is left in charge of Curious Goods for a few hours, which is always a bad idea. While alone, he buys a box full of old junk for $25. Archie enters as Johnny is going through the box and spots a factory model radio from a 1954 Chevy. He offers $100 for it, for his brother Ray, but Johnny sells it to him for $25, and tosses in a cheap little Confederate flag. Johnny is quite proud of himself and brags to Micki when she returns to the store. "Did you check the manifest first?" Of course he didn't.

Micki does, and sure enough she finds a 1954 Chevrolet car radio. She should be furious, but isn't—I guess being mad won't change the situation. Jack returns home from a trip, and he is disappointed when he doesn't get the warm welcome he deserves. Johnny, to his credit, steps up: "I bought a car radio, then sold it without looking it up."

"And it's listed," Micki fills in.

Jack sighs and asks who bought it.

"Some retarded guy named Archie," Johnny says (I guess the term "retarded" was still acceptable in 1989) but reasons that it might be okay, he wouldn't hurt a fly.

Jack doesn't quite buy that. Archie was wearing a car wash uniform, so Micki goes with him in hopes of finding Archie. Jack stays behind to see if they have a file on the radio. He is clearly mad.

Ray is very excited about his new radio, but as is always the case with Ray, his conversation with Archie comes back around to his father, who went to jail and was put to death because he killed not a man, but a "colored sharecropper," and an "uppity black lawyer" found a witness. Archie finally finds his voice and tells his brother that he doesn't like when he talks like that, and he didn't like the way Ray treated Elliott. "You may be slow Archie, but you don't have to be stupid," Ray insists, pulling out his father's photo album, filled with snapshots from his KKK rallies. "Daddy would be turning in his grave if he knew you were friends with a colored."

A drunken Ray goes for a drive and finds Elliott playing basketball at the park. It is night, there is no one around, so Ray decides he is going to mess around with the kid. He wants to shoot a few—then pulls out a gun and shoots the basket. Elliott tells him he is nuts and walks away. Ray shoots at his feet, offended. "Where do you get off talking to a White man like that?" he slurs. "All you people were ever good for was basketball and dancing."

Apparently Ray then turns into Yosemite Sam and shoots the ground at Elliott's feet, demanding he dance. Elliott is more concerned with keeping all his toes, but he trips and Ray's shot connects. Elliott is dead. Ray checks on him and lets out a low whistle, then heads back to the car.

With bloody fingers, Ray puts on the radio, I assume in an effort to calm his nerves. The radio glows, then his whole car glows, and suddenly he is driving through a decidedly old-fashioned town. He parks and checks a newspaper, discovering he is in Larksburg, Mississippi, circa 1954. He smiles when he realizes where he is, and heads into a diner with a "no coloreds allowed" sign hanging proudly in the window.

In the diner, he takes a seat at the counter and asks the waitress, Enid, about Steve and Margie Pierce. This being the 1950s, she has no problem giving him directions to their house. But suddenly the whole diner falls silent as a large African-American man, Ben (Gene Mack), enters. The tension in the diner is so thick you could choke on it. Ben approaches Enid and meekly asks if he can buy a loaf of bread from her, as the general store is closed and he needs food for his children. Enid angrily tells him she won't help, he needs to leave, it isn't up to her to feed his children. In desperation, he grabs her arm. Joe (Henry Czerny), the man sitting beside Ray at the counter, jumps up, and Ben quickly lets go of Enid. Joe demands to know what Ben thinks he is doing. "We might have to let you into our schools, but you'll be dead before we let you start pawing our women." He smacks Ben, and Ben throws Joe into a table. It turns into a melee, with all the White guys in the diner attacking Ben. Ray even manages to get in a few good punches before the sheriff saunters in and breaks up the fight. He does not, however, arrest any of the White men in the diner. Joe, impressed by Ray's punches, introduces himself and buys him a milkshake.

Micki and Johnny return to the shop. Archie won't be back at work until morning, but they got his last name and his brother's name. Jack is still pissed, and Johnny confronts him about it: "Hey Jack, why don't you just get it over with and rip my head off?"

"If it would solve anything I would." Micki is surprised by this un-characteristic outburst, and Jack justifies it: "When it comes to people's lives, sorry isn't good enough."

Johnny decides he will go look for the radio by himself and storms out. Micki and Jack call him back, and Jack apologizes. "I'm not angry with you, I'm angry at the situation. We sold hundreds of items before we found out what they could do. You haven't done anything worse."

But it is worse: Jack, Ryan, and Micki didn't know there was any-thing wrong with the antiques when they innocently started selling them. Johnny knew about the curse. Granted, the chances of anything in that box being cursed were slim at best. But after "Bad Penny," you'd think Johnny would be extra-careful to remain in Micki and Jack's good graces.

Back in 1954, Ray and Joe are sharing vehemently racist ideology. Joe vows that things will never change, that segregation will never end, but Ray warns it will: "Not just coloreds, but spics and Jews and slanty-eyes from Vietnam." The only amusing part of this exchange is when Joe asks, "Viet-who?" I guess Americans didn't learn about Vietnam until they became an imagined threat to them. Ray warns that blacks will "ride at the front of the bus, marry our women, even run for president." (And win!) Joe laughs at his wild imagination and takes him to Steve's house. As in, Ray's father.

Steve is inside, ranting about desegregation to a small collection of Klansmen. Archie, just five or six years old, sits in on the conversation, and agrees when his daddy says "no son of mine is going to school with a Colored." Margie (Melanie Miller), watch-your-shoes pregnant with Ray, brings the boys drinks before they head off to "take care of" sharecropper Ben.

Micki and Johnny visit Archie at his house. He remembers Johnny and greets him warmly, and is genuinely saddened when he hears Micki promised the radio to another customer. It's in Ray's car, and it isn't likely he will want to sell it back to them. Margie comes out and offers that sometimes Ray goes driving and doesn't come back for days. Micki leaves her card, but the pair stake out the house from across the street. Later that night, Jack brings them some food and tells them that his research suggests that they may be dealing with time travel for this curse.

Steve's Klan has gathered for a small rally, complete with burning crosses, burning effigies, and burning rhetoric. Steve is ready to lead his group to kill that sharecropper, but Ray warns him that he will be arrested for it. "You need to kill a human being to be arrested for murder," Steve says with a smile. This line actually made my jaw drop. Ray warns him about a "colored lawyer" dying for a case like this, and a witness. He suggests Steve kill the witness too, to stay out of jail.

The Klan, in full hooded regalia, have Ben chained up in a barn. One Klansman announces that the penalty for assaulting a White woman is thirty lashes. As he sets about whipping Ben, his ropes loosen. Klansmen rush to retie Ben, and Ray loses his mask. "Finish him off!" he yells, and the whipping continues until Ben is dead. The Klan is jubilant after their killing, though they wish they had strung him up for all to see. There was no witness there, and Ray thinks that maybe his being there changed things. He gets in the car and realizes there is still blood on the radio. He wipes it off, and doing so sends him back to the future.

Jack, Micki, and Johnny are still staking out the Pierce home when Ray's car appears out of nowhere. Johnny wants to go accost him, but Jack warns they need to be careful—it looks like Ray has figured out how to use the radio.

Ray is not happy about returning to the progressive 1980s and asks Margie where his daddy is. She thinks he is cracked: daddy was hanged by the state of Mississippi before Ray was born; accept this. Jack overhears this argument from outside while Micki and Johnny try to break into the garage. Ray informs Archie that he won't sell the radio back and grabs his father's photo album. "I've gotta go save daddy."

Archie is confused by this and follows his brother out to the garage (Micki and Johnny hide when they hear him coming). Ray needs to go "kill another one of your little black friends" and grabs his gun. Archie realizes it was Ray who killed Elliott and is horrified. Ray throws his brother across the garage, a warning to keep his mouth shut. Johnny is worried about his new friend and enters the garage, but it is too late: Ray has bludgeoned Archie to death. Micki runs to Archie while Jack and Johnny try to get Ray out of the car, but he wipes blood on the radio as the guys grip the door handles. All three men are sent back to 1954.

Ray leaves Jack and Johnny by the side of the road and goes straight to Steve's house, telling him that Henry Emmett (Marc Gomes) is the lawyer he needs to kill. Margie is worried, but Steve isn't. He believes he is fighting a war and has no plans to surrender. Archie starts singing "Daddy killed a negro," a song he surely (hopefully) made up, while Ray rails about how nothing good will ever happen to his family if he is put to death. Ray is so insistent that Steve relents and tells him to go find the lawyer while he speaks to the Grand Dragon. Margie leaves the room and Archie starts singing again. Steve smacks him so hard he is knocked out of his chair, and Archie's screams bring Margie back into the room. Ray hears the ruckus from outside, but thinks nothing of it and continues on his race war.

Johnny and Jack finally make it into town and they see an angry crowd gathered outside the courthouse. Henry Emmett is arguing with the White townspeople when the sheriff interrupts. Emmett wants an arrest made in Ben's murder, but the sheriff needs evidence. The lawyer vows to find a witness, and the sheriff reminds him that they must be willing to testify. "They won't live long after pointing a Colored finger at a White man." That's not a threat; it's just a fact of life.

While Johnny goes looking for Ray, Jack tries to warn Emmett that someone may try to harm him, perhaps very soon. Emmett sees this as a direct threat, though a polite one, and tells Jack that his "Klan friends" won't stop him from prosecuting.

Ray returns to his parents' house and waits for Steve. He gets a kick sitting in his daddy's chair and excitedly tells Margie that he found the man they were looking for. Margie has more important worries on her mind, as she is caring for an unconscious Archie.

Ray assures her everything is going to be okay.

"Is that because you and my husband are going to get rid of all the coloreds?"

"If we have to," Ray announces proudly.

Margie shakes her head. "When are you going to realize they're just people like us?"

Ray is shocked to hear this tolerance from his mother. Put in his place, he changes the subject and asks what is wrong with Archie.

"His daddy hits him," Margie says matter-of-factly. "Sometimes I think he might hit him just once too often."

This is not turning out the way Ray had hoped.

Jack and Johnny meet up outside the Pierce home, and Jack warns him to leave the radio where it is—it is their ticket home. They can't just leave Ray here, for fear of changing history and the impending chaos that could cause. Jack looks through the Pierce family's album of intolerance (it was in the car when they traveled back through time) and takes it to the sheriff while Johnny waits there. The sheriff promises to have a "long chat" with the boys in the photos, but that is all he can do since Jack can't testify that Steve is the man behind Ben's murder. As Jack leaves, he sees Steve's car swing into town and the Klansmen drag Emmett into the car. Jack tries to intervene and they take him, too.

The Klan takes Emmett and Jack to a field filled with burning crosses. One of them wants to kill the White boy, which the Grand Dragon is fine with, but they have other business to attend to first: there is a spy in their midst. He holds up the photo album as proof, revealing (to the audience) that the sheriff is the Grand Dragon. Ray takes off his hood, insisting that they are making a mistake, but the men strip Ray of his robes and tie him up anyway. "The only thing worse than a Negro," the Grand Dragon proclaims, "is a Negro-lover." He wants to know if Ray is a "Negro-lover, or just the FBI." I find it amusing that those are the two worst things he could be, the only two things he could be.

Johnny sneaked a ride to the meeting in the trunk of Ray's car. With the Klan distracted, he slips into the front seat and hot wires the car, driving it through the meeting while firing warning shots with Ray's rifle. The Klan scatter, and Johnny scoops up Jack and Emmett into the car. They get away and the Klan, itching to do some killing, turn on Joe for introducing Ray to them. Steve takes off his hood and addresses Ray directly: "Southern men don't need saving. We look after our own." Ray begs his daddy to stop and tells him it was his wife that acted as a witness against him. It doesn't matter. Both Ray and Joe burn at the stake.

Status: Johnny and Jack drop off Emmett somewhere safe, assuming he won't say anything after two strangers saved his life. Johnny can't imagine what it was like to be black here, and Jack reminds him that it was only thirty-five years ago. I was hoping to hear some first-hand experiences from Jack, but he offers none. They return home safely and the radio is vaulted.

* * *

"This show really looked amazing," says director Allan Eastman. "It is one of my all time favorites. I think the story was very strong, the actors were all excellent and I think we made a very good film out of it. I've been told by several people that they consider 'Hate On Your Dial' to be the best *Friday the 13th: The Series* episode ever. It was done with a lot of passion and commitment by all involved."

"I thought 'Hate on Your Dial' was one of the best things we've ever done," says Jim Henshaw. "I think it got a couple of awards from… I don't want to say the NAACP, but groups like that, just for the way it dealt with racism." Steve Monarque, production designer Stephen Roloff, and line producer J. Miles Dale also include it among their top episodes.

Eastman was offered his choice of scripts for his first episode on the series. "I chose 'Hate' because it seemed like the most interesting subject matter; a way to portray racism and hatred in a way that condemned it unequivocally. I had been involved with the civil rights movement when I was a young man. I considered it an important issue then and it is a battle that is still not completely won a half-century later."

"Hate on Your Dial" was a surprisingly difficult episode to get through. I don't think I have ever heard the term "colored" used so much outside of actual footage of the time. Having not watched it in twenty years or so, I had forgotten about how strong the depiction of the KKK was in this episode. Watching this in 2015, in a time when the Voting Rights Act is being stripped away, police are being accused of shooting unarmed African-Americans, Confederate flags still fly above government buildings, and racial tensions are headline news across the country, this episode seems especially pertinent. An exchange between Jack and Johnny holds just as true today as it did in the 1980s:

Johnny: "This place is unbelievable."

Jack: "The future isn't much more comforting."

Johnny: "Come on, we've come a long way."

Jack: "The rules may have changed, but some of the feelings haven't."

"We shot the Klan stuff in a park at night so it was never really exposed to the public," Eastman assured me. "We had this crazy stunt guy, J. J. Makaro, who loved getting burned up, so we added that for its visual appeal and to bring the fires of hell to earth."

"There was one time where there was a burning cross," Louise Robey recalls, "and one of the crew starts singing 'It's a lovely day in the neighborhood!' What kept us going was humor."

Eastman didn't feel the humor right away. "When I first came to set, I was surprised and a little unsettled by the shooting crew who seemed very grim and not given to the usual kind of joking lightheartedness that characterizes most film crews. Once I started work I realized we end up shooting a brutal murder pretty much every day—no wonder they're all so bummed out. It did kind of get you down when you have to shoot a scene where a sweet guy is beaten to death by his brother with a ball peen hammer."

It wasn't just the racism that drew Eastman to this script; it was the time travel aspect. "I suggested that we shoot the 1950s stuff on actual black and white film, as opposed to the usual method, which was to just remove the color from standard color film stock during electronic post production. That always resulted in a soft, fuzzy grey black and white. I fought to shoot it in Tri-X stock which makes a very high contrast black and white image. This worked extremely well to root the story in the past, as well as serving as a visual metaphor to the story.

"We shot in a small town outside Toronto and dressed it very well for the period. The art department did a great job on the physical appearance: the vintage gas pumps, the signage, the wardrobe and hats, all that kind of stuff. "

My brain doesn't handle time travel storylines very well. In this case, if Ray died in the past, why would Margie remember him? Wouldn't Archie still be alive? I get lost in all the logistics. I actually once asked a Nobel Prize-winning physicist if time travel was possible. Short answer? It's not.

"Night Prey"

Written by: Peter Mohan
Directed by: Armand Mastroianni
Original airdate: November 13, 1989
Cursed antique: Cross of Fire

"Night Prey" opens with a depressed Jack sitting at the waterfront, giving a defeatist voiceover. "I just don't know anymore. It used to be so simple. But now good and evil are blending together. I'm not sure I know the difference anymore. For me, the nightmares started days ago. When did it start for him? How long did it take him to lose his way?"

The voiceover leads into a flashback, August 1969. A young couple, Kurt and Michele (Michael Burgess and Genevieve Langlois), are on their honeymoon, clasping hands over a romantic dinner, getting all melodramatic about it. They finish dinner and go for a walk, Of course, they stop to kiss in the moonlight. Out of nowhere, a man jumps on the couple, knocks out Kurt, and lures Michele away. She seems bewitched by this stranger, who whispers for her to give herself to him. Kurt wakes in time to see the stranger—clearly a vampire—bite his wife and fly away with her.

Twenty years later, and Jack's voiceover continues over Kurt—now aged twenty years—sneaking around outside a nightclub. Jack ponders how he hunted them, followed them, learned them, and that maybe it was the hunt that twisted him. "On this night his hunt would merge with mine. I would join the hunt, as well."

Voiceover done for now, we see a young woman eagerly leading a man out of the club and into an alley. She can't wait to get to his place; she wants him now. She takes charge, kissing him against the wall, and he again protests. Then she lifts her skirt, and he is all in. After some kissing and heavy petting, the woman, clearly a vampire, takes a bite out of the man's neck and drains him dry. As she leaves the alley, Kurt jumps out, brandishing a cross. She swats him aside and lunges at him, but Kurt is ready. She impales herself on a wooden stake and Kurt runs.

He can hear the hissing of vampires all around him, so he breaks into a church. He sees an ornate cross in a display case and steals it. The priest comes out and tries to stop him. There is a struggle and the priest drops dead—the cross has a blade hidden in it, and it popped out the bottom during the struggle. Kurt retracts the blade and the cross begins to glow and shake. A vampire flies around outside the window, taunting Kurt. A younger priest checks on the noise, and Kurt runs outside, chasing the vampire, but he is gone, and day is breaking.

Jack and Micki go to the church the next day. The priest who died, Father McKinnon, was a friend of Jack's, and they meet with Father Finn (Don Carrier) to find out what happened. The cross that was stolen is valuable. Known as the Cross of Fire, it is a relic from the Crusades. It was common practice to hide blades in the relics to provide protection for traveling monks. The cross was a donation made in memory of a congregant, Mr. Drake. Finn gives a description of the assailant, but that is all he can do. Returning to Curious Goods, Jack goes to lay down for a bit, and Micki goes straight to the manifest. Unsurprisingly, the Cross of Fire, purchased by Walter G. Drake, is listed.

Kurt returns to the club, the Neon Gargoyle (the best-ever name for a 1980s goth club) which he has identified as the vampire's nest. Evan Van Hellier (Eric Murphy) owns the club, and he just happens to be the vampire that attacked Michele twenty years ago. Kurt tries to bluff his way into the club, but a bouncer blocks his path. He tries to sneak in through a back door, but another bouncer catches him. Hoping that the bouncer is a vampire, Kurt takes out the cross for protection. It lives up to its name by spouting fire and burning the bouncer to a crisp.

The morning newspaper reports the murder, the third in the area. The description of the suspect, a man who hassled the bouncers, matches the description Father Finn gave them. Jack hears Micki and Johnny talking about it, and sends them to speak to Father Finn again, while Jack goes to see Van Hellier. Van Hellier lives in an enormous mansion. Tom Baker (Vincent Dale), his assistant, answers the door and says his boss isn't in. (It is the middle of the day, after all.) Jack gets nothing out of Baker, but he leaves his card, just in case.

Back at the shop, Micki reports that the cross came from a Hungarian church that bordered Transylvania. Legend says it blessed a member of the congregation who then offered himself to save the village from vampires. The power of the cross was just superstition, though "one Lewis could make come true through the store." Jack thinks whoever has the cross is using it to kill vampires. The three bodies found near the Neon Gargoyle were found decapitated, staked through the heart, and burned—

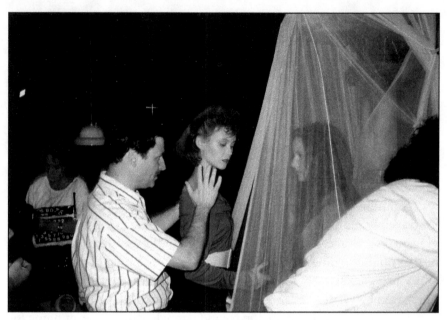

Directing a lesbian vampire scene in "Night Prey." Photo courtesy of Armand Mastroianni.

all common manners of death for vampires. Jack sends Micki and Johnny to the club to look for the "man with the beard."

But the man with the beard is waiting for Evan outside his house. A security guard gives him a hard time, so Kurt stabs him and breaks into the house. He wears sunglasses, which I assume is to prevent being compelled. Moving through the beautifully appointed home, classical music playing softly throughout, Kurt finds Evan. He accuses him of killing his wife, and Evan responds by grabbing him and baring his fangs. But the cross scares Evan back and he runs off into the night. Kurt continues into the house, upstairs, to a bedroom. He finds two women fooling around, and one, a vampire, tries to attack Kurt. He uses the cross to burn her to death. The second woman, still in bed, is about to face a similar fate until Kurt sees it is his Michele—now a vampire.

Kurt brings Michele to his "home," a dumpy, abandoned warehouse. She is chained up and put beneath a bed netting for "protection," though I'm not sure what it is protecting her from. Mosquitoes? Michele demands to be released, insisting she is not the person he remembers. But Kurt can't let go.

Micki returns home at 3:00 a.m. Jack didn't expect her home so soon (did he think she was a party animal?) but the club closed and everyone went home. "You wouldn't believe the kind of people that place attracts." Jack tells her that some of the patrons might have been vampires, as many of the bodies found around the club in the past few months had been drained of blood. He assumes that Micki and Johnny weren't attacked because the vamps didn't want to expose themselves, and their lair.

Jack tells Micki to go to bed; he is going to work on Father McKinnon's eulogy. Micki is worried about him, and he admits he is not okay with all of this. "I always think we are doing the right thing, but they always die, don't they?"

Micki reminds him that he has saved many lives, but Jack doesn't know if that really makes up for all the killing. "Yes, it does," she says, kissing him on the cheek.

Van Hellier and Baker arrive at Kurt's home. He can feel Michele in there and they break in. Michele hears this and whispers to them, but Kurt also hears, grabs his cross and runs to meet them. He jumps Baker and the two fight while Van Hellier tries to rescue Michele. She urges him to leave; he wants her to take some of his blood. The room is so full of crosses and garlic that he can't make it to her, and she again insists he leave. Baker gets the upper hand on Kurt and knocks him out. He meets Van Hellier outside, where dawn is breaking. Baker hurries his boss into the car and drives off. He suggests they turn to "the old man with all the questions" for help.

Micki and Jack return home from Father McKinnon's funeral and Jack goes to change before joining her in a drink. She notices a figure in the doorway and tells them the store is closed. Van Hellier introduces himself and asks for Jack. Recognizing the name, Micki invites him in. She is inexplicably taken with him and offers him a drink. "Not just yet," he says, brushing her cheek, but he seems ready to ask her out.

Jack comes in and breaks Micki's reverie. Van Hellier explains that he may have seen the cross in the possession of a man he rented a warehouse to. Micki offers to go check it out and Van Hellier gives her the address, but Jack is distracted by a mirror reflection on the opposite side of the store. Van Hellier does not appear in it. After Van Hellier leaves, Jack doesn't tell Micki a thing; he just grabs a bottle of holy water from the shelf and tells her they are going to pick up Johnny on the way to the warehouse.

After Van Hellier's invasion, Kurt checks on Michelle. "You have to let me go or I'll die," she insists. He won't lose her twice, and believes that once Van Hellier is dead, she will be free and they can start over. She again begs for her freedom, which Kurt won't grant. "Then feed me!" she screams.

So, he will. Kurt heads out to the hooker stroll and picks one that is sensually eating an ice cream cone. He takes her, and she gets very nervous when he pushes her towards Michelle. "I paid you. She needs you more than I do." The hooker approaches Michele, and the women start kissing each other sensually. Michele nibbles on the prostitute's ear, and she pulls away with a gasp. Kurt is right behind her, tells her not to be afraid, and holds her in place while Michele drinks deeply from her neck. When she is done, she looks at Kurt with a bloody smile, and they clasp hands like they did on their honeymoon.

Kurt hears someone enter the warehouse. He thinks Van Hellier has returned and jumps to action. Michele begs him not to hurt him. "He loves me!" Kurt ignores her and rushes out to the hall, but he is instead confronted by Micki. Johnny fights him off and Micki grabs the cross. Johnny is worried because Kurt is getting away, but they have the cross. Time to go.

They get to the car, but Micki stops. She is mad that Jack is more concerned with the cross than what is going on in the warehouse. Van Hellier tricked them into retrieving the cross so that he could move in and kill Kurt. But as far as Jack is concerned, they have done their job—the rest is none of their concern. The trio bickers for a bit, and Jack finally gets in the car. Micki and Johnny run back into the warehouse.

Michele senses that Van Hellier is near and begs Kurt to get out while he still has a chance. He refuses to leave without her and decides that he wants to be turned. It is the only way he can protect her, and the only way he can be with her forever. She initially declines, but a kiss makes her fold, and she bites.

Van Hellier and Baker are in the warehouse now. Kurt kills Baker with relative ease, and Van Hellier confronts Michele, mad that she made Kurt one of them. Michele fights back, accusing Van Hellier of lying to her when he told her Kurt was dead.

Kurt attacks, and the two vampires face off, tossing each other around the warehouse. Van Hellier gets the upper hand and is about to behead Kurt, when Michele stops him. "If you really love me, you'll let him live."

Van Hellier has to think about this for a minute, but he finally tosses the axe to the ground. Kurt uses this time to ram a stake through Van Hellier's heart. He drops dead, deflates into a mummy that turns to dust. (An all practical effect, this is much more effective than modern vampires, who tend to explode into sparkly dust when staked.)

Jack, Micki, and Johnny all come in and join the fray. Jack throws holy water on Kurt, and he is set alight, then sends Johnny and Micki out to safety, and turns his attention to a furious Michele. He is about to strike her, too, but she is scared and sad and cowers. He takes pity on her and tosses the holy water to the ground and leaves. Michele is left, physically unharmed, but emotionally damaged by the death of her two lovers.

Status: The cross is vaulted. We pick up with Jack where we came in: with him on the bench, lamenting the life of a vampire. "I wish I had their wisdom," he says in voice over. "God help me, I almost envy them."

* * *

I didn't watch this episode much as a kid. Strangely, I was never particularly into vampires, but that wasn't what kept me away. It was Jack's opening and closing voice over, and his sad face as he sat at the water's edge. I found it hopelessly depressing. That might sound a little irrational, but I had a similar response to the theme song from *M*A*S*H*. To this day, I have never seen an episode because I always found the theme song unsettling.

"Night Prey" is a very depressing episode, even without Jack's voice over (which, as an adult, sounds borderline suicidal). A man spends his whole life trying to track down his one true love, who was taken from him. He finds her and she doesn't want him. He finally convinces her to change him so they can be together forever, and both he and her other lover die, leaving her with a lifetime of nothing. It is too maudlin and overwrought for me. (I have a black hole where my heart should be.)

However, this was director Armand Mastroianni's favorite episode, and he has a lot of memories about shooting "Night Prey." "I kept saying that I wanted to do a vampire story, a different type of vampire story.

"I remember *Les Miserables* [the stage production] had opened and was playing up there. I had seen it on Broadway and I wanted to see the Toronto version. I remember being very taken by the guy who played Jean Valjean, Michael Burgess. I thought, *What are the chances of this guy getting out of the show to play our vampire hunter?* Sure enough, he had an out in his contract that if he got an offer to do TV, he could take a small window and do it. I ended up becoming good friends with him. I told him I really liked his performance and thought he would be really good as this passionate man who is in love with his wife, who was attacked by a vampire years ago. I thought, *What if he keeps her in the basement, but everything about it is beautiful and delicate… but she's a monster.* I wanted her to be kept under this beautiful veil because the light hurts her eyes, and I wanted everything to have an elegant quality about it. The music I kept hearing in my head was this piece of symphonic music, a haunting melody. I kept saying I wanted this music. I wanted this one sequence to be just music. It was a long scene, but I wanted it only music.

"[In the scene where Michele is changed] I wanted the effect of Van Hellier flying down like a bat, so we had a StediCam on a crane and we lowered it and the guy came running off it. You felt like the camera was the point of view of the vampire, and she turns and he bites her and the husband is devastated—the love of his life was taken from him. But not to lose her, he keeps her confined because he doesn't want her going out and feeding off of people. Unlike the doctor [in "Better Off Dead"] who fed his daughter prostitutes, I wanted this one wanted to be very classy. There was an elegance about it.

"I wanted to do a scene where he has to go out and get food for his wife—get blood for his wife. He goes out under the guise of picking up a girl. It should be a young girl, a waif type. She's still a prostitute, but I didn't want her to be trashy. I wanted her to be innocent—even though she wasn't. I wanted to have this almost lesbian love scene between them, and it's in there! Nobody cut it. Underneath that scene, I wanted to hear that music. I wanted him to walk the streets at night, looking at different people, and this girl is eating an ice cream cone… who is eating ice cream at night? Visually, in my head, I just had these ideas. She's licking this ice cream very slowly, very sensually. He's aroused by her and he approaches her, and she thinks the two of them are going to get it on. He brings her home, and brings her downstairs, and suddenly she sees this woman, a very beautiful woman, but she is behind this veil, so the girl thinks, 'What the hell is this?' and the guy says, 'She needs you more than I do.' No dialogue, you just see it in their faces.

"I told [Burgess] it was like he was the voyeur, he was the audience. He should be there and just watch. So, she takes her strap off and she parts the curtains and she goes in there, and the women look at each other. I tell them, 'Let the sensuality take over. Let it be very delicate, very beautiful. Think about this music.' And I kept playing the music for them on the set. They are touching each other's face and brushing her hair and she moves in to kiss her. The girl is getting into it a little bit, and the husband is just standing there, watching. Waiting and watching. We think—or she thinks—he's getting off on it, watching the two girls. Finally as the wife looks up, the embarrassment that she is going to have to do this, she looks up at her husband and her teeth are bared and the girl is unaware. The minute she bites, the girl starts to pull away and the husband grabs her and holds her so the wife can feed. This is how much he loves her. He holds the girl until she is drained.

"I thought it was a very sexual scene, and that's what I wanted it to be. The whole vampire thing is very sexual. When I did *Dark Shadows* I did the same thing: I made it more of a sexual act than just biting people's necks. I really enjoyed doing that.

"Then at the end, he decides to have her make him a vampire because he wants to be like her, wants to be with her. Then the original vampire comes for her, and there is this fight to the death. That was very difficult stuff to shoot because they were both flying around that warehouse at night, up on wires. Oh god, it took forever to shoot!

"I liked that episode because it had a nice feel to it and was kind of gothic. At the same time, it could have just been a vampire movie, but I wanted it to have a certain sense of elegance."

Genevieve Langlois played Michele in this episode. "I think Armand wanted there to be a lot of sexual energy with the other women," she said. "It was very dramatic to say the least. I think Armand loved the ambiguity of that episode and he pushed it." But it wasn't all dramatic. "One of the funniest things about the episode for me was that we all had gone to have those vampire teeth done and when we had them on, we couldn't talk. We had to redo the lines in studio. When we would talk with the vampire teeth in, a lot of times we would burst out laughing! It was hilarious."

"Femme Fatale"

Written by: Jeffrey Bernini
Directed by: Francis Delia
Original airdate: November 20, 1989
Cursed antique: 16mm film reel

Desmond Williams (Gordon Pinset) is a classic director, who specialized in Film Noir in the 1940s and 1950s. He has been married to his leading lady, Lili Lita (Kate Reid), for decades. Now, she is bedridden, forcing Desmond to care for her. He waivers between resentment and deep love for her.

One of his favorite pastimes is watching his old films. *A Scandalous Woman* is his favorite, and the role that made him fall in love with Lili. A fairly typical noir, Lili played Glenda (Chris Moore), a tough, determined, and very sensual gun moll. Not only does Desmond watch these reels over and over, but he does so with pretty young actresses. Like tonight, when he invites Tina over for a private screening. (Fun fact: *A Scandalous Woman* is a Paramount picture, with music by Frederick Mollin.) During Glenda's first scene in the film, Desmond wants Tina to show she is "as talented as my Lili!" and pushes her into the projector light. Tina is sucked into the film, into the Glenda roll. Glenda is now real, flesh and blood, and she and Desmond make out on the couch like a couple teenagers.

The film plays around Tina, never missing a step, no matter what she does. Tina is at the wheel of a car, in the climactic chase scene. Gunfire opens up and Tina is scared. She tries to duck behind the car door, but her fate is sealed. Glenda pulls away from Desmond and knows her time is up. In the film, Tina is shot. Glenda is returned to the film in time to deliver her final line: "Don't cry baby; this is funny. I always thought I'd die in bed." Desmond watches sadly as the end credits roll.

Desmond is not making any progress on his latest script, so he decides to take a break. A local cinema is holding a Desmond Williams retrospective, and the manager has invited Desmond to come speak. Lili gives her blessing.

Tonight's film is *Felony Life*, and as luck would have it, Johnny is being dragged to the theater by his date, Erin (Kymberley Huffman). She is a film student and this is her favorite film. Johnny makes no attempt to hide his boredom. He does not want to be there, but he gives in. The film screens, and Erin is mesmerized. Johnny is bored. As the film ends, the audience claps; Johnny is more interested in his hot dog. She asks him what he thought, and the best he can offer is, "It was okay." Erin is disappointed by his response, but it is short-lived because the manager announces tonight's guest. The crowd claps enthusiastically, and Erin decides to go down and ask a question. Johnny asks, accusingly, where she is going. "To share my thoughts with someone who understands." Johnny is not getting laid tonight.

Erin introduces herself to Desmond outside, with Johnny in reluctant tow. She wants to direct and is looking for advice. Desmond takes down her phone number, saying he is thinking of teaching a class and will let her know when it begins (remember, this is before email). An all-too-eager actress named Krissy insists on giving Desmond her number, too, and he ends up inviting her back to stay the night at his house and have a private screening of *A Scandalous Woman*.

Krissy is in the car chase scene, and Glenda and Desmond are back on the couch. Glenda is ready for Desmond to prove his love and put old Lili in the film, so Glenda can stay and the two can be together forever. Desmond promises he will—next time. Glenda doesn't like this answer and tells him if she can't stay next time, they are finished. She is sucked back into the film.

At Curious Goods, the disappearance of a sixth actress this month sends Micki to the manifest, looking for movie or theater-related objects. Nothing fits. There is a Victorian costume, male. The makeup case was returned; the movie camera was returned. Then there is an old 16mm film print. Not sure why Micki wouldn't think that would fit. Johnny comments that the movie he saw last night was cursed, because it cost him a beautiful girlfriend. (No, Johnny, you cost *yourself* a beautiful girlfriend. Ass.) Jack is excited to hear about the film, and was sorry he missed Desmond Williams.

The name lands with Micki, as Jack tells his younger companions about *A Scandalous Woman*, the film during which Desmond and Lili married. "She retired to be his wife," muses Jack. "It was big news back then."

Micki has bigger news: *A Scandalous Woman* is the name of the film Lewis sold, to a D.W. Johnny, watching the news while sitting cross-legged on the floor like a child, turns up the TV when a report about Krissy's disappearance comes on. Johnny recognizes her from the screening. Jack takes Micki with him to visit Desmond, an errand Johnny desperately wants to go on. Jack, perhaps sensing that Johnny would be insulting to Desmond, sends Johnny to check in with a police friend.

Glenda's words weigh heavily on Desmond. He takes Lili out for a little fresh air, and imagines throwing her off the balcony. He is shaken from his reverie by Lili's shouts, and discovers he is actually pushing her. He helps her back from the edge, apologizing profusely. After speaking briefly to the cops who came to his door, inquiring about Krissy ("Sorry officers, anyone under thirty looks the same to me"), he prepares Lili some tea. Desmond adds an entire bottle of medicine to the tea, hoping to overdose her, but as he approaches her room, his hands tremble and he drops the cup, shattering it on the floor.

The doorbell rings, and Desmond finds Micki on his porch. She says she saw his film last night, was really inspired, and wants to talk about a movie print he bought. Desmond weighs his options, then lets her in, taking her to his screening room. While Desmond checks on his wife, Jack appears at the window. Micki is about to pass the reel to him, when Desmond returns. Micki explains she is interested in buying it, and Desmond suggests they should run it first, to see if she likes it. While watching the movie, Jack is seen skulking around outside the house by the cops who just visited. They arrest him, just in time for Jack to miss Desmond throwing Micki into the movie.

Desmond and Glenda make out as per usual, until she discovers that Desmond didn't kill Lili. Then she gets mad. "If you aren't man enough to kill that old bitch, I'll find someone who will." The police return to the door, Jack in tow, claiming his friend is inside and she is in danger. They go check out the screening room and find Glenda chilling in there. Jack is astonished to see the young Lili Lita there, so much so he is at a loss for words. The cops mistake Glenda for Micki, so when she says she has never seen that man before, they leave—with Jack in handcuffs.

Desmond is furious that Glenda let the cops see her. "Why shouldn't they? You keep me locked up like a caged animal."

"You're mine!" Desmond defends. "I created you!"

When wife-Lili calls from upstairs, Desmond responds, finding his wife wheeling herself to the door. Desmond tells her the commotion was just a prowler that the cops picked up. He puts her back to bed. When he returns downstairs, he is just in time to see Glenda slip out the front door.

But Glenda was just hiding behind the ivy; as soon as Desmond leaves, she returns to the house.

This is just to teach the older man a lesson; she reminds him how easy it would be for her to leave. She again implores him to kill older Lili, but he can't. "She's my wife!"

"All you ever tell me is what a burden she is," Glenda reminds him. "I am your chance to live like a human being again." She is adamant that he kill her tonight, and set her free.

Stuck between a rock and a hard place, Desmond goes to his wife's room, gives her a kiss on the forehead, and smothers her with a pillow. Glenda kisses him happily and promises to get rid of Lili's body in the morning.

The couple return to their frantic make-out session on the couch (which has seen more action in this episode than Andy Warhol's infamous red velvet couch) when Lili limps in. She has a cane in one hand and a gun in the other. "Death scenes were always my forte," she explains, before realizing Desmond's new lover was "made up to look just like me." Glenda reveals that she is her, and points out Micki in the film, running from gangsters. "She took my place in the picture so I could be here."

After bailing out of jail, Jack and Johnny come to the house. Johnny chases Glenda out the door, while Jack remains to talk some sense into Desmond and Lili. "The film must allow your character to be freed if another takes her place," Jack explains. He also tells her that there were more before Micki, who will probably never be seen again.

Lili finally understands. "What you really loved is that pathetic character I played."

Glenda has lost Johnny on the streets and sees her name on a marquee. Tonight the theater is screening *A Scandalous Woman*, and Glenda just can't help but sneak a peek. She is utterly taken by her image on the screen, and the full house that has come to watch. Johnny finally catches up with her and quietly whispers her name. Glenda is flattered to be recognized (as Lili Lita, of course) and he tells her he needs to take her back home. Glenda can't believe that Desmond lied, didn't tell her about her legions of fans. Johnny suggests she confront Desmond, and she leaves the theater willingly.

Desmond is still trying to justify his actions to Lili, and actually trying to convince her to step into the picture, where she can be young and healthy forever. Glenda returns, and Desmond turns to her to convince her older self to return to the picture. But Glenda is on Lili's side. "She gave me life! You kept me trapped in a film, and never told me what I mean to other people. She gave me to the world; you just wanted me for yourself."

Desmond grabs for Lili's gun, and it goes off in the struggle, shooting him in the stomach. Lili decides she has "been away too long" and steps into the light, getting sucked into the film. Glenda laughs, "I'm free!" but then she turns black and white and goes up in flames like a film negative. Micki is tossed from the screen, and the elder Lili Lita dies one final death. She morphs into Glenda, and the credits roll.

Status: The film is returned to the vault.

*　*　*

I always felt I was a little too close to turning into Desmond Williams. Television (more than films) has always been escapism for me, but I always wanted to be part of the show. If there was ever a cursed object I would fall prey to, this would probably be it.

When director Francis Delia was given the script for "Femme Fatale," he could see the potential, but felt it was "unshootable" in its original form. "I am sure [writer Jeffrey Bernini] was working off of *The Purple Rose of Cairo*, to a degree. It's the same—characters came down off the screen and interacted with Mia Farrow," Delia says of the 1985 Woody Allen film. Unlike *Purple Rose*, whose movie-within-a-movie was a screwball comedy, Delia knew that his *A Scandalous Woman* had to be a classic, 1940s gangster film with a noir feel. While he doesn't remember what was in the original script for "Femme Fatale," he knew it "wasn't doing anything that was compelling." "The girls Desmond was offering to the film needed to be put in jeopardy," he says.

Both Delia and executive story consultant Jim Henshaw remember filming the *A Scandalous Woman* scenes in the tail end of a hurricane. "The night of the shoot, it bucketed rain, but we *had* to shoot it that night; we couldn't delay anything," explains Henshaw. "We were out there with six or eight stuntmen doing this incredible gun battle in a pouring rain storm. You look at the footage, and it's like, 'How did they do this?' Halfway through the night, we realized we were in trouble if it stopped raining. There aren't enough rain bars in the city to keep shooting [and keep continuity]. We finished the last shot, and it stopped raining. I thought, *Someone up there really wants this to look good*." Delia remembers that the reports back from Hollywood on the dailies were incredible. "I've seen 1940s movies and ours looked just like it came from that era!"

I refer to the young Lili Lita as Glenda for two reasons. First, it is easier to distinguish between the two women. Second, and most importantly, is that clearly, Desmond isn't in love with Lili Lita as much as he is in love with Glenda, the character he made for Lili Lita. I don't think he was just looking to get with the young, hot, healthy version of his wife, but he was living out some sort of deep fantasy, where he got to hook up with this fictional character. Clearly, he created Glenda, so he created a character that pushed all his buttons.

Delia sees Desmond as trying to recapture his youth, and the glory days of his career. "It might have appeared that there was a dalliance with a younger woman. I like the fact that the younger woman is actually his wife, who was the actress in the movie. He longed for those days." He loves the satisfying resolution in "Femme Fatale," bringing the story full-circle. "We are punishing [Desmond] not so much for cheating on his wife, but for not accepting the world as it really is," Delia concludes.

I am actually offended by Johnny's behavior in this episode. Of course Erin was going to dump him—he was being petulant and obnoxious at the movies. How in the world does he expect to maintain a girlfriend if he can't even *pretend* to have a good time doing what she wants? He will never get laid with an attitude like that. On top of everything, his attitude offends me as a film school graduate. He didn't even try to enjoy the film! Dammit, Johnny angers me so.

Fun fact: The scenes from *Felony Life* were actually excerpts from a real film, *Detour* (1945) directed by Edgar G. Ulmer. The film follows a hitchhiker who gets wrapped up in blackmail and manslaughter. Though made through a "poverty row" studio with cheap sets and bad acting, it has gained praise over the years and can be considered a classic of Film Noir. The film is now in the public domain, but it likely wasn't when "Femme Fatale" was made.

"Mightier Than the Sword"

Written by: Brian Helgeland
Directed by: Armand Mastroianni
Original airdate: January 8, 1990
Cursed antique: Fountain pen

A huge group of people have gathered outside a prison to celebrate the death sentence of Clint Fletcher. Nicknamed the Rocky Mountain Barber, Fletcher was convicted of murdering sixteen coeds and sentenced to die in the gas chamber. The crowd outside is made up entirely of death sentence supporters. It is like a football game, with people tailgating in the parking lot and holding signs with slogans like, "Breathe deep, Clint" and "How long can you hold your breath?"

Inside the prison, crime biographer Alex Dent (Colm Feore) is the envy of the other journalists because he gets an exclusive with Fletcher. "I helped catch him," he explains gleefully. Inside the holding cell, Fletcher is chained up, with an unrepentant, steely expression. When Dent asks if he has any final words, Fletcher tries to attack him. Dent stabs him in the neck with his fountain pen and pulls back a little trigger. The pen glows and Fletcher passes out for a moment. When he comes to, he has no idea where he is; Dent has to explain it to him. He freaks out, struggling and fighting the guards every step of the way to the gas chamber. He cries, begs for help, insists he is innocent. The guards ignore him, lock him up, and gas him to death.

After the execution, Dent leaves with the chaplain (Thomas Hauff) who gave the last rights. They discuss the ethics of the death penalty and the nature of evil. Dent explains that he thinks evil is a disease that has simply left Fletcher and moved on to someone else. He wants to discuss this more, and the chaplain goes to his car for a card. Dent injects him with the pen, releasing into the clergyman the evil he drew from Fletcher.

A few days later, Jack and Johnny convince Micki to come with them to a lecture Dent is giving. He again espouses his belief that evil is a disease, something that can infect a person, rewiring his chromosomes, and turning him into a madman. "You're the disease!" a man screams from the audience. "You write these books as if you enjoy the killing." He thinks Dent encourages serial killers. Dent defends himself, and the man reveals himself to be Jerry Fletcher—Clint Fletcher's brother. The two verbally spar some more, until Dent says, "All you are doing is convincing this audience that insanity runs in the family." Jerry loses it and security has to drag him away.

Dent continues his lecture, telling the audience that, although the police have kept a low profile on the case, there is a serial killer on the loose. He has killed twice and Dent predicts he will strike again, soon. He also claims the killer is a minister or priest, "driven by some twisted religious concept, hunting those he once helped." He predicts tonight will be the night he strikes. After the lecture, Johnny approaches Dent for an autograph and the obnoxious, stereotypical "I'm an aspiring writer, can you give me advice?" question that he not-so-secretly hopes will yield a mentorship. Dent, of course, is far more interested in Micki. Jerry is also waiting for Dent, and accuses him of somehow being involved in his brother's murder spree. Dent invites him to meet him at the Neon Gargoyle for drinks later that night. (Yes, the Neon Gargoyle is also the vampire club in "Night Prey.")

Back in his hotel room, Dent begins to write. He pricks his finger with the pen and writes fervently, describing the evil coursing through "his" veins, time to cleanse another soul of the sins of the world. He is referring, of course, to the chaplain, and he is sending him to kill Jerry Fletcher. (Doesn't get any more suspicious than that.) Jerry and the chaplain meet in an alley, and the chaplain shoots, just once. Jerry drops, presumably dead, and the killer gives his final benediction: "I am the resurrection and the light. He who believeth in me shall never die." He fires three more shots before he leaves. I didn't notice this until just recently, but I am pretty sure the four gun shots are meant to represent the four points of the cross. Dent drops his pen, sweaty and panting. It looks like he just had an orgasm over his last sentence: "This is the first time a killer contacted me directly." He starts writing again, and sure enough, the chaplain goes to a pay phone.

The morning paper reports that Dent's prediction came true: there was a murder last night. But there are two new wrinkles: the killer contacted Dent, and the victim is Jerry Fletcher. This is all too coincidental for Jack's taste and he sends Micki and Johnny to the press conference he is holding.

Director Armand Mastroianni with Colm Feore on "Mightier Than the Sword."
Photo courtesy of Armand Mastroianni.

Harold (Michael Caruana), Dent's manager, alibis him for the murder and won't let Micki or Johnny speak to him. So, they sit and listen in on the press conference. Detective Adams speaks first, promising that Dent has offered his services as a consultant only. Dent quickly takes over and insists that this madman must be stopped—how they do that is immaterial. Someone asks if these murders will end up in his next book. Dent isn't concerned about that; he is concerned with catching the killer. He reveals that the killer asked to meet Dent in person tonight, and Detective Adams pulls Dent back for a congressional hearing-style whisper. He continues, quite confident that if the killer is reaching out, he wants to stop. After the press conference, Detective Adams rails against Dent's showboating, and reminds him that he is calling the shots.

The trio meets up back at the store to share their findings. Dent has published three books on serial killers in the last five years, but before that he didn't exist. No other books, no other life. All three subjects of his books had no memories of the killings. Jack couldn't find Alex Dent in the manifest (though that shouldn't matter because so many of the objects ended up in other people's hands). The only writing-related implement, a pen, was sold to a Billy Frazer. Johnny has his first (and only) brilliant idea: maybe they are the same? Micki offers to talk to Harold while the guys go look around the "east side."

This is where Dent is supposed to meet the killer. He is wearing a wire, and there is a heavy police detail in the surroundings, ready to arrest the killer. The detective tells Dent they will move in when he says "This isn't good," which is the worst code ever—try jamming that into everyday conversation. As soon as Dent is out of eyeshot, he rips off the wire.

The cops know this and move in. Dent is taking a moment to write. It's time to end it, but he wants one more victim to "sweeten the climax." Detective Adams creeps down the alley alone, and Dent reveals himself, telling him he is writing the final chapter. The chaplain appears and shoots the detective dead. Dent grabs him, sucks the evil out, and recedes into the shadows as the cops swoop in. The chaplain is confused as Dent reveals himself, claiming the killer came out of nowhere, there was nothing he could do. Johnny sees this all unfold.

Meanwhile, Micki has staked out the lobby of Dent's hotel. She sees him come in with Harold, who can hardly contain himself, he is so excited about the press and the advance his next book will garner. An "old friend" interrupts, and Dent's face clouds over. He sends Harold upstairs while he chats with his wife, Marion Frazer (Donna Goodhand). He is not happy to see her and wonders how she found him. "I just turned on the television and there you were," she states. It's not like Dent has been living under the radar—he thrives on the spotlight. It should come as no surprise to him that he could be easily found. Marion flirts with him in a taunting, cat-and-mouse way, before stating the obvious: she wants money. "I supported you while you wrote this trash," she says, smacking a pulp novel into his hands. Dent is unmoved until Marion threatens to out him as Billy Frazer to his fans.

He relents, takes down her address, and tells her he will "make some plans," but never wants to see her again.

"Then make sure I don't come back," Marion quips. She gives him a kiss and takes her leave. Dent tosses his book into the trash. He takes the stairs up to his room.

Micki overheard the whole conversation, and Dent noticed her in the lobby, which is why he took the stairs. Micki collects the book from the trash then pursues Dent into the stairwell. It appears empty, but she continues—even after the lights go out. Dent grabs her, knocks her out, and injects her with his evil pen. "There has never been a female serial killer," he muses, "until now."

Johnny returns to Curious Goods and tells Jack what he saw in the alley. Jack fits the pieces together and thinks that Dent is controlling the killers with the pen. Micki stumbles in, looking rattled, and explains that she followed Dent to his room but someone knocked her out and stole her wallet. Jack puts the investigation on hold and puts Micki to bed.

Back at his hotel, Dent has started working on his next bestseller. "You will take me closer to murder than I have ever been," Dent tells Micki's license. He wants to make her something vicious. "A slasher," he says in an amused tone. He writes: "The evil multiplied quickly in her blood, slowly transforming her into the monster she was to become."

Micki is washing up before bed, but seems inexplicably drawn to the medicine cabinet, where she finds Jack's straight razor and smiles. As Jack is locking up the store, Micki comes partway downstairs, a far-away, glazed expression on her face. She says nothing until Jack notices her there and asks if she is okay. The razor is behind her back, and she flicks it with her thumb. "There is something I forgot to tell you," she says, explaining the meeting with Marion and showing him the book that Dent threw away: *Blood Madness*. This confirms that Billy Frazer and Alex Dent are the same person. Micki still stands there, blankly, and Jack asks if he can get her something. She says she is fine and will just say goodnight. This final flick of the blade draws blood and a wince, the only emotion to pass Micki's face.

Jack is reading *Blood Madness* when Johnny comes over the next morning. "The ecstasy as I slashed the life from her... the joy as the heart blood poured over my hands and filled my eager mouth," Jack recites disgustedly. "How could I be so stupid? Of course Alex Dent is using the pen to create killers. He was obsessed with brutality!" Johnny goes to wake Micki and finds she isn't in her room.

That is because Dent is controlling her: "She walked the streets as the evil in her mind enveloped her. The evil picked the time and place, and it is beginning to show its power. She doused herself in the ritualistic foreplay of torture." Micki heads into a bar, where Dent sits in the corner, writing and watching.

A man approaches Micki at the bar and buys her a drink. She takes an offered smoke. "She decided to play with him," Dent writes. The man is starting to get impatient that Micki doesn't immediately drop her panties at a free drink. "I haven't got all day. You know we will have a good time." He takes her hand and she takes out her razor, slicing his hand open. She leaves calmly as the guy screams for someone to call the cops. "The torture was part of the excitement," continues Dent's narrative. "He was the lucky one who got away. Now, she was ready to kill."

Director Armand Mastroianni makes sure things don't get out of control on the set of "Mightier Than the Sword." Photo courtesy of Armand Mastroianni.

Dent's power over Micki abates long enough for her to return to Curious Goods, frantically calling for Jack and Johnny. They have figured out that Dent used the pen on her and have rushed out to find her. But soon Dent is writing again: "She thrived on the fear she evoked in her victims." Micki takes out the razor and spins slowly. "What's happening to me…?" she worries as Dent dictates her next move. "She stepped into the night a predator, the city her prey. Her first victim was Marion Frazer. Marion's killing was the most brutal I had ever seen. It would be artistry, beauty, and symmetry… the bloodlust was maddening. Killing was the only way she could display her talents." Micki arrives at Marion's door.

Jack and Johnny have Dent's hotel lobby staked out. No one has seen Dent, and Johnny starts in with the stupid questions. "If he writes her to kill, she will kill," Jack says with frustration. Johnny redeems himself by suggesting that Micki and Dent are in the same location—he likes to watch. The next person Dent would want to kill is Marion. The two rush to find a phone book, and miss Dent slipping out of the hotel.

Director Armand Mastroianni joins the protesters in "Mightier Than the Sword."
Photo courtesy of Armand Mastroiani.

Marion is getting anxious. Micki just sits there, smoking, completely calm. "He told me to wait. He wants to be here," she explains. Jack calls but before he can tell Marion what is going on, Micki has hung up the phone and approaches with the razor bared. Marion knocks Micki back and escapes into the hall, only to run into Dent. In the struggle, Dent drops both the pen and Marion down the stairs. With her intended victim dead, Micki turns on her creator and chases Dent back into Marion's apartment, slashing at him viciously.

Johnny and Jack have arrived. They check on Marion, then hear screaming upstairs. Jack grabs the pen on the way up, where they find Micki has pinned Dent to the bed and is just going berserk over him.

Johnny begs Micki to stop, but this only succeeds in turning her murderous intentions onto him. Jack holds her back and uses the pen to draw the evil from her neck. Micki goes limp and they take her home.

Alex Dent is left dead by Micki's hand.

Status: The pen is locked up in the vault. Micki is inconsolable over the fact that she killed someone. She cries on Jack's shoulder, but it is a ruse so she can get close enough to slash Jack's neck. It is all a dream, and Micki wakes screaming. Jack rushes in and holds her, promising she is safe.

*   *   *

Another episode I loved. I think it is because I have always been fascinated with serial killers, with the psychology behind them.

Of course, when Alex Dent says "There has never been a female serial killer," he is factually wrong, but anecdotally correct. Female serial killers are not as infamous as their male counterparts because their crimes are rarely as violent, lurid, or random as men's. Most famous is Aileen Wuornos, who has been dubbed "America's first female serial killer" for shooting seven johns to death in the span of a year, but she wasn't captured until after *F13* had wrapped. Female serial killers usually fall into categories like "Angel of Mercy" or "Angel of Death" (respectively, health-care workers who believe they are killing to put people out of their misery, or occasionally revive them and become heroes; or people who join the field as an easy cover for their murders) or "Black Widows" (women who kill their husbands and sometimes their in-laws, usually for money).

Belle Gunness, suspected of killing upwards of forty victims in Indiana at the beginning of the twentieth century; Mary Ann Cotton, an English woman who may have killed as many as twenty-one people, including eleven of her thirteen children in the mid-1800s; and Marybeth Tinning, who was convicted in the death of one out of her nine children (murder could not be proven in the death of the other eight) in the early 1980s are just three examples of female serial killers who operated prior to "Mightier Than the Sword."

Armand Mastroianni directed "Mightier Than the Sword." He got along very well with Louise Robey, and listened to her when she said she wanted to do more than say, "Hey Jack, what do you think?" "I know we wanted to make her become this slasher with the razor. I loved the idea of the razor, better than picking up a knife. Everyone was using a knife. Then I threw in the twist at the end, where she wakes up and is having that dream where she is cutting up Jack at the end. It was almost like a Brian de Palma ending." I never liked this ending—I always found it kind of contrived, like a cheap shot at the audience.

Mastroianni has good things to say about his villain, Colm Feore, who played Alex Dent. "When you get an actor of that caliber, it elevates the other actors. They work harder to be that good. They see the level this guy is putting out and they want to match him. They want to be there to at least parallel his level. I like this episode. It stands up. It is moody, it is atmospheric, it has a nice quality about it. It leads you down this path... this guy is such a manipulator of people."

"What was interesting is that a lot of writers would pitch the same kind of story ideas," recalls Jim Henshaw. "Nothing against them, but because we were basing everything on cursed objects, being writers, we must have heard—from almost every writer who came in—a story about a writer who had a cursed pen. It was just a natural story thing. Brian Helgeland came in and pitched a version of it, and we said, 'Woah, no one has ever pitched that before!' So, we bought that idea."

"Year of the Monkey"

Written by: R. Scott Gemmill
Directed by: Rodney Charters
Original airdate: January 15, 1990
Cursed antique: Three monkey statues

Micki, Jack, and Johnny visit the Bushido Kendo Club, and meet with sensei Musashi (John Fujioka) to buy back a black tea set. Musashi is aware of the "magic" it possesses after he served tea to a student. There is a Japanese fable about a tea set that turned ordinary tea to poison, and it turns out that, with this tea set, the fable is true. The student recovered and Musashi never used it again. Jack promises they have a safe place for it, but Musashi wants them to prove their trustworthiness and asks them to retrieve three monkey idols. The monkey idols represent resistance to evil. Those who mastered them were given great power; those who failed were punished with death. The wealthy and powerful Tanaka clan were said to have the three idols, and Musashi wants them to go after them. He is oddly vague about the whole thing.

Patriarch Tanaka (Robert Ito) is in failing health. He is elderly, on oxygen, and living in Tokyo. He summons for his three children to come home. Each one manages an office of the Tanaka empire. Hito (Von Flores) manages the Hong Kong office; Michiko (Tia Carrere) handles the "local" office (whatever "local" is to Curious Goods); and the youngest, Koji (Leonard Chow), is in charge of the New York office. Tanaka is concerned about how his empire will be managed after his death, and that his children won't act with honor. He gives each of his children a gift, with instructions not to open them until they return home. Whoever fails the test shall not be named in Tanaka's will. The boys are annoyed and think their dad is just playing with them, but Michiko understands that their father just wants the company run properly.

There is no mention of the monkey idols in the manifest. Johnny thinks Musashi is using them to get hold of another cursed object, but Jack doesn't believe it. Musashi was one of the last samurai, and as a samurai, he would never use others for his own gain. Jack found a drawing of the three idols, stamped with Tanaka's seal, among Lewis' things. If Lewis was looking for them, Jack thinks they should be looking for them, too. He sends Johnny to New York and Micki to Hong Kong while he remains home to check into Michiko.

Koji's gift is the "hear no evil" monkey. According to the note his father included, the monkey covers its ears so it cannot hear lies or gossip. To be like the monkey is to be free of evil temptations. "Stubbornness and arrogance keeps him from understanding what he hears from others," the note continues. "You must learn to listen, distinguish truth from falsehood—such is the path of honor." He crumbles up the note and calls his dad crazy.

His secretary comes in with some papers for him to sign. The monkey uncovers his ears, and Koji can hear the secretary's thoughts: "I bet he wants me to stick around while he signs these, like I have nothing better to do. Just sign them, don't ask for the detail sheets." Koji is confused, but then hears his secretary think, "Things ran a lot smoother while you were in Tokyo." As a sort of punishment, Koji asks for the detail sheets. The monkey puts its paws back over its ears.

Koji gets some insider trading info thanks to the mind-reading monkey and is intrigued. He calls his dad to ask if he should act on it. "A wise man knows when to hear, and when to be deaf." This is not the advice Koji was looking for, and he makes a call, instructing his trader to buy as much of the stock as he can, and spread it around so they don't know where it's coming from. The monkey starts laughing, the power goes off, and Koji disappears.

Koji is transported via monkey back to his father in Tokyo. Tanaka accuses his son of abusing the gift he gave him and gives him one final chance to die with honor: commit seppuku. Koji refuses, and his father warns his death will be one of great suffering. Gongs bellow, deafening Koji, who collapses.

Johnny tries to flirt his way past the secretary, but it doesn't work. So, he dresses up as a delivery boy and forces his way past the secretary, into Koji's office. He is not there. Suddenly the lights go out and Koji appears, slumped over his desk, bloody and very dead. Shohei (Lawrence Nakamura), Tanaka's assistant, slips in, takes the monkey, and slips out. Johnny tries to follow him, but it is like he has disappeared.

Hito has the "see no evil" monkey, who hides its eyes from wicked temptations. "Those you can't exploit, you deceive, and so deceive yourself," Tanaka's note accuses. "You must become a truthful man whose word is trusted. Only then will you be a man of honor." Hito takes offense to the characterization.

He is off to his importer, and on the way Micki tries to talk to him. He blows her off, so she grabs a taxi and follows. Micki hides while Hito checks on a delivery. A customs agent comes to check on his merchandise and finds it filled with illegal ivory. "It's not what it looks like," Hito stammers. The monkey uncovers its eyes and the ivory changes into innocuous china that no animals lost their lives to make. The customs agent is dumbfounded but has no other recourse, so she leaves. Hito smiles and picks up the monkey—which swiftly transports him back to Tokyo.

Appearing before his father, who is looking subtly younger than he did when we last saw him, Hito is accused of abusing the power of the statue and his father offers him the same choice: a death of honor or a death of suffering. Hito thinks he is trying to intimidate him and takes the proffered sword. He meets Tanaka's bluff, but when his father doesn't stop him from plunging the sword into his gut, Hito holds it to his father's throat. The gongs chime and fire burns out Hito's eyeballs. Back in Hong Kong, Micki rushes into the cargo container to grab the monkey, but Shohei gets there first. He briefly knocks Micki out and disappears. When she wakes, she is laying next to Hito, eyes horribly disfigured and his mouth open in a silent scream of agony.

Jack has been having a hard time getting a meeting with Michiko. He takes the idol drawing to Musashi and asks him to translate it. It tells the story of how the monkeys were brought from the underworld to challenge mankind's virtue. Few have mastered the virtues of the idols. Those who fail are punished with death; those who succeed are granted "rejuvenation." "It is said that all men live forever through their children," he offers cryptically, but gives nothing more.

After hearing the matching stories Micki and Johnny gave, Jack is adamant that Musashi will help him. Musashi claims he is forbidden to, but then takes Jack into his library and tells him the whole story: Tanaka stole the idols from the Temple of the Monkey God in Burma. The Tanaka clan became very wealthy, but suffered from accidents which wiped out the coming generations. He shows Jack some photos and explains that the monkeys allow Tanaka to live on if he sacrifices his family to them. He has been doing this for centuries. Musashi, one of the last true samurai, was sent to kill Tanaka in 1945 and return the idols to the temple. But he fell in love with Tanaka's daughter. The two were planning on committing shimju, lover's suicide. Musashi reveals a huge scar on his stomach. "Even that I could not do properly." Now, he must live a humble life of shame. Jack is more determined than ever to see Michiko.

Michiko has been given the "speak no evil" monkey. "Learn to speak for yourself," the note says, "only someone with courage can manage my empire. Choose your words carefully. Speak only what you know in your heart to be true."

She meets with an employee who has missed thirty days of work. He apologizes, saying he and his wife have been going through hard times. He offers to make it up in overtime, but the monkey tells a different tale: he's got a mistress. "He cheats on his wife and he is doing the same to you." The monkey encourages Michiko to fire him, but she ignores the idol and promises her employee they will work something out. He thanks her and leaves.

Michiko then speaks directly to the monkey idol: "Say whatever you want, I'm never going to use your powers." The room goes dark and Michiko screams as she is transported to Tokyo. Jack, who had been waiting in the lobby the entire time, rushes in. He finds no Michiko, but he does slip away with the idol.

In Tokyo, Michiko kneels before her father, who looks younger still. No one comments on this. Tanaka is proud of her. She alone has proven she has honor, and he has waited a long time for a child such as her, one who didn't abuse the magic. "The monkeys will serve you, and I can go on, knowing my empire will be led with wisdom and integrity." He hands her the sword, like he did with all his children, but this one is not for seppuku; this is for Michiko to use on her own father, "as you must do to your own children if they dishonor you." Michiko is disgusted at the thought. "If I am to find peace, you must send me to the next life and abide by the idols. It's the only way." Tanaka encourages her to "show your courage," but Michiko cannot. Instead, she commits seppuku.

Jack puts the single "speak no evil" idol in the vault when he hears the door chimes. He goes up and finds the door open, but no one there. Shohei appears and demands the idol back. Jack plays dumb, and gets knocked out for his efforts. When Micki and Johnny finally return home, they find a note, telling them that Tanaka has Jack, and will trade him for the statue. The only natural place the idol would be is in the vault, so they retrieve it, then take it back upstairs, guessing that it will transport them to Tokyo. Johnny warns Micki that it is probably a trap, but she reminds him that it's the only chance they've got. Musashi is upstairs in his samurai gear, and announces he is here to help Jack. The monkey comes to life, laughing, and transports the three of them to Tokyo.

Musashi leads Micki and Johnny through Tanaka's compound, where they find Jack, guarded by a young Tanaka. He wants his idol and holds his sword to Jack's neck. Jack begs them not to give it up, "he has no evil power without all three." Tanaka raises his sword to strike, but Musashi jumps into action and faces off against Tanaka. The men battle while Micki and Johnny untie Jack. Tanaka comes running at Musashi with his sword, and at the last minute, Musashi drops his sword. He is impaled on Tanaka's sword, much to his horror. A samurai who kills an unarmed man has no honor. Tanaka insists he was tricked, but the monkey idols don't care. All three laugh and the gongs chime. Johnny grabs the idols and they are transported back to Curious Goods, leaving behind Tanaka, who is presumably killed.

Status: The monkey idols are stored in the vault. Johnny promises he will pick up the tea set from the kendo school tomorrow. If Johnny is in charge, there is only about a 40% chance that it will actually make it into the vault.

Mentioned but not explored: Tea set

*　*　*

I never understood why Musashi wouldn't help with the monkey idols. He has history with Tanaka, so it might be hard for him to get close. But why wouldn't he give *any* info to Jack, even after they have proven their trustworthiness? He has been shamed, sure. But isn't it more shameful to send strangers to fight your battles? And why would Musashi trust them with the idols, but not with the tea set?

I loved the scene where our heroes have sushi with Musashi. Johnny is so disgusted by sushi, which amuses me because who doesn't love sushi? I guess sushi wasn't as popular in the 1980s as it is today, where there is a sushi bar on every corner. Micki, of course, loves sushi. The tuna tartare with quail's egg is her favorite.

Production designer Stephen Roloff names "Year of the Monkey" as one of his favorite episodes. "We didn't have many writers, so the scripts sometimes arrived late," Roloff explains. "Just a few days before camera, we got a script for the next episode, which included scenes in the home of a Japanese Samurai warrior. This was pre-Internet, so a member of my art department team spent a lot of time at the library. She came back with reference material, including original blueprints for a five-story Japanese pagoda, the ones with curved roofs and elaborate carvings. As a joke, I had the drafting team print these onto our regular blueprint paper and send them down to the construction department. When Adam Kolodziej, our art director, went to check on the carpenters an hour later, they were poring over the drawings and ordering materials and manpower. There was no way that they were going to build a five-story Japanese pagoda in three days… but that didn't mean they weren't going to try!"

The notion of "see no evil, hear no evil, speak no evil" is a fairly common one, but the tale of the three wise monkeys probably originates from Confucius' Code of Conduct. The first pictorial depiction of the monkeys is thought to be the seventeenth century carvings by Hidari Jingoro at the Toshogu Shrine in Nikko, Japan. The three monkeys have names ("see no evil" is Mizaru; "hear no evil" is Kikazaru, and "speak no evil" is Iwazaru) and are Japanese macaques, monkeys that are native to Japan's snowy northern regions.

"Epitaph for a Lonely Soul"

Written by: Carl Binder
Directed by: Allan Kroeker
Original airdate: January 22, 1990
Cursed antique: Mortician's aspirator

Morticians are often portrayed as creepy loners with strange predilections. So, it is rather strange that it wasn't until season three that *F13* decided to tackle the topic.

Eli Leonard (Neil Munro) is one such stereotypical mortician. He is good at his job—even if he uses canned patter to soothe mourners. In fact, his only creepy habit seems to be keeping a scrapbook of all the corpses he has buried. That is, until another mortician brings him an overflow corpse. Eli spies an antique mortician's tool, an aspirator, in the back of the van, and asks to keep it. According to mortician gossip, Neville Morton, founder of the Glenview Mortuary (where Eli works) was using the aspirator to embalm his dead wife when he had a heart attack and died. Some say Morton murdered his wife, that she was alive when he began to embalm her.

Eli sets to work on the kid who was just brought in, a motorcycle victim whose parents insist on an open casket. He decides to give his new antique toy a try. He plunges the aspirator into the corpse's abdomen, blue light flows into him, and the corpse sits straight up on the table, screaming. This whole scene is viewed by Steve Wells (Barclay Hope), a man whose young, beautiful fiancée, Lisa (Monika Schnarre) died of a congenital heart defect. He has been having a hard time letting go, and was there late saying a final goodbye to Lisa before her funeral. He runs off, and Eli doesn't pursue. He is too busy putting the pieces together. "Morton uses it to kill his wife, I use it to revive a dead body." He re-kills the motorcycle kid.

Micki and Jack are holding a cocktail party at Curious Goods for the Antique Dealer's Association. Jack hates it, but it is his duty as treasurer to do so. The police commissioner, an ass hat married to a porcelain dealer, teases Jack about his "occult adventures" and tells him about Steve's report about a corpse coming to life on the embalming table. (It seems "right up Jack's alley.") Since the police commissioner won't look into Steve's "crazy" story, Jack decides he and Micki will.

After Steve reiterates his story to Jack and Micki, they go visit Eli, interrupting his "courting" of Lisa. Eli shows Jack and Micki the corpse, and explains that Steve is just going through a hard time right now. "It's not an easy thing to lose a loved one." Micki murmurs "I know," in a move I like to think is a subtle ode to Ryan. Micki and Jack are satisfied with this answer. Steve isn't sold, but there is no evidence otherwise, so he puts it aside and attends Lisa's funeral. It's an open casket funeral, but before heading to the gravesite, Eli slickly swaps the coffins. The coffin that is buried in Lisa's grave is empty.

That night is Eli's... first date with Lisa. (Wedding?) He lays her out on his table, surrounded by candles, and tells her "tonight my solitude will end." He removes her engagement ring and unbuttons her dress, then plunges the aspirator deep into her gut. Her fingers twitch, her body shakes, and her eyes blink open. She is submissive, completely still, until Eli begins kissing her. She gives in to the physical.

The next morning, Lisa tries to speak. It takes her a few tries, but she finally chokes out "Where am I?" Eli tells her that she is his wife, and her name is Deborah. He leaves her alone when he hears the bell downstairs. Micki has brought Steve back to show him the corpse of the motorcycle kid. Steve insists on speaking to Eli, but it devolves into an argument. He pushes past Eli into the workroom while Eli speaks to Micki outside, warning her to get him out of here or he will call the cops. Steve finds Lisa's engagement ring in the workroom and pockets it before Micki drags him out. Eli returns to Lisa, who was listening to the argument from upstairs. She recognizes Steve's voice, but Eli ignores her inquiries and puts her back to bed.

Steve goes to the cemetery that night and digs up Lisa's grave. Her coffin is empty, save for a few sandbags. He goes straight back to the mortuary, sneaks in through an open window, and goes into the upstairs residence. He wakes Lisa, who recognizes him immediately, but Eli appears behind him and stabs Steve through with the aspirator. Lisa is inconsolable.

Later, she creeps downstairs, looking for Steve, but finds only Eli in the basement, having just cremated Steve. Lisa cries, proclaims Eli as crazy, and begs to be left alone. "You should be grateful!" Eli insists. "You are alive, and Steve is dead." He insists she will grow to love him (what every

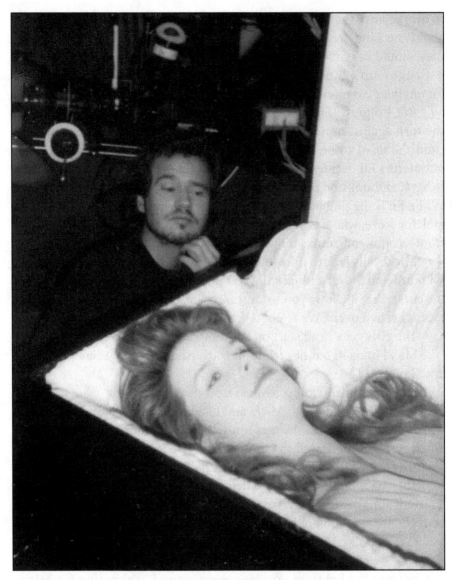

Director Allan Kroeker checks on Monika Schnarre in "Epitaph for a Lonely Soul."
Photo courtesy of Allan Kroeker.

girl wants to hear) but she runs, determined to go home. Eli fulfills her request, sort of: he seals her in a coffin.

Back at Curious Goods, Micki is getting worried because she hasn't been able to reach Steve. She finally gets around to telling Jack about Steve's story about the aspirator. Jack had checked the manifest for items sold to Eli Leonard, but decides to go back and check for anything related to morticians. The more I think about how lackadaisical they have been about checking the manifest, the more frustrated I become. By this point, they should have the manifest damn near memorized. Any time there is a strange murder, they should be combing through that manifest looking for *anything* even remotely related.

But I digress. Eli is pondering his predicament with Lisa. Why did she turn against him? What did he do wrong? (I think raising a woman from the dead to be enslaved as his "wife" pretty much answers those questions.) Eli decides that he didn't wait long enough. So, he goes back to his scrapbook and picks Linda Curry (Claire Cellucci), dead two years. While Eli is digging up Linda's grave, Micki sneaks into the mortuary to look for Steve, who has been missing for at least a day. She hears a rattling from a coffin and cranks it open. Lisa sits straight up, gasping for air.

Micki calls Jack to inform him that she found Lisa (who informs her Eli murdered Steve) and Jack fills her in on what he has figured out about the curse: that it allows you to "restore a life, only after you've taken one." Jack is headed over. "We've got to find the aspirator!"

The girls get a head start on the hunt, and head into the workroom.

Micki finds it, but her triumph is overshadowed by Lisa's frightened cry. "Look out!"

Eli comes in and knocks Micki unconscious.

When she wakes, both Micki and Lisa are tied down. Linda's corpse is lying on his slab, and Eli blames himself for the minor decomposition: "I didn't embalm her as well as I should have." He will also call her Deborah. He turns to Lisa and pointedly informs her that Linda won't turn against him, then he aspirates Linda and helps her sit up. To Micki, he muses that if he embalms her properly, she will last a number of years. "Then you will be ready for me." Before he can aspirate Micki, the doorbell rings. (Jack is always so polite.) Eli tapes Micki's mouth shut and answers the door.

Jack isn't *that* polite—he let himself in. Eli must have figured this out, because the lights go out. He creeps around, whispering for Micki. Eli comes up behind him but before he can strike, Micki screams. The tape has come off her mouth and she is begging Linda to help set her free. Jack heads towards the sound, Eli following behind. Before Jack can pick the lock to the workroom, Eli attacks. The men fight, and Jack takes the struggle down into the basement.

Micki is free from her restraints and follows the sound of the fight into the basement. She hits Eli over the head with a vase. He tumbles down the remaining steps, falls on his own aspirator, then stumbles into the incinerator. Eli catches fire. I'm not sure in what world a mortician (or any human being) would leave embalming fluid and other flammable liquids right next to a flaming cremation chamber, but Eli does. The fluids spill and the fire spreads quickly.

Jack and Micki run, making a quick stop to save Linda and Lisa, but it is too late for them. The flames have them surrounded. They hold each other and let the fire take them.

Status: Jack had to sift through the ashes of the mortuary, but he got the aspirator back and stowed it safely in the vault.

* * *

It took viewing this episode as an adult to realize just how twisted it is. As a kid, it just seemed as weird and creepy as any other episode; as an adult, you can see how this is basically TV-friendly necrophilia. Screenwriter Carl Binder says, "With this one, I really had to police myself. A friend of mine was a mortician for awhile, and it's a very strange profession. I don't remember a lot of the process during the writing of this script, but I do remember having to dial it back, because the mortician (who I named after my mortician friend) had a thing for dead bodies. It was always fun to see how far Jim [Henshaw] and his team would push it."

"To my recollection, it was outrageous and macabre and utterly absurd," says director Allan Kroeker. "'Epitaph' was all about the destructive folly of control. I don't think it was sleazy, performance-wise, owing largely to the talents of the late Neil Munro. The mortician clearly wanted a serious 'relationship' with the women. It kept going wrong and the more he tried to control it, the worse it got. It was darkly comic and sad because he was such a lonely figure."

One thing that I had forgotten about until I turned on the episode was the scrapbook that Leonard kept of all his corpses. As a kid, that seemed totally normal to me. As an adult, I realize that is not normal. Unless he was just keeping a portfolio of his work, like any artist. Leonard using the scrapbook to "shop" for his next wife is where it gets undeniably sinister.

"I was surprised to get the part of Steve Wells, as I felt I was still Lloyd," says actor Barclay Hope. He looks back fondly on working with Neil Munro. "He was truly something special. One of Canada's leading actor/directors who left us far too early."

Actress Monika Schnarre played Lisa in this episode, and agreed it was very creepy. "The only misgivings I remember having were getting into the coffin. It's not something I want to do again for a *long* time. It was very difficult to lie perfectly still. The hardest part is controlling your breath."

"I may have crawled into the coffin myself to demonstrate," says Kroeker of putting his actress at ease. "I've done that few times to convince an actor that it was all okay. What I do remember is that she was statuesque, she was of super-model height, and the coffin was too short. She had to bend her knees to fit. I recall her laughing about it. I'd never worked with a model before and she did a great job and she was fun."

The aspirator is an actual mortician's tool. A metal tube with blades on the end is plunged into the abdomen in order to drain the internal organs of liquid. A hose is attached to suck out the fluids, then an adapter attaches to the embalming fluid and fills up the organs, preventing bacteria from growing. "The aspirator was rigged to simulate penetration," Kroeker says of his prop, "like a spring-loaded knife, so he could really plunge it into the corpse and the illusion was pretty convincing and utterly gross. Our episode was 'recalled' by the sponsor, a car manufacturer, who insisted that we excise about ten frames from this effect. I thought that was pretty sensational, having my episode 'censored!'"

"Midnight Riders"

Written by: Jim Henshaw
Directed by: Allan Eastman
Original airdate: January 29, 1990
Cursed antique: None

Jack has taken Micki and Johnny out to the country to watch a planetary convergence. The last time this convergence happened was in 1972, coincidentally on the same day. According to Jack, some ancients believe that when a major configuration like this happens, the past repeats itself. Micki sees a shooting star, which Johnny's mom called "heaven's fireworks," and they would shoot off whenever an angel got its wings. (And I shot a little bit of vomit into my mouth.)

Not too far away from our stargazing trio, a pair of teenagers, Penny and Tommy (Andrea Roth and David Orth), are fooling around in a parked car. Further down the road, an older man named Cawley (Dennis Thatcher) bids farewell to a long haul trucker from whom he hitched a ride, and he walks to town.

A motorcycle gang, the Dragon Riders, appears out of nowhere. The gang stops with the kids, and Tommy gets out to deal with them, thinking it is a rival school punking them. The motorcyclists' faces are obscured by the glare of their headlights, and Tommy offers them his wallet. The bikers want to know where Randall Betz is. Tommy admits he is his father, and this leads to a beating. Seeing Penny in the car, they start making obscene gestures and one guy breaks the window in order to pull Penny out. "Leave her alone!" bellows Cawley.

"This time you lose, old man," one of the bikers retorts. "Tonight we finish it."

Micki hears the ruckus and the trio decides to check it out. They arrive as the bikers ride off. Micki and Johnny check on the kids, but Jack is frozen. He can't believe his eyes. Cawley is his father. Jack hasn't spoken to his father in a decade; he thought he was dead.

The group heads into town. Penny's mother, Cynthia (Fiona Reid), is furious. Penny isn't supposed to see Tommy, and she grounds her. Micki and Johnny take Penny home while her mother, the town's doctor, takes Tommy to the clinic. Penny fills them in on the pertinent stuff: her father died before she was born, and the town has their own version of "The Legend of Sleepy Hollow," except instead of the Headless Horseman, it is a Headless Biker.

The bikers are rampaging through the town, commenting on how things haven't changed. They also fill us in on what they are doing there: they came back from the grave for the Dragon, the leader of their gang. Until they get him, their beef is with the ones who put them here (aka killed them): the sheriff, Betz, and "the girl." If those three are dead when the last planet aligns, they get the Dragon back and they get their lives back.

Like any good small town, the residents have a nasty secret, and Cynthia meets with Randall Betz—now Reverend Betz (John Bayliss)—to discuss their situation cryptically. Cynthia is concerned that the kids are seeing each other still, and is concerned that seventeen years ago was when Cawley was last seen in town, witness to someone else getting beaten on that same road. As if summoned, Cawley appears and needs to know where they buried "him." "We have to dredge up the past or it will bury us all." Cawley informs them that the bikers are back for the Dragon, and the only way to stop them is bury him in hallowed ground, and the truth must be known.

Seventeen years ago, the sheriff was a young deputy, but he remembers these bikers—remembers they were killed. The gang just wants the Dragon, but the sheriff doesn't know where he is. They don't believe him, and one particularly rough, bearded biker grabs a chain. The sheriff shoots, but the bullet goes right through—can't just shoot something that is already dead. Beardy wraps the chain around the sheriff's neck and they drive off, dragging the sheriff behind them.

Jack doesn't understand what brought his dad to this town. Everyone seems to know him, but he loves the ocean and exotic ports, not inland backwater towns like this one. Cawley insists his son be on his way, not to worry about him. They are interrupted when the gang drives up, the badly battered and thoroughly dead sheriff dragging behind. Reverend Betz shows up and Cawley once again pleads with him to tell him where the Dragon is buried. "Everything will happen like before, only this time they won't be stopped." The reverend runs.

He goes straight to Cynthia, and like a panicking school boy, tells her what happened, the same as before. Next they will block the roads, cut off the town, and come for them. On cue, the power goes out. Penny, who had been eavesdropping, shouts for her mother and the reverend urges them to leave as soon as they can.

Jack, Micki, and Johnny congregate at the sheriff's station and Cawley finally fills them in on the whole story: Seventeen years ago, he was passing through town, hitchhiking to his new ship. The Dragon Riders were here too, and they came upon a young couple on a deserted road and roughed them up. The sheriff arrested their leader, a huge man called the Dragon, and put him in jail in the hopes the others would leave town. The gang swore that if anything happened to the Dragon, they would be back. The boy was only bruised, but the girl said she was raped. The Riders said she was lying, and when the sheriff tried to arrest them, they killed him. The phone and power lines were cut, and roads in and out of town were blocked off, then the gang came down on the townspeople. But the town was ready and wiped them out. The Dragon tried to escape in the confusion, but Cawley grabbed a fire axe and beheaded him. He could have let him go but he didn't. After it was over, they found the girl hadn't been raped; she just lied to save her reputation. The boy was off to Bible college. (If you haven't figured it out, the girl was Cynthia and the boy was Reverend Betz.) The town burned the bodies of the gang and buried the Dragon. "They were killed for what they seemed to be, not what they were," Cawley finishes. Jack asks why here, why now, though it seems that he answered that question in the cold open. "Everything is the same as it was before. The place, the date. I'm here."

The reverend thinks he sees Cawley go into church, but all he finds are the bikers, blinding him with their headlights. The gang roughs him up while taunting him with gems such as, "We kicked the fear of god into you." They decide to give the reverend the same chance he gave the Dragon. The reverend runs, screaming for help, and the bikers roar after him, quickly forming a circle around him. The reverend prays, and one of the bikers knocks him down, killing him easily. As Tommy rushes to him, the bikers peel out.

Cawley informs Jack, Micki, and Johnny that the Dragon has to be buried in consecrated ground, otherwise he will join the other bikers and they will roam together, forever. Jack is getting suspicious and asks how he knows this. Cawley dodges his son's questions and assures him that the Dragon is the only one who has a score to settle with him. They have just over an hour before the final planet converges.

Jack and Cawley take Tommy to Cynthia's house. She answers the door with a bayonet. Tommy rushes in to check on Penny, and Cynthia gives up on trying to keep them apart. Cawley needs to know where the Dragon is buried, but she is still concerned about keeping the lie. "They got what was coming to them," Cynthia offers weakly. But she finally admits to Penny that she lied about saying she was raped. She won't admit the final truth, but she will tell them where the Dragon is buried: in Weaver's Field, by the old well. Luckily Penny is a bright girl and she figures it out on her own. Reverend Betz is her real father, which makes Tommy her half-brother.

Cynthia runs upstairs for something or other before heading out with the group to get the corpse, but the bikers are waiting for her in her room. "You told them we raped you—you got one coming," one of them tells her. More bikers invade downstairs, and they force Cynthia onto one of their bikes. Johnny jumps Beardy and is knocked out easily, but it gives Cynthia a chance to run. Unfortunately, she just stands there, and a biker runs her over. But she isn't dead, and as long as she is alive they have a chance.

Jack and Micki work on digging up the Dragon while Johnny heads to the cemetery and preps a grave. The ground starts to rumble and Micki and Jack are bathed in a yellow light as a bike roars out of the ground. "My god, Cynthia must have died!" Jack surmises. He and Micki narrowly avoid the headless biker as he puts his rotten head atop his neck and wields his axe. Jack hot wires a car and they race off. The Dragon keeps up with them, hitting the car wildly with his axe. Jack turns sharply. The Dragon is about as quick to react as one might expect from a person who has been dead for almost two decades, and he runs right into the car. This doesn't stop him though, and Jack leads him to the cemetery.

Once there, Cawley finally reveals to Jack that he hasn't earned the right to be buried in hallowed ground. He died ten years ago and was buried at sea. This was his chance to redeem himself. Cawley stares down the Dragon, and the Dragon tries to chop him to bits. Again, hard to fight a ghost with a human weapon, and the axe just goes through him. Johnny is ready for the Dragon and as he enters the cemetery, Johnny whacks him with a shovel. The Dragon falls right into a grave and Johnny buries him as fast as he can.

Status: Penny and Tommy are about to be slaughtered by the bikers, but the Dragon was buried just in time, and they disappear. Similarly, Cawley disappears, which means Jack doesn't get a proper goodbye. He doesn't know what he is feeling right now. "How do you grieve for someone who died a decade ago?" Johnny goes and ruins the moment by pointing to a shooting star. "He made it, Jack."

* * *

"Midnight Riders" is the only episode without a cursed object, just a supernatural occurrence. Writer Jim Henshaw says it "was an experiment to see if we could stretch, see if we could go into this aspect of the genre and do a story there." Other episodes have been without antiques sold by Lewis, but there was a source of evil that could be identified and contained: "Wedding in Black" had the snow globe; "Doorway to Hell" had the mirror; "The Prophecies" had the book of Lucifer. But "Midnight Riders" doesn't have anything that can be locked up in the vault; nothing that can be contained.

"We always called this show 'Bikers From Hell,' among ourselves," reveals director Allan Eastman. "A better title, but the series was already under siege in the US from Christian and Southern rightists for its 'Satanic content.' I think anyone that actually believes that Lucifer and his demons are real is considerably crazier than anything we portrayed on that show." Eastman admits the content was extreme, violent, and bloody, but "like all material like that, the show was interesting to do because it was unlike anything else you got to work on." For example, Eastman remembers being shocked that the church in the little town they were shooting in actually allowed them to bring motorcycles into the church and crash out through the front door. "Everybody is fascinated by show biz, I guess."

One thing that always stuck out to me about this episode was that it was really dark. Visually dark. I think it was detrimentally dark. Hard to see what was going on. But Eastman assures me he had a reason for doing so. "Doing the show was rarely fun because of the content and the long night shoots," he admits, "but at the same time, it always felt important to do it as well as you could and to push the limits on it because it was unlikely you'd ever get the chance to work on anything like that again.

"There's no question that violence and evil exist in the world but it is humans that do it, not some outside mythical supernatural force. That's the way I tried to approach it and I just used the cursed aspect as a metaphor for human cruelty. Maybe I pushed a little harder to be dark on this episode because it was my second time around and because the material itself was so dark. As a director, I always wanted to take scenes as far as I could take them and maybe a little beyond. I loved horror movies and Lovecraft and Poe when I was a kid, so this was a chance to really engage with the Dark Side, to not be afraid of it and to see where you could really go with it.

"There were very interesting places to explore in the relationship between Jack and his dad, with the murder of the bikers and the dark acts behind the facade of the little town and its inhabitants. It was fun as a filmmaker to peel all that back. Plus, how often in life do you ever get to give the direction, 'Put more maggots on the headless biker's neck?'"

Line producer J. Miles Dale recalls one of the insane stunts they did on this episode. "That was an episode that was inspired by the Meat Loaf album cover [*Bat Out of Hell*]. We dug this tunnel to have this motorcycle come out, and Jamie Jones was going to be riding it. He hadn't done that many stunts at that point. We told him, 'Jamie, you are a headless biker, you are coming to get this guy, and you are wielding an axe, so we need you to come over a hill where your head is in your shoulders so you can't see, you need to be holding the axe in one hand, and you need to be pulling a wheelie.' And he did it! It was the greatest thing ever."

Eastman goes into more detail. "The Bat Out of Hell shot was an amazing set up. We dug a long ramp down ten feet underground, then a passage of about fifty feet with a sharp upturn at the end. The grave was covered with breakaway foam and dirt and we had two air cannons down there to fire dust into the air. I had three cameras rolling on it in slow motion. The stuntman was in the headless biker jacket, looking out from inside so it was hard for him to see. I was a little worried about him not coming out in a straight line, so I had safety spotters to protect each cameraman. I laid down next to B camera about thirty feet away. The stunt biker drove down the ramp, hit about 30 mph underground, then exploded up through the grave. He was a bit off line—the safety spotter dragged me and the cameraman out of the way and the rear wheel of the bike actually hit the camera when it landed. It was an amazing shot and everybody was safe. That's good filmmaking.

"Steve Monarque was actually pretty funny and easy to work with but he did this odd thing all the time," Eastman recalls. "He had a bum trick knee which went out on him from time to time so you'd have a tracking shot with Steve and someone else walking along and suddenly Steve would just fall down out of the shot. I found this increasingly hilarious after a while—you took what laughs you could find on *F13*—and would purposely set up shots to see if I could get Steve into a situation where he'd fall down out of the shot. Kind of my entertainment on a tough shoot.

"Steve was actually really clumsy. In 'Midnight Riders,' he had to throw himself down by Dennis Thatcher, who was supposed to be dead at that point, but the corpse suddenly sat up yelling 'Oh, the little bastard got me in the balls!' Very funny in a graveyard at three in the morning."

The incestuous relationship between Penny and Tommy is not sensationalized. "One direction I remember giving to the two young actors, David Orth and Andrea Roth, was after it was revealed that Andrea's real father was actually the priest, they had to suddenly realize that, after all their teenage sex in the backseat, they were actually screwing their half sibling," Eastman recalls. "This was never stated overtly but I thought it was a very powerful moment the way they played it. We worked hard to get that reaction right."

"Repetition"

Written by: Jennifer Lynch
Directed by: William Fruet
Original airdate: February 5, 1990
Cursed antique: Cameo necklace

Journalist Walter Cromwell (David Ferry) is celebrating his Newspaper Columnist of the Year award with his co-workers and his mother (Kay Tremblay). As the night draws on, Walter puts his wheelchair-bound mother into a cab then goes back to the office to finish his column. He works through the night and falls asleep on the drive home, where he swerves off the road, goes over an embankment, and hits young Heather (Vicki Wauchope), who is playing in the woods with her dog Tiger. Walter panics and buries the girl in a well. Tiger runs home, in a very Lassie moment, and "tells" Ruth (Sharry Flett) that her daughter is gone.

A month later, Walter's life has fallen apart. He has become an alcoholic, his mother is on her death bed, and his work has gotten so bad that his editor takes him off the payroll until he can pull himself together. He goes to confession, hoping that the priest will lead the police to Heather's body. The priest won't, and won't absolve him until he turns himself in. Instead, he goes home. Walter stumbles out of the car and falls, finding a cameo locket tangled underneath the car. The locket belonged to Heather, and now features her silhouette on the front. With her adorable speech impediment, Heather begs Walter to let her out of the locket and let her live again. He drops the locket down the garbage disposal and goes upstairs to care for his mother, who is calling for her medicine. When he returns to the kitchen to pour himself a drink, the locket begins calling again.

Heather explains how he can help: he just needs to find another soul. "Give them the cameo at the same place you killed me, then kill them at the same time. They will take my place." Between Heather and Mother nagging him, Walter decides to give it a try. He takes Mother out to the woods, hands her the cameo, and waits. The nagging persists, and Walter smothers his mom with a blanket. Heather comes crawling out of the well, filthy but alive, and rushes home.

Walter takes his mother home, pulls the sheet over her head, and informs the doctor that his mother passed away in the night. He pours himself a drink while he waits for the ambulance to take Mother—but he hears her calling. Thinking she is not dead, Walter rushes back upstairs, but she is still dead. Mother is now the one trapped in the cameo. He tries to explain to her that her life was nearly over, and takes the locket back out to the forest and drops it in the well.

He returns to confessional to tell the priest he has sinned again, but "not so bad" this time. "I killed someone else to save her, but she was on her deathbed anyway." The priest doesn't see this as a fair trade and again implores Walter to turn himself in.

Despite no longer having the locket, Mother's voice still haunts Walter, following him, begging him to save her, to "find someone the world won't miss." He wanders into a homeless shelter, run by Anne (Kate Trotter), a friend of Micki's. With his tattered clothes, the alcohol on his breath, and the voices in his head (which he responds to), he doesn't seem out of place at the shelter. A man named Bill (Aaron Ross Fraser), a regular at the shelter (when not in "the funny farm") befriends Walter. Walter offers him a place to spend the night. Rather than go back to his house, he takes him to that spot in the woods. Walter reclaims the locket from the well and drags a sleepy Bill from the car out to the correct spot. He hands Bill the locket. Bill is too distracted by the locket wrapping itself around his hand to notice Walter coming at him with a huge branch.

At the mortuary, Mother sits upright. She woke up in the middle of the embalming process, screaming. But you can't survive the embalming process, so she dies again.

So, now Walter has killed Bill, and his mother is extra-dead. Nothing seems to be working out for Walter, and here comes that damn cameo, now with Bill moaning and whining from the front. He ends up back at the homeless shelter, where a few of the regulars start asking him about Bill. They beat up Walter, and Anne breaks up the fight. She desperately wants to help Walter, promising that "every problem has an answer." He must start by "admitting you made a mistake." Walter promises that Bill will be back tomorrow and rushes out.

One more confession, promising to turn himself in as soon as he "puts things right." By putting things right, he means to kill Heather. He lures her back out to the woods with promises of giving her locket back. When Ruth realizes that Heather is gone once again, she calls Anne in a panic. Anne had helped her the first time Heather went missing. On the way out to Ruth's house, Anne recognizes Walter's car on the side of the road and pulls over.

Walter hears Anne calling, so he grabs Heather and hides. Previously, Heather had no memory of her death, but being back in that spot brings it all rushing back. She screams and races into Anne's arms. Walter reveals himself, and Bill's silhouette begs him to use Anne instead of Heather. He comes towards Anne with a broken bottle, and apologizes. But instead of stabbing Anne with the bottle, he uses it to slit his own neck. Anne pulls the bloody locket from his hand and Bill crawls out of the well.

Status: Anne takes the locket to Micki. Jack once told her that they specialize in "one-of-a-kind items" and the locket seemed to "hit the mark." One of the homeless men gave it to her, and he has since moved on. Micki finds the locket in the manifest and thanks Anne profusely. Jack calls as Anne leaves, and Micki happily informs him that they "got one back before it caused any problems at all." Anne hears this and it gives her pause. Sadness? Surprise? Bemusement? I can't quite read it, but it is definitely telling.

*   *   *

"Repetition" is a very distinctive episode in the *F13* repertoire. It doesn't follow the almost procedural formula of most episodes, where strange murders occur, the crew connects them to a cursed antique, and the investigation ensues. In this case, the cursed object flies under the radar. There is nothing for Micki to investigate; hell, she only has a few minutes of screen time this entire episode. Jack and Johnny don't appear at all.

The morality of this episode is also unique. Generally speaking, most episodes of *Friday the 13th* feature a straightforward "bad guy" who is using a cursed object for selfish gain; usually money or fame or youth. But the "bad guy," Walter, isn't really a bad guy. He wasn't even driving drunk when he hit Heather—though he did handle Heather's death poorly.

Kate Trotter played Anne in this episode, marking her third and final appearance in *F13*. Though she never saw Effy Stokes or Dr. Carter as villains (Effy was "heartbroken;" Carter was "that kind of genius that tipped into craziness"), she thought it was "wonderful to play a woman who wasn't disturbed by needs that were too great." "Her needs were to help, to fix, to be kind, to be present," says Trotter. "That was what was satisfying to her. That was wonderful. For me, it was such a beautiful way to end my time with the series. The fact that I got to play three distinct roles in a series is kind of extraordinary. That was so generous of them."

"The Long Road Home"

Written by: Carl Binder
Directed by: Allan Kroeker
Original airdate: February 12, 1990
Cursed antique: Yin-Yang charm

"The Long Road Home" begins in what would normally be the final act of an episode, with Micki and Johnny in the final rush to obtain the cursed object. The item in question is a yin-yang charm. The owner of the charm can use it to put his mind in another person—as long as that person is dead. And generally, that means that the owner must do the killing.

We open on a lifeguard, Jerry, getting out of a pool and slipping the charm into the pocket of his robe. He leaves, and Micki enters. She realizes that the dark shape in the pool is Johnny, tied up and left to drown. She dives in, shotguns a little oxygen to him while she unties him and gets him out of the pool. Jerry is on his way to Don's house. Don is a possessive man who keeps his wife, Carol, on a very short leash. Jerry and Carol have been having an affair, and Jerry goes there to kill him. Carol encourages Jerry to "do it," which means putting the charm on Don's bare chest. It starts spinning and glowing, and Jerry puts his hand on top of it. "Don" sits up, fully healed, and Carol asks if he is Jerry. I will never forget the way he says "Yes," in a way that is smug, boastful, and eager. Micki and Johnny burst in and the boys fight while the ladies look on. Micki grabs the charm while Don/Jerry goes after Johnny with a knife. He defends with a lamp, and Don/Jerry electrocutes himself. Micki and Johnny leave, with the charm, while Carol is left to weep over two dead lovers.

The pair stops for gas on their way home. Micki calls Jack to inform him that they got the charm, but they won't be home for four or five hours. (The eponymous "long road home.") The attendant warns them that a storm is brewing, but Johnny is determined to outrun it.

On the road, Micki ruminates on yin and yang. Johnny just glares, admits he has a lot on his mind, and says he is sick of people dying. The body-swapping case brought back some bad memories. He is worried that he won't know the difference between right and wrong, and that maybe—just maybe—there is a right time to use a curse. Micki assures him there isn't, then attempts to change the subject by announcing she is hungry.

They pull into a dingy bar, Henshaw's Roadhouse, with only one other customer (an old man slurping soup). Micki orders a cheeseburger; Johnny (still in a foul mood) just wants coffee. Shortly after, Mike and Eddie Negley (Angelo Rizacos and Geza Kovacs) walk in with a few dead chickens they caught in their traps. The brothers are filthy backwoods-types, straight out of a 1980s slasher film. They take an immediate interest in Johnny and especially Micki, a pair of good-looking strangers passing through town. The brothers sit down in their booth and start trouble. Mike wants to know if they are married; sensing that these two are trouble, Micki says yes and takes Johnny's hand. Eddie, who is a little slow, takes Micki's burger. Johnny grabs him by the wrist, with murder in his eyes. Mike invites the two to "ride in their truck for awhile."

Johnny stands and announces they are leaving. Mike is insulted by this, and by the treatment of his brother: "People 'round here don't take kindly to poor attitudes." Johnny gets violent, knocking Eddie out quickly before turning his attention to Mike. Doris, the grizzled waitress, breaks it up and kicks the Negley brothers out with threats of calling the sheriff. She offers Micki and Johnny a fresh meal, on the house. "It's the least I can do." That phrase has never been so dead-on. With the immediate danger gone and Johnny uninjured, Micki warns him about being careful who he picks fights with. He defends his actions, and Micki drops it. "It's just that I worry about you sometimes."

Meanwhile, Mike is outside, tampering with the gas line to Johnny's car, while Eddie keeps watch.

Johnny and Micki aren't on the road too long before the engine starts to knock, and the car stalls. A quick check of the engine, and Johnny realizes they are out of gas. Micki won't wait there by herself, but wants to go back to the diner. He claims it is too far, and that the interstate is just a few miles ahead.

"A few miles" turns out to be more than a few. "Guess I was wrong," Johnny admits.

"What else is new?" grumbles Micki under her breath.

Then they come across a huge, rambling house, set deep amongst the trees. "If they have a gas can, we're in business," says Johnny.

The two head to the house, oblivious to the name "Negley" neatly printed on the mailbox.

There is no one home, but the door is unlocked, so they let themselves in. The power is out, and the phone lines are down. They assume from a photo that a kindly, elderly couple owns the house, so they decide to stay put, at least until the storm subsides. Johnny builds a fire, and the two warm themselves beside it. She asks if his mouth is still sore. "Yeah, why don't you kiss it and make it better, like you did in the pool?"

Micki bristles: "That was business. Don't get your hopes up."

The talk turns to mothers, and Johnny didn't know Micki's mom was still alive. "I guess there are a lot of things we never talked about," she says, more coquettish than she was a few minutes ago. "After Ryan, I suppose it just seems easier not to get close to people," she admits, before continuing with "Maybe some day, after this is all over, we could take the time... ."

"... to get to know each other," Johnny finishes. He leans in to kiss her, but before their lips can meet, the fire pops and startles them back to neutral corners (while I sigh in relief). Johnny will go look for more firewood while Micki busies herself finding blankets.

Micki's search takes her to the attic, where she doesn't find blankets—she finds human taxidermy. Before she can scream, Mike Negley clamps his hand over her mouth and holds a knife to her throat. He sends Eddie to find "hubby" and start the generator while he fantasizes about what he is going to do to Micki. The power pops back on and Mike takes the time to introduce her to his family. When he starts up the record player, it makes Pa's rocking chair sway. Mike recommends that Micki compliment Ma on her hair. "She's real touchy about her looks and she just got a perm." He explains that Grandpa was "long gone" before the Negleys started stuffing things, as a way to explain his more putrid visage.

Meanwhile, Johnny has gone out to one of several sheds on the property, looking for firewood. He just finds more taxidermy, little furry creatures... and a human skull. Eddie finds him and the two men fight. Eddie throws Johnny across the shed, his leg catches in ladder rungs, and Johnny's leg snaps. He screams... and screams again when Eddie comes toward him with a knife.

Back upstairs, Micki revolts when Mike pushes her in close to the mummified Grandpa. ("He is hard of hearing.") She attempts to run, but runs right into Eddie. Caught between two Negleys, Eddie proudly shows the bloody knife and proclaims "hubby" dead. The Negleys are ready for party time.

Micki is tied to a chair. Mike assures her that his parents like her better than the last one, Theresa, and encourages Eddie to show her off. Eddie doesn't want to, so Mike gets Theresa, a young woman who has been stuffed, her arms positioned for dancing. She stepped into one of their traps, and was the first "live person" the brothers stuffed. Mike suggests Eddie get to work on stuffing Johnny while he takes his turn with Micki. Eddie wants to have a go first, he feels he earned it. It takes some cajoling, but Mike gives in. "Don't break anything," he warns before giving them some alone time.

Eddie waits until Mike is gone before untying Micki. "Are you okay? Did he hurt you?" Micki responds to this inquiry by kicking Eddie in the nuts. She then grabs one of Ma's knitting needles and slashes his face. She is about to stab him when Eddie grabs her arms. "It's me! It's Johnny!" He explains that he used the charm; that he broke his leg, and reminds her of a conversation they had in the car. Micki finally believes him and gives him a hug. Johnny's plan is to sneak back to the shed, get his body, and get the hell out of there. But when they get there, Johnny's body is gone. Mike must have taken it somewhere.

Mike surprises them. He thought Eddie was going to run away with Micki. Mike starts beating his brother (or his brother's body) with a pipe. Finally he throws the car keys at Eddie's limp body, promising that Micki is all his—after he's done with her.

During the ruckus, Micki escapes. She makes it back into the attic, where she finds Johnny's body. She hides when Mike pops in, but he doesn't stay long, and she sneaks back downstairs, back to the garage, and helps "Eddie" up to the attic. He is badly beaten, and Johnny ponders what would happen if Eddie's body dies before he can get back to his own body.

Mike is looking for Micki out in the woods, giving them enough time to do the body swap. Except neither of them have the yin-yang charm, and it's not on Johnny's body, either. "Is this what you are looking for?" Mike shows up, waving the yin-yang around. He sees Eddie's limp body crumpled next to Johnny's, and rushes to his brother's side. He blames Micki and aims a shotgun at her. She pushes Grandpa, in a wheelchair, at Mike, and it knocks him down the stairs. Micki rushes after them and finds the charm pressed between the two bodies. She uses it to transfer Johnny's mind back into his own body, his leg healing in the transfer.

Micki and Johnny rush from the house. She doesn't register that Grandpa's body is missing until he grabs her on the way out. In the fall, the charm was positioned just so, transferring Mike into Grandpa's mummified corpse. "Party time," he hisses as he grabs Micki from the shadows.

She breaks away and Grandpa strangles Johnny. Micki stabs him with a knife—all that comes out is sawdust. Johnny and Micki run while Grandpa tries desperately to hold his stuffing in.

Micki and Johnny make it out to the Negley's truck, with Grandpa close on their trail. Grandpa starts firing at them with his shotgun, and doesn't notice when he steps into one of the Negley's hunting traps. He is strung up by the ankle and the wind scatters his remaining stuffing.

Status: Micki and Johnny make it back to his car with the charm and head back home. He is disappointed that they never got the chance to finish their "talk." She promises they will have plenty of time when they get home. Luckily, they never do.

* * *

"The Long Road Home" is tied with "The Charnel Pit" as my favorite episode. The homage to *Texas Chainsaw Massacre* (1974) is unmistakable (if you can believe it, director Allan Kroeker has *never* seen *Texas Chainsaw Massacre*), but there are also shades of *Psycho* (1960) and *Last House on the Left* (1972). A dilapidated old farmhouse, visitors stranded there in a storm, creepy hillbillies, and human taxidermy are all classic horror movie tropes for a reason: they are effective. I'm not given to scares, but this episode was, to me, the scariest of the series. Story editor Jim Henshaw thought it was "one of the scariest, best things we did."

Both Angelo Rizacos, who played skeevy Mike Negley in this episode, and Carl Binder, who wrote the script, consider "The Long Road Home" their favorite episodes. "There seemed to be room to explore the horror mood and take one's time," says Rizacos. Binder explains that "this was one where Jim [Henshaw] really pushed me to make it creepy and scary. And then he made it even scarier with his pass of the script. It's just incredibly creepy and a lot of fun. I especially love the scene in the diner when the Negley brothers—who were named after a very close friend—come in and have their first confrontation with our heroes."

"The brothers had a signature 'embrace,' kind of like a wrestler's headlock," says Kroeker. "It came to be known as the 'Negley Hug.' People on the crew got into the habit of greeting each other with it."

Of course, a scary script can only go so far without a scary setting. "It was an actual farmhouse that this very old man lived in alone," says Rizacos. "It was night shoots and very cold. The house had only a wood stove in the kitchen for heat and lumber guys would drop off ends and scraps for the old man to get through winters. The farmhouse was surreal in that a metropolis had grown around it over the years, and yet it had not changed." From this description, it sounds like this may be the same farm they shot "Scarecrow" at.

"The Long Road Home" is another episode with a unique structure. Binder: "I thought it would be fun to do an episode that begins where most episodes end. The teaser of this episode is actually what would be the climax of another episode: the team has a harrowing confrontation with the bad guys, defeats them and gets the antique back. But then, as they head back home, they encounter trouble, which becomes the bulk of this story."

I always hated the idea of Micki and Johnny hooking up. As a kid, with the finer points of adult relationships far out of my grasp, it always made my stomach churn to see Micki and Johnny kiss (or almost-kiss), and I could never understand how Micki could brush off his smarmy come-ons one minute, then be ready to kiss him a minute later. Of course, now it makes sense, but it doesn't make me feel any better. I am surprised that those feelings have not gone away. Watching it twenty years later causes that same nausea to bubble up. "The romance was all done by Jim and his staff," says Binder. "I didn't really know exactly where the characters would be at this point, so I kind of just indicated romantic moments, and then they filled in the details."

Henshaw has a slightly different recollection of the potential Micki/Johnny romance: "I don't think we ever intended for there to be a romance. I think there was a natural kind of chemistry between them. I think the fans were sort of looking for something, based on the fact that Ryan and Micki had been cousins, so *nothing* could happen between them. I think a lot of people thought that, since we were bringing someone new in, something would happen there. I don't think we ever intended it. There was a lot of nice byplay between them, but I think we just left it alone. It was probably because a lot of other shows were doing that kind of stuff and we wanted to stay away from it. The reality is, if the series had gone on another season, it was an idea we were kicking around. I don't think we consciously said this was something we had to do."

Louise Robey was not shy about her feelings on a Micki/Johnny romance. "I asked Frank, 'Why on earth would Micki be dating a dolt?' There is no way Micki would have been involved with him." She remembers the opening shot that kicked off Micki's almost-romance with Johnny. "There was one time, very late at night, they let most of the crew go.

I had to run to a swimming pool, rip off my coat, leap into a pool, dive underneath—they had underwater cameras—and I had to kiss him on the mouth and give him mouth to mouth resuscitation and bring him up. Like that would ever happen in real life! But it worked—in one take. It had to have, otherwise I would have had to go back to hair and makeup. I wasn't going to do that! Plus, the poor crew that was left…. We did it."

"I think the writers were always in limbo about it," suggests Steve Monarque. "They wanted it to go that way; then they didn't. I think what they found with me was that I brought more of a physical action-packed character to the show. I was more involved with getting smacked around, punched, getting into fights, prison, all that stuff."

It's funny what you notice as a kid and as an adult. I probably watched this episode a hundred times as a kid, but it wasn't until viewing it as an adult that I noticed just how scummy the restaurant is. (I also didn't connect the name, Henshaw's Roadhouse, to story editor Jim Henshaw until I was an adult, and didn't notice that they were in Johnny's car, not the Mercedes, until this viewing.) But the burger and fries that Micki orders comes right out of a microwave. You don't see it, but you hear the beep and the unmistakable sound of a little door slamming shut. It is completely inconsequential, but as an adult, I am excited to discover little nuances that I had never noticed before.

"My Wife as a Dog"

Written by: Jim Henshaw
Directed by: Armand Mastroianni
Original airdate: February 19, 1990
Cursed item: Leash

Aubrey (Denis Forest) returns home from a dismal trip to the vet, his aging dog Kelly in his arms. He sets her down in her bed and tells her not to listen to that vet. He then heads to Soupy's Bar, where his estranged wife Lea (Kim Nelles) works. He wants sympathy for Kelly's imminent death, and wants Lea to come over and say goodbye. Lea only wants to discuss Aubrey signing the divorce papers. He becomes more agitated and Joni (Jayne Eastwood), the bar's owner, kicks Aubrey out.

Aubrey is a firefighter, and the guys in his station are worried about him. Keith (Vincent Dale), who was at the bar and helped Joni physically remove Aubrey from the premises, checks on Aubrey. All he can do is accuse Keith of dating his wife. Whatever sympathy Keith has for Aubrey is gone. Before their words can get too heated, the bells ring and they are off to a fire.

Keith and Aubrey are teamed up inside the massive house fire. Keith seems to have put aside their argument in favor of doing their job, but Aubrey hasn't. He gives Keith a shove, and the men wrestle in the inferno. Aubrey grabs a nearby braided cord and strangles Keith to death, then drags him into the flames. The other firefighters eventually find Keith and drag him out. They assume he succumbed to smoke inhalation.

The cord Aubrey used to kill Keith is actually an ornate dog leash, and he stuck it in his pocket after the murder. He comes home to Kelly and clips it to her collar, ready to take her for a walk. Kelly is suddenly alert and active. She jumps up, ready for a walk.

The fire captain is over at Curious Goods, doing a fire safety inspection. Unsurprisingly, Curious Goods is a "five alarm waiting to happen." Jack, Micki, and Johnny all offer defenses as to why the place is so cluttered, but the captain is unrelenting. He gives them thirty days to bring the store up to code. Johnny, as part of his defense of the store, mentions that they get stuff in all the time, like this letter they got from Mrs. Cox.

The captain tells him to forget about that letter—Mrs. Cox's house was the one that burned down, took one of his men with it. Everyone immediately worries that one of their items started the fire.

Dr. Gibson, the vet, calls Aubrey, worried because he missed his appointment, presumably to put Kelly down. Aubrey insists Kelly is getting better, despite the vet's diagnosis that she is terminal. He will take care of Kelly on his own. Aubrey says goodbye to Kelly before heading to work, and tells her he hopes that when mommy hears of the good news, she will come visit.

Lea is sick and doesn't have the strength to tell Aubrey to leave the bar when he comes in. He again is focused on the dog; she is focused on the divorce papers. "I'm out of your life and everything connected to it. I'm happy she's okay, but I don't care! I don't want to be anything to you!" Joni steps in and kicks Aubrey out. Again.

Jack is with Mrs. Cox, inspecting the remnants of the burned home. The inspector said the fire was caused by bad wiring, so one of the objects likely wasn't responsible. All of the items she bought from the shop were unharmed, but she couldn't find the dog leash. "I guess it couldn't survive the heat of the fire."

Jack returns home and fills in Micki on the missing leash. While he was gone, Micki found an article about the dead firefighter. Mrs. Cox

Kim Nelles begins her transformation in "My Wife as a Dog."
Photo courtesy of Armand Mastroianni.

thought he died of smoke inhalation but according to the article, there were abrasions on his neck. The official story is that Keith's mask came off and he got tangled in the air hoses, trying to get it back on.

That night, Kelly whimpers painfully, so Aubrey clips on the leash. It doesn't help. He rushes her to the vet in the middle of the night, and Dr. Gibson again advises him to put her out of her misery. "Stop thinking about yourself and start thinking of her." He prepares the injection, but Aubrey freaks out and strangles Gibson with the leash. He clips it on Kelly, and she perks right up.

Meanwhile, Lea is at work, trying to make change but having a hard time doing the math in her head. *What the hell is happening to me?* she wonders.

Aubrey wakes to playful barks from Kelly, leaping in and out of bed. She brought him his slippers, but Aubrey can't figure out why she woke him so early. Then he remembers: Keith's funeral. "How did you know about that?" She leads him to the kitchen, where his paper is laid out, and she goes into the fridge, clearly trying to make breakfast. Aubrey puts it together: "I killed once, you got healthy. I killed again, and you can think."

While Micki and Johnny fix the stairs at the shop, Jack checks the newspaper and sees an article on Dr. Gibson's death. He had the same abrasions as the firefighter. Micki suggests the leash offers communication with animals, but Jack thinks it is more. In the manifest, the leash is listed as the Leash of Dreams, of Australian aboriginal origin. Aboriginal tribes have always had great affinity with animals, Jack explains, and they don't distinguish between waking reality and dreams. "They believe whatever you envision could become real; otherwise it wouldn't drop into your head." Micki finishes the assessment: "Then it could be making someone's fondest dreams come true." Micki heads to the veterinary office, and Jack goes to the see the fire captain again.

After the funeral, Baldwin invites Aubrey to a party, promising there is a girl he wants to introduce him to. Aubrey begs out, but Baldwin insists. "I wouldn't fix you up with a dog." Hardy-har-har. Meanwhile, Jack asks the captain if it is possible one of his men could have stolen the leash. He insists his men wouldn't do that, then speaks of Aubrey directly. "He's had a run of bad luck. Wife leaves him, loses a buddy… at least I hear his dog is getting better."

Aubrey makes dinner for him and Kelly: steaks. Though Kelly sits at the table and has a napkin tied around her neck, she still eats like a dog. Lea calls and begs Aubrey for the divorce papers. She isn't feeling well, is having trouble putting things together, and just wants all this to be over. Aubrey returns to his dinner with Kelly. "I don't need anybody. I've got you."

Baldwin walks Tricia (Jennifer Griffin) out of the party, apologizing that Aubrey never showed up. She heads down the street, alone, to her car, when she hears someone. She gets nervous, but Aubrey steps out and introduces himself, calming her down. She doesn't want to go back to the party so he walks her to her car. Aubrey takes the leash out of his pocket and, off-screen, strangles Tricia with it.

He goes straight home to Kelly and clips on the leash. Her eyes turn a dazzling—and very human—shade of blue. At the bar, as Lea is closing up, she catches her reflection in a mirror and screams. Her eyes are now deep brown, just like a dog's.

Aubrey is snuggling with Kelly in bed the next morning. He asks her if she knows how many more it will take to turn her into Lea, and making sure she wants this to happen. They are interrupted by a knock, and Aubrey directs Kelly to stay in the bedroom. Jack is at the door, asking him about the fire and if he saw a braided dog leash. Aubrey doesn't remember anything like that, but he lets Jack in to talk. Jack starts telling him about the leash when the bedroom doorknob starts to turn. Kelly is trying to open the door. Both men are keenly aware of the jiggling doorknob, but neither mentions it. In order to break the uncomfortable silence, Jack asks if anyone else may have grabbed the leash.

Kelly finally succeeds in opening the bedroom door. As her nose peeks out, Aubrey shouts "No!" then shows Jack a photo album to distract him while he shuts the door discretely. Jack asks about his dog; Aubrey tells him she died and asks him to leave. Aubrey returns to the bedroom and chastises Kelly for disobeying him. Kelly looks sad, and Aubrey softens. "I forget you are still mostly a dog." Then it occurs to him: he needs to kill Lea in order for the transformation to be complete.

At work, Aubrey calls the bar and promises to bring the signed divorce papers over after closing. Lea thinks it is another excuse to see her, but he swears it isn't. She struggles to hang up the phone, clearly having coordination issues. She also whimpers like a puppy. After the phone call, Aubrey triumphantly announces to his company that he and Lea are getting back together. Lea, meanwhile, confides in Joni that she just wants this whole thing over. Joni insists she eat some dinner, and Lea does—like a dog, without the use of her hands.

Aubrey notices Jack in his car, keeping an eye on the firehouse. He reports a fire and instantly the bells in the firehouse go off. The men jump into action and roll out without Aubrey. Jack follows the fire truck, allowing Aubrey to slip away without being seen.

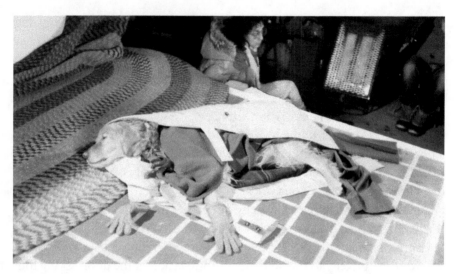

Kelly resting up before her big transformation in "My Wife as a Dog."
Photo courtesy of Armand Mastroianni.

At the bar, Joni tells Aubrey she sent Lea home. She checks the divorce papers and sees they aren't signed. Before she can start yelling, Aubrey strangles her with the leash.

Micki and Johnny are watching Aubrey's home when he pulls up. Jack, having been thrown off by the false alarm, followed Aubrey home and meets up with the others. Micki goes home with Jack while Johnny continues to sit watch. She is starting to think this is a big waste of time. "I hope we're not barking up the wrong tree," says Jack. Hardy-har-har. I don't know how he managed to say that line with a straight face.

Aubrey clips the freshly-powered leash to Kelly. At home, Lea is yelping and howling. Rushing to the mirror, she sees her canine teeth are far more canine than normal, and her hair is getting longer, darker, and shaggier. Aubrey tries calling her but she isn't answering.

Frustrations have stalled the hunt for the leash, and Jack suggests they put it on hold and go after something with a "warmer trail." The captain returns to again inspect the shop, and is impressed they were able to get up to code. He has to go straight to a meeting with the police about the woman who disappeared at Baldwin's party. He mentions that Aubrey and Lea are patching things up and when asked, he offers them the name of the bar she works at. Micki thinks maybe Aubrey is using the leash to rekindle his wife's affection.

Lea goes into the bar for her regular shift, but it quickly becomes clear she can't work. She calls Joni in a panic, needing someone to cover for her. It goes to voice mail (wait, this is 1990… so it goes to an answering machine). Her voice is high pitched and yelp-y, her hands are growing knobby, and her fingernails are turning into claws. As soon as she hangs up the phone, it rings. Aubrey has the papers, promises there won't be any trouble, and, as if to prove it, tells her Joni is there. Lea will come right over.

When Lea arrives, Aubrey warns Kelly to stay in the room and be quiet—this is almost over. Lea is anxious and Aubrey sends her into the bedroom, where he says Joni is with Kelly. Joni is in the bedroom alright—dead. Aubrey sneaks in and loops the leash around Lea's neck. "Kelly needed a body but she still doesn't have your soul!" With her new canine teeth, Lea bites Aubrey and escapes into the kitchen. He tackles her and again starts strangling her. As he does so, Lea grows more canine, and Kelly grows more human. Lea becomes hairy; human hands grow from Kelly's paws. Lea is finally dead, and a voice calls to Aubrey from the kitchen.

Micki and Jack break into the house through the bedroom, where they find Joni and Tricia's bodies. Johnny breaks in through the front door and sees Aubrey clipping the leash to "Lea's" collar. She is weak, on the floor, covered by a blanket. Johnny goes after Aubrey, who doesn't put up much of a struggle; he ends up sobbing in Johnny's arms. Micki helps "Lea" up and removes the collar from her neck. As they walk out, she notices the dog, dressed in a trench coat. She is dead.

Status: The leash is returned, but there is "a lot we are never going to understand about this one." No one knows that Kelly and Lea effectively switched places. Aubrey is in prison for multiple murders. "Lea" brings a gift to her husband: his slippers and a newspaper. He scratches her behind the ear and she pants.

Mentioned but not explored: Listed in the manifest: amber mug; solid oak cradle (maybe from "What a Mother Wouldn't Do?"); a nineteenth century musical something.

* * *

Kim Nelles, who played Lea, was on a bit of a casting roll at the time. "This was a series I was familiar with in Toronto and [when I auditioned] it was with all the girls I was always up against," says Nelles. "My friend Jennifer Griffin got the part of one of the victims but it could just as easily have been her in my part. When I got the part I got a call from Denis Forest a couple of days before the shoot. He wanted to go out for a drink and get to know me a little. I went and it was odd. He was very intense and serious and I remember thinking, 'This is a supernatural thriller show where I am turning into a dog. This isn't 'Dog Day Afternoon!' But it did actually add to the strange guy persona that was the character and I must say, it did help me act towards him in a way I might not have if we hadn't had the drink together."

"When they approached me with this one, I was like, 'Oh wow, she's going to turn into a dog,' said director Armand Mastroianni. "I told Kim Nelles I wanted her to start developing little habits, like she has fleas or something. I would have her do little scratches, and I told her to watch how a dog behaves, to pick up little idiosyncrasies. Little yelps and things like that. And she did it! A lot of it was very funny while we were shooting. We had a lot of fun watching her scratching and wearing whiskers."

"The process for my transformation into a dog was hard, I won't lie," Nelles tells me. "I had to have special contact lenses put in. They told me they were the same kind Michael Jackson used in 'Thriller.' I also had to have a plaster cast made of my face that they could build the prosthetics on. That entailed sitting in a chair for a half-hour with just two straws up my nose to breathe while the plaster set. I had a panic attack and had them rip it off. They said, 'If you can't do it this time, we'll have to cast someone else.' So, I managed to get through it the second time, but it took everything in me. It was the most claustrophobic thing I've ever been through. The actual shoot days where they put the prosthetics on my face were fun and fine. I mean, I was being tended to like I was a star. Being fussed over and worked on for sometimes up to four hours. It was exciting.

"I didn't want to [play the role] campy or over-the-top. I really tried to imagine this crazy, awful thing happening to me and thinking that it was a mental breakdown because of my awful relationship. Armand Mastroianni was wonderful and fun and warm. One of my very favorite experiences with a director. I mean, sometimes he was in hysterics when I entered with my dog face on but he was very considerate and conscious of the fact that I *couldn't* think it was funny."

While it was nothing I consciously picked up on as a child, watching this episode as an adult felt a bit uncomfortable. It certainly hints at bestiality. "There is a scene where he is in bed with a dog. Like, what are we doing, bestiality? Let's not go there, but it looks like we are going there," remarks Mastroianni. "It was an atmosphere that allowed you to explore and experiment. Nobody was telling you not to. They were all saying, 'Go for it. If we can't use it, at least we know we did it.' That is a really encouraging thing to say to a director. That makes your mind travel, go to places where you don't feel so restricted."

"Jack-in-the-Box"

Written by: Dennis Foon
Directed by: David Winning
Original airdate: April 23, 1990
Cursed antique: Jack-in-the-box

Brock (Wayne Best) is a manager at a pool club. A couple of drunk guys throw the lifeguard into the pool, causing Brock to throw them out. The drunks don't take kindly to that, so they wait until the club is empty, then sneak back in and beat the hell out of Brock. The janitor threatens to call the police, but it is an empty threat and they all know it. Brock's daughter, Megan (Marsha Moreau), comes in looking for her dad, and sees him dead in the pool. And on her birthday, too.

Micki is friends with Brock, and his wife Helen (Lori Hallier), so she goes over to comfort her. The women giggle over the old photos of Brock while Megan looks around at the forgotten birthday party her mom was planning for her. She opens the gift her father left for her: a pirate-themed jack-in-the-box. Johnny, uncomfortable watching the ladies giggle, follows the sound of the music from the jack-in-the-box and finds Megan, who quickly hides the toy. He tries to commiserate with her over losing a father (and he lost his twice!) but she just wishes the man who killed her dad was dead. Johnny tells her it won't bring him back, but Megan doesn't believe that.

Helen drinks herself to sleep that night, but Megan can't sleep. She also can't wake her mother up, so she takes her jack-in-the-box and bikes to the pool club. Megan sits at the edge of the pool, sadly playing with her toy, when the janitor grabs her. She is scared; he is drunk. Megan realizes he was drunk the night Brock died and blames him for her father's death. She swats his bottle into the pool, and the janitor falls in trying to grab it. Megan backs away, winding the jack-in-the-box. When the top pops, blue arms grab the janitor and drown him. Megan seems unfazed, until her father's ghostly visage appears over the pool. "I knew you would come back!" she exclaims.

The next morning, Megan excitedly tells her mother about visiting with Brock. Helen insists it was a dream and blows her off. Megan heads off on her bike and recognizes Mike, the drunken bully who killed her dad, walking out of a club with a skanky date. Megan returns home to tell her mother she saw the man who drowned her daddy, "coming out of the stripper place with ladies." Helen is far too drunk by this point to care, but Micki is over, and completely sober, so she asks Megan what he looks like. She can't remember and runs from the room, frustrated.

That night, Helen makes Megan put her jack-in-the-box away before dinner. Megan gets a TV dinner; Helen gets vodka. Megan suggests that if the man who killed her father was caught and killed, god would give her dad back. Helen gets annoyed, the two fight, and Megan leaves the house. Helen feels bad—but not bad enough to go after her.

After the janitor was discovered in the same pool that Brock was killed in, Johnny and Jack pledge to keep this from Micki. Jack checks the manifest and finds a listing for a drunken sailor's jack-in-the-box. Despite this, Johnny doesn't think the two deaths are related. That night, Micki wakes to see Brock's ghost standing before her. "Megan needs you, Micki." She calls out for him, and Jack responds. She tells him excitedly about her vision, but he just assumes it was a dream.

Megan has gone back to the bar she saw Mike leaving. When she sees his date, Sandra, leave with a different man, Megan asks where Mike is. Sandra doesn't want to help and gets in a car, so Megan follows her. Sandra ends up in a fancy bathroom, primping herself as she runs a bubble bath. Megan peers in through a small window and turns the box. The jack pops, and blue arms grab Sandra and drown her in the washbasin. (I guess drowning in a full tub would be too obvious.) "Let's go see daddy," Megan whispers to her jack-in-the-box and skips off.

At the pool, Megan happily splashes the specter of her father. But he grows serious and asks her not to use the box anymore—he doesn't want her hurting people for him. He encourages her to take care of her mother before fading away.

Johnny is reading up on the latest drowning death while Jack is at the sailor's museum, asking about the jack-in-the-box. Micki puts the pieces together, but her visit to Helen later is strictly a friend-helping-friend situation. She offers to take Brock's clothes to a homeless shelter, and Helen accuses Micki of sleeping with her husband. Micki is taken aback but blames the accusation on Helen's drinking. This leads to an argument, and Helen throws Micki out.

As Micki leaves, she runs into Megan, who admits that she doesn't like being home while her mom drinks. Micki asks the girl if the man who killed her father had a jack-in-the-box with him. Megan is alarmed and stomps inside to discover her mom drinking again. "I hate it when you drink. I hate everyone who drinks!" she screams.

"Then I guess you hate me too!" Helen retorts. She apologizes, saying it is hard for her to deal with Brock's death.

"It's hard for me too, but I don't drink," Megan spits. Once again, she leaves the house.

Megan waits outside the bar and confronts Mike when she sees him leave. He warns her to keep her mouth shut. She follows him to a drive-thru car wash and starts the jack-in-the-box as he goes through. Water starts leaking into the car, and Mike can't get out. The car fills and he drowns.

Megan returns to the pool and is joyous when her father returns; but he is mad at her. She insists it is okay—she killed the one who killed him. "Our time together is over," he says bluntly. "Your mom needs you. As long as she is alive, we can't be together." Bad choice of words, Brock. Real bad.

Megan returns home to an angry mother who gets nervous when Megan starts to ominously wind the jack-in-the-box. Brock's ghost floats down the stairs and asks what she is doing. Helen is speechless as the sight of her dead husband. Brock tells Megan to "love your mother like you love me, and I will always be with you." He locks eyes with Helen before vanishing. But it's not good enough for Megan. She leaves the house, insisting that she is going to be with her daddy. Micki and Johnny show up shortly thereafter, and after Helen explains what happened, they all race down to the pool.

Megan is already there, in her swimsuit, telling Brock that if he won't come back to her, she will go to him. She sits at the edge of the pool and starts winding the jack-in-the-box. Brock tries to talk her out of it, but there is only so much an apparition can do. Luckily Helen, Micki, and Johnny have arrived, but the door is locked and Megan isn't about to un-lock it. Johnny breaks the glass and they rush in, preventing the jack-in-the-box from popping. Brock smiles and waves goodbye. Micki grabs the jack-in-the-box; Helen grabs Megan.

Status: The jack-in-the-box is stowed in the vault, and Megan and Helen go on a vacation to clear their minds and reconnect.

*   *   *

The jack-in-the-box's curse is kind of murky. At first, it seems pretty straight forward: you use the box to summon forth mystery arms (in blue lycra!) to drown a victim, and in return you get time with the spirit of a dead loved one. But then Brock appears to Micki. And he appears to Megan and Helen when not summoned (although it could be a continuation of the visit where he accidentally tells her to kill her mother). Then when Megan is ready to kill herself, Brock appears. He wasn't summoned and surely his time with Megan was up by this point. If bringing back Brock's ghost is part of the curse, it seems rather benevolent. After all, it's a pretty crappy evil curse if the curse then tries to convince an "innocent" to *not* use it again.

"Jack-in-the-Box," if you can believe it, came from a PBS show, and shopping. "I had recently been given my first TV commission, writing a script that was never produced for PBS," says episode writer Dennis Foon. Coming from the theater, the PBS commission led to Foon getting an agent, which lead to lots of meetings. "I had no idea what was going on," Foon admits. "I met with the *Friday the 13th* guys, who explained the premise and structure of the show, the cursed object, the kind of stories they were looking for, and sent me away, inviting me to send them some ideas, following the template they gave me. What drew me to this show was the idea that horror was a way of looking not just at fear, but at a wide range of deep emotions. My unproduced PBS script was a realistic teleplay about a little girl who loses her dad to cancer. So, I transposed that idea to *F13*, adding a revenge motif.

"At the time I remembered the trouble I had trying to buy a cool jack-in-the-box for my kid," adds Foon. "I suspect safety issues were the reason. So, somewhere in that mix—a kid protagonist and creepy, unsafe jack-in-the-boxes—the story unfolded, with, of course, a nautical theme so people could be appropriately drowned." Foon admits that as a baby in the world of television, the whole writing process was pretty mysterious. "Once I handed the draft over to the story department, they pretty much had their way with it and made me look like I knew what I was doing. I can't remember how my original submitted script opened, but they came up with a new teaser, where the dad is drowned in the swimming pool, which I thought was pretty damn smart."

"It's always tricky working with kids," admits director David Winning. "You have to follow proper labor laws and they can't work full, long days, so they sometimes aren't available when needed. Quite often you have to shoot around kids to make the scenes work." Young actress Marsha Moreau, who played Megan, was incredible. "She made us cry when she needed to," says Winning. Moreau has since quit acting.

Foon didn't pitch the show again because he was busy directing a new stage play, but he didn't realize his episode would be one of the last. "I certainly hope it didn't curse the show!"

"Spirit of Television"

Written by: Robert Holbrook
Directed by: Jorge Montesi
Original airdate: April 30, 1990
Cursed antique: Television

It is a dark and stormy night (of course) as Ilsa Van Zandt (Marj Dusay), psychic to the stars, primps before her next clients arrive. Rock diva Jessica Francis (Belinda Metz) is there to reach her former guitarist and lover, Roger (Jed Dixon), who overdosed on pills a year ago. She has dragged along band mates Vinnie and Bruce to support her, but neither of them believes this séance stuff.

The four of them gather around a table in a dimly lit séance room. Ilsa calls for Robert to cross the dimensions of time and space. A wind picks up inside. Candles flicker, a chandelier shakes, and Ilsa feels his presence. The old television behind Ilsa turns on, and Roger appears. Jessica is excited, but she is the only one who can see or hear him. Bruce and Vinnie think she is nuts. Jessica feels responsible for Roger's death, like she pushed him into it. But Roger forgives her.

At home, Vinnie wants to cancel the next few shows—Jessica is too "strung out" and he sees the séance as a waste of $2,000. Despite being forgiven by Roger, Jessica still feels guilty. "Get over it!" yells Vinnie, "You've got a band to run!" He stomps out of the house and Jessica goes downstairs for a drink. Her TV clicks on and Roger appears, unannounced and in a decidedly not-cursed television. She is grateful—she has more to say to him. Roger is not the same sweet guy as he was during the séance. He is disheveled and angry and blames Jessica for basically nagging him to death. Jessica loves him, begs for forgiveness, but he would "see you rot first." The TV explodes and she is thrown across the room, dead.

Ilsa waits expectantly by her old TV set. Jessica appears on it and gets sucked downward, presumably to hell. "I gave you her life. Now, give me more time!" An image of Ilsa's own tombstone appears, and a one is added in front of the four. She has another ten days of life.

The TV news reports on Jessica's death, which shocks Micki—she was a fan of her music. The report says she has been battling depression (essentially trying to peg her death as a suicide). Vinnie is interviewed, and told how a séance with Ilsa Van Zandt may have pushed her over the edge. The name is familiar to Micki, not from the manifest, but because another one of her clients died. Stepping into Jack's role, Micki sends the boys to check out the scene while she talks to Vinnie.

Ten days of life really agrees with Ilsa. Her boy toy, William (Paul Humphrey), who insists he is not some "bimbo who is mooching off her," although he admits their relationship started that way, is pleased that she looks better. He is worried that she seems to take ill every few weeks and wants her to see a doctor. She declines, promising it is nothing to worry about, and the two start to fool around.

Micki, Jack, and Johnny regroup at the shop to compare notes. Jessica felt guilty about Roger's death, and Jack points out that it is usually guilt that drives people to mediums in the first place. Jessica died when her TV shorted out; Ilsa's last client Eddie also died from electrocution. Micki wants to visit Ilsa, but she doesn't just take on any client. Luckily, Micki bought a couple dresses from a fashion designer, Genevieve (Nancy Cser), who is one of Ilsa's clients. She makes a call.

That night, Micki and Johnny join Genevieve at a séance. Genevieve wants to speak to her mentor, Martina. She appears—to Genevieve only—in the television, and at her student's request, shows off her newest fashion creations. Genevieve just gets a few designs before Martina fades away. That night, as Ilsa and William are getting ready for bed, she loses a tooth. The calendar reads April 13th. William is planning a vacation for the two of them, but Ilsa is distracted and wanders off to her séance room, to her cursed television, to call for the spirit of Martina. "Get her. She is yours."

Micki and Johnny fill in Jack on what happened. They didn't see or hear anything, but Genevieve clearly did, and she wasn't faking it. Ilsa said it was because the connection between Genevieve and Martina was a private one, but Jack says that is just not true. "Everything that has ever been written about spiritualism says that the spirit is seen and heard by everyone at the table." Johnny claims "that's what I thought," which feels like such a "me too" attempt to know what is going on. Micki felt an energy in that room. Maybe she is real. Micki and Johnny go to talk to Genevieve, who disappeared the moment the séance was over.

She had to get back to her studio to sketch. Genevieve is quite proud of the designs she has stolen from Martina (dead or not, that is clearly what happened here) and draws a bath. While she waits for the tub to fill, she returns to her drawing table to marvel at the sketches. Her television turns on its own, and the trolley it sits on turns. Genevieve drops her coffee when she sees an angry Martina on the screen, and asks how she comes up with her ideas. "Why should I tell you? So you can steal another idea?" Martina sneers. She accuses Genevieve of stealing her designs and selling them as her own—before her body was even cold.

"I didn't think you'd mind," Genevieve offers weakly.

"You didn't think I'd know!" Martina accuses.

The TV chases Genevieve, and she tries to hide in the bathroom. In her panic, Genevieve trips into the bathtub and the television launches in after, electrocuting her. Micki and Johnny show up in time to hear her screams, but by the time they get inside, Genevieve is dead.

Ilsa watches Genevieve disappear into hell, then sees her tombstone come up. The date changes to April 15th. She only gets one more day. "You always give me more than one day!" The TV turns off, as if in response to Ilsa's cries. She begs, on her knees. "What has changed? Why are you betraying me?"

It is the morning of April 14th. Micki thinks a cursed object has to be involved, maybe something that gives her fame and fortune. But they have no idea what. Jack has an idea: he will call his friend Robert Jandini (Paul Bettis). The two used to have a magic act together, but he has made a vocation of debunking spiritualists as of late.

Ilsa is still concerned. Why didn't the TV give her ten more days, like it usually does? She is interrupted by William, who alerts her of two men who want a séance—and it has to be now. Jack and Jandini come in, unannounced. Jandini gives a fake name and says there is someone they must contact immediately. Ilsa assumes this is a shakedown. Of course she knows who Jandini is; what kind of psychic would she be if she didn't know him? Ilsa is still hesitant to let them in, but Jandini promises that if she refuses, he could make it "very public." "I'm a little hurt you didn't come sooner," she says and lets the men in to inspect the room.

After two sweeps, they have found no evidence of mirrors, trap doors, or any of the other tricks fake psychics use. She directs Jandini to sit directly across from her (facing the television) and the guys insist William remain in the room with them. Ilsa asks for the name of the deceased, but Jandini suggests they just wait and see "who pops out of the woodwork." He looks smug as Ilsa calls upon the dead known to Robert Jandini. The TV turns on, and Jandini's parents appear. Jandini is nearly speechless as they fawn over their son. Neither Jack nor William sees anything, but Jack does notice his eye line seems locked on the television.

After the séance, Jandini swears Ilsa is legit, even if Jack didn't hear or see anything. "But it had to be real!" Jandini insists, then admits he more or less abandoned his parents as they got older, and he always felt guilty about that. The séance let him know he was forgiven.

Ilsa, meanwhile, checks the card Jack gave her against the old business card stapled to the back of the television set. The names might be different, but the address is the same: 666 Druid Ave. Ilsa figures that someone wants the television back, and if they succeed, she can't last more than a day. "That's why you haven't given me the time I earned, and you won't until you are safe again."

William returns to the room after seeing their guests out, and he is amazed. He had never seen Ilsa work before and he wants to learn how to do it is, so he can help take some of the pressure off her. She assures him not to worry about it, that "what is beyond death is far less important than living." She sends him to bed, then calls upon Jandini's parents in the television, telling them to tell their son what they really think of him. William watches this from a crack in the door.

Jack calls Micki at the shop and tells her about their séance experience. It's the same one Micki and Johnny had. He is going to get a drink with Jandini, and Micki and Johnny continue with their research. Up until five years ago, Ilsa seemingly didn't exist. Johnny finds a stack of books about spiritualism in Lewis' files, all written by Ellie Robinson. The last one was published in 1984, which is around the time that Ilsa Van Zandt starts showing up in public records.

Johnny has a cop friend pull the file of Ilsa's last client who died—he was electrocuted when his TV fell into a swimming pool. Micki realizes all the deaths are connected to televisions. In the manifest, she finds a 1950s model black and white television set. Lewis never sold it; he donated it to a convalescence home. The pair take a road trip out to the home. (I don't know why they did this; they could have called. We don't see them visit the home. And clearly they don't remember the last ill-fated road trip they took, in "The Long Road Home.")

Jandini and Jack have a drink at the bar. Jack is bothered by the séance. Ilsa didn't start with a prayer of protection, as if she "didn't care if an evil spirit came by." Jandini had been hesitant to tell Jack what he had seen, fearing he wouldn't believe him. He finally begins to spill when the TV above the bar reveals his parents. This time they are angry with him.

"This is how you spent the time you could have been with us?" All Jack sees is the hockey game that has been on the TV the entire time.

Jandini is shaken, starts screaming at the television. This creates quite a ruckus, with Jandini becoming more distraught the more his parents accuse him of abandoning them. Jack takes him out of the bar, but is stopped by the bartender. While Jack pays the tab, Jandini wanders into the street. Pretty good trick for getting out of paying for drinks.

Jack finds Jandini across the street, in front of an electronics shop with lots of TVs in the window. They all turn on, and all are playing the same program. "You broke our hearts! We loved you, all you ever gave us was pain! We wish we never had you." When Jack finds him, talking to a wall of seemingly blank televisions, Jandini is about to throw himself through the window. Jack shakes his friend from his reverie and takes him back to his hotel room.

Ilsa has been glued to her cursed television this whole time, waiting and waiting for her next victim to appear. In frustration, she pounds on the set, and notices tumors on her hands. She feels them on her face and runs to the mirror to check. She dresses in a scarf and big sunglasses, despite being the middle of the night, and instructs William to stay there while she goes out.

In his hotel room, Jandini worries that his parents will haunt him for the rest of his life. Jack tries to get him to describe what he saw, but his friend is pretty much hysterical at this point. Jack gets a call from the front desk, claiming there is an urgent letter from Curious Goods for him. He leaves Jandini alone to pick up his "letter." Jack has been at that hotel for maybe an hour, probably less. It is the middle of the night, so clearly there is no mail delivery. How is *none* of this suspicious to Jack?

Anyway, Jack has no sooner left than Ilsa knocks at the door. She came to "see how he is." He is relieved to see her because something went very wrong at that séance. The TV flicks on again, and he begs her to make his angry parents go away. He picks up the television, and Ilsa doesn't waste any time. "Go to them," she hisses, then pushes him out the window.

Jandini lands on the pavement in front of the hotel. Jack sees the commotion from the lobby and runs out to find his friend dead. William has just driven by and is shocked to see the scene before him. Ilsa is standing just outside the hotel, watching her handiwork unfold.

Returning home, Ilsa begs the TV to give her what she wants. "I gave you the one who wanted you, now give me the time!" Her tombstone remains unchanged – and her clock has just chimed midnight on the 15th. Good thing the tombstone doesn't list a time of death. William hears her cries and checks on her. She turns away and tells him to leave, unwilling to show him her face tumors. He finally convinces her to reveal herself, and begs her to see a doctor. "They can't cure it; they've tried." William begs Ilsa to let him help her, but she isn't paying attention anymore. Normally, in a situation like this, the cursed object owner would just kill whoever is around in order to keep their curse going. But Ilsa doesn't sacrifice William; she decides she needs to kill Jack.

Jack is at Curious Goods at this point, but seems to be on his way out again. Johnny tells him about Ellie Robinson, who was a good medium, but not a great one. (So... a medium medium?) Micki shares the info about the TV being a donation; that Ellie/Ilsa must be using it to recover from a degenerative disease that literally had her falling to pieces. When she was in the convalescence home, doctors gave her a week to ten days to survive. They still don't know how she is using the television, but worry that Jack will be her next victim. Jack plans on rushing out to find Ilsa, but Micki and Johnny convince him that he is acting out of his own guilt and being selfish. They tell him to wait at the store; they will go get the television.

The pair arrives at Ilsa's house. Ilsa isn't there, and neither is the television. Johnny thinks she has skipped town, but Micki reminds him that she didn't leave when she thought Jandini was on to her. She thinks she has taken the TV to Jack, and calls him to warn him.

Well, she *tries* to call him. As Jack answers the phone, the line goes dead. Then the power goes out. He hears the front door open and goes downstairs to investigate. It is an interesting, handheld, POV shot as he descends. Jack sees the TV sitting on the counter, and as he moves towards it, William grabs him. Ilsa summons forth Jandini on the television. She is in bad shape, covered in sores and tumors. Jandini appears—in a top hat, no less—and blames Jack for getting him killed. Ilsa points out that he has spent his life searching for what is beyond death. "Here it is." Jack struggles, trying not to look at the television, not to buy into its guilt trip. If Jack won't come to Jandini, Jandini will come to him. He reaches his hand out from the television and tries to drag Jack in. Micki and Johnny arrive, and Johnny immediately tackles William. William ends up getting sucked into the television. Ilsa tries to pull him out, but it is no use. Jandini grabs her and pulls her into the television. The screen goes dark and all is still. I'm not sure if Ilsa died because the TV got the wrong victim (William instead of Jack) or if her time was up.

Status: The television is stored in the vault, and Jack tells a wonderful fable: Arabian knights have a story about a servant who saw Death across the marketplace. He was scared, and begged his master to allow him to hide across the desert, in Baghdad. The master agrees, and his servant runs. The master seeks out Death and reprimands him for scaring his servant. Death apologizes, explaining he was surprised to see him—he thought he had an appointment with the servant tonight. In Baghdad.

* * *

TV has always been a sacred thing to me. I didn't like the idea of a television set—something that was a source of comfort to me—being a tool for evil. Not that this episode would give me nightmares; nothing ever did. But I didn't want my perfect television to be sullied with evil spirits.

I'm glad they didn't go with the clichéd "TV that shows the future" plot. This is a far more unique curse, but not quite as item-specific as many of the other curses are. It makes for a perfectly average, perfectly forgettable episode.

"Tree of Life"

Written by: Christine Foster
Directed by: William Fruet
Original airdate: May 7, 1990
Cursed antique: Druid figurine

It is 1984, and Michael Eng rushes to the Oakwood clinic where his wife, Jennifer (Brenda Bazinet), is in labor. Dr. Sybil Oakwood (Gale Garnett) greets him and tells him his wife isn't quite ready to see him. She sends Michael to place a candle before a mighty oak tree to ease his wife's labor pains. He is frustrated by her mumbo-jumbo, but she reminds him that her mumbo-jumbo is what is giving him a baby in the first place. He finally agrees, and takes the candle into the night.

He comes to an altar before an oak tree and places the candle. "Superstitious garbage," he mutters. A wind picks up and the ground shakes. Roots come up from the ground, strangling Michael and pulling him into the ground.

Jennifer has given birth to a perfect baby boy. She knows she birthed twins, but Dr. Oakwood says the little girl was stillborn. Jennifer insists she heard the baby cry and panics. A nurse gives her a sedative. The little girl is, of course, not dead. Oakwood takes her down the hall to the nursery and names her Shelagh, which means "out of sacrifice comes joy." She will be a priestess for the king of the wood, a prophetess and a magician. "Soon this room will fill with her sisters, and through them the secrets of the Druids will spread through the world."

Now, a couple is at Curious Goods, buying a cradle for their unborn baby. The Sandersons (John Innes and Carole Galloway) have been trying to get pregnant for thirteen years, and it was Dr. Oakwood that finally made it happen for them. Mr. Sanderson says the treatment was basically health food—and good ol' fashioned sex. After Johnny delivers the cradle, he stops for a street cart hot dog and sees a woman trying to steal a magazine from a newsstand. Johnny steps in and pays for it. This disheveled woman is Jennifer Eng, and she has clearly fallen on hard times. The magazine she wanted had Sybil Oakwood on the cover. After her insistence that Oakwood is a witch who stole her baby, Johnny sits down to talk with her.

"It was a spell, not a treatment. It had to be," Jennifer insists. "It happened too fast." Her husband left her the night she had the baby, which seems crazy to her because he wanted a baby as much as she did. Scotty, her son, died last summer at age five. Johnny is sympathetic and seems to believe her, and she begs him to check it out.

He returns to the store and Micki reads up on the clinic while Jack checks the manifest. According to the magazine, the clinic offers a 98 percent success rate. Dr. Oakwood is not listed in the manifest, and Jack thinks that Jennifer might be having a nervous breakdown. Nonetheless, Johnny promised to check it out.

Oakwood is leading her nurses in a forest ceremony to keep the trees fruitful. She removes a skull from an ornate box and the nurses/priestesses all drink "the life blood of our forest king" from it. (So… they drink syrup?) Once the sacred oak bears fruit, each priestess will get her own seed to nurture, and her own coven of young ones to feed it.

When Johnny sneaks around the back of the clinic and peeks through a window, he finds a nursery, filled with a dozen little girls, none older than five. The eldest is Shelagh (Ashley Wood), and she seems to be the "leader" of the group. Johnny ducks when Nurse Dana comes in to put them to bed.

As he is heading away from the clinic, the wind picks up, the earth shakes, and a scream erupts. Another husband, Mr. Forbes, has just gone into the forest to give his sacrifice. Johnny rushes towards the scream, but by the time he gets to the altar, the tree has swallowed Mr. Forbes up. He calls out, but receives no answer, so he leaves. On the tree, a flower starts to bloom, revealing a tiny druid figurine.

Johnny returns to Curious Goods to share his findings. Neither Jack nor Micki really believe anything strange is going on, but Micki agrees to go back with him to check it out. When they arrive, they find the nursery empty. Oakwood has all the girls in the forest, dancing as she chants to the god Cernunos. This ceremony is for the Sandersons, who think it is adorable. Back at the clinic, Johnny sneaks in, and Micki follows. The entire place is empty. He goes through Oakwood's files, but can't find one for Jennifer.

Micki spies a fire deep in the woods and they venture out to inspect it— after Johnny grabs a stack of files. The pair spy on the ceremony, during which the Sandersons are told to drink from the skull, to ensure a "safe and gentle birth." Unsurprisingly, Mr. Sanderson looks a little weird about drinking from the skull, but he does it.

Back at the shop, Micki and Johnny fill in Jack, who thinks they were speaking ancient Gaelic, a Celtic language. In addition to offering sacrifices (none tonight) they would utilize an oak tree because Celts knew oak trees could survive most lightening strikes. They believed they stored sacred power and were symbols for rebirth and energy.

Jack returns to the manifest and finds a fertility statue of Cernunos, made of black Irish oak. The Druids believed Cernunos birthed twins that sprang out of his forehead. Lewis sold it to Dr. Frederick Cornwall (who later tells Micki he donated it to a charity event). In going through the files taken from the clinic, Micki and Johnny find that every single birth at the clinic was a boy. Several other births listed twins, but the girls were always stillborn. They also find three files stating that the fathers abandoned their families at birth. Strange that that would be in medical records.

Against Jack's suggestion, Johnny calls Jennifer and tells her he thinks he found her daughter. Jennifer doesn't hear anything after that—she immediately runs from the pay phone and heads to the clinic. Johnny thinks all the little girls there belong to women like Jennifer. Jack agrees. Julius Caesar all but wiped out the Druids. Those who remained blended in with other Pagan sects, but all held on to one thing: all the priests were women. And every employee at the clinic is a woman. Dr. Oakwood is breeding followers so the Druids can rise again. They figure that the husbands must be the sacrifices, and Jack suggests that all the husbands aren't sacrificed because it ties in with the seasons or the cycle of the moon. Tonight is a full moon *and* the winter solstice.

The girls are excited after their nap, and run outside to play. All except Shelagh, who tells Nurse Dana of a dream she had about a nice man who said he was her daddy, then said he was dead. Dana assures her they all have mommies and daddies that live in a far away country. Jennifer walks in and tells Shelagh she is her real mommy. Dana recognizes her and calls Dr. Oakwood and Nurse Morgan to help restrain her. Oakwood promises Jennifer she will be the "guest of honor" at the sacrifice of fire, and Shelagh runs off to join her sisters, concern crossing her face.

Jennifer is kept bound while Morgan works on the wicker casket. Oakwood insists it be finished by nightfall, but Morgan is concerned—she doesn't feel right about sacrificing a woman. Oakwood assures her that after Jennifer's sacrifice, each nurse will get their own coven, and surely that is worth one female life. Luckily for their ritual, Mrs. Sanderson has gone into labor.

As Mr. Sanderson is sent into the woods with a candle, Micki, Jack, and Johnny arrive. Johnny goes to check on Shelagh while Micki and Jack sneak in through the front door. Micki finds the ceremonial skull, which Jack confirms is Druidic. Johnny is heading to the nursery when he sees Mr. Sanderson going into the woods. He chases him down and gets there just as the earth is swallowing him up. Johnny attempts to pull him out, but instead he is pulled in.

Mrs. Sanderson is given an inhalant against her wishes, to "make the contractions stronger." It actually just makes Mrs. Sanderson pass out (calling it the Cloth of Dreams probably gave it away), allowing Oakwood to birth the babies. Micki hears the baby's cries and goes to investigate. Jack, left alone, sees a few nurses taking the wicker coffin out into the woods. Nurse Morgan sneaks up behind him and Cloth of Dreams him.

Micki sneaks into the nursery and asks the little girls for help looking for a "stranger like me." Shelagh approaches: "The one who said she was my mommy?" Micki confirms that this is her mommy and asks Shelagh to help her find her. The two sneak out as Nurse Dana brings in their new baby sister. The little girls all coo in obnoxious adherence to gender stereotypes. Micki and Shelagh find Jack is gone, as is the chest with the skull. Shelagh says this means they went to the tree. "That's where they send all the daddies."

Morgan alerts Oakwood to Jack's arrival. She doesn't care who he is or where he came from, she just wants him in the "wooden suit." "A double male sacrifice will guarantee the tree will bear fruit tonight." Jack is put in the wicker coffin, while Jennifer is having her blood drained. She is no longer needed for the sacrifice, but she has seen too much. Oakwood assures her death will be slow and easy, then she joins her nurses in the woods.

It is time for their ritual to begin. The flowers bloom, and in the center of each bursts forth a tiny little Cernunos figurine. The nurses hoist Jack, in his wicker coffin, up high. They chant and writhe, teasing the wicker with the flames. Meanwhile, Micki has found Jennifer and unhooks her from the IV before she loses too much blood. Jennifer and Shelagh are reunited.

Johnny is not dead. He is in an underground cavern beneath the tree, and when he tries to get out the way he came in, something causes him pain and he can't leave. Instead, he starts to explore and hears Mr. Sanderson call for help. Johnny sidesteps a rotting, putrid skull, then finds scissors (how the hell did scissors get down there?) and uses them to clip Mr. Sanderson free.

Now, they just have to get out of there. Johnny finds the main Cernunos figure and starts cutting it free of the roots. This makes the tree angry and above ground, the coven stops chanting. The blooms drop from the tree and the sky grows stormy. The women are freaking out; Jack's wicker coffin drops from the tree; and the tree is hit by lightening.

As the coven runs in panic, Oakwood tries to save the seedlings. She is too busy to notice Micki has arrived, and helps Jack out of his wicker coffin. Johnny manages to claw his way out of the earth, with Mr. Sanderson at his back and the Cernunos figurine in his arms. Oakwood is still scrambling for seedlings, and doesn't notice when lightening hits the tree again, causing an enormous branch to fall. This brings the entire oak tree down, crushing Oakwood beneath it. Jack takes the main figure while Johnny and Micki collect all the seedlings. "Don't leave any behind," he warns.

Status: The Cernunos figurine and all its seedlings are vaulted. Jennifer has her daughter back, and the Sandersons go home with twins. I wonder what happened to the rest of the little girls... .

* * *

Episode scribe Christine Foster remembers being pregnant at the time of her pitch—that was the inspiration for "Tree of Life." "My pitch was that the mothers stayed at the clinic, then gave birth to twin girls, but got to keep just one," says Foster. "The other was raised at the clinic with all the other 'donated' twins, playing in the woods, all dreamily dressed in white and living pure little lives until they were periodically sacrificed to the Tree to keep it bearing more statues."

As with so many episodes, production made a few judicious changes to the script. "The production team said no child sacrifice, even implied, so all my lovely little figures in white with flowers in their hair now trooped out and attended the sacrifice of the husbands. Nutty, really, because no one would miss a child who'd never 'existed,' but certainly families would miss a goodly number of husbands. It took a lot of rewriting to even try to justify that and I was never exactly happy with the outcome."

I certainly wouldn't have minded the child sacrifice, but I have a black hole where my heart should be. I think the way it was explained made sense. The little girls were going to start their own covens, so there is a reason for them to be around. The sacrifice of the male twin would make the most sense—then it would be the child who never "existed," but not the beloved female child.

I feel like the "cursed object" could have been better incorporated into the story. Cernunos is often considered a god of fertility, but its relationship to the mysterious fertility treatment is unknown. We only ever see couples taking place in the fertility ceremonies after they are knocked up. Does the sacrificed husband provide for the next infertile couple? That is what I have to assume: the husband is sacrificed to the tree, which sprouted from Cernunos; then the fruit of the tree is fed to the infertile couple as part of the "health food diet."

Also unique was the fact that the figurine multiplied. We have had a few irregular items in this show (the chain whose curse infects the key in "Night Hunger;" the not-quite-cursed snow globe that can break in "Wedding in Black;" the playhouse that doesn't actually kill people in "The Playhouse") but none that have multiplied. It makes sense, though: the Druids are all about the life force in nature. The figurine is carved of oak and a tree sprouts from it; why couldn't it multiply? Do you think the seedlings are cursed? Can they be destroyed?

"Tree of Life" was one of Steve Monarque's favorite episodes. "I got sucked into the ground by a tree, so I got to deal with all that. That was fun," he says. It's certainly better than being raped by a tree (as in *Evil Dead*).

"The Charnel Pit"

Written by: Jim Henshaw
Directed by: Armand Mastroianni
Original airdate: May 14, 1990
Cursed antique: A *double face* painting

Professor Webster Eby (Vlasta Vrana) is teaching a class on the Marquis de Sade, focusing on how de Sade didn't deny his darker side. One student, Larissa (Christa Daniel), takes issue with de Sade (making me wonder why she is taking the class), calling him a pervert and a sicko. She reminds Eby that there is a "sicko" in the city right now, leaving bodies in the river, and girls are disappearing—including one from the class. "Is that okay, someone just exploring their dark side?" she challenges. Eby defends de Sade weakly then dismisses the class. Another coed, Stephanie (Cyndy Preston), stays after to compliment him on the class.

Stephanie goes home with the professor. It doesn't seem to be a strictly romantic liaison, but there are no other reasons for the late night visit. They go upstairs, into his attic "playroom," lined with whips and chains. She ignores all this and focuses on a large painting on the wall. Eby informs her that the painting was from de Sade's time, and some say he painted it himself. Tired of talking, he puts a blindfold on her and kisses her, biting her lip in the process. She touches her bloody lip as Eby whispers to her: "Do anything he asks; he has all the answers we seek." He pushes her against the painting, and her blood activates it. The painting becomes a window into de Sade's dungeon and she falls in.

De Sade (Neil Munro) greets Stephanie gently, assures her there are no dangers here, except those she wishes to embrace. She spends some time chained up, then he takes her down, telling her not to confuse the pain with malice. "In life there are those who enjoy and those who endure." He hands her off to his valet, Latour (Paul Jolicoeur), to take her to his room.

With Stephanie gone, de Sade takes a parchment from his desk, then gets a peasant girl from a cell. A servant girl begs him to pass on a letter to her mistress, the Duchess Darnay, promising she made no mention of de

Sade or what has gone on there. De Sade says nothing, just puts her back in the cell and takes the first girl to the painting. He throws her through the painting, where she lands, dead, on Eby's floor. He greedily takes the scroll from her hand.

That night, Latour wakes de Sade. General Lafayette (Andrew Jackson) is here, and says it is urgent. Stephanie lies in de Sade's bed, tangled in the sheets, dead. "She thought she was strong. In the end all she could offer were her fears." Lafayette has come because another dead peasant girl was found on the grounds of Lacoste, his estate. De Sade grows defensive: "I gave no permission for soldiers to be on my property." He then suggest Lafayette look for the perpetrator elsewhere. They say proper goodbyes, and de Sade, frustrated, snuffs out a candle flame with his fingers.

In the present, Eby takes his newly received de Sade manuscripts to his classroom to study. He finds Larissa there, waiting for him. Stephanie didn't come back to the dorm last night, making her the second girl from their class who has gone missing. Eby is too absorbed in his new documents to pay much attention—until Larissa threatens to go to the police. Eby knocks her out.

Over at Curious Goods, Johnny wants to look into these missing and dead girls—the missing never turn up dead, but a dead girl appears for each one that disappears. There is no evidence there is a cursed object involved, so Jack has them do something more productive: going over Lewis' travel receipts in hopes of tracking down more objects. One name they keep running across is Arnold Eby, who flew Lewis all around the world. There is a notation about a first-class delivery from New York to a local art appraiser, Lafontaine. The boys will go check in with Lafontaine because Micki has an appointment to meet with a woman about some antique firedogs.

Micki finds a note on the door from Mrs. Hudson. She ran to the store, will be back in ten minutes. While Micki waits, she notices a man pull up to a house across the street, and sees him lug an enormous rolled carpet out of his car—with an arm dangling out the end. Micki looks around to see if there is anyone else who sees what she sees.

Finding no one, Micki follows the man—who we know is Professor Eby—into his house. Armed with a fireplace poker, Micki creeps upstairs and finds Eby tying up Larissa in his playroom. Micki tries to hit him, but he punches her and throws her across the room. Eby starts to strangle Micki, but she kicks him in the balls. She pulls herself to her feet, leaning against the wall for support, but this is the wall with the painting on it.

On the set of "The Charnel Pit." Photo courtesy of Armand Mastroianni.

Her blood opens up the portal and before she knows what is happening, she falls through into a dungeon.

The servant girl sees Micki fall through the painting and, seeing her chance, rushes up to the painting. The portal open and she falls through, no blood necessary. But the portal can only be opened in the present, and it is a one-for-one exchange. So, when Micki approaches the painting, it is just a painting. Sizing up her surroundings, Micki finds the servant girl's letter, discovers she is in the year 1790, and finds a key to Duchess Darnay's room at the inn. Latour comes down, and Micki hides, until she can sneak away.

Jack and Johnny visit Lafontaine, who remembers the painting and its owner, Arnold Eby, who died a few years ago. It was a *double face*, or two-sided painting from eighteenth century France. *Double face* paintings had images on both sides of the canvas, usually an image of life on one side; death on the other. What stuck out about the painting was that it wasn't mixed with an oil base, but applied with human blood. Legend said the artist painted it while imprisoned in the Bastille.

Back at Curious Goods, Johnny is worried. They haven't heard from Micki all day. Jack isn't worried (at least, he acts like he's not) and focuses on Arthur Eby. He bought an eighteenth century writing box about a year before he started paying for Lewis' travel, but there was no mention of a painting. Jack thinks the curse opens a window in time, but Lewis could have had that done to any painting; this one must have a power of its own. Now, Jack reveals his concern for Micki. He calls Mrs. Hudson, who tells him Micki never made it over. Johnny returns with a new worry: police found another body in the river.

Micki has found her way to the inn and looks around the Duchess Darnay's room, finding it filled with lavish wigs and gowns. With few options, Micki steps into the role of Duchess Darnay, squeezes into a fancy frock, and finishes buttoning herself into a corset.

Latour enters, with de Sade at his heel, proving his valet wrong about the duchess's arrival. "I'm the Marquis de—well, I'm sure my disgraceful reputation precedes me," he offers once Latour has left them.

"It does…? It does!" comes Micki's reply. She scarcely speaks as de Sade rambles on about the ball tonight and insists she attend.

Micki falters, but de Sade locks eyes with her. "Lacoste offers pleasures few have experienced, but none can resist." Micki softens, and agrees to attend. Remember, she still does not know she is keeping company with the Marquis de Sade.

Countess Deville (Nancy Cser) arrives at the ball with Lafayette in her carriage, warning her to keep her eyes open and report back to him. The countess thinks it is "a lot of fuss over a dead peasant girl." As she enters Lacoste, she stops to greet her host, who is chatting with Micki. "Everyone knows the finest parties are thrown by the Marquis de Sade," the countess compliments. Micki's face grows worried.

Inside the ball, Micki loads up her plate at the buffet, clearly more than a woman of the eighteenth century would eat (or could eat in those corsets) when the countess chats her up. Micki is not his houseguest, and the countess admits she has been sent to see what he is up to. "It's a wonderful intrigue. Everyone knows he is between lovers, and that is not possible for long." She is a gossipy one, telling of Lafayette's suspicions. Micki gets a little tense and excuses herself. De Sade, from across the ballroom, sees her leave and follows.

Micki sneaks around, trying to figure out how to get back into the dungeon, get back to that painting. De Sade catches her trying to open a secret doorway. "Are you always in the habit of going through a gentleman's chamber?"

Micki plays along: "That depends upon the gentleman." Behind that wall is a place for de Sade's "private pleasures," and Micki asks to see it.

De Sade takes her face into his hand, roughly pulling her closer, but she does not blink, does not pull away. Test passed, de Sade opens the door and the two descend. Micki goes straight to the painting. "You enjoy seeing people in pain, don't you?" she asks.

"It is only when one is in pain that one's true self is revealed." He explains that what happened in this room helped him endure the "anguish of captivity."

Micki turns coquettish and asks what happens here now. "Whatever we wish." Their eyes lock, and they probably would have kissed, but Latour interrupts. Lafayette is ordering the guests away.

De Sade rushes back to the party, and Micki turns to the painting, hoping that if she doesn't see Latour, he won't see her. It doesn't work, and he insists she leave. Upstairs, de Sade defends himself to Lafayette, claiming that he has never harmed anyone. Another body was found in de Sade's woods, and Lafayette decided his reputation is enough to clear the guests under the guise that he is helping de Sade save himself. As Micki leaves, she looks like she wants to say something to de Sade, wants to stay, but the guard is insistent that she leave.

The guys are really worried about Micki, but at least that wasn't her in the river. Johnny wants to report Micki missing, or do *something*; Jack agrees but doesn't know what. The police have been looking into the missing girls and the dead girls for months with no suspects. The guys theorize that they are the victims of the same person, and Johnny finally chooses to mention that, in talking to the cops earlier, none of the dead girls have any dental records to speak of. A few missing teeth, but no fillings or bridges or braces. That is all it takes for Jack to be certain the painting is behind this. But he worries the painting only gives you a one-way ticket: a live girl goes in, a dead girl comes back.

Some checking reveals that the pattern fits: a woman disappears the same day a body appears. It takes some time, but the guys track down Arnold Eby's sole heir, his son Webster. His last known phone number has been disconnected, but maybe he moved into his father's house. And his father lived on the same street as Mrs. Hudson.

Back at the inn, Micki sits down and writes a letter: "My name is Micki Foster. I was born in the twentieth century and I find myself trapped in 1790. I came here through a two-sided painting, one created by the Marquis de Sade." Though this part isn't verbalized, a shot of the parchment Micki writes on reveals the entire story, how she saw the girl in the carpet being brought into the house, how her blood activated the painting, how she hopes the same will bring her back. "I'll do anything I have to get back into that room and try." I find this sentence odd. It seems a "way out" for Micki, a way for her to explore those darker desires she clearly wants to explore, while being able to say, "Hey, I was just trying to get home." I wonder if this part had been verbalized at some point, but then cut out because it seems like an "escape route" for Micki—one she does not need, and one that kind of vilifies female sexuality. "I'll do anything I have to get back into that room and try [to get home]" pretty much negates any claim Micki has to her sexuality. I would like to believe that director Armand Mastroianni realized this and decided not to keep the line in the voice over. His episodes are often overtly sexual in a positive way. (The sex scene in "Mesmer's Bauble;" the notion of a subservient wife in "My Wife as a Dog;" the lesbian vampirism in "Night Prey.")

As Micki ruminates on these feelings she has never felt before, on de Sade's cruelty and willingness to "embrace evil," and the magnetism she finds "irresistible," de Sade and the countess are playing in his dungeon. She is chained up and seems to be enjoying the cat o' nine tails whipping her back. Micki writes all through the night. On the last line, "He makes you doubt everything you hold dear... ." Her huge feathered quill dances down her chest—until she is startled from her reverie by a knock at the door. She quickly puts the letter away and finds de Sade at her door, there to offer more hospitality since they were rudely interrupted last night. Micki tries to hold back a breathy smile.

The two return to Lacoste and ride horses very fast across the grounds. They slow, and he reveals his surprise at how well she rides. She admits she is fascinated by how unrepentant he is. De Sade has been told that before but, as Micki points out, "by peasant girls who fear you; never by your equal." De Sade's horse begins to rear up, and he instinctively raises his riding crop to the beast. Micki grabs his arm, preventing him from hitting the steed. The two stare at each other, waiting for the other to break.

"I can devise tests that will break you, Duchess," he warns.

"Let's see," she dares him. He lowers the crop.

The dynamic between de Sade and Micki changes suddenly when they go back to his dungeon. She is not scared and he wants to know what makes her different, why she chooses to be a victim when she doesn't have to be. "You choose to be a torturer when you don't have to be," she challenges.

De Sade points out that his role doesn't feel pain, then drops the accusation: "You think your bravery will provide you with escape, but there is none." He opens up one of the prison cells to reveal the countess inside, dead.

Micki backs away, now showing fear, and Latour catches her. De Sade has had someone watching the inn since the duchess's servant escaped. She didn't go the one place she surely would have, which means that she went through the painting, and Micki would have had to come through the painting first to open up the wormhole. "Life, like the charnel pit, offers no escape but death." Latour drags Micki away and chains her up.

De Sade is pissed. "You teased me for two days with your courage. Now, we will see how much you really have." He gets a whip.

She spits in his face; he rips her dress open. I'm not sure why de Sade believes her courage was fake, or why that should matter.

Through all of this, Eby has kept Larissa locked up as his sex slave. He thinks that, because the servant girl came through without a scroll, de Sade was displeased with him. So, Eby plans to break Larissa in: "If you are going to be of any use, you have to learn to be a friend of pain." Creepier still, he promises that they will do everything twice: once to get over the shock, and again to "see what it offers." He pulls a whip off the wall as Jack and Johnny break in. Eby hears them and hides behind the door. When the guys come in, he knocks out Jack easily and whips Johnny

Neil Munro and Louise Robey on the set of "The Charnel Pit."
Photo courtesy of Louise Robey.

back against the wall. Johnny bleeds onto the painting, and the portal opens up. He sees Micki in the dungeon, and without a second thought, jumps in.

In the dungeon, Latour immediately grabs a sword and starts to battle Johnny. Johnny kicks the sword out of his hand, but he still has a dagger. De Sade tells Latour to drive him into the painting, but Johnny gets to it first. Latour falls through into the present, and right into Eby, stabbing him with his dagger. The two men fall to the floor, dead. De Sade picks up where Latour left off. Johnny grabs a sword, but has no idea how to use it. Instead, he punches de Sade and grabs a length of chain to defend himself with—to no avail.

Micki watches the men fight, while chained up, which is an odd "damsel in distress" image that almost negates the sexual power Micki held earlier. Eventually Johnny kicks de Sade, knocking him out, allowing him to uncuff Micki. De Sade reaches for his sword, but Micki takes it and holds it to his neck.

Jack takes some blood off Eby and wipes it on the painting. The portal opens. From Micki and Johnny's point of view, the bodies of Eby and Latour drop through. "Jack found us a way! C'mon!" shouts Johnny and, again without thinking, he throws himself through the painting. Despite his anger at Micki's deceit, de Sade makes one final play to keep Micki. "He could be dead for all you know. If you go, you could be dead, too." Micki would rather be dead than trapped here with de Sade. She drops the sword and jumps through the painting. Micki falls into Jack's arms and the three of them embrace.

Back at Curious Goods, the painting goes into the vault. Jack is still troubled by the fact that he doesn't know how Lewis found the painting. Micki sees the writing box and is intrigued. Jack tells her it was something else Lewis sold to Eby. They don't know what it does but figured it belonged in the vault. Out of curiosity, Micki opens the writing box and finds her letter. The envelope has been opened. Micki is worried that her letter caused all this. "Thoughts don't cause pain; it's what people do with them," he assures her. "If people are looking for evil, they are going to find it."

Status: The painting is locked up. The writing box is locked up. And the vault is closed one final time.

*   *   *

"The Charnel Pit" is my favorite episode. It ranks among Louise Robey's favorites, as well ("I love riding horses and to be able to ride sidesaddle was interesting"). Initially, I think it was my favorite because of the sumptuous sets and beautiful gowns. But it was more than that. Micki was so in command, even in a foreign country, a foreign time, and in an actual dungeon. As a kid, I had no idea who the Marquis de Sade was or what sexual tension was; I just knew that Micki was giving this "bossy" man a run for his money. I respected that.

I showed this episode to a friend once. We couldn't have been more than twelve or thirteen years old. She couldn't understand why Micki was so attracted to the Marquis de Sade in the episode: he was fat and bald. "It's not about his looks," I insisted. It was about his tone, his intensity, something unspoken that, as a kid, I could not put into words. At this age, I had never heard of the Marquis de Sade and had no knowledge of the S&M lifestyle. But there was something I understood, instinctually.

The scene in which Micki and de Sade are riding horses is an intriguing one. It is as if Micki has worked through any misgivings she may have felt about her attraction to de Sade. She approaches him as an equal, something that de Sade has probably never faced, even among women of his own social standing. When Micki prevents him from whipping his horse, de Sade doesn't like this—*he* is supposed to be the dominant—but he seems intrigued by someone, a woman, standing up to him. Interestingly, in the BDSM community, it is often considered the submissive who truly controls the relationship, because he or she is the only one who can stop the game.

The depiction of the Marquis de Sade is an interesting one to me. Outside forces try to vilify de Sade's "libertine" proclivities, but de Sade defends them with an honesty and a philosophy that feels very true to historical depictions of the man. But at the same time, he is clearly fucking these women to death, without an ounce of pity or emotion. The real Marquis de Sade may have taken his sex games too far (for example, cutting a prostitute) but he was never accused of murder. Among the aristocracy and ruling upper class of the time, deviant sexual activity was not unusual. It seems to me that the reason de Sade was made such an example of was because he was proud and outspoken about his proclivities, and because he was a blasphemer—a serious crime in those times. Had he not incorporated crucifixes into sex with prostitutes, or spent hours railing against the existence of a god, his deviance may very well have gone unnoticed.

"The Marquis de Sade angle came from Frank," says Jim Henshaw, who wrote this episode. "I had pitched the story, and had been doing some research on the Marquis de Sade, just putting it all together. When we got killed, Frank called and said, 'We might as well be hung for sheep as a lamb. If they say we are being as rough and tough as we are, we might as well do that.' So, we did it to show them where we could have gone, and what we could have done."

"I remember being told the show was going to be canceled," says director Armand Mastroianni. "Frank Mancuso Jr. himself came to me and said, 'Listen, I want to go all-out on this episode. I don't care what it costs. I want to go big. I want this to be the end-all show.' Jim said we were going to do the Marquis de Sade, the *double face* painting, and Micki would be pulled through the painting and back through time. I love those time travel episodes.

"Again, this was a very dark and sexual episode because it dealt with S&M and the Marquis de Sade. It seems appropriate that I started with Neil Munro and ended with Neil Munro. I enjoyed making that episode because we were really allowed to create a period, which I hadn't done before, especially in that show. We pulled out all the stops. The production budget was not limited because Frank said to go all-out. I didn't want to shoot everything the same way. I wanted to do a lot of *Citizen Kane* shots, where the camera is low and coming around things. I wanted to give it the perspective of grandeur.

"That episode actually got me *Dark Shadows*," Mastroianni says of the 1991 reboot of the vampire soap opera. "I got a telephone call after ['The Charnel Pit'] aired from [executive producer] Dan Curtis. I will never forget this: 'I watched a show you did and I was very impressed with it. *Friday the 13th*. I loved the way you shot it.'"

Fun fact: In the scene in the art appraiser's office, the assistant is played by director Armand Mastroianni. He doesn't actually remember doing the cameo, but says he often does cameos in his projects. "If it looked like me, it probably was me."

Epilogue

FRANK MANCUSO JR. (creator, executive producer) – The reason why the show was so successful was because we had big sponsors: Mc-Donald's and Proctor & Gamble, those guys. It wasn't like a bunch of local things. So, when Donald Wildmon started writing those places and saying that he has all these followers and he's going to tell every single one of them not to use their products if you continue to support this Satanist show and blah blah blah.... I kept on thinking that this was a joke, until the McDonald's guys came around and said they love the show, they love the demographics, they love everything else, but "we don't need this guy attacking us. It's easier for us to find another show than it is to go ahead and fight this guy, whether he has a premise or not." I thought this was really amazing. I knew that this would be the end of it, even though I was firmly of the belief that this guy had never seen the show.

STEVE MONARQUE (Johnny Ventura) – From what I remember there was a rumor about some sort of organization that was trying to get us off the air. I think I was a little naive about what was going on because I was interviewed by the Associated Press, and I said things that got kind of twisted. I actually got a call from Frank Mancuso Jr. himself, asking me why I said the things I said. I told him I never said those things.

They interviewed me and asked if I ever get a chance to watch my show. I said that I really don't get a chance because I'm working all the time. I shoot at night and sleep during the day. And it's hard because it's actually a year behind in Canada. So, I don't get to watch the show. Then they asked what it was that I don't like about the show. I said it was those cold mornings when you are shooting in just a T-shirt with candy-coated blood all over you. It gets a little uncomfortable, but that's about it. Then they asked me what show I was doing, and I said we were doing one about vampires.

What came out was "Steve Monarque, the new star of *Friday the 13th*, doesn't have time to watch his own show, thinks there is too much blood, and thinks the people he works with are vampires."

That happened when the beginning of the rumors were first going around. So, I get a call from Frank, freaking out, asking why I said that. I told him that is not what I said. He said I need to be really careful when I speak to the media because if there is some sort of organization behind it that wants to ruin something, they will just change what you said.

So, that was kind of my part in the downfall. It wasn't because of me, solely. I believe there were these organizations out there that really felt the show was cultish and demonic and evil.

LOUISE ROBEY (Micki Foster) – I secretly was sort of happy about [the show ending] because I was fed up.

JIM HENSHAW (executive story consultant) – We had material in place for the two shows [in season three] that we never did. I remember we paid out the writers and probably paid out a few other people who were contracted for the episodes. We had four or five stories we were working on [for season four]. There were a couple of really big effects things we were going to try. The show was basically done before CGI really came through. So, we were doing some stuff, but not a lot. There were some new techniques and new software we thought we could use and do some interesting things with. We also, I think, had run across a couple other actors that we wanted to use more. They had been minor characters on other episodes, and we started talking about bringing them back. At one point, we had even discussed having a thing where all the antiques that had been captured in the vault got out, so we could revisit some of those cursed objects, but do something different with them, and really complicate the universe. This stuff could change and have different powers, depending on who is attached to it. You could have a cursed object that would operate one way for one person, then another way for someone else. It would really complicate the detective story, and give the audience something they weren't expecting.

It was like, "We've got a cursed camera, and it does this, but for a different person it could do something completely different." The audience and our characters would have gone into the search knowing what it does and knowing what to look for, then suddenly being taken in a completely different direction.

I don't remember any of the episodes that were cut. I know we would have been at outline stage for them, but probably not much further along.

STEVE MONARQUE – I was kind of bummed that it ended the way it did. I felt like it really could have gone for another year or two, maybe three. I think the ideas were really good. When it happened, it happened really quick. It wasn't like, "This is our last season." It was like, "Nope, it's over. This is our last week." That's not how it's supposed to happen.

People, to this day, still contact me about the show. It plays around the world. Someone sent me an episode in which [I was dubbed] into Japanese. That was fun to watch! I didn't understand what I was saying.

JOHN LEMAY (Ryan Dallion) – Looking back, I do regret [leaving the show]. I wish I had been more mature and understood how to make the experience one that I could continually grow from. I wish I had found a mentor who would help me find that. I was put into different situations every week. There is no reason why I shouldn't have found that to be interesting and fun to do on a regular basis. We learn our lessons the hard way sometimes.

LOUISE ROBEY – I have some of the items. I have a manifest. I did keep the doll from "The Inheritance." Made of porcelain, unfortunately during a move, she broke into pieces. I'm not quite certain where Veda is. I do have my little rabbit, the one that used to lay on my bed in close-ups, with the little bow tie and vest.

RODNEY CHARTERS (cinematographer, director) – I still have the sword from "Year of the Monkey." I got to keep the samurai sword. It was nothing special, but it was kind of fun to have around the house. The kids were scared of it. I might have gotten the snow globe, but I don't know where it is now. They made a very lovely model of the castle in the globe.

JIM HENSHAW – In a lot of ways, I looked at *Friday the 13th: The Series* as the show on which I finally learned to write. It was that kind of thing where the demands made of you every week were things you had never conceived of before. You would suddenly have to make things make sense, make it work in a dramatic story, and it has to get done in a week. That kind of thing really forces you to dig and find the stuff that makes you a better writer.

TIM BOND (director) – It was so much fun to do *Friday the 13ᵗʰ*. Every episode was like a little movie. It was a different world. So many series you do, it's back to the same police station. *Friday the 13ᵗʰ*, except for "back to the store," was a whole world. It was in the early days of computer-generated imagery—or, in those days, computer *assisted* imagery—so it was really fun to work out a new optical trick for each show. That was the most fun that I had with it—inventing those things.

WILLIAM TAUB (executive story consultant) – *Friday the 13ᵗʰ* probably could have had a longer life. It was designed as a late-night show, and when it started pulling really good numbers they decided to move it up, and I think moving it up wasn't a smart thing to do. Because once it started moving up, it started getting parental attention and it became a popular cause.

J. MILES DALE (line producer) – I seriously used to be able to name all seventy-two episodes, in order. It's perverse.

ALLAN EASTMAN (director) – *Friday the 13ᵗʰ* was a unique show and a unique gig. I'm not sure whether I would have gone back to it even if it hadn't been canceled. The long night shoots were brutal and I did get nightmares sometimes from some of the things we had to shoot. But at the same time, just as it is always fun to make an audience laugh, it is also really fun to scare the shit out of them. That part of it was something I really enjoyed.

ARMAND MASTROIANNI (director) – In *Friday the 13ᵗʰ*, each episode was about a different thing. Yes, our characters were the same, but we would go into the past, we would do all sorts of crazy things. It allowed each show to have a signature. The beauty of working in that environment is that it allowed a director total creative freedom, and the ability to take the chances you wanted to take and not worry that someone will scold you. The people who ran that show were some of the best.

LOUISE ROBEY – I'm very, very proud of the show. I believe it is a classic. It's timeless in the sense that it doesn't fit into the 80s with big shoulders and stuff. There is nothing pointing to what era it would be in. Therefore, I think there is a lot to be said about the reruns. It seems to go on and on and on. So, I am proud of it as a body of work.

FRANK MANCUSO JR. – I always maintain I could have done another 150 of those shows and never gotten stale on it.

STEPHEN ROLOFF (production designer) – The magic for me of the *Friday the 13th* experience stemmed from the fact that we achieved the miraculous on a daily basis. We were on a tight seven day per episode shooting schedule, and in each episode the cursed object took us into worlds ranging from London in 1880 to Alabama in 1950 to voodoo temples, Chinese dynasties, the Marquis de Sade's pleasure palace, cursed playhouses... even the gates of hell. This took a lot of incredibly talented people working at their best, and I'm very proud of what we achieved together.

LOUISE ROBEY – When the series finished, Chris sat down with me on the front steps [of Curious Goods] and said, "You have passed your apprenticeship, my dear." That was some apprenticeship!

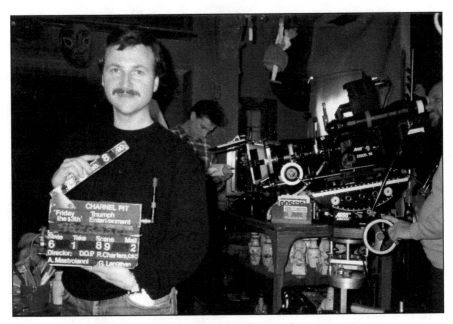

That's a wrap! Photo courtesy of Armand Mastroianni.

An Interview with Frank Mancuso, Jr.

FRANK MANCUSO JR. had a lot to share about the series. A lot of it was "shop talk" that is not particularly interesting to everyone, so I have included his full, uncut interview here.

How did *Friday the 13th: The Series* get started?

Mel Harris, who used to be the head of television at Paramount came to me and said that he wanted to create a *Friday the 13th* television series. They had a great deal of success in syndication with *Star Trek,* so they were looking through their sci-fi/horror catalogue, saying "what titles do we believe we could get traction on, that have enough name value that it wouldn't require sizable casting or a lot of advertising dollars spent on making people aware of what the show is." At the time, I felt as though I'd kind of done *Friday the 13th* and I wasn't really interested in revisiting it. I felt like it ultimately was limiting how people perceived what I was capable of doing. So, I said, "Yeah, I really don't want to do this."

He asked why. I said first of all, I don't watch television, so I don't think I'd be very good at making it. Second of all, I've made these other films now and people are finally starting to put that *Friday the 13th* thing behind me. Now, all of a sudden, I would be jumping right back in the middle of it. Then there was the obvious part of it: the certain limitations of what you could put on television. *Friday the 13th* movies are known for certain scenes of real aggression, and that would be a real limitation if you brought it to television.

He basically said, "Look, we really want to do this, and you are really the only one who can do it. I don't care *what* the show is, just call it *Friday the 13th.* You make it anything you want for an hour, and we will put it on the air." I told them I get it, but I just don't want to do it.

My dad, who was, I think, the chairman of Paramount at that time, said, "Look, this is a real opportunity to do something you've never done before. Theoretically, they can sell this thing." So, I said, "It can be *anything* we want?"

He said, "Absolutely. Because it is syndication, you aren't going to get a lot of notes, you aren't going to get a lot of structure from us. You are just going to get a budget from us, then you can go do whatever the hell you want."

That, ultimately, made me curious enough to start thinking about, *Well, if I was going to do this, what would the show be?* I started meeting with some people and talking to some people about various scenarios in which this might be fun. I was certainly drawn towards a sort of anthological premise because I felt like that most naturally suited the way my head worked. They kept wanting some common openings and closings, then it will feel more like a TV series and less like a movie. So, we started thinking about *The Twilight Zone* and how that had common elements and they were bound thematically but they weren't necessarily a traditional series. We started riffing off that, and that's sort of how it all got going.

In Canada it was called *Friday's Curse*, and a lot of people have complained about the title being "confusing." Looking back, would you have preferred a different title?

I'm not a big fan of going back and saying, "Well, if this would have happened… ." because you don't know what the other sequence of those events are. I think it's unwise to say, "Oh, if you called it *Friday's Curse* you wouldn't have had the stigmatism of *Friday the 13th*, of people saying "where's Jason?" and all that stuff. So, that's one side of it. The other side of it is, if you called it *Friday's Curse*, no one might've shown up. You might not have had the opportunity to do it. So, I don't think you can necessarily change one thing and then assume everything else would have stayed the same. What I can say is that the thinking was right. There are titles out there that carry enough weight, in and of themselves, to attract an audience. If you can find the means by which to satisfy those people, watching that show, then you have a core that you can build off of. Again, you have to realize, this is syndication – this isn't network television. You are relying on barter economy. You are relying on people buying spots as opposed to getting network support. So, the paradigm of how it works is different.

It's really pretty simple: if you have enough advertising support to warrant making the show, you make it. The president of the network can say, "I don't care if this gets a zero rating, we're so proud of this show we're going to put it on anyways." That doesn't happen in syndication, because there is no "guy." There's just a bunch of individual guys who say, "Well it works for us in Philadelphia at seven o'clock." "Well it works for us in Kansas at eleven o'clock at night." Everybody sort of find their own niche where they feel like this particular piece of programming serves them best. It has to do with what other holes they have, it has to do with what they think the show can do, what they think the audience will be, so forth and so on.

There were certainly times where I felt as though we were being limited by defining something in a negative way. I never like to do that, but like I said, if not for that title, I don't think it ever would have lived. What I mean by "defining something in the negative" is like to say, "Well, it's not the movies." That doesn't really help anything. You are calling it the movie, so why would you start off your definition by saying it's not the movie? It sounds like a mistake from the get-go. What you have to do is try to find some means by which to define it that allows you to express what it is and recognize the fact that, like I said, the economics were built off what they thought the movies would bring to it. If it wasn't for the movies, truthfully, it never would have happened. I realize that.

There was a time, much later in the show, midway through the third year, where this guy Donald Wildmon, who was this kind of religious right kind of guy, really started attacking the show. It was clear to me in seeing some of his attacks that he had never seen the show. It was also clear to me that he was using the movies as the reason to kill the show. I remember doing a test, where I said to Paramount, "Let's just go out there and put an alternate title on the show, and show two focus groups the same show. One with the *Friday the 13th* title, and one with another title." Just to see how the two of them react differently to the show. It would tell us one of two things: it will either tell us that *Friday the 13th* is a big part of the reason why people are watching the show, and/or it will tell us something else. What it kind of told us was the reason why people enjoyed the show called—something else—I don't even remember the title we used. It may have even been *Friday's Curse*—was the narrative and the stories. And then when pushed, a lot of the reason people didn't sample the show was because they thought it was the movies. I went back to Paramount and said, "Look, it seems to me that this is the best news you could have gotten. What it says is, you could change the show's title and position it differently and perhaps expand the audience." At that time, there were enough advertisers that got affected by Donald Wildmon.

The reason why the show was so successful was because we had big sponsors: McDonald's and Proctor & Gamble, those guys. It wasn't like a bunch of local things. So, when Donald Wildmon started writing those places and saying that he has all these followers and he's going to tell every single one of them not to use your products if you continue to support this Satanist show and blah blah blah… I kept on thinking that this was a joke, until the McDonald's guys came around and said they love the show, they love the demographics, they love everything else, but "we don't need this guy attacking us. It's easier for us to find another show than it is to go ahead and fight this guy, whether he has a premise or not." I thought this was really amazing. This is going to be the end of this. I was firmly of the belief that this would be the end of it, even though I was firmly of the belief that this guy had never seen the show.

I always maintain I could have done another 150 of those shows and never gotten stale on it. What happened was they started this third series called *War of the Worlds*. It started off like gangbusters, like bigger than *Friday the 13th*, but not as big as *Star Trek*. It was more like true science fiction, but then the show was falling every wee. It appeared that the core audience that they initially peaked with what it was going to be, was not satisfied with the show. I remember being at NATPE, one of these television conventions, in Houston, and a few of the station groups that had the *Friday the 13th* TV show said they were so excited about *War of the Worlds*, this is great, this is really good news, so on and so forth. I said, "What are you talking about?"

They said that I was going to get involved in *War of the Worlds*.

I said, "I'm not getting involved in *War of the Worlds*. I've never even seen *War of the Worlds*. I don't know what you're talking about."

After the fifth person who came up to me, I went to my dad and said, "What the hell is going on?"

He said, "Well, I think some of the people in the television group, because they were really unhappy with the way the show was being made, sort of started to tell them that you were going to get involved."

I said, "That's great, but nobody's had that conversation with *me*."

They came and we talked and we talked and we talked. Again, it was one of those things that I didn't want to do. It just didn't appeal to me, and I had literally never seen the show. They told me I could take *War of the Worlds*, do whatever I wanted, then I'd have two hours in a row, that's almost like a block of television, nobody has that. I told them I wasn't really in the television business.

I only did this one thing: long story short, they kind of convinced me that this would be a remarkable opportunity, and they were both in Canada and I could use some of the same people we were working with on *Friday* and swap them over, go back and forth. So, we tried it, but it was pretty clear to me, five shows in, that this is kind of a closed idea. You're either going to have this war or not. How long can you dance around it? I thought the premise of [*War of the Worlds*] kind of sucked. I don't see how they could continue to make this dance work. We just did it for one year. It wasn't like there was anything wrong with the people, it just felt to me like... *Star Trek* could have gone on for a thousand years because you could keep coming up with different adventures. But when you have two groups and there is supposed to be this war, there's only so many ways you can dance around it. How many years can you not have this war? How long can you threaten and promise, threaten and promise, and allude to? It just got to be kind of closed-ended. Even though there was nothing wrong with the people involved, it just wasn't fun because, five shows in, I felt like we were repeating ourselves.

So, was *War of the Worlds* the reason *Friday the 13th* ended?

I think it was really that enough major sponsors that got threatened by Donald Wildmon. When the sponsorship changed, because there is no network, everything went south.

Also, what happened, too, is because the show got so—the way a barter show works is that different day or night parts have different intrinsic values to them. A show at three o'clock in the morning is less valuable than a show at eight o'clock at night. But it is up to the individual station group to position the show where they think it will be most successful. My vision, to the extent that one wanted to call it a vision, was that I wanted it to be the last thing you saw before you went to bed. That was my sort of reference to how I was framing the show. Ultimately, and I don't think this is necessarily a bad thing, but the nature of enterprise is to be successful. When we originally started [we were on at] twelve o'clock at night in a lot of places—which was perfect for me—and then some people said, "Well, if twelve o'clock works, since our news is on at ten o'clock, why don't we put it on at eleven? At eleven would be even better than twelve, because we have bigger groups, so on and so forth." All the way down to where people were putting the repeat shows on Saturday at seven o'clock.

All of a sudden, the show just feels different on Saturday at seven o'clock than it does Friday at eleven o'clock. It just does. It sort of belongs, in my view, in one place, and it kind of doesn't belong in the other place. However, the people at Paramount were making a lot more money on Saturday at seven o'clock than they were Friday at eleven o'clock. What you have is a network, but it's only a network in the loosest possible definition, because what it really is a series of individuals, all across the country, all who put it in their own place, where they think it belongs. That is what becomes a network. But the guy in Philadelphia isn't calling the guy in Los Angeles to ask what they think they should do. They are serving their own. If they have a show that drops out, and they think *Friday the 13th* solves that problem, that's what they're going to do, and they have the right to do that. So, you can't really control, or at least, if you can, I'm unaware of how you can—where the show goes.

As they moved it around, it started hitting different pockets of viewers. Like I said, I never wanted it to be a seven o'clock or eight o'clock show that kids could see. That was never what it was supposed to be.

Tim Bond said you wanted it to be a date night show, so kids would come home and have to watch it in the dark.

Yeah. I remember growing up, on Friday nights, late, late night, they would play monster movies. That was my reference. That was what I wanted to create for the generation that was watching television then.

Can you talk a bit about casting the leads?

It was kind of a normal process; I say normal because part of the economic structure of the show was that it was being filmed as a Canadian content show. So, that had certain obligations. Aggregately, you had to end up with half the directors Canadian and half… or maybe it was two-thirds/one-third. I forget. But there was the relationship in order to make the tax qualifications that you had to have a presence of Canadian talent, both in front of and behind the camera. That didn't particularly scare me because I had wanted to go to Toronto. I had lived there for a number of years. The budgets were severely limited, so my feeling was because the budgets were so limited, you had to go to a place where, for *nothing*, you could get something. You couldn't make this a studio show because you would have to build everything that people saw. Therefore you had to go to a place that had enough varied looks and varied locations and varied seasons so that your show would have the opportunity to exploit those things, essentially for nothing; for just being there. I wasn't necessarily bothered by the—restrictions is not the right wore—but the definition of what made a Canadian-content show never really worried me.

The casting process was a pretty normal thing. The only good thing about it was because there was no network, we weren't having to keep running people by the network executives who might say, "Well, we don't want a red head" or "we don't want this." There was none of that. It was really just who we felt could bring the qualities we're looking for.

Chris [Wiggins] to me was more like the emotional and spiritual anchor of things. The kids, Robey and John LeMay, were more involved in doing the heavy lifting. But the truth of it is, after Chris, it was easier. We always knew that he would sort of ground the show in a way that I thought was important. The guest stars were more the "sexier" parts, for lack of a better word. They were the ones that had the most fun associated with them because the Robey-LeMay parts were more of the "procedural" aspect of trying to get the thing back. So, Chris kind of grounded it, then they were our protagonists that were out there trying to save the world from whatever it was that was being unleashed. Then you've got the guys who are making the deals with the devil, who were the more fun people to watch. They are the ones benefiting in some real way from the implementation of the device.

In some ways the LeMay-Robey parts were—thankless is the wrong word—but they were the more gumshoe aspect of what it is we were doing. I felt like both of them worked off each other well. In a lot of the episodes we featured one or the other, some both, but I never really felt like we had to steer towards certain kinds of things because I didn't feel like they would be able to do this, or she can't do that. I didn't feel limited in that way.

What happened with John LeMay's exit?

He would be infinitely better equipped to answer than I would. I guess what I would say is that anything that I can offer would really be a matter of conjecture. Here's the thing that I know: syndication television is tough. It takes a lot of time, and any television series you are going to do, whilst providing you work, opportunity, and some money, it does limit what else you can do, just by virtue of the time it takes. So, I feel as though perhaps—and this isn't uncommon—but some people think, *Well, I've made my mark here, now it's time for me to go and exploit that and jump into this other thing.* More often than not, it doesn't. More often than not, people look at you in a certain way, they like you doing what it is you are doing, then all of a sudden you are doing this other thing and they don't necessarily follow. Sometimes they do, and I don't really know what happened to John after that, but I don't think he found himself in the center of something like that.

I don't think you can blame people for making choices. It is what it is. Every one of these shows is put together with a matrix of personalities. For some people, it works great, and for some people, it works less great. Obviously there was some part of that show that was not satisfying to him. I don't know necessarily what it was, whether it was the time thing, or whether it was not challenging enough, whatever it is, I don't know. But I do know that you can't really convince somebody to do something that they don't want to do when it is performing on screen. You will be reminded daily when you watch them that they don't want to be doing this. In my view, in those kinds of situations, the best thing to do is to suggest what you think is best and live with whatever it is. This is not a shot at Steve [Monarque], but I don't think we were ever able to recapture that same dynamic – but then again, how could you? The whole vibe in the beginning was based on the three of them, and how they reacted to whatever it was that was going on. You take one of those pieces out and you insert a different piece and you assume it will all go on the same, and it doesn't. It can't.

When Johnny was introduced in the middle of season two, did you know at that point that John LeMay was leaving? Was that your way of setting up Johnny to take his place?

We knew that he didn't want to be doing it, so we had to start dealing with it in some way. I didn't think it was fair to just go in and swap him out. It was a conscious awareness that we had to start dealing with this, and figure out something that feels right.

How did Steve fit in, in your opinion?

Well, I always thought that the original Darren was better than the second Darren on *Bewitched*. If there hadn't been an "original Darren"—and the second guy was the first guy—you can't go back and wish. What became obvious was that it wasn't the same. That should be obvious because they weren't the same. I don't think that, had we initiated the show with Steve instead of John, that we wouldn't have found the same thing had it been reversed. It had nothing to do with Steve—he was just a guy trying to do a gig. I thought he was absolutely fine. Had there not been a show with John LeMay before it, nobody would be complaining. But because it's not the same, people were complaining. You couldn't pretend it's the same—it's not. But it doesn't mean that it can't be whatever it is. It's that definition by a negative inference: "It's not what it was." Well, right! That is indisputable. That's not how you should be defining it because it is something else. You can like it less, or you can like it more, but use the context you are supposed to in order to come up with a view on what it is. I got a little frustrated that people were taking shots at him, like "John LeMay wouldn't do it that way." Right. So what?

The one thing I notice about television is that when people invite you into their home, they make you [part of the family]. The number of people, during that period of time, that would get my credit card at a restaurant, would see my name and say, "Oh my god, you did that *Friday the 13th* television show." They would go on and on and on. "You know, in episode nine… ." Blah blah blah. It's really different with movies. Movies they see once, then they go have pizza or go do whatever they do. Every once in a while you do something that really effects people in a special kind of way, and I've been lucky enough to do a couple of those where it felt like certain people *really* got affected by it, but television, they really make you part of their life, especially in those days. There wasn't TiVo, so they had to rearrange their lives to some degree to experience what it is you were showing that week. That's all changed, but in that time period, if you wanted to watch the show, you had to stop whatever you were doing at a certain time and say, "Okay, now this is my time to be doing this." [Laughs] Then tomorrow we'll all meet around the water cooler and talk about it. In that way, people become more emotionally connected to how they perceive the show. If you are doing something that fucks with that, they're not happy. "I loved it the way it was: now you did this." It's like, the guy didn't wanna do it anymore, whaddya want me to do? [Thick NY accent, laughs] I can't change his mind. That's not my gig. My gig is to come up with stories that you're going to find appealing, and that's what I'm going to continue to try to do.

You mentioned you could have done 150 episodes more, and cancellation seemed to come upon you pretty quickly. Were you guys plotting out a season four?

Not really. This Wildmon thing started getting traction. Here's the thing. You've got to realize the size of this show was miniscule, compared to what people know television shows to be now. We essentially had one writer, this guy Jim Henshaw. He was the real guy, then we had people come in and out and we would get help on every episode, but the way that the show would work was we would meet at the beginning of the year. I would have, for lack of a better word, "sketches" of a lot of shows. Some of them would be as simple as, "I want to do a black and white vampire show" and some of them would be like "Here's the story of the show." It would be all over the place. We would go sit in a hotel for three days and just talk about it. Because we didn't really have anybody to go to, story-wise, content-wise, other-wise, that was sort of what the year became. To the extent with which that notepad was filled with good ideas, it was a good season. To the extent of which it was not-so-good ideas, we had to sort of do a lot of vamping mid-year.

What would happen is like, I would want to do a black and white vampire show. So, Jim Henshaw would go ahead and sketch it out, then he would go and meet with a bunch of spec writers in Canada and say, "Here are the next five shows we are doing." One guy would say, "Let me bring you back a take on this one." So, we would sort of work with them on creating that show, then Jim and I would bounce back and forth with each other until we felt happy with them.

That's kind of the way it worked for all the years. Sometimes it was location-oriented; sometimes it was season-oriented. Like [someone] would remember going to this place where there was this Amish-like village, let's go do a couple of shows there. And I love this object—let's lose it and find it in another episode. So, there were things like that that I felt like I wanted to play around with. Since there was nobody to say no, we did whatever we wanted to do. The one thing I can say about Paramount is that they really did stick with their original thing: "We're not going to tell you anything. Just go do whatever the hell you want." Maybe it was because it was successful from the beginning, and they just left us alone, but there was never any, "Nah, you can't do that." The only thing they originally said was, because of the nature of syndication, they didn't want two- and three-parters. It will just screw it up. I remember—and I don't remember which one—but I said, "This isn't really a two-parter, it's an unresolved show." Then we resolved it in the next show!

The thing is, when you start these things, you have to start with rules because if you don't, you are opening the world of infinite possibilities. Unless you have some kind of a framework... It's like, here is what this thing needs to look like within forty-seven minutes, so that we feel like it is our show. They were really object-guest star-premise-driven. They really were, by definition, more anthological than most continuing series. When we started off, we probably had more rules than we did at the end because the one thing that I found out about television that was different from movies is that television is kind of this working laboratory. You do a show, then it's like, "Well, that didn't turn out so good" and "Where did we screw up?" "We should never give her these kinds of lines, it just doesn't sound good coming out of her mouth" or "He's terrible when it comes to this kind of stuff, let's not give him those things to do." You learn that in television; you can't learn that in movies because you get one shot through. You finish one day's shooting and you're on to the next. You can't pretend that that day before didn't exist. They are all interrelated to one entire piece, whereas with [television] you end up with twenty-six little pieces every year.

Are there any episodes or antiques that hold a special place for you, or that you especially like?

There were, obviously, and there are people we worked with that I'm really proud of. Atom Egoyan did one of our early shows; we kind of found him. And Cronenberg, who I am friendly with, so I brought him in to do a show. Some of our best shows were just kind of like this special connection between a guy and a premise. Francis Delia did some really good—I think he did the black and white vampire show. [He didn't; Bradford May did.] Just stylistically. We kept trying to say we don't have any money, but we do have freedom and that's worth a bunch. I kept saying to everybody, "Look, I don't care how smart we are, if we are making a show for $475,000, and Michael Mann's making one for $1.4 million, we ain't that smart, where it can look like *Miami Vice* can. It just will never be that. So, we have to make sure we don't make *Miami Vice* because we're going to end up looking bad." What we had to do was make something nobody else was making, and we do it in our way, and we do it according to our rules. Then at least we will be the best of what we are. People won't care about what it costs because there won't be something standing next to it that costs three times what we're spending and it will become apparent as to what our limitations are.

I think that, as the guy who was creating the architecture of what the show was, I think that was a valuable contribution, which was, if we frame our references to what it is that exists now, we're in trouble. They are all making their shows for a lot more money than we are. We have to find a different vernacular to use. If we do that successfully, then like I said, there will be no other reference, or it will be one from a long time ago, and that's fine with me.

There are a lot of shows that I have felt, stylistically and aesthetically, were beautiful and really great and pushed people's emotions, and I thought that was great. Then there were shows where you were just kind of disappointed with how they turned out. Again, because we had flexibility in how we delivered the shows, if we were really disappointed with a show, we kept screwing around with it until we were happier. I would say, "I know this was supposed to be up next, but it's not going to be, so we are going to give you this show instead." Because there was no sequence necessarily, it didn't really matter. We would keep messing around with it, messing around with it, messing around with it, go buy some stock footage, we gotta dress this up a bit, it's gotta look better. We kept on playing with things until we at least thought they were better and we had taken things as far as we could.

That sounds like fun.

Yeah, it was. It was a TV laboratory. I don't know the way other television shows work, but in that context, we really did have a tremendous amount of freedom. Because we had a tremendous amount of freedom, we didn't send it out until we felt like this was it. This is what we want.

You said the budget per episode was roughly $475,000?

The first year, that's what it was. I remember having this moment, before we started. I'm not really prone to freaking out, and I kind of freaked out. I said to myself, "What am I doing? I don't even watch television, and I'm now responsible for twenty-six hours of television." It really hit me hard, before we had started show one. I made peace with myself by saying, "It's twenty-six little movies." That is something I understood, and that is something I knew I could do. So, that is kind of the way, in my head, how I created the infrastructure, was around that premise: twenty-six little movies, we'll find some directors that we like, we'll give them multiple episodes, we'll create this little family amongst ourselves. There are enough locations, there are enough seasonal changes. If you start breaking it down that way, it's like, "Okay, I can do this. This is gonna be okay." It was more just to make my own head work. I needed to find that key because if I didn't, I was afraid the whole thing would come down. It really was on me. There was nobody else. There wasn't a whole team of us that was involved at the Paramount level because nobody in Canada knew anybody at Paramount. It wasn't built that way. It wasn't built like a traditional network show, where you've got nine producers and fifteen writers and they all sit around and talk in a room. There was no room—there was no nothing! It was us. Me and Henshaw, and some people we found along the way, both creatively and from a production standpoint that really started contributing more and more. We brought them up through the ranks and got them more involved on a day-to-day basis. It was a fun moment in time.

Afteword

LOUISE ROBEY QUIT ACTING after appearing in the direct-to-video thriller, *Play Nice* in 1992. She married into British royalty in 1994 and had a son, James, but the marriage ended in 2001. (Can you imagine the flame-haired, outspoken actress being pegged into a *Downton Abbey*-style life?) Louise married again, a photographer, who passed away in 2010. She currently lives in France, where she is working on a variety of music and writing projects.

John D. LeMay never quite became the movie star his agents wanted him to become. After leaving *Friday the 13th: The Series*, John had a handful of television guest spots and returned in *Jason Goes To Hell: The Final Friday* (1993). He is still acting, though focusing on musical theater, most recently appearing in a musical version of James Joyce's "The Dead" in Los Angeles. John has entered the filmmaking space with feat1stfilms, directing videos and documentary shorts. He is married and has two daughter.

Steve Monarque continued acting and added writing and directing to his resume. Most recently, he has written, directed, and starred in *Simpler Times,* a short film starring Jerry Stiller that has been gaining acclaim on the festival circuit.

I was unable to speak to Chris Wiggins about his role as Jack Marshak. While still alive as of June 2014, he was in poor health and his caregiver said he was "not available." I hope that he gets a chance to know about this book, and know that he has left a legacy that lives on with fans.

There were a few guest stars who, unfortunately, have passed in the years since *Friday the 13th: The Series* aired. R. G. Armstrong (Uncle Lewis) died in 2012 of natural causes. Denis Forest ("Brain Drain," "The Mephisto Ring," "Cupid's Quiver," "My Wife as a Dog") died in 2002 after suffering a massive stroke. Neil Munro ("The Charnel Pit," Better Off Dead," "Epitaph for a Lonely Soul") died in 2009 after a long struggle with cancer. Cliff Gorman ("Doctor Jack") died from leukemia in 2002.

Others have retired from the limelight and I could not get in touch with them (Carolyn Dunn, Susannah Hoffmann, Tara Meyer, producer Jon Andersen); very few outright declined to speak with me (Vanity, John Bolger, Gordon Pinset, Tom McCamus), and all said they had nothing to add.

■

Printed in the USA
CPSIA information can be obtained
at www.ICGtesting.com
LVHW022315081223
765728LV00005B/141